Universities as Political Institutions

Higher Education Research in the 21st Century Series

Series Editors

Pedro Teixeira (*CIPES and University of Porto, Portugal*)
Jussi Välimaa (*University of Jyväskylä, Finland*)

International Editorial Advisory Board

Mari Elken (*University of Oslo, Norway*)
Gaële Goastellec (*University of Lausanne, Switzerland*)
Manja Klemenčič (*Harvard University, USA*)
Simon Marginson (*University of Oxford, United Kingdom*)
Emanuela Reale (*Institute for Research on Firm and Growth CERIS – CNR Rome, Italy*)
Creso Sá (*University of Toronto, Canada*)

VOLUME 12

The titles published in this series are listed at *brill.com/cher*

Universities as Political Institutions

Higher Education Institutions in the Middle of Academic, Economic and Social Pressures

Edited by

Leasa Weimer and Terhi Nokkala

BRILL
SENSE

LEIDEN | BOSTON

All chapters in this book have undergone peer review.

The Library of Congress Cataloging-in-Publication Data is available online at http://catalog.loc.gov

Typeface for the Latin, Greek, and Cyrillic scripts: "Brill". See and download: brill.com/brill-typeface.

ISSN 2542-8837
ISBN 978-90-04-42256-8 (paperback)
ISBN 978-90-04-42257-5 (hardback)
ISBN 978-90-04-42258-2 (e-book)

Copyright 2020 by Koninklijke Brill NV, Leiden, The Netherlands.
Koninklijke Brill NV incorporates the imprints Brill, Brill Hes & De Graaf, Brill Nijhoff, Brill Rodopi, Brill Sense, Hotei Publishing, mentis Verlag, Verlag Ferdinand Schöningh and Wilhelm Fink Verlag.
All rights reserved. No part of this publication may be reproduced, translated, stored in a retrieval system, or transmitted in any form or by any means, electronic, mechanical, photocopying, recording or otherwise, without prior written permission from the publisher.
Authorization to photocopy items for internal or personal use is granted by Koninklijke Brill NV provided that the appropriate fees are paid directly to The Copyright Clearance Center, 222 Rosewood Drive, Suite 910, Danvers, MA 01923, USA. Fees are subject to change.

This book is printed on acid-free paper and produced in a sustainable manner.

Contents

Foreword VII
   Jussi Välimaa
Acknowledgements VIII
List of Figures and Tables IX
Notes on Contributors XII

Introduction 1
   Leasa Weimer and Terhi Nokkala

PART 1
Geo-Political Influences

1 Powershift: Universities and the Seismic Winds of Change 11
   Susan L. Robertson

2 The Rise of Nationalism: The Influence of Populist Discourses on
  International Student Mobility and Migration in the UK and US 33
   Leasa Weimer and Aliandra Barlete

3 Pursuing Ideal Partnerships: The Discourse of Instrumentalism in the
  Policies and Practices of Sino-Foreign Higher Education Cooperation 58
   Heather Cockayne, Jie Gao and Miguel Antonio Lim

4 The Challenges of Brexit: UK Higher Education Governing Councils
  Responding to Sudden Change 81
   Heather Eggins

PART 2
Political Analysis, Action and Power

5 Keynote Conversation: Advancing the Conversation on the Politics of
  Higher Education 107
   Brian Pusser and Imanol Ordorika

VI

6 Universitas Reformata Semper Reformanda: A Political Parallelogram of
Continual University Reform   138
Susanne Lohmann

7 Student Protests and Higher Education Transformation: A South African
Case Study   165
Magda Fourie-Malherbe and Anneke Müller

8 University Third Mission as an Organisational and Political Field: Evidence
from Three Case Studies in Italy   189
Giacomo Balduzzi and Massimiliano Vaira

9 Teaching Staff in Non-University Higher Education in Japan: Career
Experience, Competencies and Identities   213
Yuki Inenaga and Keiichi Yoshimoto

PART 3
Societal Values, National Regimes and Higher Education

10 Inclusion and Fairness in Access to Higher Education: Theoretical
Distinctions, Measurement and Patterns of Interaction   237
Pepka Boyadjieva and Petya Ilieva-Trichkova

11 Academic Career, Mobility and the National Gender Regimes in
Switzerland and Finland   262
Terhi Nokkala, Pierre Bataille, Taru Siekkinen and Gaële Goastellec

12 The Applicability of Two Graduate Employability Frameworks: How
Possession, Position, Integration and Engagement Shape Graduate
Employability   287
*Martina Gaisch, Victoria Rammer, Silke Preymann, Stefanie Sterrer and
Regina Aichinger*

13 Universities in the Complex Setting of the West Bank: Entrepreneurial or
Engaged?   311
Huub L. M. Mudde

Foreword

This book is based on the papers presented during the 30th Annual Consortium of Higher Education Researchers (CHER) conference hosted by the Finnish Institute for Educational Research at the University of Jyväskylä in August 2017.

The conference focused on 'Universities as Political Institutions – Higher Education Institutions in the Middle of Academic, Economic and Social Pressures'. 'Political' is defined in many different ways throughout the chapters in this book. During the conference, 'Political' was used as a broad and descriptive concept which may refer to definitions, uses and users of power or more broadly to a variety of relationships among different actors and agencies responsible for making, executing or resisting decisions concerning higher education institutions.

The main reason for the selection of this topic was the notion that universities are, in fact, political organisations and social institutions which consist of a variety of conflicting definitions and practices on how to organise, plan and implement academic and managerial decisions and processes. Similar variety occurs with the multiple relationships higher education institutions may have in their networks, formal agreements and practical cooperation with the actors and agencies in and of the surrounding societies. However, higher education institutions have been studied or problematised only rarely as political social entities in the field of higher education research. With recent changes in societies, politics and economy it is high time to open discussion and debate on HEIS as political institutions because the post-truth period has seriously challenged not only the validity of research-based knowledge but also the role of higher education in societies. We should have a better understanding on the tensions inside institutions and between higher education and societies.

I would very much like to thank all the authors who contributed to the book, with special thanks to Dr. Leasa Weimer and Dr. Terhi Nokkala for their hard work in editing the volume.

Jussi Välimaa
Professor and Director
Chair of CHER and the CHER Conference in 2017

Acknowledgements

We would like to thank many individuals who contributed to the eleventh volume of the annual Consortium of Higher Education Researchers (CHER) book series. This book would not be possible without the contributing authors who worked diligently to turn their conference papers and plenary presentations and debates into thought-provoking chapters. We thank them for their time, responsiveness to feedback, and for meeting tight deadlines. We also wish to acknowledge Jussi Välimaa for writing the foreword and more generally for his unconditional support in ensuring the success of this publication. We are also grateful to those who peer reviewed the chapters and offered relevant and constructive feedback to the authors and to Sini Tuikka and Timo Hautala for editing the APA style and to Kate Sotejeff-Wilson who copy edited the final version of the chapters. A special thank you to the Finnish Institute for Educational Research and the University of Jyväskylä for sponsoring the conference. Finally, we wish to acknowledge over 200 colleagues from 30 countries who attended and actively participated in making the 30th annual conference in Jyväskylä (Finland) intellectually stimulating.

Figures and Tables

Figures

2.1   Tweet from Donald Trump: Make America great again (Trump, 2016b).   41

2.2   Tweet from 'vote leave' (Vote Leave, 2016).   43

2.3   Tweet from Nigel Farage (Farage, 2016).   43

2.4   Tweet from Donald Trump on Mexican immigration (Trump, 2015).   46

2.5   Tweet from Donald Trump on muslim immigration (Trump, 2016a).   46

2.6   Tweet from Donald Trump on travel ban (Trump, 2017).   47

3.1   Institutions involved in the SBC partnership (Source: SBC, 2015).   68

6.1   A parallelogram of forces consisting of a point of origin, two component forces, and a net resultant force (Source: Brews ohare, https://en.wikipedia.org/wiki/Parallelogram_of_force, under license CC BY-SA 3.0, https://creativecommons.org/licenses/by-sa/3.0/deed.en).   146

6.2   The individual university at the centre of the isomorphic cross.   148

6.3   Vertical and horizontal isomorphism.   148

10.1   Students of low social background (in %) in two waves of EUROSTUDENT (IV and V). Source: EUROSTUDENT IV 2008–2011 (Orr, Gwość, & Netz, 2011, p. 47) and EUROSTUDENT V 2012–2015 (Hauschildt, Gwość, Netz, & Mishra, 2015, p. 56).   247

10.2   Students of high social background (in %) in two waves of EUROSTUDENT (IV and V). Source: EUROSTUDENT IV 2008–2011 (Orr, Gwość, & Netz, 2011, p. 47) and EUROSTUDENT V 2012–2015 (Hauschildt, Gwość, Netz, & Mishra, 2015, p. 56).   247

10.3   Index of inclusion in participation in higher education for people of low and high social background for the period 2009 and 2013, by country. (Source: ESS 2008–2010 and ESS 2012–2014).   248

10.4   Scores for fairness of representation in higher education by people of low and high social background as of 2009, by country. (Source: EUROSTUDENT IV, 2008–2011 and Eurostat, LFS data for 2009 extracted on 14.03.2018, code: edat_lfse_03). Note: The Czech Republic was excluded from the figure as an outlier with regard to the low social background group with low social background. The value is 5.23. For the high social background one, it is 0.46.   249

10.5   Index of fairness in participation in higher education for people of low and high social background for the period 2009 and 2013, by country. (Source: EUROSTUDENT IV 2008–2011 and EUROSTUDENT V 2012–2015 and Eurostat, LFS data for 2009 and 2013 extracted on 14.03.2018, code: edat_lfse_03).   250

10.6 Indices of inclusion and fairness for people of high social background (Source: EUROSTUDENT IV 2008–2011 and EUROSTUDENT V 2012–2015 and Eurostat, LFS data for 2009 and 2013 extracted on 14.03.2018, code: edat_lfse_03 and ESS 2008–2010 and ESS 2012–2014). 251

11.1 Doctoral degree obtained in the country of current employment (European academic staff, 2010). (Source: EuroAC). 267

11.2 Labour market participation patterns of couples aged 29–45 years, by family labour market configuration (Finland & Switzerland) 2016. (Source: UNECE). 269

11.3 Swiss and Finnish HE staff gendered composition (2014). (Source: FSO and Vipunen, Education Statistics Finland). 270

12.1 Comparison of the models of graduate employability by Holmes (2013) and Clarke (2017). 291

12.2 Adapted model of graduate employability. 297

12.3 Human capital of graduates in Austrian and Czech HEI. 298

12.4 Social capital of graduates in Austrian and Czech HEI. 299

12.5 Identity process of graduates in Austrian and Czech HEI. 301

12.6 Personal attributes of graduates in Austrian and Czech HEI. 302

Tables

3.1 Advice for the CFCRS ideal model. 66

3.2 Constrictions for the CFCRS ideal model. 66

3.3 Highlights China's HE policy developments with developments at SBC. 70

6.1 Societal polarisation in the age of Trump and Brexit. 159

8.1 Case study main features. 197

8.2 Case study departments at the three institutions. 198

8.3 People interviewed for each case study and institution of membership. 198

9.1 Basic data of tertiary education system in Japan (2015). 217

9.2 List of variables and categories analysed. 222

9.3 The type of academic and vocational experiences. 224

9.4 Determinants of competencies required and possessed at recruitment. 226

9.5 Determinants of identity and satisfaction during work. 228

10.1 Tendencies of interaction between inclusion and fairness in higher education for people of low and high social background in the period between 2009 and 2013. 253

11.1 Sample composition. 271

13.1 General profile of the five universities assessed. 313

13.2 Employment Indicators of the West Bank, Palestine. 317

FIGURES AND TABLES

13.3 Variables per dimension of the HEInnovate framework. 319

13.4 Number of respondents per university. 320

13.5 Mean per dimension of the analytical framework, students and staff, by university (n = 256). 321

13.6 Summary of entrepreneurial university assessment of the four Palestinian universities. 328

Notes on Contributors

Regina Aichinger
holds a Master's degree in Economics and Social Sciences (major field of study: organisational learning and development, human resource management) from Danube University Krems. She obtained her PhD in Pedagogics at the University Koblenz/Landau. Her research focuses on governance structures and mechanisms in higher education systems with particular regard to dialogical management. She is Vice Executive President of the University of Applied Sciences Upper Austria responsible for organisational development, quality management, diversity management, accounting and head of the department of higher education research.

Giacomo Balduzzi
is a post-doctoral fellow at the Department of Political and Social Sciences, University of Pavia. He collaborates with the Centre of Studies and Researches on Higher Education Systems (CIRSIS) at the same institution.

Aliandra Barlete
has a PhD in Sociology of Education at the Faculty of Education, Wolfson College, University of Cambridge. She holds a Master's in Higher Education from the Universities of Oslo, Tampere and Aveiro (joint European degree). Her research interests focus on the international dimension of higher education and its relationship with multi-governing and multi-spatial projects in Latin America and Europe, in particular regional and inter-regional arrangements.

Pierre Bataille
received his PhD at the University of Lausanne on the life course of graduates of the French grandes écoles in 2014. He is a junior lecturer at the University of Lausanne and has previously been a SNSF Postdoctoral Researcher at the Université Libre de Bruxelles. His main research interests include the sociology of education, sociology of elites, sociology of work, cultural sociology, gender perspective, and longitudinal approaches in mixed-methods research design. His research has been published in *European Sociological Review, European Educational Research Journal,* and *Sociologie and Sociétés contemporaines.*

Pepka Boyadjieva
is Professor at the Institute of Philosophy and Sociology, Bulgarian Academy of Sciences, and Honorary Professor of Sociology of Education at the University of Nottingham. She is a member of the Editorial Board of the ISA's SSIS series,

Journal of Social Science Education and *International Journal of Lifelong Education*. Her research interests are in the field of education with an emphasis on higher education, educational inequalities, lifelong learning and school/university to work transitions. Currently, Boyadjieva is a member of the Network of Experts working on the Social Dimension of Education and Training (NESET 2019–22) and leads the Bulgarian team of the "Encouraging Lifelong Learning for an Inclusive and Vibrant Europe" (ENLIVEN) project. Among her latest articles is "Invisible higher education: Higher education institutions from Central and Eastern Europe in global rankings" (*European Educational Research Journal*, 2017).

Heather Cockayne

is a researcher and Senior Tutor in the Manchester Institute of Education at the University of Manchester. Her research interests include transnational education, internationalisation and the student experience in higher education. Previously she worked within a Sino-UK partnership in Shanghai, China. She has 12 years of experience teaching internationally in the UK, South Korea, Spain and China.

Heather Eggins

is Visiting Professor and Senior Research Fellow at Staffordshire University, UK, and Fellow Commoner at Lucy Cavendish College, University of Cambridge. Her areas of higher education research include policy and strategy, gender issues, access and equity, quality assurance and enhancement, and globalisation. She was a Fulbright New Century Scholar in 2006, and has served as Director of the Society for Research into Higher Education, and a consultant to UNESCO. She has considerable editorial experience, and her books include, as editor and contributor, *The University as a Critical Institution?* (Sense Publishers, 2017); *The Changing Roles of Women in Higher Education* (Springer, 2017); *Drivers and Barriers to Achieving Quality in Higher Education* (Sense Publishers, 2014); and *Access and Equity: Comparative Perspectives* (Sense Publishers, 2010).

Magda Fourie-Malherbe

is Professor of Higher Education Studies in the Centre for Higher and Adult Education, Faculty of Education, Stellenbosch University. She is a former Vice-Rector: Teaching and Learning at Stellenbosch University, and before that, she was Vice-Rector: Academic Planning at Free State University in South Africa. She holds qualifications from the University of the Free State and Stellenbosch University, and has worked for almost 30 years at various public higher education institutions in South Africa as a lecturer, academic developer, researcher, supervisor and higher education manager. Her research includes work on higher education governance, leadership and management, teaching and learning, and transformation. She has authored and co-authored more than 40 contributions to scholarly journals, books and research reports. She has been a guest lecturer at universities in Botswana, Uganda and China, and has presented/co-presented 33 papers at international conferences.

Martina Gaisch

is Professor of English, intercultural competence and diversity management at the University of Applied Sciences Upper Austria, Austria. She completed her doctoral studies in philosophy at the University of Vienna. As an applied linguist and academic head of diversity management working at the school of informatics in Hagenberg, her main research areas are at the interface of educational sociology, higher education research and sociolinguistics.

Jie Gao

is a researcher at the Danish School of Education, Aarhus University in Denmark, studying cross-border partnerships in higher education. Her research interests include anthropology of education, higher education policy and internationalisation of higher education institutions. Previously she worked in a Sino-Nordic partnership in Shanghai, China.

Gaële Goastellec

is a sociologist. Her main research interests lie in the relationship between education and society, analysed through the comparative socio-history of access to higher education. Among her latest publications are "Inequalities in access to Higher Education and degrees: methodological and theoretical issues" (*Social Inclusion*, 2019, co-authored with Jussi Välimaa); "Revisiting the issues of access to Higher Education and social stratification through the case of refugees: A comparative study of spaces of opportunity for refugee students in Germany and England" (*Social Sciences*, 2018, Marie-Agnès Détourbe); and Kamanzi and France Picard (Eds.), *L'envers du décor, Massification de l'enseignement supérieur et justice sociale* (Presses de l'Université du Québec, 2017). As Professor of Sociology at the University of Lausanne, she is the Director of the Laboratory Capitalism, Culture and Society. She is also the President of CHER and the Vice-President of the AISLF CR20 on International Comparisons.

Petya Ilieva-Trichkova

is an Assistant Professor of Sociology at the Institute of Philosophy and Sociology, Bulgarian Academy of Sciences. Her research interests include educational inequalities, social justice, higher education and lifelong learning. Currently, Ilieva-Trichkova leads the project: 'Social inequalities in education, human

NOTES ON CONTRIBUTORS

capital and opportunities for individual development: theoretical and methodological aspects' funded by the Programme for support of young researchers and doctoral students in the Bulgarian Academy of Sciences – 2017. Her latest articles include, among others: "From conceptualisation to measurement of higher education as a common good: challenges and possibilities" (*Higher Education*, 2018) (co-authored) and "Higher education systems and institutions, Bulgaria", in J. C. Shin, P. Teixeira (Eds.), *Encyclopedia of International Higher Education Systems and Institutions*, 2018 (co-authored).

Yuki Inenaga
is an Assistant Professor at the Research Centre for University Studies (RCUS) at the University of Tsukuba, Japan. Prior to joining the RCUS in 2005, she worked at Kagawa University, the Research Institute for Higher Education (RIHE) at Hiroshima University, and Kyushu University. She majors in sociology of education and her research interest lies in the current changes and challenges facing higher education, including the non-university sector, further education, vocational education and training, and (outside) stakeholders and their impact on higher education. One of her publications include *Competencies, Higher Education, and Career in Japan and the Netherlands* (Springer, 2007), which she co-edited with Keiichi Yoshimoto.

Miguel Antonio Lim
is Lecturer in Education and International Development, Programme Director of the Master's programme in Education (International) and Research Coordinator at the Manchester Institute of Education at the University of Manchester. His research interests include performance metrics, internationalisation, and reputation management in higher education. He is task force leader on migration and higher education at the EU-Marie Curie Alumni Association. Previously, he was EU-Marie Curie Fellow at Aarhus University, Denmark. He has worked on international partnerships for Sciences Po-Paris and taught at the London School of Economics (LSE). From 2010–2012, he was the Executive Director of the Global Public Policy Network Secretariat.

Susanne Lohmann
is Professor of Political Science and Public Policy and Director of the Jacob Marschak Interdisciplinary Colloquium on Mathematics in the Behavioral Sciences at the University of California, Los Angeles. Professor Lohmann received her PhD in Economics and Political Economy from Carnegie Mellon University in 1991. She was the John M. Olin Fellow at Carnegie Mellon University; Alfred P. Sloan Fellow, also at Carnegie Mellon University; James and Doris McNamara Fellow at Stanford University; John M. Olin Fellow at the Univer-

sity of Southern California; Fellow of the Center for Advanced Study in the Behavioral Sciences; and Fellow of the John Simon Guggenheim Memorial Foundation. Professor Lohmann's research on collective action and central banking has been published in leading economics and political science journals. Her current research addresses the institution of the university. Professor Lohmann teaches ethics and governance. Her fully online course "Diversity, Disagreement, and Democracy" employs an innovative game play pedagogy to teach civics. She is the recipient of four teaching awards.

Huub L. M. Mudde

is a Senior Project Consultant and Lecturer of Institutional Entrepreneurship at the Maastricht School of Management (MSM). He holds a Master's in Sociology from the Wageningen Agricultural University, the Netherlands. Currently, he is pursuing his PhD at Maastricht University on "Entrepreneurial Universities in Developing Countries". Mudde is manager of several multi-year education and research programmes. He is team leader and expert in several agribusiness and WASH projects in Indonesia, Palestine, Sierra Leone and Ethiopia, and was responsible for a leadership and management capacity development programme in Ethiopia. He has managed entrepreneurship development programmes in Liberia and Rwanda. Mudde is advisor and trainer on partnerships, project management, dialogue, communication planning, vision development and fund raising for organisations working in the area of international relations. Before working for MSM, Mudde was coordinator of, Europe's Forum on International Cooperation (Euforic) and worked at the Information Department of the Dutch Ministry of Foreign Affairs.

Anneke Müller

has worked in academic development at Stellenbosch University for more than 20 years. She became interested in a broader definition of student success after witnessing the remarkable improvement in students' NSC results after attending a one-year bridging programme where they received good teaching. She realised that the final school results cannot be the only criterion to allow students' access to higher education – as is the case in South Africa - and determine prospective students' potential. In her research, she examined alternative factors to be considered in this regard. Since Müller had been reflecting on a broader definition of student success for some years, she understood the barriers to student success when they were raised by disgruntled students during the #FeesMustFall movement. Her scholarly work is informed by students' real-life experiences and their ability to succeed against the odds. Müller currently works in the Development and Alumni Division of Stellenbosch University.

NOTES ON CONTRIBUTORS

XVII

Terhi Nokkala

is a Senior Researcher at the Finnish Institute for Educational Research (FIER), in the research team Higher Education Studies (HIEST), University of Jyväskylä, and an Adjunct Professor of Higher Education Administration at the Faculty of Management, University of Tampere. Her research focuses on the interplay between higher education policy, technological developments, organisational parameters and networks, and individual experiences in various aspects of higher education, with a specific interest in comparative methodology and discourse analysis.

Imanol Ordorika

received his undergraduate degree in Physics from the Universidad Nacional Autónoma de México in 1991, his Master's degrees in International Development Education (1993) and Sociology (1998) from Stanford University, and his PhD in Education (Social Sciences, Policy and Educational Practice) from Stanford University in 1999. He has been a full Professor of Social Sciences and Education at the Universidad Nacional Autónoma de México since 1993. He has numerous publications, including books, book chapters and articles on the politics of university governance, higher education politics and policies, as well as globalisation and higher education.

Silke Preymann

focuses her research on human resources development and leadership in both, higher educational and corporate settings. She completed her doctoral studies in economics at University of Linz. She is a lecturer at the University of Applied Sciences Upper Austria concentrating on leadership and human resource development, change management and qualitative research methods.

Brian Pusser

is Associate Professor of Higher Education in the Curry School of Education at the University of Virginia. His research focuses on the politics of higher education, the organisation and governance of postsecondary institutions, national and international postsecondary policies, and international and comparative higher education. He has authored or co-authored articles published in such journals as *Journal of Higher Education, Educational Policy, Research in Higher Education*, and *Higher Education: Handbook of Theory and Research*. He is the co-editor of *Critical Approaches to the Study of Higher Education* (Johns Hopkins University Press, 2015), which received the American Educational Research Association's Division J (Higher Education) 2016 Outstanding Publication Award. He is also co-editor of *Universities and the Public Sphere: Knowledge Creation and State Building in the Era of Globalization* (Routledge Press, 2012).

Victoria Rammer

is a research associate at the University of Applied Sciences Upper Austria, Campus Hagenberg, working on a three-year INTERREG project named "Content and Language Integrated Learning" (CLIL). The project seeks to enhance graduate employability at the Austrian-Czech cross-border region by enriching the study programmes in the fields of informatics, logistics, civil and mechanical engineering with foreign language elements of German, Czech and English.

Susan L. Robertson

is Professor of Sociology of Education in the Faculty of Education, University of Cambridge and Fellow of Wolfson College, Cambridge. Prior to her appointment to Cambridge in 2016, Susan was Professor of Sociology at the University of Bristol, UK. She has also held academic posts in New Zealand and Australia. Susan is a leading scholar on education policy and governance, with a focus particularly on global and regional higher education, and the implications for social justice. Susan has published well over 100 papers. Her recent books include *Global Regionalisms and Higher Education, and Public Private Partnerships in Education*. Susan is the founding co-editor of the journal, *Globalisation, Societies and Education* (with Roger Dale) and currently editor in chief. She convenes the research cluster "Culture, Politics and Global Justice".

Taru Siekkinen

is a PhD student and a project researcher at the University of Jyväskylä, Finnish Institute for Educational Research (FIER), in the research team Higher Education Studies (HIEST). Her research focuses on the academic profession, academic work and careers. She is currently finalising her PhD related to these themes and working as a researcher in a project funded by the Academy of Finland: "Exiting Academics in Networked Knowledge Societies" (EANKS).

Stefanie Sterrer

focuses her research on higher education, its third mission and the key role in regional innovation systems. She focuses on the roles of different institutional types in higher education systems and governance. She studied Sociology and Economics and is currently a pre-doc researcher in the Higher Education Research and Development department at the University of Applied Sciences Upper Austria.

Massimiliano Vaira

is Associate Professor of Economic Labour and Organizational Sociology at the Department of Political and Social Sciences, University of Pavia. He is a

NOTES ON CONTRIBUTORS

member of the Centre of Studies and Researches on Higher Education Systems (CIRSIS) at the same institution.

Leasa Weimer

is a researcher in the Finnish Institute for Educational Research at the University of Jyväskylä (Finland). In 2018–2019 she was principal investigator for a Ministry-funded project, "Investigation of internationalisation at home in Finnish higher education and research institutes". She holds a PhD from the University of Georgia (USA) and a joint Erasmus Mundus Master's degree in Higher Education from the University of Oslo (Norway), University of Aveiro (Portugal) and the University of Tampere (Finland). With over 20 years of experience in higher education, she has been active in the field of international education as a Fulbright Fellow, President of the Erasmus Mundus Association, and an expert consultant for European higher education projects and evaluations. Her work bridges international higher education research with practice.

Keiichi Yoshimoto

(PhD in Education) majors in sociology of education and conducts research on tertiary education. He is a Distinguished Professor and the Director of the Research Centre for Tertiary Education and Qualifications at Kyushu University. He also served as Program Officer at the Research Center for Science Systems, Japan Society for The Promotion of Science (2015–2018) and President of the Japan Society of Internship and Work Integrated Learning (2009–2017). He has a wide range of international project experience, including as the national coordinator of Japan at the OECD thematic review of "Transition from Initial Education to Working Life" (1996–2000), and the Graduate surveys in Europe (CHEERS) project (1998–2000). One of his publications is "Pedagogy and andragogy in higher education – A comparison among Germany, the UK and Japan" (*European Journal of Education*, 2007), which was co-authored by Yuki Inenaga.

Introduction

Leasa Weimer and Terhi Nokkala

Universities can be viewed and studied as political institutions; especially considering that they sit at the crossroads of social, cultural, and economic pressures. The internal and external environment of higher education brings with it multiple and complex relationships as well as power struggles. Within these contested political spaces, there are phenomena to be studied. While the field of higher education draws from a multitude of disciplines, some scholars argue that only recently has scholarship focused on the political perspectives of higher education (Pusser, 2018). To better understand the politics and policies of higher education this book illuminates a variety of ways that researchers view and study universities as a political institution, from considering the national and international political pressures shaping higher education to the analysis of responses and political action from within the ivory tower.

The 2017 annual CHER conference in Jyväskylä (Finland) brought together 213 scholars from 30 countries to discuss and debate political dimensions of the study of higher education. The conference marked a milestone in the history of CHER, as we celebrated the 30th annual gathering. This book includes a selection of papers and keynote presentations from the annual CHER conference. The thematic approach of the book reflects the 2017 conference theme: 'Universities as Political Institutions – HEIs in the Middle of Academic, Economic, and Social Pressures'.

The call for papers highlighted the conference theme:

> The 30th Annual CHER conference theme focused on multiple and often complex relations and relationships, internal and external, to higher education institutions. In this context, political referred not only to definitions, uses, and users of power but more broadly to a variety of relationships among different actors and agencies responsible for making, executing, or resisting decisions concerning HEIs. Discussions at the conference offered fresh perspectives for HEIs as political institutions consisting of a variety of conflicting definitions and practices on how to organise, plan, and implement academic and managerial decisions and processes. Papers may highlight varieties with the multiple relationships HEIs, staff or students have in their networks, formal agreements, and practical cooperation with the actors and agencies of surrounding societies. The papers may also address the broader local, national, regional

© KONINKLIJKE BRILL NV, LEIDEN, 2020 | DOI: 10.1163/9789004422582_001

or global levels of policy, politics, governance, activism and resistance that impact and shape higher education. Papers that explore theoretical, empirical and methodological approaches to the theme are preferred.

Together, the selected papers and keynotes illuminate a variety of political dimensions in higher education. Some chapters focus on and analyse the external geopolitical influences on higher education, while other chapters stay within the national or institutional borders and draw attention to the relationship and tensions between higher education and national societal norms, policies, regimes, and political ambitions. Within each of these contexts, politics and power struggles among actors internal and external to higher education institutions are analysed and theorised.

In this book, 28 authors use a diverse range of theoretical and methodological perspectives in equally diverse local contexts to research and discuss the political nature of higher education. In thirteen chapters, the book is geographically diverse as it presents data and insights from unique higher education settings around the world: Finland, Switzerland, Japan, South Africa, Italy, Austria, the Czech Republic, China, United Kingdom (UK), United States (US), and Palestine. The content of this book will be of interest to graduate students, policy makers, researchers in the field, and practitioners in higher education administration, leadership and management and at the same time has potential to inform and improve policies and practices.

This year's CHER annual book is organised in three parts:
1. Geo-Political Influences
2. Political Analysis, Action and Power
3. Societal Values, National Regimes and Higher Education

1   Geo-Political Influences

The first part focuses on 'Geo-Political Influences' with four chapters. The opening chapter is based on a plenary address at the conference, presented by Susan L. Robertson. In this chapter, Robertson skillfully 'sets the scene' for the book as she illuminates how global 'ruptures' through the years influence and shape higher education. She argues that four major powershifts, since the 1970s, have resulted in deep social, political and economic consequences impacting higher education and the wider society. *Powershift 1* focuses on the 1970s global economic crisis and the advent and growth of neoliberalism. *Powershift 2* occurs with new forms of imperialism, state surveillance, conflict, and refugee movement surrounding events of 'September 11', 2001. *Powershift*

INTRODUCTION 3

3 explores the 2008 financial crisis leading to student indebtedness and constricted university finances. *Powershift 4* brings us to contemporary issues, 2016 onwards, with the rise of authoritarian power, xenophobia, and disenfranchised lower and middle classes. She leaves us with a provocative question, 'what could a 5th and 6th powershift look like that does not repeat the past thirty years?' and suggests that higher education actors, including us, need to stimulate debates, challenge practices, offer new alternatives and make way for active engagement by the younger generations.

Following Robertson's chapter, Leasa Weimer and Aliandra Barlete dive deeper into *Powershift 4* as they critically analyse how political discourses influence the international dimension of higher education. International higher education is inherently political as people and knowledge move across and between national borders. National discourse and policies related to immigration and education directly impact international student mobility. Weimer and Barlete investigate contemporary modes of political nationalisms in the UK and US. They problematise how political discursive elements during the Brexit referendum campaign and Trump presidential election may influence international student mobility to these top host destinations.

The third chapter focuses on how national policies steer and influence higher education international collaborations in China. Heather Cockayne, Jie Gao and Miguel Antonio Lim analyse the discourse of national policy documents and focus in on two case studies, the Sino-Danish Center and the Sino-British College, to explore different understandings of national policy changes and how these changes impact practice. Chinese national policy changes promote 'alliances between giants' (encouraging higher education institutions to collaborate with highly reputable partners), Chinese institutions to remain dominant throughout the collaboration and the partner must contribute at least 33% of the collaboration (teaching hours, teachers, courses, curriculum design, etc.) The authors point out that the shifting instrumentalism of Sino-foreign partnerships coincides with the evolution of China's position in the global order. They argue that China mobilises these partnerships to internationalise the higher education sector and at the same time to further national ambitions to be an active player in the global knowledge economy.

In the final chapter in Part 1, Heather Eggins explores how the UK referendum vote to leave the European Union (EU) has deep and wide implications for UK higher education. She examines potential effects on university funding and research collaboration, academic staff mobility and research capacity, and student access, from the perspectives of 16 university Councils and Vice-Chancellors/Principals. Data were collected during the moment of uncertainty, within the first year after the referendum vote, as actors discussed and strategised possible scenarios and responses. This phenomenological study focuses in on how actors experienced the phenomenon of Brexit and how they prepared to develop and take future decisions. Findings suggest that actors were already working through possible scenarios and in doing so were concerned about financial viability, attracting and retaining international students and EU staff.

2 Political Analysis, Action and Power

The second part of book, entitled 'Political Analysis, Action and Power' focuses on two areas: how political analysis is used to study higher education and how internal and external political power and action shape higher education. This chapter provides an overview of how higher education has been researched as a political institution. To open the 2017 CHER conference, a keynote debate between Brian Pusser and Imanol Ordorika addressed the evolution of the study of higher education in terms of lacking political analytical frameworks as well as the contemporary role of critical political theory in understanding higher education comparatively. This chapter is an edited transcript of the debate and also features key questions posed by conference participants. During the debate, Pusser and Ordorika discuss why the scholarly approach to understanding politics of higher education is limited. They focus in on the role of the state and civil society in shaping higher education, understandings of power and governance as well as the conceptualisation of the university as both a site of political action and an instrument in the national and global political contest. Questions from participants shaped the conversation from the macro-level to the micro-level, as the discussion moved from higher education as a critical institution in a politically-charged environment to how early-career researchers are trained to study higher education.

The next chapter includes a thought-provoking essay analysing the politics of university reform. Susanne Lohmann highlights cases of university reform in the US and UK to illustrate the complex set of political forces impacting change. She designs a political parallelogram to showcase how political forces tug at the force field influencing a political outcome. She uses 'punctuated equilibrium' to describe university reform whereby there are long periods of institutional stasis followed by occasional bursts of change. In conclusion, she calls for universities to nurture their relations and serve the cities and nation states where they reside which is a correction to excessive cosmopolitan. In the end, Lohmann argues that universities can be local, national and cosmopolitan.

INTRODUCTION 5

Moving from university reform to student movements, this chapter takes us to South Africa where student unrest has a long history. This study focuses in on the 2015-16 student protests against increasing student fees in South African higher education. Known as the #FeesMustFall student movement, Magda Fourie-Malherbe & Anneke Müller analyse the complexity of issues driving the movement and the overarching ongoing struggle for social justice in post-apartheid South African society. They conduct a case study of the movement at one particular university and analyse how the university management responded to issues raised by the students. While institutional transformation was not evident in this case, the movement did defend 'free' higher education and raised awareness around the university's language policy. Overall, this chapter highlights internal power struggles in a politicised higher education environment embedded in a complex context.

From South Africa, the fourth chapter in Part 2 takes us to Northern Italy, where Giacomo Balduzzi & Massimiliano Vaira study the university third mission. As higher education institutions face decreasing public funding, there is pressure for institutions and academics to enact the university third mission to seek economic resources and relationships with external organisations and actors. Balduzzi and Vaira conduct a multiple case study of three universities in Northern Italy examining how universities respond to the increasing expectation to pursue third mission activities and how this leads to internal institutional changes, tensions, and struggles. Drawing from new institutionalism and Bourdieu's social field theories, the authors argue that the university third mission is not just a set of activities, but it's a complex politically constructed field. A relational network of actors, the State, higher education institutions, academics and organisations come together to create third mission activities which leads to structuration of a new area of institutional life. Important to the analysis is the political interactions and tensions that take place in the internal and external dimension during field construction.

The final chapter in this part examines the competences and professional identities of Japanese teaching staff in vocational institutions. With the expansion of the Japanese higher education sector a non-university sector was created in the 1960–1970s. Yuki Inenaga & Keiichi Yoshimoto design a research framework to assess the academic experiences, qualifications and competences of teaching staff in these vocationally-oriented education institutions to better understand the political arena between academic oligarchy and the labour market. Using national survey data on teaching staff in junior colleges and professional training colleges, the authors develop quantitative models to analyse career variables in the data. From the data analysis, four professional expertise model types emerge: dual, academic, vocational, and other. The findings suggest that there are tensions between the professional identities of the teaching staff and institutional demands.

3 Societal Values, National Regimes and Higher Education

The third and final part considers the relationships and influences between 'Societal Values, National Regimes and Higher Education'. The first chapter focuses on the politically-charged topic of access to and equity of higher education. This tends to be a topic of tension between different actors, many of whom are external actors. National policies for access to higher education reflect a societal value, whether higher education is viewed as a public or private good. Since the early 2000s, European policies have emphasised the social dimension of higher education. Pepka Boyadjieva and Petya Ilieva-Trichkova argue that the massification of European higher education did not reduce inequalities in access to higher education and thus a social justice perspective is needed. The authors design a way to conceptualise and measure the social justice dimension of access to higher education by examining creating two indices: inclusion and fairness. Using European data, the authors test the indices and find different relationship patterns between inclusion and fairness in higher education for two social groups across Europe.

The next chapter explores how national gender regimes shape academic labour markets in Finland and Switzerland. Societal structures, policies-in-action and norms surrounding gender roles and expectations may facilitate or constrain career choices. Terhi Nokkala, Pierre Bataille, Taru Siekkinen and Gaële Goastellec focus in on the internationalisation of the academic career, particularly the international mobility of early career academics. They explore how mid-career academics (male and female) with children view international mobility depending on the national gender regime. Using qualitative interviews, the findings suggest that there are differences between academics working in these two national contexts. International mobility is less contested in Switzerland than in Finland where academics were critical of enforced international mobility. In Finland there was little difference, when compared with the Switzerland data, in terms of how men and women talk about balancing their career and family. The authors conclude that combining family with an academic career is more difficult in Switzerland than in Finland.

The third chapter in this part considers the relationship between a regional labour market and graduate employability. Employers and, more broadly, society have come to expect that higher education graduates possess work-ready

INTRODUCTION

skills and competences for the labour market. Martina Gaisch, Victoria Rammer, Silke Preymann, Stefanie Sterrer and Regina Aichinger explore graduate employability in the cross-border region of Austria and the Czech Republic. Using graduate perspectives (possession of skills, social capital, identity and personal attributes) as a focus of narrative analysis, the findings of this pilot study suggest that current models of employability do not reflect all related factors, especially context-specific elements. The authors design a renewed framework, taking into account the socio-economic dynamics inherent in the Austrian/Czech Republic region.

From Europe, we travel to Palestine to explore the entrepreneurial nature of universities in light of a complex local context. Higher education institutions are rooted in local social dynamics; these contexts largely influence the development of education, research, and teaching. One such higher education system that's embedded in a complex social dynamic is the Palestinian university system. Palestine is an occupied territory with political tension, economic stagnation and high unemployment rates. Within this context, Huub L.M. Mudde examines the entrepreneurial nature of Palestinian universities. Employing a mixed methods study at four universities, he conducted questionnaires, interviews and content analysis. Entrepreneurial activities, in the form of entrepreneurial courses and incubators for students, were offered in the four universities as a tool for employment and economic growth. However, Mudde argues that these activities alone do not make the four universities 'entrepreneurial universities', rather they should instead be viewed as 'engaged' as they increasingly stimulate their students to act entrepreneurially.

All together the chapters in the book seek to foster reflection and debate on the analytical power of 'Universities as political institutions'. The authors in this volume illustrate various methods and theoretical lenses, drawing from such disciplines as political science, sociology, economics, and anthropology, to analyse political spaces in the study of higher education. We hope that these novel approaches give insight into future research as well as inform policy and practice.

Reference

Pusser, B. (2018). Political perspective, research in higher education. In P. Teixeira & J. Shin (Eds.), *Encyclopedia of international higher education systems and institutions*. Dordrecht: Springer.

PART 1

Geo-Political Influences

∵

CHAPTER 1

Powershift: Universities and the Seismic Winds of Change

Susan L. Robertson

Abstract

In order to understand the rise of authoritarian populist politics and the reassertion of nationalisms in the contemporary era and their relationship to higher education I argue we need to historicise our accounts, and place universities in their wider contexts. To do this, I introduce four 'powershifts' which I argue are central to understanding these changes. Powershift 1 examines the 1970s global economic crisis, the emergence of neoliberalism as a political project, its expansion outward. Powershift 2 explores the events surrounding the now iconic moment – 11 September 2001 – giving rise to new forms of imperialism, conflict, an intensification of state surveillance and securitisation in universities, in the face of a global movement of refugee populations. Powershift 3 addresses the consequences of the rise of finance capital and weak state oversight leading to the global financial crisis in 2008, the bailing out of the banks, and subsequent effects on student indebtedness and university finances. A final Powershift 4 brings us to the present conjuncture – 2016 onwards – marked by a rise in authoritarian power, rising racism and xenophobia and a worsening situation for the lower and middle classes that can be read through parallel education biographies and qualifications.

Keywords

globalisation – populism – security – migration – inequalities – politics – universities – imperialism

1 Ruptures

In a blog entry written in the days that followed the result of the June 2016 Referendum in the United Kingdom (UK) – whether to remain in or leave the

© KONINKLIJKE BRILL NV, LEIDEN, 2020 | DOI: 10.1163/9789004422582_002

European Union (EU) – I wrote: "somehow the earth seems to have shifted off course – by a tilt in its axis" (Robertson, 2016, p. 1). Though the margins were not overwhelming, with the Leave vote at 51.9% and Remain at 48.1%, nevertheless, the leave campaigners insisted that 'the people' had spoken. In the days that followed, a pattern became clear.

Whilst 'the people's' vote to leave coalesced around migration (intra-European and refugee) and national sovereignty issues, close scrutiny of the voters and their patterns of voting revealed an underlying structural issue. These were socio-economic groups who had been left behind as a result of neoliberal policies that had delivered deindustrialisation, the 2008 global financial crisis, and a decade of austerity (Dorling & Tomlinson, 2019). Rather than all boats rising, which had been the mantra of neoliberal evangelisers, those voting to leave were significantly poorer than they had been a decade earlier (ibid). They were also less well educated, or whose education had not translated into the promise of a well-paid job. It could be argued, therefore, that the Brexit vote was symptomatic of deeper transformations that had taken place over the past forty years. The relatively well-off Brexiters within the Eurosceptic political elite had managed to touch the raw nerve of resentment amongst those who had been left behind, turning this into a venting against an imagined enemy; refugees and migrants, and Europe (Eco, 2013).

Brexit, as the organised 'Leave' campaigners had come to name it, was set to take both the UK and the EU into unchartered waters. No European member country had tried to unravel the multiple entanglements and interdependencies arising from years of integration between themselves and their continental European neighbours. For the UK, great swathes of activity – from security and defence, to the movement of people, goods and services – would all have to be unpicked and new kinds of expertise had to be found quickly.[1]

If Brexit was a very British affair, it was also global. And as Nancy Fraser (2017, p. 1) remarked, "there is no shortage of analogues elsewhere". From the election of Trump in the United States (US) in November 2016, to the disintegration of the social democratic centre right parties in Europe, and the election of far right and populist candidates in Latin America, a new world order and its 'disorder' was becoming apparent. If this was a global political crisis, what were its causes?

Closer to home, and the focus of this chapter, such questions are big and important and need to be understood both up close now, and with wisdom of a longer arc of time looking backwards. How did we get here? And what might this mean for the future of European higher education and its various instruments and processes, and for the UK? Is, and if so how, higher education implicated in these developments given that one line of cleavage is what is called educational segmentation (Bovens & Wille, 2017)?[2] By this Bovens and Wille mean that the nature of one's education qualifications maps pro- and anti-Europe; pro- and anti-Brexit; pro-and anti-Trump.

And this was not the only line of fracture. Growing divisions between communities in the UK, particularly around Islam, were fanned by a hostile government department whose tightening immigration and surveillance projects which were having profound effects on those within the higher education sector in the UK. What do these cleavages tell us about the new forms of imperialism, and the cultural politics of neoliberalism and its material effects, and how this complex and shifting set of dynamics has both shaped and been shaped by higher education policies, programmes and practices?

In the rest of this chapter I will argue that in order to make sense of these dynamics, we need to trace out a series of ruptures and crises that have had deep social, political and economic consequences for their wider societies, as well as on the higher education sector within. In the following section I frame these as a series of distinct and discrete, though internally related, powershifts.

2   Powershifts

What is a powershift? 'Powershift' is the title of a highly influential popular book by Alvin Toffler published following the collapse in the Soviet project in 1989, and with it the end of the Cold War which had structured relations between the West and the Soviet bloc from the 1950s onward. What might the future look like, with socialism no longer a threat, asked Toffler. He notes: "The end of the Cold War not just brought about mere adjustments among states, but a novel redistribution [of power] among states, markets and civil society. The steady concentration of power in the hands of the states that began in 1648 with the peace of Westphalia is over, at least for a while" (Toffler, 1991, p. 1).

In short, the collapse of the Soviet empire opened the door for the novel redistribution, or shift, of power upward, outward and downward. This included the further expansion of capitalist markets into the post-Socialist countries as well as previously decommodified spheres of social policy, an extension of US dominance in the global economy and society, a reinvigorated set of regionalisms across the globe (Robertson, Olds, Dale, & Dang, 2016) and the ramping up of the governing by the multilateral institutions (Sassen, 2006). In this chapter I will draw upon Toffler's use of the idea of a 'powershift' to signal significant ruptures in existing institutional and social arrangements, opening space for the recalibration of the redistribution of power and control amongst competing social forces operating at multiple scales.

In this section I introduce four powershifts which are central to understanding contemporary higher education in the UK particularly, and with consequences for Europe. Powershift 1 refers to the 1970s global economic crisis, the emergence of neoliberalism as a political project, its expansion outward. Powershift 2 means the events surrounding the now iconic moment – 11 September 2001 – giving rise to new forms of imperialism, conflict, an intensification of state surveillance and securitisation, and the global movement of refugee populations. Powershift 3 encompasses the inevitable consequences of the rise of finance capital and weak state oversight leading to the global financial crisis in 2008, the bailing out of the banks, and subsequent effects on redistribution. The final Powershift 4 brings us to the present conjuncture – 2016 onwards – marked by a rise in authoritarian power, populist politics, rising racism and xenophobia and a worsening situation for the lower and middle classes. I will be arguing that each powershift emerges out of a crisis in the spheres of the economy, politics and the cultural or lifeworld. Interventions are efforts to contain and stabilise those crisis tendencies through spatially strategic governing projects. In short, as we will see, whilst neither Trump nor Brexit were planned, they could well have been predicted as the likely outcomes of political projects and their material consequences for daily lives and life-worlds (Sayer, 2011).

These shifts can be broadly traced via three logics of power. The first two are what Arrighi (1994, pp. 33–34) calls 'territorial' and 'capitalist' logics. I would argue that there is also a third logic – the making of the 'social individual' – whose lifeworld and world-view emerges out of social interaction, sense- and identity-making (Bernstein, 2000; Fourcade, 2016). Each is different from the other in that the motivations and desires, situations and processes of these agents differs in relation to these logics, and what is to be focused on. For example, whilst the capitalist holding money will wish to put it where-ever profits can be had in order to accumulate more capital, territorially-located politicians and statesmen will typically seek outcomes which sustain or augment their own state vis-à-vis other states, and in relation to its citizenry. The social individual, however, emerges out of reflexive, semiotically-mediated, encounters with others/ideas/objects, whose structuring categories produce social selves, ways of seeing and being, and social orders. These three logics may well tug against the other as profit making, state-making and identity-making do not always map onto each other. At the same time, these logics can also reinforce each other; for instance, when the territorial state guarantees political structures that enable the accumulation of property, where particular kinds of identities legitimate the state's capacity to govern, or when particular worldviews reinforce the prioritising of particular logics in new spheres of social life.

2.1   Powershift 1: Insurgent Markets/Individualising Minds

A great deal has been written both about this first powershift both more generally and in relation to higher education. At the heart of this account is the instituting and embedding of neoliberalism as an organising ideology, the making of market societies (Leys, 2003; Slater & Tonkiss, 2001) and market civilisation (Seabrooke & Bowden, 2004). How and why did this happen, and what have been the implications for higher education in Europe both at the time and in relation to present developments?

The reference point for this first powershift was the iconic global 'oil shocks' in the 1970s (Harvey, 1989). In truth, however, by the late 1960s it was evident that economic growth in the industrialised world had begun to slow, with internal markets saturated and profit margins falling (Streeck, 2014b). Firms went in search of new export markets for their surplus output, for places with lower labour costs, with fewer government regulations (Harvey, 1989, pp. 141–142). More generally, the period from 1965 to 1973 was characterised as one in which the development model of Fordism and Keynesianism after the Second World War were unable to contain the internal contradictions of capital. The economic engine – capital – that powered capitalism, was in trouble (Harvey, 2014, pp. 10–11). The hegemony of the Keynesian National Welfare State and Fordist production model was now is crisis (Jessop, 1999).

The 1970s global recession that followed opened up new terrain for struggles – between Hayekian neoliberals and Keynesians (Hobsbawm, 1994, p. 409), and subaltern groups (gender/ethnicity/race) opposed to their subordination by bureaucratic, patriarchal and racial structures they deemed forms of violence. Though a Hayekian victory was not immediate, as Peck (2013) reveals in his book *Constructions of Neoliberal Reason*, the continuing shortfalls of Keynesianism (one size fits all bureaucratic governing/state patriarchy), as well as potent claims about the exploitation of the public commons (overloaded government thesis), played on and to, both those claiming liberal freedom through the market and the politics of recognition and difference.

Yet the basis for a new economic and social development model was not immediately obvious, though there were a number of contenders; these included the idea of a learning economy (Lundvall & Johnson, 1994); a network society (Castells, 1996), and a knowledge society (UNESCO, 2005). However, by the mid-1990s, the idea of a 'knowledge-based' economy was increasingly embraced by the OECD (Foray, 2004), with the OECD and World Bank respectively investing in sets of indicators to 'measure' knowledge-based economies (Robertson, 2009).

If knowledge economies were dependent upon boosting knowledge stocks (as human capital), their decisions were also shaped by the view that the West had a comparative advantage in sectors like education, which might form the basis of new trade arrangements. Targets for higher education enrolments were set so as to increase both enrolments at home and to open up education sectors to full-fee-paying students from overseas. In the case of the UK, this meant leaning upon old colonial ties, such as Hong Kong, Malaysia, India, Pakistan and Nigeria to recruit full-fee-paying students to UK universities (Robertson & Kedzierski, 2016). Those countries opening up their higher education sectors to international fee-paying students also had active government departments and allied interests (firms seeking to enter public service sectors in sectors that had been largely government monopolies) who were busy negotiating at the multilateral level to include education services in trade agreements, such as the World Trade Organization's General Agreement on Trade in Services (Robertson, Bonal, & Dale, 2002).

In this new context of global competition and the development of an education services sector, universities were now charged with driving the development of a competitive knowledge economy through the creation of knowledge rich products (as a result of ideas leading to innovations), a new breed of entrepreneurs, and by boosting a culture of small start-ups, spin out firms and the creation of intellectual property. They would also be sites for new forms of financialisation; of loans and other forms of credit to students, institutions and nations.

The broad detail of this narrative is now a familiar story, but what kind of powershift was this? In essence it was to effect a change in the very fabric of the society and its constituent social relations (Leys, 2003); as a market society (Slater & Tonkiss, 2001). Neoliberalism as a political project would set in motion the unravelling of the old social contract, whilst the extension of capitalism into decommodified social policy realms, such as education, was set to reshape both institutional life and the life-worlds of individuals. This was the culture of the new capitalism (Sennett, 2006), with education itself tasking with both producing and reproducing this new culture.

Higher education would be both globalised and regionalised. Regionalisation projects emerged as a protection against the turbulence of neoliberal globalisation (Hettne & Söderbaum, 2000). Most notable for higher education in Europe was the Bologna Process (1999). This entailed putting into place a single framework that redefined degree structures across Europe and beyond. A competitive European higher education sector was intended to limit the movement of graduate students to the US (Robertson & Keeling, 2008). In doing so, it would also help boost the European Commission's Lisbon Agenda (Robertson et al., 2016). This Lisbon Agenda was a strategy aimed to create a dynamic and competitive economy, and a socially cohesive Europe through a programme of nationally-coordinated growth and investments in research, higher education, and new technologies (Robertson et al., 2016). Lisbon provided a mandate and agenda for extending the reach of Europe's policy responsibility deeper into national territory – education – and ultimately outwards to the rest of the world. The Lisbon Agenda also confirmed a neoliberal understanding of higher education's contribution to the socio-economic well-being of the region; building and securing human capital.

Arguably the most successful European country in transforming key aspects of social life into a market society has been England.[3] In higher education the creation of a higher education market gained considerable momentum following the dismantling of its funding for 'home'/EU undergraduate places in universities and the establishment of a system of student loans legitimated by narratives like public savings, fairness to those not accessing universities, and a 'graduate premium'.[4]

According to the government, the urgent policy question was about how to "widen access and sustain and improve standards of university excellence in an increasingly pressured global context and in a more constrained public spending environment" (BIS, 2009, p. 3). In other words, how best to open up more places in higher education without increasing the longer-term financial burden on government.

It was this issue that set the terms of reference for the *Independent Review of Higher Education Funding and Student Finance* (the 'Browne Review' led by John Browne, formerly Chief Executive of the oil and gas multinational, BP) in 2010. Under arrangements at this point, the Higher Education Funding Council for England (HEFCE) partially funded each place. However, HEFCE limited its annual outlay by imposing a total recruitment cap on student numbers on each institution. The Browne Review (Browne, 2011) built into its recommendations the withdrawal of the block grant to social sciences, humanities and arts (with sciences and technology areas, and vulnerable subjects like languages protected). It also recommended lifting the ceiling on student fees to enable universities to recover their lost block funding via significantly increased student fees.

Fee increases were justified with the following observation; that in 2006, the ceiling of the Graduate Student Contribution had been raised to £3,000 but contrary to popular opinion, this had not discouraged students from seeking places. Instead, demand for student places had increased (Browne, 2011, p. 20). The Review also proposed a readjustment of the student loan system, which placed the ultimate burden on students of the costs of their undergraduate degrees. Repayments would only begin at the rate of 9% of income on salaries over £21,000 over a period of 30 years after graduation. Monies not paid back during this period would be written off by the state.

However, the effect of setting an upper limit (£9,000 at the time) meant most universities in the sector, irrespective of their mission, status or social class intake, expected to charge students at or close to the ceiling, and not the recommended £6,000. This not only created new problems for the state in terms of the overall costs of underwriting the student loan book until students paid back the loan, but the determination to institute a competitive, consumer-driven market in England has presented the government with other headaches. As McGettigan (2012) shows, these 'savings' are nothing more than an accounting trick. In moving the funding of higher education from an institutional subsidy to a student loan underwritten by government, the government was using 'off-balance accounting' techniques, meaning that the money would not show up on the government's books as a deficit.

More importantly, these new funding arrangements have opened the door to for-profit private providers of higher education, for example the FTSE listed Pearson Education, to enter the sector, with their students able to access the state-backed student loan book.[5] Prior to this, these providers had been excluded. Through commodification and financialisation of the English higher education sector was inching closer toward being more fully marketised.

Streeck (2014b) shows that this first crisis and its subsequent socio-political and spatial shift in power, from the state to the market, has eventually given rise to new levels of both public and household debt. Efforts to expand and service sectors like education to meet the demands of a knowledge-based economy are, at the same time, undermined by government deals with corporations to lower the rates of corporate tax (faced with the threat that the corporations would go elsewhere). The privatisation of education debt to households was made possible by more generous opportunities for access to credit and unprecedented levels of indebtedness (Streeck, 2017, p. 7).

These distributional inequalities have come to matter in several ways, as we will see with the third and fourth powershifts. The question is why and how? To begin, the contradictory unity between production and realisation becomes far harder to keep in balance when the reliable non-discretionary habits of the working poor are eclipsed by the vagaries of the wealthy. For capitalism to work there needs to be a circuit of capital; those consuming need financial resources to ensure what is produced can be paid for (Harvey, 2014, p. 168). Greater and greater levels of indebtedness need to be serviced, at cost. This places limits on the purchasing power of graduates – including starting families, buying homes

POWERSHIFT 19

and so on. Second, the promise of a return on education as an investment – the graduate premium – failed to be realised for many groups leading to a stalling if not reverse in social mobility. Such developments pave the way for a loss of confidence in the system that seemed to leave them worse off, and resentment toward those elites who seemed to have disproportionately benefitted from redistribution upward.

2.2   *Powershift 2: Insurgent Minds/States of Surveillance*

But there were other dynamics at work in reshaping higher education sectors in Europe, and particularly the UK. The potency of their effects on higher education were, in part, because of the closer integration of higher education into the global circuits of capital. Any political disturbance would also send tremors into the world of higher education via its expansion as a global market, and accusations that higher education institutions might be harbingers of insurgent minds. This was most visible in the days, weeks and months that followed Al Qaeda's attack on the World Trade Towers in the US on 11 September 2001, the subsequent invasion of Iraq in 2003, and the waged and civil wars over the decade in Libya, Syria and Yemen.

It is tempting to view these events through the prism of Al Qaeda, '9/11' and the invasion of Iraq. However, this was far from the case. Ali (2003) points out that in 1997 the *Project for the New American Century* was published. The Project argued that America could not be complacent with the end of the Cold War. Notable signatories to the Project included Dick Cheney, Jeb Bush and Donald Rumsfeld (Ali, 2003, pp. 7–8); key members of the Bush Administration which presided over the war in Afghanistan and Iraq. In 2001 Western forces invaded Afghanistan – sanctioned by the UN, backed by NATO. It was the first port of call in "the global war on terror" (Ali, 2008, p. 19). Two years later, the "national trauma of 9/11" was used to pursue an audacious imperial agenda of which the occupation of Iraq promised to one out of a series that launched a new imperialist agenda for the US (Ali, 2003, p. 7).

Harvey's (2003) account of the attack on Iraq is also insightful – and should be read through the predatory logics of capital, on the one hand, and the US' state's management of its own internal crises, on the other.

> The recession that began early in 2001…would not go away. Unemployment was rising and the sense of economic insecurity was palpable, Corporate scandals cascaded over each other, and seemingly solid corporate empires were literally dissolving overnight…The current account balance with the rest of the world had gone from bad to worse as the United States

became the biggest debtor nation of all time. Social inequality had long been on the increase, but the tax-cut fetish of the administration seemed set to increase it further. (Harvey, 2003. p. 12)

Similar to Ali (2003, 2008), Harvey argues that a combination of the absence of the threat of the Cold War and thus no clear enemy, and in the context of rising precarity, and fear, that the US government needed a new enemy. Add to this the geo-political and economic interest of the US in oil, and a controlling presence in the Middle East, and the stage was set for a new stage of US imperialism (Harvey, 2003, p. 22).

The unleashing of oppositional forces, and the disintegration of civility, set in motion the unravelling of fragile relationships and complicated alignments across the Middle East that was to ricochet back to the West with fury. The war on terror had become a war of terrors. Importantly for my account, the displacement of large numbers of civilians as a result of wars in Central Asia and the Middle East, together with conflict in North and Sub-Saharan Africa would fuel one of the largest movements of people toward Europe since the end of the Second World War. According to the UNHCR, there were around 68.5 million forcibly displaced people in the world, including 25.4 million refugees (UNHCR, 2017). Students and academics were caught up in this mass of displacement, either concentrated in camps or in search of a new life in Europe.

This imperialistically-motivated power shift had foreseeable and tragic consequences in multiple locations around the globe – from the violence waged in war, and the war waged on those it now assumed to be violent. Attacks in London, Madrid, Indonesia…and later Paris, Brussels, Manchester, Istanbul and London, triggered new rounds of surveillance. With many of these bombers and sympathisers grown at home and in some cases well educated – universities were identified as potential sites for radicalisation. The effects were immediate both in terms of the relationship between selected citizens and their state, and on higher education. Dependent as it was on the flow of students across its borders, any deliberate crack down on 'terrorist' centres and Islamic countries, or identification and containment measures, all contributed to the experience of being under surveillance. A new politics of insecurity and surveillance emerged in the heart of Europe, with major consequences for everyday social life. Visas took time or were rejected. Queues in airports lengthened, as did efforts to detect the next insurgent. The US and the UK leaked students as they turned to new destinations viewed as less hostile; Canada, Australia, Germany.

CONTEST was launched in 2003 as a security strategy aimed at countering terrorism, with Muslims and Muslim neighbourhoods regarded as particularly 'at risk' (Heath-Kelly, 2013). 'Prevent' is one of four strands within this overall approach, though over time its focus has changed, with higher education institutions being drawn into its implementation. Statutory "Prevent duties" include monitoring in ways that prevented "people being drawn into terrorism" (HEFCE, 2017, p. 4). As Glees and Pope (2005) note, the Home Office were persuaded by the finding that some of the homegrown terrorists responsible for the London bombings in July 2005 had studied at British universities. As a result, universities were seen as places where extremist views might be fostered and thus a recruiting ground for potential Jihadists. Faculty were given new roles; to report on suspicious behaviour presumed to be evidence of radicalisation, and to declare all invitations to outside speakers so as to ensure radicalisers were not given a platform.

'Prevent' was rolled out not only in the UK, but across Europe. 'Prevent' strategies in relation to higher education have been particularly controversial, especially amongst students and faculty. Prevent reporting requirements on higher education institutions in the UK have stirred up feelings of alienation amongst ordinary Muslim students. There is also an inference that any critique of the UK State and British values is seen as a tendency toward an extremist position. This in turn places new kinds of limits on academic freedom (Saeed & Johnson, 2016).

The construction by the state, media and fearful populations, of Muslim communities as harbourers if not nurturers of the enemy within (Eco, 2013), had now set in motion a divisive xenophobia that reinforced new divisions of 'us' against 'them'. In the academy, the effects were pernicious. As Saeed and Johnson (2016, p. 39) note, the Counter Terrorism and Security Act (2015) makes it a legal obligation on universities to report on such potentially suspicious students, but "the idea of being monitored, the feeling of considered guilty because of religious association, is a familiar sentiment for Muslim students". In Saeed and Johnson's (2016) study, students report feeling singled out, being watched and fearful of what might happen. This sense of threat was not only the preserve of students. Academics too felt vulnerable. Within the wider academy it also placed limits on academic freedom and thinking, where extremism was defined as opposition to fundamental British values, including democracy and the rule of law, individual liberty and mutual respect.

With this second powershift, new sets of collusions and collisions had been set in motion in the knowledge powerhouse; ones that have created a new set of divisions in the higher education landscape. Compliant administrators and academics were seen as colluding with the state. There was also a collision of logics – between the expansion of a global higher education services sector and the UK a desirable destination, and the UK state's preoccupation with surveillance and terrorism within the academy. Taken together they display the multiple registers of violence that have led to seismic changes in the social relations within the academy.

2.3   *Powershift 3: Resurgent Finance Capital/Compliant State*

On 15 September 2008, what had been brewing as a veritable storm over subprime mortgages in the housing sector in the US in 2007, erupted into a full-blown global banking crisis when the investment bank, the Lehman Brothers, filed for bankruptcy. The excessive risk taking by the banks around lending, the lure for the banks of profits to be made from a range of new financial products, and lax government regulation of the sector in financial centres like London and New York, were the ingredients of a perfect storm. Like a house of cards, the accumulation and high default rate of these sub-prime mortgages led to a rapid devaluation of financial instruments (mortgage backed securities, bundled loan portfolios, derivatives and credit default swaps). As the value of these assets plummeted, the market for these securities evaporated and heavily invested banks began to experience a crisis of liquidity. A slew of banks was tipped to follow, with savers scrambling to withdraw what they could. High level negotiations were the stuff of hour on hour brinkmanship, as the Federal Reserve Bank, the Bank of England, the European Investment Bank and International Monetary Fund sought to fill the liquidity crisis with an injection of billions. The knock-on effects for the global stock market were deep and profound. This was the most serious financial crisis since the Great Depression of the 1930s. The scale of the failure promoted Alan Greenspan, former head of the US Federal Reserve to point to what ought to now be an existential crisis for the economics profession given their penchant for economic forecasting models (Green & Hay, 2015). 'How come no-one saw this coming?' was a common refrain.

As Streeck (2014b) reminds us in his account of the period, one of the problems of those analysing capital accumulation and its crisis tendencies is that they failed to think of capital as being capable of having a strategic purpose. Instead we treat capital as a means of production, rather than a class whose interests and motivations are to pursue economic activity so as to generate profits. In such a framing, capital had become a source of creative destruction rather than a player in the years that followed the 1970s crisis. Streeck (2014b, p. 19) argues: "When capital proved to be a player instead of a plaything; a predator instead of a working animal with an urgent need to break free from the cage-like institutional framework of the post war 1945 social market economy" – we tend to be surprised.

Yet the evidence was there for all to see. This was a class war; one being waged by financial capital, aimed at reversing the post-war project of distribution. This can be seen in the New York Times interview with Warren Buffett in 2006, the fourth wealthiest person in the world: "sure there is a class war, and it is my class, the rich, who are making it, and we are winning" (Stein, 2006, p. 1). But this is not just a story about the rise of finance capital, and its predatory and unchecked behaviour. Rather it was the inevitable outcome of neoliberal restructuring described in the powershift one elaborated earlier. Whilst advocates of neoliberal restructuring had promised a big increase in investment as business was unshackled from state regulation, high taxes and trade union pressures (Kotz, 2018, p. 39), apart from the boom in the 1990s around information technologies, the expansion through the 1990s and 2000s was large propelled by debt-financed consumer spending. Kotz (2018, p. 4) argues that these processes created three developments that were unsustainable that would eventually lead to the structural crisis of neoliberal capitalism: (i) growing private sector debt; (ii) new derivative securities by rent seeking banks which made huge profits from initiating and trading in them, and (iii) a declining rate of profit and excess capacity in manufacturing. Taken together, these developments created a new fiscal crisis of the contemporary state reflected in an escalation in public debt since the 1970s. Streeck argues that by replacing tax revenues with debt,

> governments contributed further to inequality, in that they offered secure investment opportunities to those whose money they would or could no longer confiscate and had to borrow instead. Unlike taxpayers, buyers of government bonds continue to own what they pay to the state, and in fact collect interest on it, typically paid out of ever less progressive taxation; they can also pass it on to their children. Moreover, rising public debt can be and is being utilized politically to argue for cutbacks in state spending and for privatisation of public services, further constraining redistributive democratic intervention in the capitalist economy. (Streeck, 2014a, p. 43)

It took the economist, Thomas Piketty, to point to the workings and outcomes of resurgent finance capital in his book *Capital in the 21st Century* (2014). Piketty (2014) concludes that, if left to its own devices (weak institutional arrangements for redistribution through progressive taxation; pressure for high wages, high taxes and high skill arrangements), wealth distribution will tend toward the concentration in wealth accumulation, in turn producing inequalities. In other words, inequality is produced by both inequality from labour (wages differences) and inequality from capital (previously owned wealth).

As a public service, education has been a casualty of the debt state, with wages, investment in infrastructures and redistribution to close inequality gaps, all under pressure. Paralleling the rise of public debt is the rise in private debt, and this matters again for education equality, as more and more, households are asked to shoulder the cost of running the highly competitive education race. The ready availability of credit, coupled with downward pressure on wages, has led to what Colin Crouch calls 'privatised Keynesianism'; the replacement of government debt with private debt as a mechanism for expanding the resource inventory in the national economy (Crouch, 2011, pp. 97–124). No-where is this more evident than in the higher education sector in the UK and also the US. Figures for the US (2015) show that more than $1.2 trillion is owed in student loan debt, involving 40 million borrowers, with an average balance of $29,000 (Holland, 2015, p. 1). In 2017 in the UK it was reported that outstanding debt on loans jumped by 16.6% to £100.5bn at the end of March 2017, up from £86.2bn a year earlier, with England accounting for £89.3bn of the total (Monahan & Wiele, 2017). It is not just tuition fee hikes which have placed pressure on household budgets and created unprecedented levels of debt. Students are pushed to do more and more to thicken their CVs which involve additional resources. This has created a space for private lenders to offer new kinds of financial products to enable mobility, extension activities and tutoring.

Getting ahead via education in a highly competitive world is an expensive business, as it means increasingly significant amounts of resources being assembled and invested in those cultural, social and political capitals that will make a difference to your position in the status hierarchy and competition for talent. But in a world that has come to link 'talent' to very high salaries, and to justify very high salaries as the reward for talent, winning that race is worth the investment (Brown et al., 2011; Newfield, 2010). Like any race, however, there are winners and losers, though the size of the pool of losers is widening as the 'winner takes all'. Like all races too, the rules for engagement are always strategically selective of some over others. This is power that matters, with bite! As Brown and colleagues observe: "if the capitalist system has no loyalty to American workers, much the same can be said of American corporate elites. They have not simply played a game of winner takes all; they have created one" (2011, p. 115).

The issues are compounded when considering the changes that have occurred in the reorganisation of work globally, and what this means for economic returns. Brown and colleagues (2011) show in their book *The Global Auction*, how national labour markets, production and wages have been transformed by global processes. A key dynamic at work here is the way in which relatively low-cost locations around the world – India, China, Indonesia, Vietnam and so on – can reduce the market price of technological know-how. They point to the availability of a well-educated (often in the West) workforce available for outsourced and local operations who are willing to work for lower wages, relative to the centre, but which are higher relative to the wages of the other locals.

What has made this possible have been innovations – like digital technologies – which enable routine professional work (such as health, legal or educational) to be off-shored, completed and returned around the clock for a fraction of the price. Brown and colleagues refer to this process as 'digital Taylorism':

> This involves translating the knowledge work of managers, professionals and technicians into working knowledge by capturing, codifying and digitizing their work in software packages, templates and prescripts that can be transferred and manipulated by others, regardless of location... Unlike mechanical Taylorism, which required the concentration of labor in factories, digital Taylorism enables work activities to be dispersed and recombined from anywhere in the world in less than the time it takes to read a sentence. (Brown et al., 2011, p. 72)

These global production work processes are, in turn, creating a middle class in countries like India and China. And whilst these employees "with a college education working in managerial and professional jobs for international companies may have to work long hours and constantly feel the pressure of tough financial targets, they are among the winners in a global auction" (Brown et al., 2011, p. 129).

One effect of digital Taylorism on education is that it challenges a key ideological underpinning of the 'national' social contract. Because national economies now exert less influence on the provision of jobs, they can no longer claim to provide a meritocracy with its promise of a secure job and decent wages in return for self-discipline, hard work and learning. That link is broken, and with it a key mechanism of social control, and legitimation for a system of social stratification suited to capitalist economies. The globalising of the capital-labour relation thus has huge implications for national education systems, including how best to ensure ongoing commitment to 'doing well', when the returns are visibly meagre for some, and a veritable cornucopia for tiny group of highly privileged others. The shared sense of worlds that secure a commitment to a wider social project, and with it forms of social cohesion for the state, have been ruptured. The fracture lines and frayed hopes have fed into a powershift that has thrown up an insurgent populism, and a paradoxical hardening nationalism.

2.4 Powershift 4: Insurgent Populism/Resentment

In the early hours of the 24th June, the direction of travel of the UK Referendum was visible. By 4.00 am, the decision was there for all to see. The UK had voted Leave. After months of turbo-charged boosterism by both Eurosceptics and Europhiles about the economic and political benefits to be had from leaving or staying, the distinct feeling was that if not sanity, then the tendency toward the status quo would hold the day.

But when a decision that big has the capacity to change the course of a nation, not only has the earth's axis moved, but so, also, has the very fabric of the lives, fortunes and futures of whole groups. The incumbent Prime Minister, David Cameron, resigned immediately. Nursing an ambition to be of the UK Prime Minister from her teenage years, Theresa May stepped into the breach, donning the crown and pronouncing in her new role, Brexit Means Brexit.

However, it took the election of Donald Trump in November 2016 to the US Presidency for the full weight of this fourth power shift to take hold. In aligning himself with 'the ordinary people' Trump drove a divisive and populist political campaign that vilified the cosmopolitan elite living in the cities and universities (Fraser, 2017) who had benefitted from globalisation. Whether described by Cohen (2019) as the rise of authoritarian populism, or Fraser (2017) as regressive neoliberalism, both agree that what is needed is a cultural, political and economic analysis if we are to understand the rise and appeal of populist politics.

Across, the EU, UK and the USA, voter profiles tell us that in many ways this was a vote made by those who had been left behind in the globalisation and education races, whose futures now looked even bleaker following the 2008 crisis, and a decade of austerity policies (Bovens & Wille, 2017; Dorling & Tomlinson, 2019). As argued in Powershift 3, falling wages, fewer opportunities for decent, properly-paid work, and the collapse of the promise of social mobility has changed social and life-worlds (Streeck, 2014, 2017; Fraser, 2017). Multiple deficits – democratic, welfare and social status (Cohen, 2019) have created precisely the new economy of worth and value – of us and them – that could and should have been predicted from decades of neoliberal policies and its politics.

Social identities, emotional resentment, economic insecurity and a sense of political irrelevance and status anxiety mobilise misleading stereotypes and use a politics of denigration (Cohen, 2019). A new politics of resentment is now visible, and palpable. It is visible in that has emboldened those peddling hate. It is palpable in the uncontrollable social media. Ethno-nationalisms, racism and xenophobia are mobilised and amplified in a context where insecurity and surveillance are the stuff of everyday life, including the academy.

Whilst the challenges facing the world of higher education are all too clear, there is sense of helplessness, and an eerie sense of waiting for the final implosion. For universities in the UK, the basic economic facts of the matter are all too stark. Some 13% of undergraduate students, 38% of postgraduates, and 28% of academic staff come from outside the UK. And whilst clearly not all these students and academics are from Europe, many are.

The UK university sector is a major beneficiary of research funds – around GBP £0.8 billion per year go into the sector. With the UK set full sail ahead with its compass set in the direction of becoming a competitive knowledge-based economy, much of its necessary ballast – funds, brains, confidence in the future – is in jeopardy. The university sector has not just depended on these continental labour markets, but European students have buoyed the universities dwindling coffers with much needed finances, whilst its towns and cities have benefitted from the revenues that are spent in simply getting on with normal life; rents, services, food. Under Brexit fees would be set for European students to that of international students, whilst job applicants to UK universities would have to apply for work visas. These economic and technical challenges are accompanied by a deep sense of unease amongst academics and students regarding their status as migrants and the new politics of resentment. What had been an expanding Europe was now set to reverse gear, with Europe itself facing a new wave of nationalisms and a ratcheting up of the politics of fear, exclusion, re-bordering and resentment (Yuval-Davis, 2018). It is clear that the expansion of European regionalism and the role of higher education in this is now confronting new challenges (Robertson et al., 2016). This power shift had been seismic, and the winds of change continue to blow, its vortex twisting here and there, as the impossibility of the task and the uncertainty of the future is confronted on a daily basis.

3   What Is to Be Done?

I began this chapter with reference to the work of Toffler (1991), and his argument that the end of the Cold War would bring about a shift in power in the world order. Trajectories of development and the arc of time are not linear. Nor do developments unfold in an inevitable way, though clearly there are path dependencies which shape unfolding developments in structuring ways as well as sets of contradictions that set the seeds for ongoing change.

I make this point so as to remind us of the role that those in higher education should be playing right now in stimulating debates, challenging practices, proposing new alternatives and developing and embedding new ways practices. We need to challenge the excess of individualism and competition, the enclosure of knowledge, surveillance practices, fear of the other and limited academic freedom which now defines the contemporary academy. Our desire for recognition and respect, when crushed by the weight of winning at any cost, fuels and fans blame and resentment.

But we need more than words. If we are to overcome these societal, ethnic and educational cleavages, then higher education needs to be rethought in not just wider social, cultural and political terms, but ways that include active engagement with a range of social movements that increasingly are being engaged with by a new generation of young people who are rightly making demands. What could a fifth and sixth powershift look like that does not repeat the past thirty years? What might it take in our own institutions in higher education – to walk away from regressive neoliberalism? One thing is clear. Our analysis also needs to account not just for the dynamics of capital and the state, and the ways in which life-worlds and worldviews are shaped and lived, but a thinking through of what might be done in ways that value equality and fraternity and not simply liberty. What political decisions and actions do we want which create the conditions for producing critical, open-minded individuals, who value rather than vilify those whose fortunes and futures are at the end of the day not much different to their own. If there is any vilifying, the target could be the unchecked nature of unfettered capitalism and forms of new imperialism, and those it has benefitted.

Acknowledgements

I am indebted to Professor Jussi Välimaa for the invitation to present this keynote at the 2017 CHER Annual Conference Jyväskylä, Finland, and to the anonymous referee who invited me to join up the dots and don't pull any punches. This version of the chapter has benefited hugely from these two invitations, plus from opportunities to discuss its overall argument with conference participants and other colleagues. For all this I am deeply grateful. Any errors are mine.

Notes

1 For example, the Department for Trade in the European Commission was the sole negotiator on behalf of all of its member countries. As a result, the UK had very little specialist trade negotiation expertise in its government departments.
2 In other words (with the exception of Scotland), in the UK referendum those voting Remain had higher educational qualifications, whilst those voting Leave largely had lower educational qualifications.
3 It should be noted that Wales and Scotland have different HE policies and fee structures as compared to England.
4 The justification for the increased burden on students was that having a degree generated a significant increase in salary (graduate premium), of well over £100,000 over a lifetime. However, reporting an average in this way removes from view the fact that some professions (such as medicine, law, dentistry and business studies), generate significant returns which distorts the average. Students enrolled in areas such as the arts tend to earn significantly less than this over a lifetime.
5 There were 51,930 undergraduate students on designated courses at alternative providers (APs) in 2016/17. Of these, 25,785 were in their first year of study (HESA, 2019).

References

Ali, T. (2003, May–June). Re-colonizing Iraq. *New Left Review, 21*, 5–19.
Arrighi, G. (1994). *The long twentieth century: Money, power and the origins of our times.* London: Verso.
Bernstein, B. (2000). *Pedagogy, symbolic control and identity.* London: Rowan and Littlefield.
BIS. (2009). *Higher ambitions: The future of universities in a knowledge economy.* London: BIS.
Brown, R. (2011). The new English quality assurance regime. *Quality in Higher Education, 17*(2), 213–229.
Brown, P., Lauder, H., & Ashton, D. (2011). *The global auction: The broken promises of education, jobs and income.* Oxford: Oxford University Press.
Browne Review. (2010). *Securing a sustainable future for higher education: An independent review of higher education funding and student finance.* London: BIS.
Bovens, M., & Wille, A. (2017). *Diploma democracy: The rise of political meritocracy.* Oxford: Oxford University Press.
Castells, M. (1996). *The rise of the network society.* London: Blackwell.

Cohen, J. (2019, January). Populism and the politics of resentment. *Jus Cogen: A Critical Journal of the Philosophy of Law and Politics*.

Crouch, C. (2011). *Strange non-death of neoliberalism*. Cambridge: Polity.

Dorling, D., & Tomlinson, S. (2019). *Rule britannia*. London: Biteback Publishing.

Eco, U. (2013). *Inventing the enemy*. London: Vintage Books.

Foray, D. (2004). *The economics of knowledge*. Boston, MA: MIT Press.

Fourcade, M. (2016). Ordinalization: Lewis a coser memorial award for theoretical agenda setting. *Sociological Theory, 34*(3), 175–195.

Fraser, N. (2017). From progressive neoliberalism to trump and beyond. *America Affairs, 1*(4), Retrieved February 7, from https://americanaffairsjournal.org/2017/11/progressive-neoliberalism-trump-beyond/

Glees, A., & Pope. C. (2005). *When students turn to terror: Terrorist and extremist activity on British campuses*. London: The Social Affairs Unit.

Green, J., & Hay, C. (2015). Toward a new political economy of the crisis: Getting what went wrong right. *New Political Economy, 20*(3), 331–341.

Harvey, D. (1989). *The condition of postmodernity*. Oxford: Blackwell.

Harvey, D. (2003). *The new imperialism*. Oxford: Oxford University Press.

Harvey, D. (2017). *Seventeen contradictions and the end of capitalism*. London: Profile Books.

Heath-Kelly, C. (2013). Counter-terrorism and the counterfactual: Producing the 'radicalisation' discourse and the UK prevent strategy. *British Journal of Politics and International Relations, 15*, 394–415.

HEFCE. (2017). *Framework for the monitoring of the prevent duty in higher education in England*. Bristol: HEFCE.

HESA. (2019). *Higher Education Statistics: Alternative providers*. Retrieved February 28, 2019, from https://www.hesa.ac.uk/news/15-02-2018/sfr249-higher-education-student-statistics-APs

Hettne, B., & Söderbaum, F. (2000). Theorising the rise of regionness. *New Political Economy, 5*(3), 457–472.

Hobsbawm, E. (1994). *Age of extremes: The short twentieth century 1914–1991*. London: Abacus.

Holland, K. (2015, June 15). The high economic and social costs of student loan debt. *CNBC News*. Retrieved June 18, 2015, from http://www.cnbc.com/id/102742696

Jessop, B. (1999). The changing governance of welfare: Recent trends in its primary functions, scale and modes of coordination. *Social Policy and Administration, 343*(4), 348–359.

Kotz, D. (2018, September–October). End of the neoliberal era? Crisis and restructuring in American capitalism. *New Left Review, 113*, 29–55.

Leys, C. (2003). *Market-driven politics: Neoliberal democracy and the public interest*. London: Verso.

Lundvall, B.-A., & Johnson, B. (1994). The learning economy. *Journal of Industry Studies, 1*(2), 23–42.

McGettigan, A. (2012). *False accounting: Why the government's higher education reforms don't add up.* London: Intergenerational Foundation.

Monahan, A., & Wiele, S. (2017). *UK* student loan debt soars. *Guardian.* Retrieved February 7, 2019, from https://www.theguardian.com/money/2017/jun/15/uk-student-loan-debt-soars-to-more-than-100bn

Newfield, C. (2010). The structure and the silence of the cognitariat. *Globalisation, Societies and Education, 8*(2), 175–189.

Peck, J. (2013). *Constructions of neoliberal reason.* Oxford: Oxford University Press.

Piketty, T. (2014). *Capital in the twenty first century.* Cambridge, MA: Belknap/Harvard.

Robertson, S. L. (2009). 'Producing' the global knowledge economy: The World Bank, the KAM, education and development. In M. Simons, M. Olssen, & M. Peters (Eds.), *Re-reading education policies: Studying the policy agenda of the 21st century.* Rotterdam, The Netherlands: Sense Publishers.

Robertson, S. L. (2016, October 25). Vote Brexit, or Capexit [Blog]. *Globalisation, Education and Social Futures Blog.* Retrieved December 18, 2019, from https://edgesf.wordpress.com/2016/10/25/vote-brexit-or-capexit-by-susan-robertson/

Robertson, S., Bonal, X., & Dale, R. (2002). GATS and the education service industry. *Comparative Education Review, 46*(4), 472–496.

Robertson, S., & Keeling, R. (2008). Stirring the lions: Strategies and tactics in global higher education. *Globalisation, Societies, and Education, 6*(3), 221–240.

Robertson, S., Olds, K., Dale, R., & Dang, Q.-A. (2016). *Global regionalisms and higher education.* Cheltenham: Edward Elgar.

Robertson, S., & Kedzierski, M. (2016). On the move: Globalising higher education in Europe and beyond. *The Language Learning Journal, 44*(3), 276–291.

Saeed, T., & Johnson, D. (2016). Intelligence, global terrorism and higher education: Neutralising threats or alienating enemies. *British Journal of Educational Studies, 64*(1), 37–51.

Sayer, A. (2011). *Why things matter to people.* Cambridge: Cambridge University Press.

Seabrooke, L., & Bowden, B. (2004). *Golden standards and the making of market civilisation.* London & New York, NY: Routledge.

Sennett, R. (2006). *The culture of the new capitalism.* New Haven, CT: Yale University Press.

Slater, D., & Tonkiss, F. (2001). *Market society.* Cambridge: Polity.

Stein, B. (2006, November 26). Class warfare, guess which class is winning. *New York Times.* Retrieved June 18, 2015, from http://www.nytimes.com/2006/11/26/business/yourmoney/26every.html?_r=0

Streeck, W. (2014a, May–June). How will capitalism end?" *New Left Review, 87*, 35–64.

Streeck, W. (2014b). *Buying time: The delayed crisis of democratic capitalism*. London & New York, NY: Verso.

Streeck, W. (2017, March–April). The return of the repressed. *New Left Review, 104*, 5–18.

Toffler, A. (1991). *Powershift*. New York, NY: Bantam Books.

UNESCO. (2005a). *Towards knowledge societies*. Paris: UNESCO.

UNHCR. (2017). *World migration report*. New York, NY: UNHCR.

Yuval-Davis, N. (2018). Contemporary politics of belonging and everyday bordering. In M. Schulz (Ed.), *Frontiers of global sociology*. Berlin: ISA Research.

CHAPTER 2

The Rise of Nationalism: The Influence of Populist Discourses on International Student Mobility and Migration in the UK and US

Leasa Weimer and Aliandra Barlete

Abstract

With the rise of nationalism and populism in Western countries, international higher education operates in a changing and precarious environment. Values of cosmopolitanism and multiculturalism, which are central to internationalisation, are under scrutiny and being challenged by the ideology of right-wing nationalism. This study investigates modes of political nationalism in the United Kingdom and United States; populist discursive elements are analysed according to their influence on international student mobility. Adopting a largely critical approach, the authors present a multi-case study analysis of the European Union Referendum (Brexit vote) and the 2016 US presidential campaign and election of Donald Trump. In each case, a variety of texts (papers, regulations, policies, and news) are analysed by means of critical discourse analysis. The analysis reveals populist discourses depicting specific populations as the 'other' which shapes and changes national attractiveness and migration policies, thus potentially impacting the future flow and lived experiences of international students.

Keywords

international higher education – international student mobility – international student migration – populism, nationalism – critical discourse analysis

1 Introduction

With the recent rise of nationalism and populism in Western democracies (Alden, 2016), the internationalisation of higher education operates in a

© KONINKLIJKE BRILL NV, LEIDEN, 2020 | DOI: 10.1163/9789004422582_003

changing and precarious political environment. Values of cosmopolitanism and multiculturalism, which are central to internationalisation, are under scrutiny and being challenged by the right-wing dogma of nationalism. Nationalism, as an ideological political doctrine, places the interests of the nation first and in many cases, is discursively operationalised by the employment of right-wing populism. According to Mudde (2000) the core elements of right-wing populism includes racism, xenophobia, anti-democracy and law and order. However, populism takes different forms according to a nation's history and culture (Greven, 2016; Inglehart & Norris, 2016). This study analyses modes of nationalism via populist discursive elements in the United Kingdom (UK) and the United States (US) and explores possible impacts these regimes have on the international higher education (IHE), in particular on student mobility.

The UK and the US have significant cultural, political and economic influence in student mobility. The US and the UK are respectively the first and second destinations for international student mobility in the world. In 2013, 26% of international postgraduate students chose the US to study abroad, whereas 15% elected to study in the UK (OECD, 2016). At the same time, both countries have experienced a surge in right-wing nationalism. Populist discourses were used in both the UK's 2016 referendum to leave the EU – i.e. the Brexit vote and Donald Trump's election in the 2016 US presidential campaign. The UK Leave campaign and Prime Minister Theresa May's government espoused discourse against immigration, supported sentiments of Euroscepticism and advocated for a strong nation-state. Across the Atlantic Ocean, Trump's platform included anti-immigration sentiments, exacerbated feelings of disfranchisement ('we, the people'), and built an 'America First' approach.

The study illustrates tensions between populist discourses and the values of IHE, during select political junctures. Researchers in the field of IHE have explored possible implications of Brexit and Trump. Several authors are speculative of the possible changes (Altbach & Wit, 2017; Marginson, 2017), while others offer new research themes on the political dimensions of the international student experience (Rose-Redwood & Rose-Redwood, 2017). Aline Courtois (2018) recently edited a volume on the impact of Brexit on European Universities. Contributing to the literature, the results of our exploratory study show that political discourse depicting specific populations as the 'other' shapes and changes national attractiveness and migration policies, thus potentially impacting the future flow of incoming international students. The consequences may be grim for two higher education systems that are heavily dependent on international students.

2   Nationalism and Populism

Since the emergence of the nation-state in Europe at the end of the eighteenth century, nationalisms have existed in various forms with unique contextual characteristics (Brubaker, 1996; Smith, 2010). Smith defines nationalism as, "an ideological movement for attaining and maintaining autonomy, unity and identity for a population which some of its members deem to constitute an actual or potential 'nation'" (2010, p. 9).[1] Differently than the early process of the 'growth of nations' in the eighteenth and nineteenth centuries, modern nationalism can be viewed as an ideology and a political doctrine that promotes and protects the sovereign nation from the impact of global processes.

Andreas Wimmer (2002) expands on the modern definition of nationhood as "'the idea and practice of a state representing the people in its threefold meaning of nation, citizenry and sovereign" (p. 2). Introducing the idea of 'politisation of ethnicity', Wimmer explains how aspects such as a shared cultural heritage, ethnic homogeneity and political representativeness guarantee 'membership rights', for the fellow nationals – and consequently result in exclusionary practices and xenophobia for those who do not meet these criteria.

Tensions emerge when modern nationalistic ideals meet globalisation. As globalisation evolves there is a new temporal-scalar dimension to social life, not only across borders, but across space (Held & McGrew, 2003; Olssen, Codd, & O'Neill, 2004). An increased flow of people, goods and capitals across borders leads to a disruption in the paradigms of nationalistic territorialised political life (Koch & Paasi, 2016), impacting the local and global. As global markets become more interconnected, economic crises in one region or country have a wider impact and may spill into other spaces, either bringing economic consequences or displacement due to (sometimes forced) migration. Locally it has been noted how neoliberal policies have widened the social-economic gap between the rich and the poor within many nations (Harvey, 2005).

When globalisation is not a preferred approach, what is the alternative? One response is to turn inwards and return to focusing on the nation(al). In Western countries, this shift towards nationalism manifests in different ways. For example, in the UK recent political events have connected nationalism with "a conservative perspective, particularly when employed to justify barriers to immigration, or (in the case of English conservatives) opposition to European integration" (Buckley & Parisi, 2004, p. 409). Discussions about disintegrating the EU, the rise of right-wing parties in Europe, and referendums to separate sub-regions in nations are all manifestations of the disenfranchised.

One significant expression of modern nationalism can be evidenced by how current leaders use populist discourse to promote their nationalistic ideology. The study of populism has gained considerable scholarly interest recently; it has been analysed from various theoretical perspectives and methodological approaches (Gidron & Bonikowski, 2013). Yet, social scientists do not agree on one single definition or theory of populism. "We simply do not have anything like a *theory* of populism, and we seem to lack coherent criteria for deciding when political actors turn populist in some meaningful sense" (Müller, 2016, p. 2).

Gidron and Bonikowski (2013) present a literature review outlining three ways that populism has been analysed and studied over the past few decades, taking into consideration theoretical assumptions and methodological implications. First, some scholars approach populism as, "a thin-centered *ideology* that considers society to be ultimately separated into two homogeneous and antagonistic groups, 'the pure people' versus 'the corrupt elite', and which argues that politics should be an expression of the *volonté générale* (general will) of the people" (Mudde, 2004, p. 543). As an ideology, populism, combined with nationalist ideologies, become a set of ideas that guide political action. The second approach views populism as a *form of discursive style* that employs rhetoric, discourse and language that socially constructs struggle between two homogenous groups in society perpetuating a binary 'us vs. them', in other words, creating a discourse of 'othering'. Hawkins argues that "unlike ideology, populism is a latent set of ideas that lacks significant exposition and contrast with other discourses and is usually low on policy specifics" (2009, p. 1045). Studies focused on discursive elements consider political expression rather than political party ideas (Bos, van der Brug, & Vreese, 2013) and are more concerned with populist characteristics rather than whether a party is considered to have a populist ideology (Deegan-Krause & Haughton, 2009). Third, populism is approached as a *political strategy* that considers policy choices, political organisation and forms of mobilisation. Rather than focusing on the political party ideas or discourse, this method analyses the relationship between political actors and their constituents.

In spite of these conflicting approaches to studying populism, a few characteristics converge. The populist narrative creates juxtaposition between two groups, the 'corrupt elite' and 'we, the people'. It is assumed that the two groups are homogenous and there is antagonistic tension. This binary construction feeds into an 'anti-establishment' discourse that places the people ('we/us') against the corrupt elite ('them'). Another common characteristic is that populism crosses all ideologies, right and left, as well as extreme and mainstream (Gidron & Bonikowski, 2013), however in this paper we focus on right-wing

THE RISE OF NATIONALISM

populism. Finally, modern populism feeds into an overall disenfranchised feeling of the citizenry. As Kalb and Halmai explain, "populism refers to the moods and sensibilities of the disenfranchised as they face the disjunctures between everyday lives that seem to become increasingly chaotic and uncontrollable and the wider ongoing disenfranchisement" (2011, p. 14).

Although all three schools of thought have legitimacy in the study of populism, this study draws from the second approach by analysing discursive elements in the Brexit and Donald Trump's campaigns. While differences exist in the way populism manifests in both cases, the foundations of the rhetoric and style have a similar root: political nationalism. We argue that the Brexit vote, and the successive discourse pertaining to EU exit negotiations, as well as Trump's campaign, and subsequent rhetoric on his campaign promises, used populist discursive elements to 'other' groups that do not meet the shared criteria of national citizenry. The question remains on how such 'othering' populist discourses affect student mobility in the two cases.

3   International Higher Education: International Student Mobility and Migration

IHE is understood here as the flow of people and knowledge across borders, translated specifically as student and academic mobility, cooperation and research programmes. The concrete expressions of internationalisation strategies are most often defined either at an institutional or national level. International collaborations for student and staff mobility and research cooperation are made possible by an agreed upon specific set of rules that govern the relationship and strategic partnership, again defined by institutional or national conditions. Therefore, IHE exists as a result of cooperation among and between institutions and/or countries.

It can be argued that international activities have been a feature of higher education, since the medieval times when European scholars and students travelled to study in faraway lands in the region. Today, increased IHE is connected to the idea of the global knowledge economy (Brown & Lauder, 2010; Robertson, 2005) and the processes of globalisation mitigating more cross-border interconnectivity. More generally, the internationalisation of higher education is defined as "the intentional process of integrating an international, intercultural or global dimension into the purpose, functions and delivery of post-secondary education, in order to enhance the quality of education and research for all students and staff, and to make a meaningful contribution to society" (de Wit, Hunter, Howard, & Egron-Polak, 2015, p. 29). As the definition points out, internationalisation is much more than students moving across borders. Student mobility is, however, an important manifestation of how higher education becomes more international (Caruso & de Wit, 2015).

International student mobility refers to the (physical) cross-border mobility activity at both undergraduate and postgraduate levels. Immigration policies directly impact IHE for they allow the basic condition for the mobility of international students to happen: movement between borders. Changes in immigration legislation affects the basic conditions for IHE to operate: who is able to move, under what circumstances and for how long. Immigration policies can be viewed as a governmental selection mechanism that controls and/or guides who and how many migrants enter the country, usually occupation, national origin and wealth are used as criteria during the selection process (Czaika & de Haas, 2014).

A migrant is defined as "any person who lives temporarily or permanently in a country where he or she was not born, and has acquired some significant social ties to this country".[2] According to the United Nations (2013) when well-managed, international migration contributes to social, cultural and value exchanges between origin and destination countries. On the contrary, when poorly managed, its negative consequences can reflect poor integration, discrimination, rising xenophobia and a loss of valuable human resources and skills in the country of origin (i.e. 'brain drain'). As migration for higher education continues to evolve, national immigration policies and integration efforts become increasingly important especially for countries and institutions that actively recruit international students.

Considering the growth of international student numbers and the increased political, economic and academic significance of international student mobility, international student mobility and mobility is becoming a key field of study in migration research (Van Mol, 2014). Riaño, Van Mol, and Raghuram (2018, p. 285) identify five political discourses used by politicians to influence their agenda concerning international students:

1. International students as economic agents or drivers of knowledge and eventually of economic growth;
2. International students as sources of income for the higher education sector;
3. International students as temporary subjects;
4. International students as doubtful value; and
5. International students as part of soft power.

Depending on the national discourses employed, these discourses shape the environment for international student mobility and migration. "[S]hifting discourses clearly have an impact on the trajectories of international students, on their lived experiences, and on their subjectivities" (Riaño et al., 2018, p. 287).

THE RISE OF NATIONALISM

4   Methodology

To conduct the analysis, an entry point was established acknowledging the historical significance of both the Brexit vote and Donald Trump's campaign and election. Scollon and Scollon's (2004) nexus analysis offered a methodological guidebook to focus in on a 'nexus of practice' in which to study. A "nexus of practice" is the "the point at which historical trajectories of people, places, discourses, ideas and objects come together to enable some action which in itself alters those historical trajectories in some way as those trajectories emanate from this moment of social action" (Scollon & Scollon, 2004, p. viii). By identifying and analysing key social actors, objects and discourses, the social action can be understood.

The period analysed in the UK case begins in February 2016, when the referendum vote was announced, and extends until March 2017 when the Parliament approved triggering Article 50.[3] It includes the launch of the referendum by Prime Minister Cameron, and followed the discourses emitted during the election campaign and initial policies enacted by Theresa May's government. The historical trajectory was the result of the vote to leave the EU. In the case of the US, Donald Trump's declaration of his candidacy for President, as the Republican nominee, in June 2015 marks the beginning of the 'nexus of practice'; it ends in January 2017, as Trump assumes the presidency (the legacy). Locating the case studies in time and space also indicates a historical period in which the interdiscursive analysis was developed.

The texts collected were analysed using critical discourse analysis (CDA) (Fairclough, 2003). CDA is "a theory of and methodology for analysis of discourse understood as an element or 'moment' of the political, political-economic and more generally social which is dialectically related to other elements/moments" (Fairclough, 2003, p. 178). CDA highlights the radical changes taking shape in contemporary social life. Its *relational* features highlight the relationships between the internal (semantic, grammatical), external elements (social structure, social practices) or interdiscursive (text and its social context). By referring to a 'moment', CDA illuminates the relevance of elements of temporality and spatiality of the discursive action – which reinforces the pertinence of 'networks of practice' as analytical tool. According to Taylor (2004, p. 436), "CDA is particularly appropriate for critical policy analysis because it allows a detailed investigation of the relationship of language to other social processes, and of how language works within power relations". Discourses, as a representation of the world tied to processes of change (Fairclough, 2013), provide "a particular and pertinent way of understanding policy formation, for policies are, pre-eminently, statements about practice – the way things could or should be – which rest upon, derive from, statements of the world – about the way things are" (Ball, 1990, p. 22). This analysis focused on the interdiscursive elements: "a mediating level between the text [words] *per se* and its social context (social events, social practices, social structures)" (Fairclough, 2003, p. 37).

Data collection consisted of a two-phase process. We did an initial search for discourse that socially constructed struggle between migrants and 'us' on the Twitter pages of key social actors:

– Donald Trump (candidate for US presidency),
– Nigel Farage (during the Brexit referendum campaign he was a UK Independence Party leader and a key figure in the Leave campaign),
– Boris Johnson (during the Brexit referendum campaign he was the Mayor of London and an advocate for the Leave campaign, he was then named Foreign Secretary of Theresa May's government in July 2016), and
– Theresa May (became Prime Minister in July 2016 and the leader in Brexit negotiations with the EU).

As a second step, we conducted google searches for policies, speeches, white papers and television interviews that were mentioned in tweets. We relied on samples of discourses in different genres, from politicians' speech transcripts to Twitter text to policy documents. The genres explored were: political discourses (available in video, transcriptions or social media text), proposed or finalised policies (legislation, regulations or white papers), policy and research briefings, newspaper articles, letters, commentary. The various texts were catalogued, coded and categorised. Using analytical insights from the literature on nationalism, populism, IHE and migration, the data were analysed by identifying key themes and patterns in the data.

4.1   *The Brexit Vote: 'Take Back Control'*

On 23 June 2016 a majority of 51.9% voters chose to leave the EU treaty. The EU Referendum was proposed by then Prime Minister David Cameron, leader of the Conservative party (Tories). The main voices of the Leave campaign included: Nigel Farage, former London Mayor Boris Johnson, and the newspaper The Daily Mail. Evidences of a 'failed' EU, coupled with promises of transferring the EU funds to the National Health Service and anti-immigrant rhetoric were constant themes in their discourses (BBC News, 2017).

The public appeal of Farage and Johnson, in particular, were key in the result of the referendum. Both attracted considerable media attention by using populist arguments during the campaign. The motto 'take back control' was effective to attract voters, in particular in the Northern regions in England. Another rhetoric used circulated around the many 'losses' the EU brought for British citizens, especially in the power of decision-making, economy and EU migration – building upon the 'us vs. them' divide.

The result of the vote impacted the EU as well, for it opened an unexpected precedent: a member state leaving the region. With regards to higher education policies, the consequences are still in discussion. It is assumed that the impact of Brexit on higher education will significantly change the funding and conditions of regional programmes, such as Erasmus, Marie Curie, FP7 and Erasmus Mundus. The future prospects for the region has alarmed higher education institutions and sectoral institutions in the UK, who have published surveys, manifestos, and briefings to inform actors and the public of transformations to come (e.g. UUK, 2017; Russell Group, 2017a, 2017b).

4.2   Donald Trump's US Presidential Campaign: 'Make America Great Again'

The 2016 US presidential elections caused another moment of change. The campaign and election of Republican candidate Donald Trump came with divisive nationalist discourse in less than 140 characters flooding Twitter feeds with messages challenging the national environment towards anything international. "We will no longer surrender this country or its people to the false song of globalism", Trump claimed during a speech in Washington (Hattem, 2016). The mottos 'America First' and 'Make America Great Again' were used throughout Trump's presidential campaign and continue to be central to his narrative (see Figure 2.1).

Donald J. Trump
@realDonaldTrump

In trade, military and EVERYTHING else, it will be AMERICA FIRST! This will quickly lead to our ultimate goal: MAKE AMERICA GREAT AGAIN!

6:16 PM · 23 May 2016

FIGURE 2.1   Tweet from Donald Trump: Make America great again (Trump, 2016b)

Similar to the UK, the main policy issues that sparked the US campaign were economic issues, healthcare and immigration. The focus of these strong national mottos connected to economic prosperity and more specifically to the idea of bringing jobs back to US soil that had been outsourced to other countries by globalisation. These discourses were especially relatable for the 'citizenry' who felt disenfranchised by the employment losses of moving from an industrial society to a knowledge society (e.g. those no longer employed in the coal industry). With regards to immigration, Trump's platform included a project for a 'great wall' on the border with Mexico, which came with both public support and criticism. Trump's platform provided more evidence for the populist discourse that there is an 'enemy', which should be kept away (even if literally by building a wall).

4.3 Parallels Between Brexit and Trump

Even though Brexit and the Trump presidency are fundamentally different political events, given the temporal overlap of both cases, there are a few parallels between Brexit and the US election worth noting. The similarity in populist approaches was reinforced by the main actors. According to Farage, the then US candidate was interested in "emulat(ing) Brexit by upsetting the political establishment" (BBC News, 2017). The New York Post published a cover in June 2016 that demonstrates the connections between these two historical moments (New York Post, 2016, June 25). The front cover of the 25 June edition – a few days after the result of the Brexit vote – illustrates two fists held in the air, each displaying the UK and US flags, illustrating a 'cry out' for 'power to the people'. The cover highlights three aspects that link Brexit and the US election: (1) the 'us vs. them' divide perpetuating a movement against the 'corrupt global liberal elite' which is a core feature of populism; (2) the link between the US and the UK as global powers and; (3) the role of the media in disseminating populist discourses.

5 Findings

5.1 The UK: Seeking Control, Strategic Student Selection

Analysis of the discourse revealed one central theme: immigration. In the UK, the motto for the Leave campaign, 'Vote Leave, take back control' (Figure 2.2) painted a picture that the UK lacked control of their laws, borders and economy. This discourse framed the Leave campaign, as evidenced in a tweet by Nigel Farage (see Figure 2.3). After the results of the vote were made public, Farage referred to 23 June 2016, the day of the Brexit vote, as #Independence-Day for the UK.

Although having campaigned to remain in the EU, new UK Prime Minister Theresa May employed similar discourse in numerous speaking engagements after the referendum vote. May declared that the UK would "leave the European Union and take control of our money, take control of our borders and take control of our laws" (Hope, 2017). Furthermore, she adopted a right-wing nationalistic ideology against globalism, "If you believe you're a citizen of the world, you're a citizen of nowhere. You don't understand what the very word 'citizenship' means" (Spectator, 2016).

FIGURE 2.2   Tweet from 'vote leave' (Vote Leave, 2016).

FIGURE 2.3   Tweet from Nigel Farage (Farage, 2016).

The Brexit vote seems to have a direct connection to the country's approval of stricter immigration policies (Alden, 2016; Czaika & de Haas, 2015). Polls led by Ipsos Morris (2016) indicated that concerns about immigration were the main reason to vote Leave by voters in both main parties in the UK: Conservatives (61%) and Labour (41%). Immigration policies offer conditions for IHE, thus changes in immigration laws are one way to restrict access to incoming migrants, whether they be asylum seekers, international students or European workers.

Nigel Farage was a key figure driving immigration as a defining issue in the campaign; in particular he linked immigration to national sovereignty (BBC News, 2016). For example, Farage used a controversial campaign billboard/

poster with a large photo of a crowd of refugees/migrants queuing to enter European borders with the words scrolled across it, "Breaking Point: The EU has failed us all. We must break free of the EU and take back control of our borders". The BBC News story classified it as the Leave campaign's most appealing argument for suggesting a lack of control over the number of migrants coming into the country, especially in light of the mass migration of refugees arriving at European borders in 2015. In addition, the imagery and its accompanying narrative of refugees/migrants rushing to enter the open European borders, conjures up an 'us vs. them' binary construction; the 'us' being UK 'citizenry' protecting their borders and 'them' as the 'other' trying to enter the national borders. This particular piece of propaganda was reported to the police by the Unison Union who stated,

> To pretend that migration to the UK is only about people who are not white is to peddle the racism that has no place in a modern, caring society. That's why Unison has complained about this blatant attempt to incite racial hatred and breach UK race laws. (Stewart & Mason, 2016)

This particular interaction highlights how the 'other' was created and visualised as non-white, thus racialising the 'other'.

While the discourse painted refugees and Eastern Europeans as unwanted migrants, international student migration was treated differently in the discourse. Highly-skilled migration tends to have a positive connotation when compared to lower skills migration: "Movements of the highly skilled were celebrated as professional mobility, while those of the lower-skilled were condemned as unwanted migration. Mobility equalled good, because it was the badge of a modern open society; migration equalled bad because it re-awakened archaic memories of invasion and displacement" (Castles, 2010, p. 1567). One of the earliest addresses focused on international student mobility was given by Home Office Secretary Amber Rudd, who in 2016 claimed to be:

> passionately committed to making sure our world-leading institutions can attract the brightest and the best. But a student immigration system that treats every student and university as equal only punishes those we should want to help. So our consultation will ask what more can we do to support our best universities – and those that stick to the rules – to attract the best talent...while looking at tougher rules for students on lower quality courses. (Conservatives, 2016)

The speech revealed a discourse of strategy and selection. Selecting a group of the 'brightest and best' students can have two distinct consequences for

THE RISE OF NATIONALISM   45

international students and for the UK universities. First, the opportunities for mobile students are likely to be linked to their prior education, which usually implies that they have experienced high quality secondary education, particularly if coming from non-English speaking countries. It points to a reproduction of class structures, wherein the 'high flyer' students, those students who have the capital and privilege, benefit the most (Choudaha, Orosz, & Chang, 2012). Second, the selection of students could result in IHE becoming an activity of the elite higher education institutions given that they might be attracting the best students for their prestige and international marketing.

In 2017, Theresa May called for the 'brightest and best' students once again, yet with the focus on control, power and sovereignty:

> We will leave the European Union and take control of our money, take control of our borders and take control of our laws [...] so while we continue to attract the brightest and the best to work or study in this country, we can be confident that we have control over immigration and that our immigration system serves the national interest. (May, 2017)

A parallel debate to selection and strategy had to do with the composition of the migrant data. There was a debate about the government's approach to include international students in the net migration numbers – as *figures* (UCU, 2017), or as a *target* (UUK, 2017). According to the UK's Office for National Statistics (ONS), "overseas students coming to the UK are included in immigration, emigration and net migration figures, in line with international best practice, meaning that they are included in the figures used to produce national and local population estimates and to monitor the government's aspiration to reduce net migration to the tens of thousands" (ONS, 2016, p. 1). Universities and Colleges Union (UCU) called for the international students to be removed from net migration figures (UCU, 2017), whereas Universities UK (UUK) had less of a problem with the category they were counted in, and more with having (EU and non-EU) student migrants number as part of the overall target in the government's policies to reduce migration. Using as example other global destinations for student mobility, such as Australia and Canada, UUK claimed that those countries actually have targets to *increase* student intake.

5.2 *The US: Changing the Environment and the Number of International Applicants*

On the campaign trail, Trump's populist discourse continually vilified specific groups and individuals that were to be feared and/or part of the 'corrupt global liberal elite'. He framed Mexicans, Muslims, Hillary Clinton, Barack Obama and several others as the enemy of the US 'citizenry'. More specifically his inflammatory tweets 'othered' specific groups, such as when he portrayed Mexicans as "druggies, drug dealers, rapists and killers" (Figure 2.4). His discourse also spotlighted violent crimes committed by undocumented Mexicans, as a way to further justify his claims. He painted a picture that undocumented immigrants from Mexico were crossing the border and bringing violence and crime with them. These discourses were countered by cities and higher education institutions offering sanctuary to undocumented Mexicans.

FIGURE 2.4   Tweet from Donald Trump on Mexican immigration (Trump, 2015)

At the same time, Trump's discursive elements depicted Muslims as 'terrorists' (Figure 2.5). As he used divisive populist discourse and vividly described the 'other', his base of voters, which were less-educated white Americans, became more loyal and embodied 'we, the people' sentiments.

FIGURE 2.5   Tweet from Donald Trump on muslim immigration (Trump, 2016a)

Trump's first attempt at limiting immigration, came in the first month of his presidency. An executive order (The White House, 2017) from January 2017 banned citizens from seven Middle Eastern and North African (MENA) countries[4] from travelling to the US for 90 days, suspended the US refugee programme, and banned Syrian refugees. The rhetoric surrounding the first executive order, focused on fear and the need to secure the national borders against "bad dudes" (see Figure 2.6). This executive order was drawn up and implemented hastily causing confusion in airports around the world and impacting the travel plans of anyone from the seven Muslim-majority countries, including international students. Protesters assembled at airports around the nation. One day after the executive order was implemented a judge in New York

THE RISE OF NATIONALISM

temporarily blocked part of the order and the following day a judge in Massachusetts issued a temporary restraining order (Almasy & Simon, 2017). This was certainly not the end of the travel ban, but just the beginning of exclusionary policies of the 'other'. Trump continued to defend his policy, "This is not about religion – this is about terror and keeping our country safe" (Almasy & Simon, 2017), while higher education institutions and professional associations responded with public letters urging the Administration to release students and scholars from the executive order (e.g. AAU, 2017).

FIGURE 2.6   Tweet from Donald Trump on travel ban (Trump, 2017).

Portraying specific groups with derogatory language and excluding them with policies illuminates national power structures. Mexico and the selected seven MENA countries are all considered to be developing countries yielding limited global power, while the US is a developed nation with considerable global influence. The dramatic populist discursive elements reflect this power imbalance and further exacerbates it.

As Trump developed his populist discourse throughout the campaign, his right-wing nationalistic ideology was reflected as he repudiated elitist, liberal globalism. "There is no global anthem. No global currency. No certificate of global citizenship. We pledge allegiance to one flag and that flag is the American flag", claimed Trump in his 'thank you' rally tour after being elected (Hains, 2016).

6   Discussion: How the Discourse Influences International Student Mobility

In both cases, the discourse ostracised select migrants as a burden on and potential threat to society, who are not welcome to enter the national borders. Negative political communication deconstructs 'political correctness' creating space for the identification and ostracisation of the 'other' (Greven, 2016). In the UK case, the 'other' migrants were identified as refugees and Eastern

Europeans taking advantage of the EU freedom of mobility. In the US discourse, Muslims and Mexicans were 'othered' using explicit negative lexicon, such as "bad dudes", "druggies, drug dealers and killers". In both cases, the employment of discursive elements that 'other' specific groups exacerbate feelings that lead to anti-immigration sentiments, rejection of multiculturalism and resentment of cosmopolitan cultural elites. By 'othering' specific groups, the majority, those in power, constructed the identities of minorities. These socially constructed identities reflect the way minority groups are seen and treated in society.

One of the 'pull' factors that attract international students to a certain host country is the perceived safety in that country. Anti-immigration rhetoric, on the contrary, has a way of feeding the fear of prospective students when it comes to their personal safety, especially around issues of discrimination. Research shows that international students may experience discrimination based on their nationality. Lee and Rice (2007) applied a 'neo-racism' framework to a study investigating the discrimination of international students studying at a university in the USA and found that some of the challenges international students faced were due to their foreign national status.

As the discourse in both cases used immigration as a platform to create an 'us vs. them' binary, select international students holding specific passports and 'highflyer' credentials are the exception. This is where IHE and economic development meet. Mathies and Weimer (2018) argue that some international students will become part of a 'protected class' due to national economic strategies. They further explain that the current international student population, with high academic preparation and financial resources, may become even more selective by adding a neo-racism lens: "(N)ot all highfliers would be welcomed regardless of their academic ability or ability to pay as those who are identified as the 'other' would either be denied entry (via immigration legislation) or face discrimination (environment)" (Mathies & Weimer, 2018, p. 11).

At the same time, migrants and international mobility are treated differently in the UK case. Castles (2010) claims that migration is seen as a problem that needs to be fixed by policies, whereas international mobility is encouraged by politics. This was especially made clear in the UK case, as the discourse specifically addressed remaining open to the 'brightest and best' students. On the other hand, Trump did not make exceptions for international students. He simply categorised the 'other', migrant or international student, as someone to be feared.

The impact that populist discourse has had on actual mobility numbers is difficult to quantify. However, it's important to note that in both the UK and US, international student applications decreased following the referendum vote and presidential election. In the UK, for the 2017–2018 academic year,

THE RISE OF NATIONALISM   49

undergraduate applications from EU (non-UK) students decreased by 5% in comparison with the same period in 2016 (UCAS, 2017). However, some programmes (disciplines) showed distinct differences; apart from increases in applications in Mathematical Sciences (7%) and in Computer Sciences (1%), all other fields received fewer applications in 2016.

In the US, there has been a small decrease in the number of international applications. The Institute of International Education (IIE, 2017) reported there are over one million international students pursuing higher education in the US, contributing more than $36 billion to its economy. Numbers from the first application round since Trump's election showed a two-percentage point decline in application numbers compared to 2016, from 26% to 24% of international applicants (Farrugia & Andrejko, 2017). Although this decrease is not substantial in numbers, what is significant is that the last decrease in international student enrolments in US higher education was 12 years ago.[5] Another study, focusing on the perception of 300 institution-based professionals working on the recruitment of international students, asserted that "the political rhetoric of the 2016 election and the Executive Orders of the new administration have added complexity to the international recruitment efforts of U.S. higher education institutions" (AACRAO, 2017, p. 11). To illustrate, there has been a decrease in 40% of undergraduate applications, and 31% in graduate applications coming from the Middle East for academic year 2017–2018.

The reaction from the higher education sector in both cases has been expressive, as they fear the xenophobic discourse may decrease the sector's attractiveness of potential international students hence causing important cultural and economic losses to the sectors. Higher education institutions, professional associations, research councils, and networks in both the US and UK responded to this isolationist and anti-immigration discourse with statements and even counter social media campaigns. For example, in the UK, after the Brexit vote, the University of Sheffield launched a social media campaign: #WeAreInternational[6] that was soon adopted by other UK institutions. The campaign advocated for universities in the UK to remain cosmopolitan spaces, open to and welcoming students from across the globe. Meanwhile, in the US, Temple University launched the marketing and social media campaign #YouAreWelcomeHere[7] in December 2016. More than 250 institutions have joined the initiative.

A final topic to address is the discourse highlighting the difference between the global and the national. The shift in the scale of action – the fact that two internationally-connected nations are renouncing their 'globalism' in favour of a nationalistic discourse (i.e. 'Make America Great Again') – may cause an important shift in social relations (Cox, 1998; Jessop, 2005; MacKinnon, 2011;

Sheppard, 2002). Both May and Trump have argued against the idea of globalism and global citizenship in particular. Even though the very literal meaning of global citizenship is problematic, it is common language in IHE and thus belittles the value of gaining intercultural and international competencies.

7 Conclusion

Overall, political nationalism has impacted the national narratives in the UK and US from outward-looking and globally-open to more inward-focused with explicit calls for more emphasis on national sovereignty and an overall retreat to national borders. By analysing populist discursive elements of both the UK's Brexit vote and Trump's election, the findings reveal key intersections between nationalistic populist discourse and IHE wherein immigration emerges as the central theme. In both cases, the populist discourse constructs specific groups in society as the 'other' which has key implications for the recruitment of international student. Because the events analysed are fairly recent, and taking into account that changes in higher education are rather sluggish (yet revolutionary) (Clark, 1983), we are aware of the impossibility of providing final conclusions on the analysis of the legacy of these nexuses of practice. In both cases, the policies and discourses are still unravelling.

Populist discourse framed by a nationalistic ideology is evident in both countries. The discourse has brought a lot of anxiety to the higher education sectors in the UK and in the US. Its impact on immigration policy reveals not only a deepening of the 'us vs. them' divide, but also a change in the perception of the global vs. national. Even though IHE has been credited as being a positive asset for students, academic life and the knowledge economy as a whole, future immigration policies may not entirely reflect these ideas. Rather, future policies may only validate IHE in a positive light when mobility is reserved for the 'brightest and best'.

While this study has identified key discursive elements 'othering' specific populations, future research in this area could deepen understanding of the consequences. As potential students consider studying in the UK or US higher education institutions, does the xenophobic discourse impact their decisions in selecting host countries or their lived experiences as international students in these countries?

Finally, in reference to the possibility of a return to the national as hinted by Robertson, de Azevedo, and Dale (2016), the UK and US are interesting case studies to consider. We argue that as these two countries – who have historically been players in global geopolitics as well as top destination countries for

THE RISE OF NATIONALISM

51

international students – renounce their 'globalism' in favour of a nationalistic discourse brings important changes. First, it may impact the scale of action in IHE and second it may have wider implications in geopolitical relations. What this will mean for IHE, though, may depend on how and to what impact higher education institutions actively engage in national policy making on these issues as well as the institutional policies they implement to safeguard recruitment efforts and incoming international students from being 'othered'.

Acknowledgements

The authors would like to thank the contribution of Charles Mathies and the book chapter editors for the comments on the chapter. Warm thanks to Professor Roger Dale for the engaging discussion on populism in Cambridge.

Notes

1 For a detailed theoretical account on nationalism, its categories and evolution in the Western world, please refer to Brubaker (1996), Woolf (1996). For a historiography of nationalism, see Smith (2010, pp. 2–15).
2 http://www.unesco.org/new/en/social-and-human-sciences/themes/international-migration/glossary/migrant/
3 https://eur-lex.europa.eu/legal-content/EN/TXT/?uri=CELEX%3A12012M050
4 Iraq, Syria, Iran, Libya, Somalia, Sudan and Yemen.
5 The last decrease in enrolments for international students in the US Universities and Colleges was in academic year 2005–2006 (–0.05%) (IIE, 2016).
6 http://www.weareinternational.org.uk/
7 https://www.youarewelcomehereusa.org/

References

AACRAO. (2017). *International applicants for fall 2017 – Institutional & applicant perceptions* (Survey Data Release). Washington, DC: ACCRAO. Retrieved August 13, 2017, from https://www.iie.org:443/en/Research-and-Insights/Publications/International-Applicants-Fall-2017

AAU. (2017, January 28). *AAU urges quick end to administration order barring returning students and faculty.* Retrieved August 13, 2017, from https://www.aau.edu/newsroom/press-releases/aau-urges-quick-end-administration-order-barring-returning-students-and?id=18366

Alden, E. (2016). *What Brexit reveals about rising populism*. Retrieved July 18, 2017, from https://www.cfr.org/interview/what-brexit-reveals-about-rising-populism

Almasy, S., & Simon, D. (2017, March 30). *A timeline of president Trump's travel bans (CNN)*. Retrieved October 2, 2018, from https://edition.cnn.com/2017/02/10/us/trump-travel-ban-timeline/index.html

Altbach, P. G., & Wit, H. de. (2017). Trump and the coming revolution in higher education internationalization. *International Higher Education, 89*, 3–5. https://doi.org/10.6017/ihe.2017.89.9831

Ball, S. J. (1990). *Politics and policy making in education: Explorations in policy sociology*. London: Routledge.

BBC News. (2016, June 24). Eight reasons leave won the UK's referendum on the EU. *BBC News*. Retrieved July 18, 2017, from http://www.bbc.co.uk/news/uk-politics-eu-referendum-36574526

BBC News. (2017, August 15). Nigel Farage: Why hollywood is interested in TV series about me. *BBC News*. Retrieved July 18, 2017, from http://www.bbc.co.uk/news/uk-politics-40934834

Bos, L., van der Brug, W., & Vreese, C. H. de. (2013). An experimental test of the impact of style and rhetoric on the perception of right-wing populist and mainstream party leaders. *Acta Politica, 48*(2), 192–208. https://doi.org/10.1057/ap.2012.27

Brown, P., & Lauder, H. (2010). Economic globalisation, skill formation and the consequences for higher education. In M. W. Apple, S. J. Ball, & L. A. Gandin (Eds.), *The Routledge international handbook of the sociology of education*. Abingdon: Routledge.

Brubaker, R. (1996). *Nationalism reframed: Nationhood and the national question in the New Europe*. Cambridge: Cambridge University Press.

Buckley, F., & Parisi, F. (2004). Political and cultural nationalism. In *The encyclopedia of public choice* (pp. 734–736). Boston, MA: Springer. https://doi.org/10.1007/978-0-306-47828-4151

Caruso, R., & de Wit, H. (2015). Determinants of students in Europe: Empirical evidence for the period 1998–2009. *Journal of Studies in International Education, 19*(3), 265–282.

Castles, S. (2010). Understanding global migration: A social transformation perspective. *Journal of Ethnic and Migration Studies, 36*(10), 1565–1586. https://doi.org/10.1080/1369183X.2010.489381

Choudaha, R., Orosz, K., & Chang, L. (2012). *Not all international students are the same: Understanding segments, mapping behavior*. New York, NY: World Education Services.

Clark, B. R. (1983). *The higher education system: Academic organization and cross-national perspective*. Berkeley, CA: University of California Press.

THE RISE OF NATIONALISM 53

Conservatives. (2016). *Rudd: Speech to conservative party conference 2016*. Retrieved August 5, 2017, from http://press.conservatives.com/post/151334637685/rudd-speech-to-conservative-party-conference-2016

Courtois, A. (2018). *Higher education and Brexit: current European perspectives*. London: Centre for Global Higher Education, UCL Institute of Education. Retrieved from https://www.researchcghe.org/perch/resources/publications/he-and-brexit.pdf

Cox, K. R. (1998). Spaces of dependence, spaces of engagement and the politics of scale, or: Looking for local politics. *Political Geography, 17*(1), 1–23.

Czaika, M., & de Haas, H. (2014). The globalization of migration: Has the world become more migratory? *International Migration Review, 48*(2), 283–323. https://doi.org/10.1111/imre.12095

de Wit, H., Hunter, F., Howard, L., & Egron-Polak, E. (2015). *Internationalization of higher education*. Luxembourg: Publications office of the European Union, European Parliament. doi:10.2861/444393

Deegan-Krause, K., & Haughton, T. (2009). Toward a more useful conceptualization of populism: Types and degrees of populist appeals in the case of Slovakia. *Politics & Policy, 37*(4), 821–841. https://doi.org/10.1111/j.1747-1346.2009.00200.x

Fairclough, N. (2003). *Analysing discourse: Textual analysis for social research*. Abingdon: Routledge.

Fairclough, N. (2013). Critical discourse analysis and critical policy studies. *Critical Policy Studies, 7*(2), 177–197. https://doi.org/10.1080/19460171.2013.798239

Farage, N. (2016, June 12). *It is time to take back control of our country* [Tweet]. Retrieved August 23, 2017, from https://twitter.com/nigel_farage/status/744787641036505088?lang=en

Farrugia, C., & Andrejko, N. (2017). *Shifting tides: Understanding international student yield for fall 2017*. Washington, DC: IIE. Retrieved October 2, 2018, from https://www.iie.org:443/en/Research-and-Insights/Publications/Shifting-Tides-Understanding-International-Student-Yield-for-Fall-2017

Gidron, N., & Bonikowski, B. (2013). *Varieties of populism: Literature review and research agenda* (Weatherhead Working Paper Series, No. 13–0004). Cambridge, MA.

Greven, T. (2016). *The rise of right-wing populism in Europe and the United States*. Washington, DC: Friedrich-Ebert-Stiftung. Retrieved from http://www.fesdc.org/news-list/e/the-rise-of-right-wing-populism-in-europe-and-the-united-states/

Hains, T. (2016, December 1). *Trump: There is no global flag, no global currency, no global citizenship. We will be United as Americans*. Retrieved October 2, 2018, from https://www.realclearpolitics.com/video/2016/12/01/trump_there_is_no_global_flag_no_global_currency_no_global_citizenship_we_are_united_as_americans.html

Harvey, D. (2005). *A brief history of neoliberalism*. Oxford: Oxford University Press.

Hattem, J. (2016, April 27). *Trump warns against "false song of globalism"*. Retrieved August 22, 2017, from http://thehill.com/policy/national-security/277879-trump-warns-against-false-song-of-globalism

Hawkins, K. A. (2009). Is chávez populist? Measuring populist discourse in comparative perspective. *Comparative Political Studies, 42*(8), 1040–1067. https://doi.org/10.1177/0010414009331721

Held, D., & McGrew, A. (2003). The great globalization debate: An introduction. In D. Held & A. McGrew (Eds.), *Global transformations reader* (pp. 1–50). Cambridge: Polity.

Hope, C. (2017, May 18). Britain faces "dire consequences" without a clean Brexit, warns Theresa May. *The Telegraph*. Retrieved August 22, 2017, from http://www.telegraph.co.uk/news/2017/05/18/britain-faces-dire-consequences-without-clean-brexit-warns-theresa/

IIE. (2017). *IIE survey of college admissions 2017*. Retrieved August 16, 2017, from https://www.iie.org:443/Why-IIE/Announcements/2017-07-06-IIE-Survey-of-College-Admissions-International-Students-Fall-2017

Inglehart, R., & Norris, P. (2016). *Trump, Brexit, and the rise of populism: Economic have-nots and cultural backlash* (SSRN Scholarly Paper No. ID 2818659). Rochester, NY: Social Science Research Network. Retrieved August 16, 2017, from https://papers.ssrn.com/abstract=2818659

Ipsos Mori. (2016). *Concern about immigration rises as EU vote approaches*. Retrieved August 13, 2017, from https://www.ipsos.com/ipsos-mori/en-uk/concern-about-immigration-rises-eu-vote-approaches

Jessop, B. (2005). The political economy of scale and European governance. *Tijdschrift voor Economische en Sociale Geografie, 96*(2), 225–230.

Kalb, D., & Halmai, G. (2011). *Headlines of nation, subtexts of class: Working-class populism and the return of the repressed in neoliberal Europe*. New York, NY: Berghahn Books.

Koch, N., & Paasi, A. (2016). Banal Nationalism 20 years on: Re-thinking, re-formulating and re-contextualizing the concept. *Political Geography, 54*, 1–6. https://doi.org/10.1016/j.polgeo.2016.06.002

Lee, J. J., & Rice, C. (2007). Welcome to America? International student perceptions of discrimination. *Higher Education, 53*(3), 381–409. https://doi.org/10.1007/s10734-005-4508-3

MacKinnon, D. (2011). Reconstructing scale: Towards a new scalar politics. *Progress in Human Geography, 35*(1), 21–36. https://doi.org/10.1177/0309132510367841

Marginson, S. (2017). Brexit: Challenges for universities in hard times. *International Higher Education, 88*, 8–10. https://doi.org/10.6017/ihe.2017.88.9682

Mathies, C., & Weimer, L. (2018). A changing narrative for international students? The potential influence of Brexit and Trump. In D. Proctor & L. Rumbley (Eds.), *The

THE RISE OF NATIONALISM   55

Future Agenda for Internationalization in Higher Education: Next Generation Insights into Research, Policy, Practice. Routledge Press: New York, NY.

May, T. (2017, January 17). Theresa May's Brexit speech in full. *The Telegraph*. Retrieved August 23, 2017, from http://www.telegraph.co.uk/news/2017/01/17/theresa-mays-brexit-speech-full/

Mudde, C. (2000). *The ideology of the extreme right*. Manchester: Manchester University Press.

Mudde, C. (2004). The populist Zeitgeist. *Government and Opposition, 39*(4), 542–563. https://doi.org/10.1111/j.1477-7053.2004.00135.x

Müller, J.-W. (2016). *What is populism?* Philadelphia, PA: University of Pennsylvania Press.

New York Post. (2016, June 25). *Covers for June 25, 2016*. Retrieved August 23, 2017, from http://nypost.com/cover/covers-for-june-25-2016/

OECD. (2016). *Education at a glance 2016: OECD indicators*. Paris: OECD Publications. Retrieved August 17, 2017 from http://www.oecd.org/edu/education-at-a-glance-19991487.htm

Olssen, M., Codd, J., & O'Neill, A. M. (2004). Reading education policy in the global era. In *Education policy: Globalization, citizenship and democracy* (pp. 1–17). London: Sage.

ONS. (2016). Long-term international migration: International student migration – what do the statistics tell us? *Office for National Statistics*. Retrieved September 17, 2018, from https://www.ons.gov.uk/peoplepopulationandcommunity/populationandmigration/internationalmigration/articles/longterminternationalmigration/internationalstudentmigrationwhatdothestatisticstellus

Riaño, Y., Van Mol, C., & Raghuram, P. (2018). New directions in studying policies of international student mobility and migration. *Globalisation, Societies and Education, 16*(3), 283–294. doi:10.1080/14767724.2018.1478721

Robertson, S. L. (2005). Re-imagining and rescripting the future of education: Global knowledge economy discourses and the challenge to education systems. *Comparative Education, 41*(2), 151–170.

Robertson, S. L., de Azevedo, M. L. N., & Dale, R. (2016). Higher education, the EU, and the cultural political economy of regionalism. In *Global regionalisms and higher education: Projects, processes, politics* (pp. 33–55). Cheltenham: Edward Elgar Publishing.

Rose-Redwood, C., & Rose-Redwood, R. (2017). Rethinking the politics of the international student experience in the age of Trump. *Journal of International Students, 7*(3), I–IX. https://doi.org/10.32674/jis.v7i3.201

Russel Group. (2017a, March 29). *Article 50—open letter*. Retrieved August 16, 2017, from http://russellgroup.ac.uk/news/article-50-open-letter/

Russell Group. (2017b, May). Russell Group universities and Brexit. Retrieved August 16, 2017, from http://russellgroup.ac.uk/media/5512/russell-group-universities-and-brexit-briefing-note-june-2017.pdf

Scollon, R., & Scollon, S. W. (2004). *Nexus analysis: Discourse and the emerging internet.* London: Routledge.

Sheppard, E. (2002). The spaces and times of globalization: Place, scale, networks, and positionality. *Economic Geography, 78*(3), 307. https://doi.org/10.2307/4140812

Smith, A. D. (2010). *Nationalism: Theory, ideology, history* (2nd ed.). Cambridge: Polity.

Spectator. (2016, October 5). *Full text: Theresa May's conference speech.* Retrieved October 2, 2018, from https://blogs.spectator.co.uk/2016/10/full-text-theresa-mays-conference-speech/

Stewart, H., & Mason, R. (2016, June 16). Nigel Farage's anti-migrant poster reported to police. *The Guardian.* Retrieved August 17, 2017, from http://www.theguardian.com/politics/2016/jun/16/nigel-farage-defends-ukip-breaking-point-poster-queue-of-migrants

Taylor, S. (2004). Researching educational policy and change in "new times": Using critical discourse analysis. *Journal of Education Policy, 19*(4), 433–451. https://doi.org/10.1080/0268093042000227483

The White House. (2017, March 6). *Executive order protecting the nation from foreign terrorist entry into the United States.* Retrieved August 16, 2017, from https://www.whitehouse.gov/the-press-office/2017/03/06/executive-order-protecting-nation-foreign-terrorist-entry-united-states

Trump, D. J. (2015, June 7). Druggies, drug dealers, rapists and killers are coming across the southern border. *When will the U.S. Get Smart and Stop This Travesty?* [Tweet]. Retrieved August 23, 2017, from https://twitter.com/realdonaldtrump/status/612083064945180672

Trump, D. J. (2016a, March 7). *Incompetent Hillary, despite the horrible attack in Brussels today, wants borders to be weak and open-and let the Muslims flow in. No way!* [Tweet]. Retrieved August 23, 2017, from https://twitter.com/realdonaldtrump/status/712473816614772736

Trump, D. J. (2016b, May 6). *In trade, military and everything else, it will be America First! This will quickly lead to our ultimate goal: Make America great again!* [Tweet]. Retrieved August 23, 2017, from https://twitter.com/realdonaldtrump/status/73474 2416494845952?lang=en

Trump, D. J. (2017, January 5). *If the ban were announced with a one week notice, the "bad" would rush into our country during that week. A lot of bad "dudes" out there!* [Tweet]. Retrieved August 23, 2017, from https://twitter.com/realdonaldtrump/status/826060143825666051

UCAS. (2017, July 12). *UCAS 2017 cycle applicant figures – June deadline.* Retrieved August 13, 2017, from https://www.ucas.com/corporate/data-and-analysis/ucas-undergraduate-releases/2017-cycle-applicant-figures-june-deadline-0

UCU. (2017). *UCU response to HEPI report on impact of Brexit on universities.* Retrieved August 13, 2017, from https://www.ucu.org.uk/article/8589/UCU-response-to-HEPI-report-on-impact-of-Brexit-on-universities

United Nations. (2013). *International migration policies: Government views and priorities.* New York, NY: United Nations.

UUK. (2017, April 13). *What the British public really think about international students.* Universities UK. Retrieved August 17, 2017, from http://www.universitiesuk.ac.uk/blog/Pages/What-the-British-public-really-think-about-international-students.aspx

Van Mol, C. (2014). *Intra-European student mobility in international higher education circuits. Europe on the move.* Basingstoke: Palgrave Macmillan.

Vote Leave. (2016, June 22). *Let's take back control* [Tweet]. Retrieved August 23, 2017, from https://twitter.com/vote_leave/status/745696135377981440

Wimmer, A. (2002). *Nationalist exclusion and ethnic conflict.* Cambridge: Cambridge University Press.

Woolf, S. (Ed.). (1996). *Nationalism in Europe 1815 to the present: A reader.* Abingdon: Routledge.

CHAPTER 3

Pursuing Ideal Partnerships: The Discourse of Instrumentalism in the Policies and Practices of Sino-Foreign Higher Education Cooperation

Heather Cockayne, Jie Gao and Miguel Antonio Lim

Abstract

There have been evolving models of international higher education cooperation with China, with earlier studies (Tang & Nollent, 2007; Fazackerley, 2007) outlining entry approaches of non-Chinese education providers into China primarily through joint-venture partnerships. This study argues that such partnerships are not clearly defined, nor understood. Using an analysis of policy documents and two case studies: the Sino-Danish Center and the Sino-British College, this chapter considers the changes in Chinese policies with respect to Sino-foreign partnerships and explores differences between Chinese and foreign understandings of partnership in higher education in order to propose a new understanding of the Chinese policy ideal. By diagnosing the defining discourse of *instrumentalism* (Stier, 2004) that characterises both the shifting policies and daily practices of these partnerships, we highlight how policies interact with the practices and give rise to different modes of Sino-foreign higher education partnerships. The pursuit of 'equal partnership' is highlighted as part of this instrumentalist evolution. Our work has implications for those involved in and considering partnerships in China but also a cautionary guide to those contemplating a partnership 'on the cheap'.

Keywords

Sino-foreign partnerships – transnational education – international partnerships – higher education policy – policy borrowing

---

© KONINKLIJKE BRILL NV, LEIDEN, 2020 | DOI: 10.1163/9789004422582_004

1 Introduction: Sino-Foreign Partnerships in Higher Education

As a new form of internationalisation of higher education (HE), cross-border partnerships between Chinese and foreign educational institutions have greatly increased in the last decade in mainland China (HE Global, 2016). While the older forms of internationalisation feature the movement of people, knowledge, policies and educational services moving across borders, many Sino-foreign partnerships in HE are mainly characterised by the movement of foreign educational programmes, providers and campuses into China. Joint ventures (JV), double-degree programmes, franchise and twinning arrangements are mushrooming as Chinese and foreign universities, commercial providers, government agencies and international organisations rush into bilateral or multilateral partnerships. With rapid growth in both scale and impact, Sino-foreign partnerships have risen from a supplement to a component of China's higher education (HE Global, 2016). Partnerships have also taken on more important and complicated roles that have gradually taken shape in China's national strategies.

Along with the rapid growth of these education provisions there have also been changes in the related regulations. In June 2018, China's Ministry of Education (MOE, 2018) announced the closure of some Sino-foreign joint educational programmes and institutions. It was officially announced that five institutions and 229 programmes had been shut down in the past few years. The last time such a scale of closures took place was in 2014 when 252 programmes and institutions were closed. Both incidents have caused concern; there are increasing worries that China is imposing more limits and control over its educational partnerships with the rest of the world.

There is, however, an alternative interpretation of the closures: the shutting down of 'unqualified' programmes or institutions and announcing their demise to the public could be seen as just 'routine' practice for the MOE (CRCFCRS, 2018), which takes place every few years. Most of these JV are closed by the partners themselves because they failed to enrol enough students (CRCFCRS, 2018). The MOE facilitated the closing procedures for 'the unfit' to maintain a good arena for other Sino-foreign partnerships to develop (Zhao, 2016). The regulations of these partnerships have been recognised as heading towards a 'Chinese solution' for foreign partnerships – 'seemingly tighter but de facto looser' – meaning that the system would remain open and favourable to high-quality foreign educational resources, though more barriers are set for those who prove to be less so (Lin, 2018).

These new developments give rise to many important questions regarding transnational education (TNE) partnerships in China. In this chapter, we aim to answer two sets of questions. The first, descriptive, set of questions concerns the changes in policy. The second, more analytical, set of questions concern why these changes are being made and what could account for the differences in some of the responses to Chinese policy changes. Finally, our early findings led us to develop the last question concerning the different understandings of HE partnerships.

- What are the changes in Chinese policies with respect to Sino-foreign partnerships? What have been the responses among Sino-foreign HE actors to these changes?
- Why are these changes being made?
- Are there differences between Chinese and foreign (and particularly 'Western' or European) understandings of partnerships in HE? If so, what are these?

This chapter contributes to the understanding of Sino-foreign HE partnerships by diagnosing the defining discourse that characterises both the shifting policies and daily practices of these partnerships – the instrumentalism – which shifts its form with China's changing positioning of itself in the global order. We argue that the Sino-foreign HE partnerships have always been instrumentalised as a means to an end by China's MOE. Yet at different phases, the instrumentalisation of these partnerships takes different forms and serves different purposes (MOE, 2013), depending on what dominates China's discourse of self-positioning and developmental strategies. This discourse also deeply influenced by the economic and political coordination or rivalry between China and the country involved in the partnerships.

The structure of this chapter initially provides a brief review of the historical development of HE partnerships and situates them in the context of China's drive to become a globally competitive "knowledge economy" (Jessop, 2012). The study of the Sino-foreign HE partnerships not only shows how China mobilises such partnerships to internationalise its HE sector, but also opens a window into a much larger process of China's transformation: from a relatively passive importer of foreign educational programmes to a more proactive player in the global knowledge economy. Next, we show how the conceptual terms by which foreign scholars, university organisations, think tanks[1] and Chinese policymakers refer to these partnerships and reflect important differences in understanding the nature of these initiatives. To achieve this, we completed a discourse analysis of the relevant Chinese policies and examined the evolution of the policy framework developed by the MOE that defines, regulates and steers the Sino-foreign partnerships in HE in China. It is by tracing the shifting foci of the policy framework that we map out the actors and dynamics that shape the development of Sino-foreign HE partnerships. Then we outline important policy changes in China, which demanded increased regulation of these partnerships in the form of increasing quantifiable targets

PURSUING IDEAL PARTNERSHIPS

for the involvement of foreign and local partner. Two cases are introduced: the Sino-British College (SBC) and Sino-Danish Center for Education and Research (SDC); they illustrate how the discourse of instrumentalism in polices interact with the practices and give rise to different modes of Sino-foreign partnerships in HE. By analysing and comparing these two cases, we trace the evolution and creation of these partnerships and how they reflect on the responses to Chinese policy initiatives. Finally, we end by exploring what our proposed perspectives mean for the study of HE partnerships in China.

2 New Ways to Understand Educational Partnerships in China

By using an inductive analysis of the themes arising from the Chinese policy discourse as well as from policy documents and case study notes, we propose two key arguments for understanding HE partnerships in China. First, that there is a difference between the ways in which outsiders and the Chinese system understands these partnerships. This difference is best expressed in the analysis of the terms by which these initiatives are often described: 'TNE' by 'Westerners' and 'Sino-foreign' partnerships by the Chinese. Second, we argue that Chinese policy makers are developing a moving target of their ideal HE partnership with foreign institutions. One way to understand this ideal is through a quantitative policy language used to describe the various aspects of the partnerships. The ideal appears to be that an *equal* or *50–50* partnership and policy guidelines, with a minimum level of resource contribution, to encourage movement towards this ideal. One of the policy goals was to ensure that foreign partners actively contributed at least a third of the resources (e.g. teachers, curriculum, etc.) to the partnership. The rationale being that partnerships, whose foreign involvement was below this ratio, could easily allow low-quality Chinese colleges or vocational schools to sell fancy foreign diplomas with limited foreign engagement.

The second argument for understanding the HE partnerships in China is to consider the role of internationalisation. Stier (2004) argues that there are several understandings of the term internationalisation. He offers three examples: internationalisation as a state of things, as a process and as a doctrine. We draw on the latter understanding of internationalisation as a 'doctrine' to investigate its normative nature. Linked closely to Stier's framing of internationalisation as a doctrine are the ideologies of internationalisation: idealism, instrumentalism and educationalism.

Stier's framework describes idealism as an ideology in which internationalisation is a good per se. In educationalism, internationalisation enriches the overall academic experience of staff and students and leads to their "Bildung"

(Stier, 2004, p. 92) or lifelong learning, which extends beyond the classroom. We draw, in particular, on the proposed understanding of instrumentalism (in internationalisation). Here, HE is a means to an end, which could include maximising profit, promoting economic growth and development and shaping culture and society by "transmitting desirable ideologies" (Stier, 2004, p. 90).

Through these two lenses – the differing labels on partnerships and the pursuit of 'quantitative' parity or the setting of a minimum contribution of the foreign partner – we propose that the study of Chinese HE partnerships can be usefully understood as the pursuit of 'equality' between partners, with repercussions for the ways in which foreign and Chinese universities cooperate in the future. It also shows a shift in the instrumental benefit of these partnerships to China and we argue that the previous partnerships reflected the need for China to expand provision whereas current needs demand more value from foreign partners.

2.1   *HE Partnerships: China's HE Policy*

China's HE system evolved according to its own logic following their perceived humiliation when Western powers looted China during the Opium Wars (1840–1842); China then became an importer of education. Chinese education policymakers looked to others for new innovative ideas, but this often favoured one particular style, for example Soviet system in the 1950s and the American system in 1990s (Yang, 2010). Over the past few decades the internationalisation of HE has become a growing trend and many students in China, who were financially able, have sought HE abroad or have enrolled in TNE programmes offered in China in a bid to gain globally competitive labour market skills. This trend coupled with lower teaching and research quality at many Chinese universities enhanced the Chinese governments drive to reform the HE landscape and avoid possible brain drain (Mok & Han, 2016).

The Chinese government have sought varying ways to improve quality and they have incorporated overseas practices through partnerships. In 2014 there were more than 1,600 tertiary level partnerships operating across 25 of the 31 provinces in China (HEFCE, 2014). University partnerships in China have been described by Li (2017, p. 245) as a key dimension in HE development and while they have been a key means to restructure the education system since the 1950s there has been a considerable increase in partnerships in recent years. With the increase of university partnerships and TNE provisions now being sought out and provided globally, this growing trend has been described as an evolutionary phase in the global development of HE in the context of new trade agreements for services and the opening up of new education markets (Yang, 2008).

PURSUING IDEAL PARTNERSHIPS 63

3   Different Understandings of Partnership

China has implemented major projects to enable some high-ranking, flagship universities to become world class with the aim of developing key research bases and knowledge production capacity. As China wanted to import 'good practices' from abroad, partnerships with foreign universities were seen as a way to not only boost Chinese society's exposure to HE, but also allow China to access the world's most advanced education systems (Yang, 2008, p. 274). Bringing the Sino and foreign partners together could carry mutual benefit and many scholars began to apply the label of TNE to this process in China (Helms, 2008; Huang, 2003; Yang, 2008).

While 'Western' literature (which also includes Chinese scholars publishing in English journals) often uses the term TNE to describe the growth of partnerships in China, there is often a different term used in the Chinse policy language to describe and guide the development of these partnerships; here the term 'CFCRS' (Chinese-Foreign Cooperation in Running Schools) is more commonly used. CFCRS refers to the cooperation between foreign and Chinese educational institutions to establish educational institutions within the territory of China, which are created for the purpose of providing education services mainly to Chinese citizens. Our analysis of this language shows a changed emphasis in the term CFCRS which highlights the fact that there are two aspects of the partnership – that there is a clear distinction between the foreign partner and the local (Chinese) one. Both partners have their roles to play.

In contrast to TNE, the distinction between foreign and local partner is much more pronounced in the Chinese understanding of partnership than what is often understood by 'transnational' education. On the other hand, our reading of the term TNE in the literature, shows that the emphasis is often placed on connecting the two partners, a production of a new kind of education that draws from both parties, and a fluid passage back and forth of ideas all of which are depicted and implied by the use of the prefix *trans*.

3.1   *Transnational Education*

As Healey (2015) discovered, with partnerships becoming multidimensional and the boundaries of types blurring, it is becoming increasingly difficult to create a typology of educational partnerships. With the expanding globalisation of HE, more partnerships are crossing borders and continents, resulting in more international collaborations. In the 'West' the collaborations in which "the education provision for students based in a country other than the one in which the awarding body is located another" is called TNE (HE

Global, 2016, p. 9). However, "with over forty different definitions currently being used for TNE and each definition varying with the type of programme offered and the providers moving across different national borders" (Knight & McNamara, 2017, p. 1), an univocal understanding of TNE is difficult to pin down.

A standard typology for TNE is often to classify by activity, whether it is distance learning, an international branch campus, franchise, or form of external validation (Healey, 2015). These types of activities can differ depending on the host country regulations in place and the partnership motivations. What's more, TNE has changed drastically over the last 10 years as new actors, partnerships and modes of delivery have come into play. This has brought along an increase in the research in this area as well as on the various regulations being imposed on TNE partnerships (Knight, 2016). Recent research (Knight, 2016; Knight & McNamara, 2017) has focused on devising a classification framework for TNE programmes globally and while this may address some of the confusion surrounding TNE activities globally, it does not address specific host country issues.

TNE is a now a global term; it emphasises the location of both the student and awarding body (although it need not be specific about either). However, we argue that in the case of China, this understanding is insufficient. The Chinese policy making focus is not principally about location but the bringing together of foreign and local (Chinese) provisions to provide educational services for Chinese citizens. Chinese policy guidelines highlight the expectations of the provision and the requirements of the collaboration (Lin, 2012), rather than the requirements of travelling between global locations. This example is just one of the ways in which the literature on TNE can fail to capture the local context and the local policy priorities.

3.2 Chinese-Foreign Cooperation in Running Schools – CFCRS

One main reason for implementing the CFCRS policy was to regulate the expanding HE partnerships in China (Iftekhar & Kayombo, 2016). The CFCRS, in contrast to TNE, has different principles set out by the Chinese central government. The *People's Daily*, the official newspaper of the Chinese Communist Party and a platform to declare the official stance on fundamental issues about China, clarified that there are two basic principles for CFCRS: (1) The CFCRS has to adapt to and serve the overall development and reform of China's own political and economic system; (2) The CFCRS has to adapt to and serve the growth and development of the Chinese students (Lin, 2012). The CFCRS is then a highly developmental policy that draws upon foreign expertise where is desirable for national development purposes.

The interim provisions on CFCRS (1995) emphasised the enrolment of Chinese citizens as a main objective of the partnership between foreign bodies (corporate or individual) or other relevant international organisations and Chinese educational institutions. However, China eventually recognised that there were some quality issues with CFCRS programmes and this was later redefined in 2003 (Iftekhar & Kayombo, 2016), emphasising that there had been a change in the requirements for the foreign partner. This was followed with the implementing regulations, which focused on programmes that awarded degree certificates to Chinese citizens and those that did not (QAA, 2013). In 2006, China was still unhappy with the quality of foreign provisions and they suspended approval of CFCRS (QAA, 2013) and the MOE then released the policy document, *Proposals on Further Enhancing the Quality Assurance of the CFCRS* (hereafter referred to as Proposal 2013), which called for greater awareness of educational sovereignty as well as political sensitivity among the Chinese institutions. Moreover, this also introduced additional guidelines surrounding the operations of the CFCRS entities.

According to *Proposal 2013*, the ideal and "coveted" partnerships should not only be "alliances between giants" in which the foreign partner is strong, desirable or even famous but also that the Chinese partners should remain *dominant* in the collaboration. In the Proposal, we see the emergence of a *policy ideal* or a model JV as set out under the "imperative advice" for those running these ventures (see Tables 3.1 and 3.2).

These guidelines show a different understanding from 'Western' TNE. In one of the guidelines, it is made clear that the Chinese partner should be leading the partnership (be dominant) and that the outputs of the JV must redound to the 'service of China'. In addition to issuing guidelines as to what kinds of activities should be promoted and encouraged, the guidelines also set out what activities should be reduced (see Table 3.2). In particular, efforts were made to curb activities in which Chinese students were seen as customers not receiving good value or where they were in such large groups with few teachers and this could affect the quality of the education. Another area of concern was the introduction of any resources that might undermine Chinese educational sovereignty.

This type of advice and guidance is typical in Chinese policy documents, to trigger and guide actions. Such documents work a similar way to top-down orders and instructions, which carry with them the authority from the top or centre: a feature of governance in China that cannot be ignored.

TABLE 3.1   Advice for the CFCRS ideal model

CFCRS "positive advice"

Insist on the collaboration between strong partners, set up role-models for demonstration...
Make sure that the foreign partners are great or famous universities...
Encourage the collaboration to take place in those disciplines that China is either wanting, weak or blank...
Complement each other's advantages, install essential integration...
Maintain the dominance of the Chinese institutions in the partnerships and utilize the foreign resources to the service of China...
Enhance the attraction, introduction, digestion, integration and innovation of the high-quality resources...
Promote the innovation in operating schools...
Build high-level, CFCRS programmes or institutions as flagships as "best practice"...
Encourage more financial and property investment from HEIs in different areas to set up a cohort of exemplary CFCRS institutions, majors with brand effects and exemplary courses...
Enhance the study and communication of the experiences of high-level, exemplary CFCRS praxis...

TABLE 3.2   Constrictions for the CFCRS ideal model

CFCRS "constrictions"

Impose strict control over the CFCRS in the disciplines of business, management and other disciplines that China has tried to curb...
Impose strict control over the entry of foreign resources; protect China's educational sovereignty...

SOURCE: PROPOSAL (2013)

4   The Minimum Third: Towards an Equal Partnership?

These Chinese policies, the *Proposals on Some Current Issues of the CFCRS* (2006), were designed to ensure adequate foreign resources were brought into partnerships and also to facilitate integration between the Chinese institutions and their foreign partners. The guidelines set *quantified* standards that enforce a guaranteed proportion of foreign contribution in every CFCRS programme. The logic behind this shows that a programme with a ratio of less than a third (33%) of foreign components, whether this be in terms of teaching hours, foreign teachers, courses or aspects of the curriculum as a whole, could not qualify as a truly collaborative programme between China and a foreign partner.

The change towards this minimum third rule is a step towards a more equal partnership: exemplified by new JVs that have a rhetorical commitment to an equal or 50/50 partnership (as presented in one of the cases below). The movement and pre-occupation of being regarded as an equal partner rather than being seen as the struggling laggard is a theme that has grown. A developing Chinese nation now demands more equality in its dealings with foreign partners in all areas as it continues through its modernisation process. In light of the discourse on the value and primacy of knowledge in the knowledge economy (Jessop, 2012), there is an added importance given to the validation of China's own knowledge products, development and the strength of its education system.

The move towards the minimum third rule means that it has become more challenging to set up a JV. There are significant differences between currently operating Sino-foreign partnerships, some of which cannot achieve the minimum third rule. Some partners were happy to collaborate with foreign partners even with a small contribution on the overseas partner's part for the sake of an improved reputation for the local university through the JV. In other cases, overseas partners were unwilling to shoulder the risk of committing too many resources. The result is that many Chinese higher education institutions (HEIs) were forced to forego the opportunity to collaborate with foreign institutions because they could not adequately meet the new guidelines. The new regulations appear to have hindered Chinese HEIs in terms of potential development and expansion via a CFCRS partnership (Li & Huang, 2015).

Even until recently, a large proportion of CFCRS programmes still failed to meet the minimum third standard mentioned in the 2006 Proposals. For example, in the evaluation of the CFCRS programmes by MOE in 2014, among the 73 programmes that took part in the evaluation, about 41% of these programmes could not fulfil the "Four Indices of 1/3" (Xue, 2016). In October 2014, 252 CFCRS programmes or institutions were shut down, the list of names were announced publicly by the MOE and no applications for independent CFCRS institutions were approved in 2013 and 2014 (Lin, 2015).

The two case studies which follow show how the Chinese CFCRS policies are put into action and how the 'Western' term TNE is used and viewed in relation to two very different Sino-foreign partnerships. These two cases highlight how one partnership (established in 2006) has undergone various changes in line with the changing Chinese policy ideal and how a much newer second partnership (established in 2014) has established itself as a very different, but 'ideal', kind of Sino-foreign partnership. Both cases show how the partners understood and then adapted to their understanding of the new goals – the instrumentalist needs – set out in the CFCRS policy.

5 A Tale of Two Partnerships: The Sino-British College and the Sino-Danish Center

The various policy changes within Chinese HE have resulted in both Chinese and Western HEIs, but more importantly Sino-foreign partnerships, making changes or being designed from the very start with particular features for more parity and to comply with the local standards and requirements. This has resulted in an ever-changing field with partnerships constantly adapting to meet instrumentalist Chinese policy.

5.1 *The Sino-British College*

The Sino-British College (SBC) became fully licensed as a university college in 2006 and is one of the many JV partnerships in China. It is a partnership between a college of the University of Shanghai for Science and Technology (USST) and a United Kingdom (UK) university consortium, called the Northern Consortium UK (NCUK) (see Figure 3.1). The consortium comprises of eleven-member UK universities.[2] Due to this unusual collaboration, Mok and Ong (2013) described it as a highly complicated product of TNE; each of the nine

FIGURE 3.1   Institutions involved in the SBC partnership (Source: SBC, 2015)

PURSUING IDEAL PARTNERSHIPS

individual universities, rather than the collective consortium (NCUK), are considered as the foreign collaborators under the CFCRS regulations.

The Northern Consortium was created in 1987 to facilitate collaboration between its members in order to establish and run courses overseas to prepare students for studying abroad (QAA, 2013, p. 11). The purpose of this registered charity was to provide both academic programmes and university placement services for international students. NCUK, a registered trading arm owned by the charity, has been organising places for students at UK university partners for some time, as well as providing preparatory programmes for students who wanted to study overseas (NCUK, 2015). These preparatory programmes were designed to provide a foundation of the subject knowledge and prepare students to study in the UK, they lasted for one year and were based in the student's home country. Once completed, students would transfer to a partner university in the UK for a further three years of undergraduate study, this is known as the 1+3 route. When NCUK collaborated with USST, a public university that originated from the University of Shanghai in 1906, the JV formed (the Sino-British College – SBC) becoming one of the 100+ HE collaborations USST had established (USST, n.d.).

As curriculum and content were provided by NCUK the original 1+3 route was adapted for delivery at SBC to become a 2+2 route. This meant that students would spend two years at SBC (in China) and then they would go to a NCUK partner university for the final two years, ending with a university degree from that partner university. However, since the initial establishment of SBC in 2006 there have been various changes relating to the course delivery, which seems to have fallen in line with China's education policy developments. Table 3.3 highlights some of the main developments along with the relevant policy changes.

Initially when SBC was set up in 2006 the CFCRS regulations were under review and a proposal concerning current issues with CFCRS programmes was released. SBC was able to provide foundation programmes and deliver a UK curriculum. This meant that foreign providers were operating in China and that potentially some revenues for local providers were being diverted because the SBC's provision of UK education relied somewhat on a perceived superiority of the foreign brands and pandered to the Chinese customers' preference for what they saw as authentic Western education.

In 2006 SBC moved from the 1+3 to the 2+2. This meant that on the 2+2 programmes, students would spend an equal amount of time in UK and the China. The move to offer the 2+2 route is but one potential example of how the SBC and USST JV moved towards more 'parity'. By dividing the time that students spent equally between China and the UK, one concrete result was that more fees were paid and collected in China relative to the earlier system in which

TABLE 3.3 Highlights China's HE policy developments with developments at SBC

Year	SBC developments	China policy developments
2006	SBC – JV formed and licence approved (for 2+2 preparation programmes)	'Proposals on Some Current Issues of the CFCRS' released. Policy document calls for enforcing more control over the CFCRS entities
2008		The Chinese government granted a licence for degrees in Events Management to be taught in China (QAA 2013:12).
2009	Approved delivery of University of Huddersfield BA (Hons) Events Management (3+1 / 4+0). Approved delivery of Liverpool John Moores BEng (Hons) Industrial electronics and BEng (Hons) Manufacturing systems Engineering (3+1 / 4+0).	From 2006 to 2009 MOE suspended its process of examining and ratifying CFCRS programmes and these procedures were only reinstalled again in 2010 (Xu, 2014).
2010	University of Sheffield Business Management programme launched (2+1+1). First students arrive in Sheffield September 2013	The pause 2006 – 2009 was related to quality. Many CFCRS programmes were small-scale, low-level colleges in pursuit of profit, they did not have the capability or motivation to appeal to high-level overseas (often Western) partners. The Proposals on Some Current Issues of the CFCRS (2006) imposed the policy of "Four Indices of 1/3", which built up a set of quantified indices
2012	Government approval for a 4+0 Accounting and finance (Leeds Met) course was not secured. The last students for the 3+1 course were recruited in September 2012 (QAA 2013:13).	

(*cont.*)

PURSUING IDEAL PARTNERSHIPS   71

TABLE 3.3   Highlights China's HE policy developments with developments at SBC (*cont.*)

Year	SBC developments	China policy developments
2013		In December 2013, the MOE released: Proposals on Further Enhancing the Quality Assurance of the CFCRS. "a comprehensive summary of the construction of quality assurance system in the past 3 years and a clear statement of the future goals for the construction of QA system (Xue, 2016)
2017	1 to N Consortium model 1+3 / 2+2 / 3+1 / 4+0	

more money was remitted to the UK. Students at SBC on this 2+2 route could complete a pathway programme focusing on either business or engineering (QAA, 2013).

There are other aspects of significance in the SBCs operation. By working with a large set of UK universities in NCUK, the JV seems to have given rise to the prevalence of 'collaborative' modes of CFCRS entities but which feature, on the contrary, the dominance of the curricula and pedagogies from the foreign provider. This means that the foreign provider appears to contribute more than 50% but this is not ideal either. Within such a collaboration, the Chinese HEIS' roles as content provider in the programmes are reduced to a minimum and they mainly perform as the local administrators and take on logistical responsibilities. However, with students spending 50% of their time at SBC in China and 50% in the UK (2+2: two years in China and two years in the UK), there was still an equitable balance of sorts maintained.

From 2006 to 2009 there was a pause in the approval of additional CFCRS as there were issues related to quality. Many CFCRS programmes were small-scale, low-level colleges in pursuit of profit and it was felt that they did not have the capability or motivation to appeal to high-level overseas partners. As the MOE continued to design and promote diversified paths for the different levels of CFCRS entities, it seems that there was a process of stratification. China's MOE top-down designed allowed for partnerships established in China, by some private colleges or vocational schools, to focus on the need in terms of subject area and geographical location and then bring in foreign resources to fill the gap. This can perhaps be seen in terms of the Chinese government, in 2008, granting a licence to SBC for degrees in events management to be taught in China (QAA, 2013, p. 12). This ratification of CFCRS programmes led to SBC being able to deliver an events management degree (in 2009) along with the other NCUK pathway programmes. This meant that students could stay in China for the full four years of their study, or they could choose to study part of their programme in the UK.

This change allowed students to be able to obtain a double degree, one from USST and another from the University of Huddersfield (the UK TNE provider) and they would be able to do this without leaving China. The double-degree system means that the Chinese and foreign curricula can be run side by side. Often it is common for the Chinese HEIs to be insufficiently motivated or prepared to integrate the Chinese and foreign curricula, which may call for additional effort in building mutual understanding and common ground between the two or more educational systems.

The approval of events management degrees coincided with major events being held in China, such as the World Expo in 2010, the summer youth Olympics in Nanjing in 2014 and perhaps owing to a knowledge gap in the field of hospitality and event management services and the positive CFCRS advice of encouraging collaboration in disciplines where China is either wanting or is weak, there was a strategic choice to approve the provision of the events management degree. Another such approval was that of two engineering degrees delivered by Liverpool John Moores University. As China works to become a leader in STEM subjects, which include engineering, these also fell into the CFCRS category of strategic need.

With regard to the prohibitions of the CFCRS Proposals, which were included in the *im(position) of strict control over the CFCRS in the disciplines of business, management and other disciplines that China has tried to curb.* These controls were indeed felt at SBC when government approval for a 4+0 accounting and finance course were not secured. The SBC provision had been running as a 3+1 course, but the final students were recruited for that programme in September 2012 (QAA, 2013, p. 13) with the programme to close down soon after, indicating further developments at SBC based on the policy developments in China.

The most recent change and development can be linked to China becoming a centre for international students which has given rise to the 1-to-N Consortium model which provides differing options for non-Chinese citizens. The 1-to-N Consortium model means that international (non-Chinese) students can study for the foundation level at SBC (year one) and then move to one of the NCUK partners for their undergraduate degree. This distinction between

Chinese and non-Chinese citizens allows the CFCRS to provide varying education programmes for different reasons, but all in line with China's overarching plans.

5.2 The Sino-Danish Center (SDC)

The SDC is a joint project for education and research between eight Danish universities,[3] the Danish Ministry of Science, Innovation and Technology (now named the Ministry of Higher Education and Science), the University of the Chinese Academy of Science and the Chinese Academy of Sciences. It was initiated by the Danish Ministry of Science, Technology and Innovation as one of the many initiatives included in the Strategy for Knowledge-based Collaboration between Denmark and China published in 2008 (called the China Strategy from here on). At the time the Danish Ministry was working as a driving force in conceiving the China Strategy and soliciting the commitments from the eight Danish universities as well as financial support from the industry foundation before the establishment of SDC. As a platform for the Sino-Danish exchange and collaboration, the SDC was intended to guarantee the *equal* or even symmetrical presence of the two countries in the partnership. After its establishment the ministry remained a stakeholder in the SDC collaboration as it provided the funding and oversaw the construction of SDC building (Bech, 2016). Therefore, the conception of SDC's roles and missions reflect, were heavily influenced by the national developmental strategy of Denmark from the very beginning. The SDC was a political project intended to guarantee the *equal* or even symmetrical presence of the two countries in the partnership. At the core of SDC's operation there was an implicit 50–50 policy which guided the organisation of its resources and the composition of its structure. This 50–50 principle reflected the intended equal division of obligation and benefits between China and Denmark (SDC, 2015). Clearly, this operating principle meets the minimum third required of foreign partners.

The Danish Ministry legitimised and emphasised the knowledge-based collaboration with China as a coping strategy to "create substantial value for the Danish society and contribute towards positioning Denmark in the global knowledge economy" (DMoS, 2008, p. 4). The main premises for such an argument in China Strategy were (1) the statistics-informed discovery of China's rising capability as a producer of new knowledge and the prediction of China becoming one of the main knowledge producers in the future (ibid) and (2) the recognition that it was a prerequisite for future growth that Danish businesses exploit international collaboration and sales potential and have access to the required manpower. As a result, the China Strategy made it clear that its vision of the Sino-Danish collaboration had a focus on knowledge, education and innovation and it must support the activities of Danish business in China.

The Danish Ministry of Science, Technology and Innovation's China Strategy aimed to facilitate access for Danish universities, business enterprises and institutions to create knowledge and innovation in cooperation with Chinese partners as well as attract Chinese students to Danish universities and businesses (DMoS, 2008). It was in this context that the proposal of establishing a Sino-Danish university came about. Other initiatives developed at the same time such as: block grants for Danish universities offering doctoral programmes for the purpose of financing the stay of Chinese researchers in Denmark, scholarships for the exchange of talented Master's students between Denmark and China, and cooperation with industry to promote student mobility between Denmark and China. The establishment of SDC is but one piece of a larger national strategy that Denmark initiated to forge knowledge-based alliances with China. The SDC was designed in a different way from previous partnerships so it could enable the collaboration between Denmark and China to be equal, mutually beneficial and strategically complementary in the first place.

As a project initiated by the Danish government, the SDC needed to be sensitive to the Chinese policy idea of equal partnership from its very inception. As such the SDC's 50–50 policy is central to the design of the institution as a platform between China and Denmark (SDC, 2015). This equality served a *political* and instrumental purpose. It was an instrument of diplomacy between Danish and Chinese governments.

Even though this 50–50 principle was not formalised, it was acknowledged in the organisation's application documents submitted to the MOE of China (in 2010) and in the narratives of SDC's legal documents and its website (SDC, 2015). Our analysis of the SDC, including the observation of how things operate on the ground, shows that this 50–50 policy is embedded as an innate and omnipresent premise even though it can sometimes be difficult to achieve in practice. In the interviews with SDC workers by one of the authors, there was frequent reference to the 50–50 principle as a basic policy.

Unlike SBC, the SDC did not evolve as an institution in response to Chinese policy but rather was created to specifically address the new policy goals of the CFCRS. It is as if Danish policy makers sought to create the right institution that would fit the guidelines. The SDC was to be a well-recognised instrument that fulfilled the CFCRS and wider Chinese HE goals. The SDC can therefore work not only as a standard for comparison with older CFCRS programmes and institutions, but also as a blueprint for new applicants to initiate and construct their own CFCRS proposals.

PURSUING IDEAL PARTNERSHIPS

6 The Evolution of HE Instrumentalism in Sino-Foreign Partnerships

Our analysis of the development of equal partnership in HE JVs points to the different perceived needs of China's HE sector and the wider economy. Our diagnosis shows a discourse of instrumentalism in the regulative polices of the Sino-foreign partnerships. We have particularly highlighted this instrumentalist strand following Stier's earlier (2004) identification of an ideology of instrumentalism that clearly views internationalisation as being a means to an end. In the cases that we have shown above, the need to fulfil the guidelines of the CFCRS seemed to be the primary motivation to with respect to the evolution (SBC) and development (SDC) of partnerships with China with other aspects (education or international contact as 'good' in themselves) being less emphasised.

This instrumentalist discourse constructs the CFCRS as an instrument mobilised by the MOE to achieve *different purposes* at *different times*. This insight also allows us to extend Stier's analysis by proposing the temporal element to his framework. Internationalisation can indeed be merely an instrument to meet wider policy goals, but it is important to understand how the shifting goals lead to a sifting understanding and practice of internationalisation. The shifting weight assigned to the different aspects of the functions of CFCRS purposes can be summarised as follows:

- Early period (1995–2006): The mechanism to effectively bring in foreign resources for domestic needs;
- Middle period (2006–2013): The instrument to raise quality and diversity of Chinese HE and to force the reform of the current system.
- Recent period (2013-present): The detailed categorising of the partnerships and proactive design of their developmental paths to achieve multiple ends, such as; better capacity, better structure and a design that enables the optimal coordination of HEIs at different levels.

The case of the SBC's earlier establishment shows how this Sino-British partnership responded to the instrumental need in the earlier two periods. The evolution of the SBC to provide more parity and, more evidently, the principles on which the more recent Sino-Danish venture was founded, reflects the more recent active participation of Chinese policy makers in the characteristics of new partnerships.

The discourse of instrumentalism takes different shapes across time and set limits on what the CFCRS can and should do. Its shifting not only reflects the changes in the social context of CFCRS and new economic-political imperatives identified by the MOE for the CFCR. This shift in also in accord with

China's transformation in its positioning of itself in the global order from passive and defensive receiver of foreign expertise to aspiring equal partner, and then to proactive mobiliser, and even initiator.

7 Concluding Remarks: Moving Forward

HE partnerships between China and international partners are not straightforward. Chinese HEIs may sometimes be insufficiently motivated or prepared to integrate the Chinese and foreign curricula, this process calls for a lot of effort in building mutual understanding and common ground between the two (or more) educational systems which can be vastly different in many respects. Chinese partners are often attracted by the cultural capital that comes from being associated in name with a reputable overseas institution as this can attract more students. Meanwhile the partnerships also increase the amount of financial capital that the overseas partner reaps through such cross-border collaboration (Postiglione, 2011). This can be seen as a win-win situation for the universities, but not necessarily for the overall development of the HE sector of China.

As such the Chinese MOE has worked hard to ensure that partnerships do contribute to China's development in expected ways. Rather than marginalising the Chinese curricula and posing a threat to China's educational sovereignty, *Proposals 2013* depicts both the positive and negative features of partnerships in CFCRS to distinguish right from wrong to sketch out desirable practices. By establishing that existing partnerships, such as the SBC, develop in line with policy changes and that newer partnerships, such as the SDC, are a more *equitable* provision from the very beginning, Chinese policy makers can ensure that only high-quality resources which the country needs and can benefit from are brought in. They can avoid programmes being repetitive and dumped into China by foreign HEIs in pursuit of profit. The explicit pursuit of these goals by China through its CFCRS policy lead to the practice of internationalisation in specific, instrumental, ways.

For partnerships established among elite universities, especially the Sino-foreign universities or colleges such as the SBC and SDC, the goal was to push for innovation and excellence to enhance the synergy of the partners and to set up models for other CFCRS partnerships to follow. The stratification of CFCRS partnerships is the outcome of MOE's design; it is also a process of coordinating the different roles of CFCRS and aligning them with the national strategy of development.

While this blueprint provided a relatively clear outline for the development of CFCRS programmes or institutions set up after *Proposal 2013*, for the

CFCRS programmes and institutions established before 2013, it raises quite a few challenges. The design and refinement of the structure and developmental paths for the CFCRS has been a historical process, the requirements and evaluation standards have evolved and sometimes even changed dramatically. Those programmes or institutions which were rendered 'non-ideal' by the new regulations needed time and space to adapt to the new standards. The evolution and responses of these institutions should be the subject of further study and our proposed framework is one way to understand the coming changes.

Our approach shows the development of a discourse of instrumentalism that China adapted to position itself in the global economy. Further study of other JVs in China could add a deeper insight into this policy ideal which could be used for future partnerships. This chapter contributes to our understanding of the evolution of Sino-foreign HE partnerships and in particular highlights the differences between the ways in which some 'Western' academics and Chinese policymakers view these partnerships. We show how these different understandings of partnership as well as the ways of interpreting China's instrumentalist policies affect the practice of internationalisation, specifically in the ways that Sino-foreign partnerships are run. It offers a cautionary guide to those who wish to partner with China. Chinese HE partnerships are costly to build up and maintain and the value they bring to China will increasingly be put under scrutiny. This increased understanding of difference could also be used to consider how China conducts its own JVs abroad.

Notes

1 We reference, for instance, the work of HEGlobal, an arm of Universities UK (UUK), an umbrella organisation of all UK universities.
2 These include: University of Bradford, University of Huddersfield, University of Leeds, Leeds Beckett University, University of Liverpool, Liverpool John Moores University, University of Manchester, Manchester Metropolitan University, University of Salford, University of Sheffield and Sheffield Hallam University. However, both the University of Manchester and the University of Liverpool were both pursuing their own interests in China at this time and were therefore not part of the founding partners at SBC (QAA, 2013, p. 11).
3 These include the following: Aalborg University, Aarhus University, Copenhagen Business School, IT University of Copenhagen, Roskilde University, Technical University of Denmark, University of Copenhagen, and the University of Southern Denmark.

References

Bech, M. (2016). *Creating collaboration – Human hubs and go-betweeners in Sino-Foreign University collaboration, an ethnographic and organizational perspective* (PhD dissertation). Aarhus University, Aarhus.

CRCFCRS, Center of Research on Chinese-Foreign Cooperation in Running Schools (China). (2018, July 20). *Shush the 'noise'! understanding the MOE's approval of abolishing CFCRS programmes* (Published online). Retrieved from https://www.wowodx.com/fujian/shamendaxue/smdxzwhzbxyjzx/3404412376c145 2e9023dbfcfdf3ea30.html

DMoS, (Danish) Ministry for Science, Technology and Innovation. (2008). *Strategy – The knowledge-based collaboration between Denmark and China.* Retrieved from https://ufm.dk/en/publications/2008/files-2008/strategy-knowledge-based-collaboration-denmark-china.pdf

Fazackerley, A. (Ed.). (2007). *British Universities in China: The reality beyond the Rhetoric* (An Agora discussion paper). London: Forum for Culture and Education. Retrieved from https://academiccouncil.duke.edu/sites/default/files/u6/AC-pdfs/09-10/11-19-09/Agora-China-Report1.pdf

Healey, N. M. (2015). Towards a risk-based typology for transnational education. *Higher Education, 69*(1), 1–18.

HE Global. (2016). *The scale and scope of UK higher education transnational education.* Retrieved from http://heglobal.international.ac.uk/media/3780659/Scale-and-Scope-of-UK-HE-TNE-Report.pdf

HEFCE, Higher Education Funding Council for England. (2014). *Transnational education in China.* Retrieved from http://blog.hefce.ac.uk/2014/11/27/transnational-education-in-china/

Helms, R. (2008). *Transnational education in China: Key challenges, critical issues, and strategies for success.* Redhill: The Observatory on Borderless Higher Education. Retrieved from http://www.obhe.ac.uk/documents/view_details?id=11

Huang, F. (2003). Transnational higher education: A perspective from China. *Higher Education Research & Development, 22*(2), 193–203.

Iftekhar, S., & Kayombo, J. (2016). Chinese-Foreign Cooperation in Running Schools (CFCRS): A policy analysis. *International Journal of Research Studies in Education, 5*(4), 73–82.

Jessop, B. (2012). A cultural political economy of competitiveness. In D. Livingstone & D. Guile (Eds.), *The knowledge economy and lifelong learning* (pp. 57–83). Rotterdam, The Netherlands: Sense Publishers.

Knight, J. (2016). Transnational education remodeled: Toward a common TNE framework and definitions. *Journal of Studies in International Education, 20*(1), 34–47.

Knight, J., & McNamara, J. (2017). *Transnational education: A classification framework and data collection guidelines for International Programme and Provider Mobility (IPPM)*. British Council. Retrieved from https://www.britishcouncil.org/sites/default/files/tne_classification_framework-final.pdf

Li, J. (2017). Ideologies, strategies and higher education development: A comparison of China's university partnerships with the Soviet Union and Africa over space and time. *Comparative Education, 53*(2), 245–264.

Li, J., & Huang, K. (2015). Dui Gao Xiao Zhong Wai He Zuo Ban Xue Xiang Mu Ping Gu Zhi Biao De Shang Que – Guan Yu Jin Yi Bu Wan Shan 'Si Ge San Fen Zhi Yi' Zhi Biao De Jian Yi [The debate of the indicators for the CFCRS appraisal – Advice for further improving the 'four indices' of 1/3]. *Higher Education of San Jiang University, 1*, 6–9.

Lin, J. (2012). Zhong Wai He Zuo Ban Xue Zhong Yin Jin You Zhi Jiao Yu Zi Yuan Wen Ti Yan Jiu [On the introduction of educational resources with high quality in Sino-foreign cooperative school running]. *Educational Research, 10*(393), 34–38.

Lin, J. (2015, November). *To balance quantity, quality and benefits in oder to push the development of CFCRS—Where is its policy going*. Paper Delivered at the 6th Annual Conference of CFCRS.

Lin, J. (2018). On the policy goal and its implementation conditions of Chinese-Foreign cooperation in running schools. *Educational Research, 10*, 70–76.

MOE, (Chinese) Ministry of Education. (2018, June 21). *The announcement of the general office of the moe on the approval of abolishing some CFCRS institutions and programmes*. Retrieved from http://www.moe.gov.cn/srcsite/A20/moe_862/201807/t20180705_342056.html

Mok, K., & Ong, K. (2013). Transforming from "economic power" to "soft power": Transnationalization and internationalization of higher education in China. In Q. Li & C. Gerstl-Pepin (Eds.), *Survival of the fittest: The shifting contours of higher education in China and the United States* (pp. 133–156). London: Springer-Verlag.

Mok, K. H., & Han, X. (2016). From 'brain drain' to 'brain bridging': transnational higher education development and graduate employment in China. *Journal of Higher Education Policy and Management, 38*(3), 369–389.

NCUK, Northern Consortium United Kingdom. (2015). Working together. Retrieved from https://www.ncuk.ac.uk/wp-content/uploads/2016/11/NCUK-Working-Together.pdf

Proposals, (Chinese) Ministry of Education – MOE (2013). *Jiao Yu Bu Guan Yu Jin Yi Bu Jia Qiang Zhong Wai He Zuo Ban Xue Zhi Liang Bao Zhang Gong Zuo De Yi Jian [Proposals on further enhancing the quality assurance of the CFCRS]*. Retrieved from http://io.ruc.edu.cn/displaynews.php?id=21

Postiglione, G. (2011). East asian knowledge systems: Driving ahead amid borderless higher education. In D. Chapman, W. Cummings, & G. Postiglione (Eds.), *Crossing borders in East Asian higher education* (pp. 25–46). Dordrecht: Springer.

QAA, Quality Assurance Agency. (2013, May). *Review of UK transnational education in China 2012: Overview.* Retrieved from http://www.qaa.ac.uk/en/Publications/Documents/TNE-China-Overview.pdf

SBC, Sino-British College. (2015). *Introduction to SBC.* Retrieved May 8, 2017, from http://www.sbc-usst.edu.cn/en/AboutSBC/AboutSBC/IntroductionToSBC

SDC, Sino Danish Center. (2015a). *School profile.* Retrieved May 7, 2015, from http://sdc.ucas.ac.cn/Schoolprofile/Pages/committee.aspx

SDC, Sino Danish Center. (2015b). *Quick links.* Retrieved May 7, 2015, from http://sdc.ucas.ac.cn/QuickLinks/Pages/default.aspx

SDC, Sino Danish Center. (2015c). *Master's programmes.* Retrieved May 7, 2015, from http://www.sinodanishcenter.com/master's-programmes

Stier, J. (2003). Internationalisation, ethnic diversity and the acquisition of intercultural competencies. *Intercultural Education, 14*(1), 77–91.

Stier, J. (2004). Taking a critical stance toward internationalization ideologies in higher education: Idealism, instrumentalism and educationalism. *Globalisation, Societies and Education, 2*(1), 1–28.

Tang, N., & Nollent, A. (2007). *UK-China-Hong Kong trans-national education project British Council.* Retrieved from https://www.britishcouncil.org/sites/default/files/uk-transnational-education-in-china-and-hong-kong.pdf

USST, University of Shanghai for Science and Technology. (n.d.). *Brief of USST.* Retrieved August 19, 2017, from http://isoe.usst.edu.cn/s/17/t/69/p/1/c/410/list.htm

Xue, W. (2016). Zhi Liang Jian She Jin Cheng Zhong De Gao Deng Jiao Yu Zhong Wai He Zuo Ban Xue – Ji Yu De Si Kao [CFCRS in the QA construction – Thoughts based on the third-party assessment report of higher education]. *China Higher Education Research, 2*, 12–19. [in Chinese]

Yang, R. (2008). Transnational higher education in China: Contexts, characteristics and concerns. *Australian Journal of Education, 52*(3), 272–286.

Yang, R. (2010). International organizations, changing governance and China's policy making in higher education: An analysis of the World Bank and the World Trade Organization. *Asia Pacific Journal of Education, 30*(4), 419–431.

Zhao, X. (2016, November 12). Enhancing the exit mechanism for CFCRS programmes. *China Education Daily.*

CHAPTER 4

The Challenges of Brexit: UK Higher Education Governing Councils Responding to Sudden Change

Heather Eggins

Abstract

This chapter examines the impact on UK higher education of the UK referendum decision to leave the European Union on 23 June 2016. A study of the individual responses of members of governing bodies of the UK institutions and their collective decisions is presented. The likely effects on university funding and research collaboration, on academic staff mobility and research capacity, and on student access are considered. Analysis of the findings indicates that a range of new strategies are being mooted, including the development of new income streams and the expansion of student markets. However, the problem of how best to respond to uncertainty remains.

Keywords

institutions – governing bodies – policy – uncertainty – Brexit – change – strategy

1 Introduction

The apparently settled condition of United Kingdom (UK) higher education institutions was thoroughly shaken by the result of the referendum held on 23 June 2016, in which the British electorate voted to leave the European Union (EU) by a majority of 52% in favour to 48% against. This was a wholly unexpected result, and the Prime Minister, David Cameron, resigned the following day. On 29 March 2017, Article 50 of the Lisbon Treaty was triggered by a letter to the EU signed by the Prime Minister, Theresa May, which established a two-year window to negotiate terms. That window closed on 29 March 2019.

© KONINKLIJKE BRILL NV, LEIDEN, 2020 | DOI: 10.1163/9789004422582_005

This chapter considers the position that the institutions found themselves in, and discusses the response of the university councils and vice-chancellors/ principals to the unexpected circumstances. The role of councils is to enable and support the aims of the university: to teach, research and innovate. It includes the preservation of financial stability, investment in the university estate and its maintenance, contributions to its local, national and international communities and the development and oversight of the strategic plan for the university. Decisions made by councils are delivered by the vice-chancellor/principal working in tandem with the council.

The role of strategic decision-making undertaken by university councils is frequently underestimated. The impacts of such decisions, particularly at a time of uncertainty, can be crucial for the future health of the institution. The topic of this research, while recognising that Brexit is both a political moment and one of economic uncertainties (Simon, 1955, 1957) has been chosen to highlight the process of making strategic responses to a situation. Oliver (1991) offers helpful insights into the range of strategic responses seen in institutions. She argues that organisations may engage in manipulative strategies to shape their social or political effectiveness, particularly when under pressure. Resistant strategies, where organisations 'think outside the box' can enable institutions to be more flexible, innovative and adaptive. Investigating the range of responses available to organisations makes more sense than conforming to the rules and expectations of institutional environments, when the future cannot be in any way anticipated.

The theoretical framework proposed by Oliver (1991) offers a useful approach to understanding the immediate responses of governing bodies; Oliver's paper, 'Strategic Responses to Institutional Processes' draws on the work of Di Maggio (1988) and Powell (1985). In this paper, she argues that there are four main strategic responses to the prediction of institutional change, namely the identification of different strategic responses, the development of a conceptual framework "to contribute to our understanding of the behavior of organisations in institutional contexts", the role of organisational self-interest, and active agency in organisational responses to institutional pressures and expectations (Oliver, 1991, p. 145).

This chapter presents the first phase of the research, explored soon after the event of Brexit, when decisions have not yet been taken by councils. It is a phase of 'scouting the territory' before being in a position to move to decisions. The second phase, whose follow-up interviews have been almost completed, will explore Herbert Simon's (1955) ideas of bounded rationality to examine the efficacy of the decision-making in a continuing environment of uncertainty.

THE CHALLENGES OF BREXIT

2   UK Funding Arrangements

Each country of the UK has its own Higher Education Funding Council which regulates fee levels at universities, ensures a framework is in place for assessing the quality of higher education and scrutinises the performance of universities. Public funding is provided for a range of institutional allocations including research, part-time undergraduate courses, certain full-time undergraduate subjects and capital developments, but each government controls the total amount allocated, for instance the Welsh government allocated £21.4m to higher education (HE) providers for the 2017/18 year.

UK tuition fees vary depending on one's home country. English universities can charge up to a maximum of £9,250 per year for an undergraduate degree, which is paid to the individual student as a repayable loan. HE institutions in Wales can charge up to £9,000 for home students and £3,925 for EU and Northern Irish students (THE, 2017). Welsh students can apply for a non-repayable grant towards the cost of tuition fees. Northern Irish universities charge £4,030 for home students and £9,250 for other UK students.

Scotland has no charge for home or EU students at undergraduate level, but those from elsewhere in the UK pay up to £9,250 a year. However, there is a cap on the total monies paid to Scottish universities by the government to cover costs, and this can be varied from year to year.

In England there is now no cap on the number of undergraduate students that a university can take: an open market. The overall effect of the very varied funding regimes of UK countries has a bearing on the overall stability of university institutions in the four nations.

One other point is significant: although each country takes its own decisions on the level of tuition fee, or none, each country is bound by the UK central government's policies on immigration and control of visas. Thus, the number of international student visas granted for any of the four countries is tightly controlled by central government. This has major knock-on effects on the numbers of international students allowed into the country and, as they pay higher fees than all other students, is a factor in the overall capacity of the institution to expand income.

However, although the contextual background of HE institutions varies considerably in terms of income streams, each institution is affected by the Brexit decision, albeit in different ways, and the councils are faced with how best to respond to the challenges as they impinge on their institution. DiMaggio and Powell (1983) argued that bringing about change in organisations is by no means easy in a situation where all organisations are affected by resource centralisation and dependency, uncertainty and goal ambiguity. Thus rational arguments, in an irrational world, may not necessarily lead to successful outcomes.

3 Methodology

The research was conducted during a tight time scale, from 24 April 2017 to 7 June 2017, a window ending before the general election of 8 June 2017, whose results changed the outlook yet again. The Prime Minister, far from expanding her majority, found herself leading a hung parliament with no majority, and only managed to rule by agreeing a confidence and supply relationship with the small Northern Irish Democratic Unionist Party (DUP). Under this arrangement, the government agreed on a financial package with the DUP in exchange for support on certain issues. The methodology used was a series of detailed interviews held during those dates, with interviewees drawn from England, Scotland, Northern Ireland and Wales. Every type of university was represented: the ancient universities, Russell Group universities (the research-intensive institutions), 'modern' universities more recently founded, and 'teaching only' universities. Those interviewed were all active in contributing to the strategic plan of their institution and were either members or chair of the board/council of governors, or vice-chancellor/principal/provost of their institutions.

The study can be characterised as phenomenological (Husserl, 1901), in that it examines how members of university councils experience the phenomenon of Brexit; it notes the feelings and responses to the shock of Brexit, but moves on to examine how members of the councils are preparing to take decisions relating to the new situation. The author used maximum variation sampling whereby interviewees were chosen from the most prestigious and wealthiest universities and from the poorest universities in areas of deprivation in order to maximise the diversity of responses to the research question. Two respondents were chosen from Northern Irish institutions, two from Wales, six from Scotland and six from England. Those in Scotland and England were drawn from different types of institutions: research-intensive; teaching centred with research; and 'teaching only' institutions. Those interviewed included one leading member from the university council, usually chair or committee chair, and one vice-chancellor/principal or provost. Interviews lasted up to an hour each, and were usually done in person, with the occasional telephone interview. All were recorded. A constant comparative method of coding was applied, in terms of categories, themes and concepts.

THE CHALLENGES OF BREXIT

The documentation drawn on was culled from a range of publications from government bodies and other relevant source such as the Royal Society, Universities UK (UUK), Russell Group and specialist journals and websites dealing with Brexit issues in relation to HE. These included the Higher Education Policy Institute, the Centre for Global Higher Education, Wonkhe.com, *Times Higher Education,* London School of Economics (LSE) Centre for Economic Performance, blogs of HE institutions such as LSE and university websites. Because the timescale was deliberately confined to the first year after the vote, information was used that only relates to that period. An iterative sampling approach was employed while collecting public domain documents, consisting of newspapers, blogs and journals published during the period of the interviews. Other documents referred to include government reports published after the interviews but they give valuable information relating to the position immediately before the Brexit vote. Follow-up interviews to chart developments after the Brexit vote are ongoing and will be used for future research on this topic.

4 The Context Pre-Brexit

The context of HE in the UK was already complex before the referendum vote, principally because the shape of the HE sector in the UK was very diverse and hierarchical. A number of universities are ranked in the top ten in the world for research and teaching, and others are in the top 100 (THE, 2017). The World University Rankings for 2016–2017 announced that Oxford University had become the top world-class university, with Cambridge in fourth place and Imperial College London in eighth place. However, the bulk of universities concentrate on a mix of research and teaching. These tend to have some specialist areas of high performing research; and a few are characterised as teaching only institutions which undertake little funded research. The latter categories have, as a result, a very different pattern of income from those dependent on research.

The growth of the knowledge economy had a major impact on the core activities of the universities. New funding mechanisms had been introduced. Some researchers considered that the more utilitarian approach to research which had been heralded in the 1990s (Clark, 1998) was itself weakening the institutions (Etzkowitz & Leydesdorff, 2000). During the period of retrenchment and austerity, public funding had been steadily withdrawn from the universities, so that a major part of university income now depended on the students who paid £9,000 per annum. Competition between universities for students was becoming more marked every year, particularly when the caps on numbers were lifted (Bagshaw, 2017).

The other source of funding from the public purse was for research, which was rewarded according to the level of merit. All HE institutions could submit their research in the national Research Assessment Exercise. The last one had been held in 2014. Under this system the old established institutions were rewarded with research income to a larger extent than those who were deemed to have achieved fewer research outcomes. Failure to attract research monies under this system could have unsettling consequences for those institutions and lead to cutbacks in the faculties affected.

New societal expectations have put further pressure on institutions. One emphasis has been on the exploitation of knowledge in the form of intellectual capital and intangible assets (Sanchez, Elena, & Castrillo, 2006; Secundo, Margherita, & Passiante, 2010). Alongside that has come the demand that all stakeholders of HE should be consulted on and included in the work and outreach of the institution in the expectation that there should be social impact from which they could benefit (Goddard & Vallance, 2011).

Regulatory checks can consume hours of preparation: quality assurance agencies oversee the standards of delivery of courses on a country basis; accreditation and evaluation of institutions are similarly conducted on a country basis. The Office for Standards in Education, Children's Services and Skills (OFSTED), inspects all Faculties of Education who provide teacher training. Their findings affect the income and viability of those faculties to a large extent.

The model of universities as collegial communities which lead themselves had given way in many instances to the efficient objectives of New Public Management (Bleiklie, 1998; Deem & Brehony, 2005). Change management approaches had already been developed in an effort to respond to the changes thrust upon institutions (Senior, 2002). Cummings, Bridgman and Brown (2016) note that change itself is highly complex: he sees it as going through the stages of unfreezing, changing and refreezing. The new discourse within UK universities, pre-Brexit, was already that of national and international competitiveness for funding and for student recruitment. EU research funding added to UK funding; EU and international students supplemented those from the home countries. The sector had become marketised; students had become 'consumers of higher education services' for which they paid, in England, a high price, and business models of accountability had been adopted (Mansour, Heath, & Brannan, 2015; Lumby, 2012). Leaders were expected to meet targets which aligned with measurable indicators. As a result, the leadership and management of institutions had assumed a more important role (Bleiklie, Enders, Lepori, & Musselin, 2011) and the formal structures of leadership had been strengthened (Bryman, 2007; Bleiklie & Kogan, 2007; Stensaker et al., 2013).

THE CHALLENGES OF BREXIT

The 40-year close relationship between the UK and the EU had engendered a range of interconnections between them (Frölich, Huisman, Slipersaeter, & Stensaker, 2013).

The three key areas were those of research, students and academic staff. Each will be considered.

4.1   EU Research Funding Pre-Brexit

The research programmes funded by the EU have been a source of important funding for institutions over the years since they were established. Framework Programmes have been operating since the late 1990s. In the EU Seventh Framework Programme cycle (FP7, 2007), British universities and other UK-based research organisations attracted €8.8 billion in grants of which UK universities took over 71%. (The UK contribution to the EU research and development budget was some €5.4 billion.)

The UK's four national academies – the Academy of Medical Sciences, the British Academy, the Royal Academy of Engineering, and the Royal Society – commissioned a report from the Technopolis Group to assess the role of EU funding in UK research and innovation, following the vote. The report was published in May 2017. The evidence and analysis provided exhibits the importance of EU funding to the sector, and drew on the most recent figures available. All academic disciplines received some funding, ranked by the proportion of total research funding gained from EU government sources.

Archaeology received the most (38%), followed by Classics (33%) and IT (30%). Seven of the top fifteen research areas were social sciences, six arts and humanities and two were natural and physical sciences. In terms of the disciplines which attracted the most money, they were ranked in the order of clinical sciences (£120m); biosciences (£91m); physics (£55m); chemistry (£55m) and IT (£46m). The Royal Society, commenting on the findings, wrote "Given the high numbers, these fields may find it challenging to replace this income from other sources if the UK no longer had access to EU funds" (Royal Society, 2017b, p. 1).

Universities have also benefitted from EU research and innovation funding. The EU collaborative research budget aims to provide leverage for business, and centres are often based in universities. One such example is the Ulster University Nanotechnology and Integrated Bio-Engineering Centre (DCLG, 2014). Research networks on specific initiatives are also funded by this means: an example is the EuroCoord Network of Excellence, working on pan-European HIV research. Such initiatives not only bring money into the institutions involved, but also offer the possibility of creative, interactive collaboration with those from other European countries (Universities for Europe, 2016a).

4.2 *Students Pre-Brexit*

The reputation of the UK HE system for excellence has attracted non-UK based students for many years, many of whom were from the EU. The diversity of the student body, drawn from EU and other non-UK countries has provided a valuable international community on campuses (Universities UK, 2017). British students learn to relate to those from a huge range of countries, and this in itself provides a part of their education in fitting them for the global world of today. In 2016 over 125,000 EU students were studying in the UK. These generated £3.7 billion for the UK economy, supporting 34,000 jobs in HE institutions (Universities for Europe, 2016b).

The spread of EU students through the UK system, however, was very uneven. The universities which attracted the largest percentages of EU students were in Scotland with the University of Aberdeen, which has historically strong connections with Scandinavian and Baltic countries, attracting 19.2% EU students. Its accessible geographical location combined with the fact that there were no tuition fees for EU students in Scotland was particularly attractive (Highman, 2018a).

The second group of UK universities with a large number of EU students were those at universities belonging to the Russell Group, a group of 24 universities noted for their research output. Examples include the LSE, which had 17.6% students from the EU, Imperial College 16.2%, and Cambridge 12.8% (Highman, 2018a). The numbers involved are considerable, with University College London with 4,470 students topping the list. These non-UK EU students represent around 10% or more of the student body in most of the high achieving research-focussed universities: an important factor in economic and cultural terms (Conlan, Ladher, & Halterbeck, 2017).

Over the years, the UK has benefitted from the EU Erasmus exchange programme, which has served as an important factor in the cultural preparation of UK students for a global world. Over 200,000 UK students have taken part in these programmes, spending a year in the European country of their choice. Likewise the same number have come to Britain to study, and developed an understanding of British culture (Universities for Europe, 2016b).

The student curriculum was likely to be affected by Brexit; many courses included study periods in Europe, and the span of these was wide-ranging: not only languages but business, catering, estate management, political science, history, economics. Some courses specialised in topics of particular interest for those from Europe such as European Studies and European Law. A number of courses include important elements of European knowledge: the law is a case in point, in that both English and Scots Regulations require EU law: one research participant explained. "In early years' courses, the whole cohort spends weeks in European countries. The ease of travel to Europe opens up a world view for the students".

4.3 *University Academic Staff Pre-Brexit*

UK universities employ a large number of academic staff, of whom 35,920 (17.4%) are from EU countries (HESA, 2018). They are particularly present in the highest achieving research universities – Oxford and Cambridge, University College London, Imperial College, King's College London, Manchester, Edinburgh and Glasgow. The LSE is notable in having 39% of non-UK EU academic staff. The subject areas represented encompass many of the disciplines important for the ongoing prosperity of the country, i.e. physics, chemical engineering, mathematics, economics and modern languages. All of these subjects have over 25% EU academics: economics has 36.4% of EU staff (British Academy, 2017).

By attracting the best academics in Europe, the universities have been enabled to harness the highest research power in the Research Excellence Framework (2014) and Horizon 2020. In 2014 over 50% of European Research Council Consolidator Grants were awarded to academics from the EU who worked at UK universities. It is clear that the contribution to research, and hence to research money, from EU academic staff at UK research-based universities was invaluable (Universities for Europe, 2016a).

Northern Ireland also has a very high percentage of EU academics at its two universities: 35.3% at Ulster University and 29.7% at Queen's University, Belfast. The ease of movement within the island of Ireland has been an important factor (Highman, 2018b).

5 Interviewees' Immediate Personal Responses to the Referendum Decision

The period running up to the EU referendum on 23 June 2016 was one of noisy, raucous campaigning, particularly by the Leave campaign whose bus claimed in large letters on its side that 'We send the EU £350 million a week. Let's fund our NHS instead. Vote Leave. Let's take back control'. This and other advertising claims inflamed emotions. The result was that the vote itself became a highly charged emotional matter. For many, the vote to leave was a protest vote, rather than an anti-Europe vote, by those living in areas that were economically struggling: the majority of university towns were prosperous, perhaps partly as a result of the employment and commerce provided by the institution's presence.

Reissner (2010) noted that there was little research which examined the emotional aspects of change, and the effects of a major emotional and intellectual shock such as the vote to leave. This small piece of research attempts to delineate the reactions of leaders in a particular sector, that of HE, to a decision which will be likely to bring major change to the society of which they are an integral part. Universities UK, who describe themselves as the voice of universities, had campaigned in a modest way to support the Remain point of view. They published a series of leaflets setting out in a measured tone the value of the EU to the UK universities: *Universities for Europe: The UK's membership of the European Union makes our outstanding universities even stronger, benefiting everyone* (2016b); *Universities for Europe: The EU supports researchers to collaborate internationally: working together they can achieve more than they can alone* (2016a); *Universities for Europe: The EU supports universities to drive innovation, generating local growth and jobs* (2016b). The expectation of the leaders of universities, the majority of whom supported UUK's viewpoint was that the outcome of the referendum would be to remain in the EU.

Leaders of the UK institutions were asked in the interviews to describe their immediate, personal response to the Brexit vote, emotionally and intellectually. They were also asked to comment on whether they discerned any difference in the responses of female and male leaders. The over-riding response was one of anger directed at the UK government: "we had been duped by other interests"; "we should have been given the costings to stay in. Scotland had a fully costed 500-page manifesto"; "lying bastards"; "the Prime Minister chose to introduce the referendum but failed to inform the public of the context" (research participants). The faulty communication by government or failure to communicate to the public was frequently cited.

The women who were interviewed were particularly aware of the likely effect of the vote on families: it was seen as the closing down of access to opportunities for young people: "my daughters in their late teens were devastated"; "my son has already googled how to become an Irish citizen"; "my daughter is 12 and wants to go on the Erasmus scheme when she is old enough – but it may be gone"(research participants). The intrusion of emotional responses into intellectual matters in HE is a general research topic that could be examined further.

Many of the interviewees expressed their complete shock and hurt at the outcome; they found it difficult to comprehend: "my human rights are torn up and thrown away. Culturally I am European" (research participant). However, one vice-chancellor recognised while he himself was hugely disappointed, he was "not entirely surprised. A protest vote. Many of my family voted out" and, from another, "people are feeling excluded". One can argue that one factor in

THE CHALLENGES OF BREXIT

the vote was the effect of several years of austerity, with little wage growth or improvement in the cost of living, combined with the impact of globalisation.

There was a recognition that the populism demonstrated in the vote had little concern for "informed judgement"; "evidence-based policy is regarded as an insult in certain circles" (research participant). Several respondents commented on the possible long-term effect: "it imperils the economic prosperity of the UK"; "the poor will bear the brunt of the outcomes of Brexit, threatening the stability of society and causing unrest"; "it is a vote to be poorer and nastier" (research participants). Another argued "it was a bad decision but let's make the best of it. If we are offered a terrible deal, we should hit the red stop sign".

What can be discerned even at this early stage is that some vice-chancellors were responding to the shock by seeking to understand the vote, and beginning to develop policy to meet the situation: "Universities should be embedded in their communities – isolated and poor communities feel excluded from the economic success of many university towns" (research participant). This approach has been followed through by that institution.

Other intellectual responses were concerned with the welfare of the particular institution they were leaving; "the vote has huge implications. What guarantees can we get?"; "can we manage to secure a good settlement for the university?" and "What about all our collaborative work?" (research participants).

5.1   *The Immediate Responses of Governing Bodies*

The effect of the Brexit vote was to create huge uncertainty: the possible loss of much research funding; the possible loss of students and their income; the possible loss of the EU academic staff who contributed so much to the wealth of the university. At the time of the interviews no answers had been found to any of those questions, and uncertainty was paramount. Institutional aims had been established in Di Maggio and Powell's work (1983): stability and predictability; legitimacy; the reduction of uncertainty; and the survival of the institution. The environmental uncertainty of Brexit exerts huge pressure on each institution to develop strategic responses. It is an unusual situation in that uncertainty affects the whole of society, and all institutions. The universities are merely a part of general uncertainty affecting every individual and every institution.

Most universities had not prepared for a Leave vote, thus the shock of the decision came out of the blue for council members and was very unsettling. In some universities the chair of governors instituted an immediate overhaul of the membership of council:

We recognised that we should co-opt certain skill sets on all our committees. External advisers reviewed the executive and advised council on marketing strategy. We started a massive recruitment campaign to add expertise – banking, investment, experience in managing a huge organisation. Two more members were added to council and others were co-opted to join the committees. (Research participant)

The same respondent considered that the actions had been successful:

The VC and the chair of council have an excellent relationship – skilful, inclusive... council was thus enabled in its role to challenge the executive to make sure there has been robust consideration, research and thought in exploring all relevant options. (Research participant)

The behaviour of governing bodies can be seen to align with each of the four responses named by Oliver (1991). All reported that work was carried out on the identification of different strategic scenarios, the first response named by Oliver. In one case, members of council were given training in understanding risk scenarios, and then scenario planning was undertaken, indicating detailed possible outcomes for the next five years. Outside consultants were engaged to offer robust testing of scenarios, and to challenge the council's assumptions. The institution set up a Strategy Day in which all stakeholders were involved. A full day of strategy development and evening dinner took place, followed by a council meeting the following day. Formal presentations were made by the Deans of every faculty. "Stakeholders were all involved in robust challenging of strategic and financial plans" (research participant).

Oliver's (1991) second response, that of developing a conceptual framework, produced some evidence, but as the interviews were held early on in the Brexit process, most councils had not fully developed their conceptual framework by the close of this phase of the research. However, the little evidence collected on this topic showed wide variations of view. One university council expressed the belief that the institution should become more community-centred, and should concentrate on the needs of the local area. Another council considered that the university should position itself clearly as international, and, indeed, has developed this with a decision to build an international campus.

The third response, suggested by Oliver (1991), is the role of organisational self-interest, and this has been spelled out by councils who feared for their future financial stability. Several members recognised that the institution would find itself in a situation of cut throat competition for students. This has come to pass with a number of universities now offering (in 2018/19) unconditional offers to undergraduate students, in order to meet the universities' target number. Each student brings money into the institution, and the number brought in is crucial to the overall financial health of the university.

The fourth response listed by Oliver (1991) is that of active agency in organisational responses to institutional pressures and expectations. Councils have taken part in active lobbying of relevant government agencies at every level, and have instructed their vice-chancellors/principals to do so. Very extensive engagement with peers, ranging from meetings with local councillors, through UUK to parliamentary lobbying of the UK, Scottish and Welsh governments to meetings with the Prime Minister herself. Much effort was put into 'manipulation' which Oliver (1991) defined as "the purposeful and opportunistic attempt to co-opt, influence, or control institutional pressures and evaluations" (p. 157). Continual pressure had been put on government since the vote, in an effort to ameliorate some of the uncertainties.

Vice-chancellors, in contrast, responded in part by sending out a great deal of data on a huge range of institutional aspects to council members. "When the environmental context of institutional influence is highly uncertain and unpredictable, an organisation will exert greater effort to re-establish the illusion of reality of control and stability over future organizational outcomes" (Oliver, 1991, p. 170).

Other institutions responded to the unpredictable environment by attempting to forecast trends or stockpiling inventories (Oliver 1991; Pfeffer & Salancik, 1978; Scott, 1987b). One interviewee noted that the immediate response from the executive was to rework all elements of the exposure of the university: all financial plans with robust scenarios; revisiting the implications of Brexit for international students; and revisiting the implications for research. This provides the institution with a buffer to protect itself from the risks of having to operate in an unknown environment. The institution is forced to adapt to uncertainty and finds itself having to actively manage and control resource flows (Pfeffner & Salancik, 1978).

Another institution, where unusually an extensive briefing by an independent governor was given *before* the vote, acted very rapidly on knowing the outcome. Within 24 hours a letter was sent to all EU students and all EU staff, promising to protect the positions of students and of staff. Hotline guidance advice was set up, and the council was alerted to this action. The Risk Register was updated and a detailed discussion was held in council immediately following the vote, and then every six months. The executive was expected to be proactive and engaged. A full report was presented to council every three months on all activities.

One interviewee reported that there had been "12 hours of meetings in the last few weeks alone". Consideration of the reconsidered strategic plan showed that "there was a need to replace a quarter of the income" (research participant).

Oliver (1991, p. 149) opines that in situations where change is likely "institutional theorists have tended to focus on conformity rather than resistance, passivity rather than activeness and pre-conscious acceptance rather than political manipulation in response to external pressures and expectations". All interviewees exhibited resistance to the Brexit vote; all were active, rather than passive, in dealing with the problems posed by it, and most were making use of political manipulation in some measure to attempt to modify its effects. A number of institutions recognised the major risk to their survival if they did not take action. Oliver (1991, p. 174) points out that "resistant organisations are likely to be more flexible, innovative, catalytic and adaptive", a description that can be applied to the institutions under scrutiny.

Lobbying both the UK, Welsh and Scottish governments on key issues had become of particular importance: "The vice-chancellor is instrumental in leading lobbying"; "the VC had dinner last week with Theresa May"; "Theresa May needs to rethink: students should not be included in the immigration count"; "Proper revision of immigration policy is needed as it relates to students" (research participants). The Scottish government had been lobbied for an assurance on the 2017 student intake, which had been granted. And the 2018 intake had recently been agreed.

Another major topic of lobbying was for assurances on research funding. One university reported that Horizon 2020, the most recent of the EU's Research Programmes, was already affected. Two research groups had been dropped from their collaborative groups. "There is unease"; "the UK will need to commit to invest" (research participants). Respondents argued that research expertise was of great importance for the economy of the country, and of the local area.

Those involved in lobbying were both individual universities, and also the bodies that represented them. The Russell Group (2017a) published a document which, in their view, listed the key priorities for the UK government:

- Guarantee the continued rights of current EU national (and their dependants) at UK universities;
- Ensure the UK's full access to Horizon 2020 from the date of EU exit to the end of the programme;
- Enable the UK's full access to and influence over future EU research and innovation programmes;
- Secure a good deal for future UK participation in the Erasmus programme;

THE CHALLENGES OF BREXIT   95

- Reach a rapid and satisfactory arrangement for the land border between Northern Ireland and the Republic of Ireland to sustain and enhance current north-south collaboration.

The above list of aims exemplifies the 'active agency' referred to by Oliver (1991), which provided an agenda for lobbying by its members.

5.2 *Meeting the Challenges*

The environmental uncertainty remained as the overwhelming problem faced by all councils, and this study concentrates on the time period of the first year following the vote; "there is a huge raft of uncertainties" (research participant). However, some decisions were already taken by councils in an effort to address the major challenges posed by the Brexit vote.

5.3 *Financial Viability*

The major driver of organisational self-interest (Di Maggio, 1988) was named by interviewees in informing council's decisions, and the financial viability of the institution was central to that: "Protecting our financial viability is our priority issue. We have had four meetings of the board already. It is a topic of detailed analysis" (research participant).

The diverse responses by members of different institutions indicate that the sector may be becoming more differentiated as a result of the vote. Risk analysis, undertaken by every council interviewed, has provided an indication of the extent to which each institution will be affected by the loss of EU research funding, the loss of EU funding from other sources, such as Development Funds, the likely diminution of students, and the possible loss of those research academics who may no longer have the opportunity to attract EU research funding.

During the 2016–2017 academic year EU contracts continued, so that one would not expect a major loss of EU funded research. However, one figure, reported in *Times Higher Education* (THE, 2018) notes that EU funded research recorded a deficit: it recovered only 65% of its funding costs overall. Furthermore, the article stated, "According to a report from the Office for Students, research activity in UK universities in 2016–2017 was in 'deficit' by almost £3.9 billion, compared with £3.2 billion the year before". These figures underline the vulnerability of research funding and are likely to become very much worse when the EU research funding stream dries up. The UK received €8.8 billion in research grants in the Seventh Framework Programme of which universities secured 71% (THE, 2018).

Universities have huge financial turnovers, generating £31 billion in revenue ("Research funding deficit", 2018). Many had recently undertaken capital expenditure on a large scale, for instance building new campuses based on the expected expansion of student numbers. These have been paid for by raising long-term loans from a number of sources, some of which are Euro loans from the European Investment Bank. It is likely those will need to be paid back in full on leaving the EU. Both interest and capital will need to be repaid. Other sources of funding used by some institutions were Private Finance Initiatives used, for instance, to build facilities such as student accommodation. In piece in *The Sunday Times* entitled, "It's survival of the fittest as Britain's universities head for trouble" Luke Johnson stated:

> Overall, I estimate that the sector has approaching £10bn of debt, compared with a fraction of that a decade ago. It also suffers from an actuarial deficit in the university pension scheme, which is more than £7bn and rising ... If income for the system drops, then a number of the roughly 160 HE institutions with weaker balance sheets and reputations may fail. (Johnson, 2017, p. 10)

It is clear that the financial risks are not to be underestimated.

The present position, outlined by those interviewed, a number of whom are Chairs of Finance, is that each HE institution has a high fixed cost base. In the face of the weakness of sterling, which was a result of the Brexit vote, the cost of borrowing commitments is rising, and likely to continue to become more expensive. With this comes the necessity for higher minimum cash levels to be maintained. In the situation of uncertainty in which the institutions find themselves, it is vital to have contingency funds available; "there is little communication from government on the direction of travel" (research participant).

Institutions that have been successful in attracting investment from industry are indicating that less money is likely to be available from that source. And the loss of almost £1billion a year in EU research funding makes a number of institutions vulnerable. "Money brought in by EU students will be lost from the 2018 intake in England and from 2019 in Scotland" (research participant). Some interviewees considered that their own institutions were likely not to be financially viable after Brexit was enacted; "we shall need to consolidate, to have less global ambition and become smaller. Mergers will have to be considered. We shall be reversing what Thatcher did" (research participant). However, others, who were less at risk financially, attracting little EU research funding and taking in fewer EU students, were confident that their institutions would survive almost unscathed.

Decisions taken and acted upon by the date of the interviews included the diversification of funding sources to avoid over-dependence on income flows from the EU that were likely to be at risk and increased effort to fund-raise and to search for donors. Several institutions had expanded the number of staff in the development and marketing sections. Marketing strategies had been developed to target particular groups, and in one institution marketing officers worked 80% of their time in one faculty, and 20% in the general marketing team in order to improve targeting. More money was being set aside for marketing: efforts were now being made to speak in more schools about the courses offered, and international targeting of alumnae was becoming much more widespread. Targets were being set for those holding the post of vice-chancellor/principal/president of colleges to reach from development sources. One vice-chancellor mentioned with satisfaction a trip to the United States which had resulted in two million pounds being raised for the university from one donor. "All available funding opportunities are now being taken" (research participant).

Several new approaches to expanding the influence and presence of universities had been established: partnerships with other institutions were being negotiated, particularly in the EU, e.g. in Dublin and in Paris. The Netherlands universities were being explored. "Forming partnerships with EU countries is likely to be more on the agenda" (research participant). Transnational education and making use of modern technology was mentioned by several interviewees. The franchising out of courses was being expanded not only to European countries but also to places such as Singapore, Malaysia and Hong Kong, where good connections had already been established: now, these were being expanded. Two ideas were being mooted at the time of the interviews and were beginning to be actively explored. One was the establishment of university campuses in the EU. This had been used historically for specific purposes for many years; for example Monash had an outpost in Italy where fine art students could study, but a campus delivering a wide range of subjects had not been previously envisaged. Paris had been named as a possible venue, but no agreements had been reached. Linked to this was the idea of accessing EU funding from outside the EU. This would be of particular importance if this could be done; the Ninth Framework Programme proposed to run from 2021 to 2027 will examine aspects of climate change among other topics, and will likely be very well endowed. All British universities expressed an interest in accessing those research funds: "Our research exposure is a worry"; "Our top researchers are already being excluded from collaborative groups" (research participants).

Considerable effort was also being put into developing links with local colleges. Several institutions aimed to expand the number of Articulation Agreements with local colleges. This could boost the numbers of students attending the local university and attract some students to consider university courses who would not previously have done so. Others intended to build up the capacity to offer apprenticeship training, a policy favoured by government.

However, there were some respondents who were considering a strategy to downsize. Financial modelling had indicated that there could be a 25% loss in income. That was unsustainable. Downsizing and mergers needed to be under consideration. "Mergers may have to be explored by those whose financial stability is at risk" (research participant).

5.4 Students

Income for universities in England related to teaching comes from two main sources: tuition fees and government grants to providers. The fees for UK and non-UK EU students have been capped at £9,000 a year for a number of years. EU students are treated as home students and are expected to pay back the fees in future years, after graduation. Non-EU students, however, can be charged the full cost for their courses.

The numbers published by the Universities and Colleges Admissions Service in June a year after the referendum (UCAS 2017) underline a number of issues: the first is the demographic dip in the age group applying to university, which has affected the UK population of 17 and 18-year-olds. Applicants were down 4% at 529,620. However, and probably partially as a result of changes to fees, mature applicants over 25 were down 23%. EU applicants showed a slight drop, down 5% to 49,250, non-EU applicants were up 2% to 70,830. The international figure is therefore some 20,000 more students than the EU, and brings in considerably more in full cost fees.

Interviewees raised the topic of internationalism and international students. Some institutions are putting major funds into expanding international provision, providing new buildings dedicated to that purpose. Several respondents noted that while the growth of international students was to be welcomed, the initiative was beset by problems with visas. Pressure was being put on government to ease this: "The principal has extensive engagement with the Home Office. India is badly hit by visa problems, and quotas now make it extremely difficult" (research participant). Home Office data of August 2017 showed that 97.4% of all students on visas do not outstay them. Respondents felt strongly that "students should not be included in the immigration count"; "the goodwill of people from these countries has been squandered and lost. It is a great loss to Britain" (research participants).

Several institutions have developed a strategy of ongoing internationalisation since the vote. Contacts with African countries are expanding, and further effort is being put into the growth of links with China, though anxiety

THE CHALLENGES OF BREXIT

was expressed that the Chinese government could well limit the number of Chinese exit visas for their students in future years. UUK has valued the contribution of international students to the economy in 2014–2015 at £25.8 billion.[1]

Several Interviewees mentioned the #WeAreInternational campaign[2] begun by Sheffield Hallam University: it already had over a hundred HE institutions as members. Its credo, quoted below, is a commitment to the diversity of institutions and to global scholarship: "We are committed to ensuring our universities remain diverse, inclusive communities of international scholarships open to students and staff from across the world" and "our commitment to the UK remaining a welcoming home of global scholarship, which provides a superb education to the most talented people from around the world remains firm".

All institutions gave clear support to their EU students, with opportunities to discuss and debate the decisions of government relating to their situation. New programmes were being developed which might meet their needs, such as negotiation studies. Efforts were being made to continuously update the courses offered.

However, a few interviewees mentioned that they had concerns about the "poaching" of UK students. "Our biggest concern is that bigger universities will take our students" (research participant). Because every student brought money with him or her to the university, the more students the university could attract, the better would be the balance sheet. Those universities higher up the pecking order might use their reputations to attract more UK students, and might lower their entry requirements. Student debt in England stands at over £100 billion; the clamour for change is growing but the £9K fees per student per year are viewed by institutions as essential. "Even middle tier universities are making unconditional offers (not even two E's, the lowest pass in the examinations that enable entry into universities). The pool is becoming smaller and smaller" (research participant). Other universities are offering grants or bursaries to students which will have the effect of lowering the final debt level for successful individuals. However, one respondent remarked "already, in June 2017, applicants are dropping off; there is more clearing, and a dip in the tariff" (research participant). councils are recognising the urgency of the situations in which some institutions find themselves and are taking what action they can to survive, in line with Oliver's (1991) argument.

5.5   *University EU Academic Staff*

EU research staff, representing 16% of total EU staff, currently have contracts which will end at the conclusion of the Horizon 2020 projects on which they are working. This poses a loss to the intellectual academic community that several respondents recognised, and is particularly acute in those Russell Group universities that have attracted the most research funding. Universities are already finding it difficult to attract top researchers when no guarantee of funding can be given. In a January 2017 survey (Russell Group, 2017b) 75% of EU researchers indicated they were likely to leave, and indeed, the possibility of further contracts at EU universities in view of the huge sums being put into the Ninth Framework make it likely that their services will be in great demand. Universities are offering support to those research staff they are employing and are exploring research partnerships with the EU even though UK universities can no longer lead.

EU research staff are of particular value to the top research universities, notably Oxford, Cambridge and London, in that their skills enable many millions of research monies to be drawn into the institutions. They generate large numbers of research papers, which enable those universities to top the world in terms of research rankings. (Oxford is first in the world, and Cambridge fourth in the World University Rankings, 2017; THE, 2017). One department in one university, for instance, has 25 faculty on permanent contracts and 200 research staff on fixed term contracts (research participant). The loss of such posts is likely to endanger the standing of those universities in global terms.

EU teaching staff, on the other hand, are being offered permanent contracts and being supported by their universities to enable them to remain. Following a decision made since the interviews, but relevant, the British government has decided to bring in arrangements for all EU staff, both academic and non-academic, to stay and most institutions have indicated that they will pay the costs incurred by those staff.

6 Conclusion

Organisations such as universities need to be responsive to external demands in order to survive (Meyer & Rowan, 1977; Pfeffer & Salancik, 1978). For some HE institutions, the shock of Brexit could be a matter for survival: "If income for the system drops, then a number of the roughly 160 HE institutions with weaker balance sheets and reputations may fail" (Johnson, 2017, p. 10).

The search is for the reduction of uncertainty, and the maintenance of legitimacy – social worthiness; conformity to external criteria; conformity to collective norms; reputation (Di Maggio & Powell, 1983). The university institution has the advantages of non-compliance in responding to urgent situations, using Oliver's (1991, p. 150) criteria: "the ability to maintain autonomy over

THE CHALLENGES OF BREXIT

decision-making; the flexibility to permit continual adaptation; the latitude to alter or control the environment".

The leaders of UK HE institutions are, by their response to Brexit, exhibiting clear-sightedness and flexibility. They are choosing to think imaginatively (research participants): "council is responding to Brexit calmly with the recognition that there are some problems"; "we will be poorer, and not financially secure. It will be hard work. The EU has helped us to be part of something bigger than just the UK".

Notes

1 www.universitiesuk.ac.uk
2 www.weareinternational.org.uk

References

Bagshaw, A. (2017). The Brexistential threats universities now face. *Wonkhe.* Retrieved June 26, 2017, from https://wonkhe.com/blogs/analysis-the-brexistential-threats-to-universities/

Bleiklie, I. (1998). Justifying the evaluative state: New public management ideals in higher education. *Journal of Public Affairs Education, 4*(2), 87–100.

Bleiklie, I., Enders, J., Lepori, B., & Musselin, C. (2011). New public management, network governance and the university as a changing professional organization. In T. Christensen & P. Laegreid (Eds.), *The Ashgate research companion to new public management* (pp. 161–176). Farnham: Ashgate.

Bleiklie, I., & Kogan, M. (2007). Organization and governance of universities. *Higher Education Policy, 20*(4), 477–493.

British Academy. (2017). *Brexit means? The British academy's priorities for the humanities and social sciences in the current negotiations.* London: British Academy.

Bryman, A. (2007). Effective leadership in higher education. *Research and Development Series.* London: Leadership Foundation for Higher Education.

Clark, B. R. (1998). *Creating entrepreneurial universities: Organizational pathways of transformation.* Oxford: I.A.U. and Elsevier Science.

Cummings, S., Bridgman, T., & Brown, K. G. (2016). Unfreezing change as three steps: Rethinking Kurt Lewin's legacy for change management. *Human Relations, 69*(1), 33–60.

Deem, R., & Brehony, K. J. (2005). Management as ideology: The case of 'new managerialism' in higher education. *Oxford Review of Education, 31*(2), 217–235.

DCLG (Dept for Communities and Local Government) and the European Union. (2017, November). *European development fund: Operational programme 2014–2020*, London: DCLG.

DiMaggio, P. J. (1988). Interest and agency in institutional theory. In L. G. Zucker (Ed.), *Institutional patterns and organizations: Culture and environment* (pp. 3–21). Cambridge, MA: Bollinger.

DiMaggio, P. J., & Powell, W. W. (1983). The iron cage revisited: Institutional isomorphism and collective rationality in organizational fields. *American Sociological Review, 48*(2), 147–160.

Etzkowitz, H., & Leydesdorff, L. (2000). The dynamics of innovation: From national systems and "more 2" to a Triple Helix of university-industry-government relations. *Research Policy, 29*(2), 109–123.

EU Seventh Framework Programme. (2007). Retrieved from https://ec.europa.eu/research/fp7

Frölich, N., Huisman, J., Slipersaeter, S., & Stensaker B. (2013). A reinterpretation of institutional transformations in European higher education strategizing pluralistic organisations in multiplex environments. *Higher Education, 65*(1), 79–93.

Goddard, J., & Vallance, P. (2011). *Higher education in cities and regions: For stronger, cleaner and fairer regions*. Paris: OECD.

HESA (Higher Education Statistics Agency). (2018). *Academic staff numbers 2016–2017*. Cheltenham: HESA.

Highman, L. (2018a). *EU students at UK universities: Patterns and trends* (Policy Briefing No. 5). London: Centre for Global Higher Education, UCL/Institute of Education.

Highman, L. (2018b). *University staff demographics: The fabric of UK universities at risk from brexit* (Policy Briefing No. 6). London: Centre for global higher education, UCL/Institute of Education.

Husserl, E. (1901/2001). *Logical investigations* (Abridged edition of 1st edition 1901). London: Routledge.

Johnson, J. (2017, August 6). It's survival of the fittest as Britain's universities head for trouble. *The Sunday Times*, p. 10.

Lumby, J. (2012). *What do we know about leadership in higher education?* London: Leadership Foundation for Higher Education.

Mansour, H. F., Heath G., & Brannan, M. J. (2015). Exploring the role of HR practioners in pursuit of organizational effectiveness in higher education institutions. *Journal of Change Management,15*(3), 210–230.

Meyer, J. W., & Rowan, B. (1977). Institutional organizations: Formal structure as myth and ceremony. *American Journal of Sociology, 83*(2), 340–363.

Oliver, C. (1991). Strategic responses to institutional processes. *The Academy of Management Review, 16*(1), 145–179.

THE CHALLENGES OF BREXIT

Pfeffer, J., & Salancik, G. R. (1978). *The external control of organizations.* New York, NY: Harper and Row.

Powell, W. W. (1985). The institutionalization of rational organisation. *Contemporary Society, 14*(5), 564–566.

Reissner, S. C. (2010). Change, meaning and identity at the workplace. *Journal of Organizational Change Management, 23*(3), 287–299.

Royal Society. (2017a). *The role of EU funding in UK research and innovation.* London: Royal Society.

Royal Society. (2017b, May 24). *Report lists UK universities and disciplines most dependent on EU research and innovation funding* (Press Release, p. 1).

Russell Group. (2017a, February). *Russell group: Brexit briefing.* London: Russell Group.

Russell Group. (2017b). *Russell group universities and Brexit.* London: Russell Group. Retrieved from http://www.russellgroup.ac.uk

Sanchez, M. P., Elena, S., & Castrillo, R. (2006). The intellectual capital report for universities. In Prime Network (Ed.), *Observatory of the European University – Methodological Guide* (pp. 223–252). Lugano: Prime.

Scott, W. R. (1987). The adolescence of institutional theory. *Administrative Science Quarterly, 32*(4), 493–511.

Secundo, G., Margherita, A., Elia, G., & Passiante, G. (2010). Intangible assets in higher education and research: Mission, performance or both? *Journal of Intellectual Capital, 11*(2), 140–157.

Senior, B. (2002). *Organisational change* (2nd ed.). London: Prentice Hall.

Simon, H. A. (1955). A behavioural model of rational choice. *The Quarterly Journal of Economics, 69*(1). Boston, MA: MIT Press.

Simon, H. A. (1957). *Models of man: Social and rational.* Hoboken, NJ: Wiley.

THE. (2017). *World University Rankings 2016–2017.* London: Times Higher Education.

THE. (2018, July 19). UK universities' research funding deficit soars to £3.9 billion. *Times Higher Education,* 9.

Universities UK. (2017, March 13). *International students now worth £25 billion to the UK economy – new research.* Retrieved from https://www.universitiesuk.ac.uk/news/Pages/International-students-now-worth-25-billion-to-UK-economy---new-research.aspx

Universities for Europe. (2016a). *The EU supports researchers to collaborate internationally: Working together they can achieve more than they can alone.* London: UUK.

Universities for Europe. (2016b). *The UK's membership of the European Union makes our outstanding universities even stronger, benefiting everyone, No. 2.* London: UUK.

PART 2

Political Analysis, Action and Power

CHAPTER 5

Keynote Conversation: Advancing the Conversation on the Politics of Higher Education

Brian Pusser and Imanol Ordorika

Abstract

This edited transcript of the keynote presentation at the 2017 Consortium of Higher Education Researchers (CHER) conference addresses the evolution of research on the politics of higher education, and the contemporary role of critical political theory in understanding post-secondary education in comparative perspective. It turns particular attention to the roles of the state and civil society in shaping higher education, understandings of power and governance, and the conceptualisation of the university as both a site of political action and an instrument in national and global political contest.

Keywords

higher education – university – state – politics – power – governance – critical theory

Jussi Välimaa (Chair):   I would like to introduce our keynote debaters, Professor Imanol Ordorika from Universidad Nacional Autónoma de México and also Visiting Professor in the University of Johannesburg, South Africa and Associate Professor Brian Pusser from the University of Virginia, United States (US). The format is that I will ask them a couple of questions. They will try to answer them, and then if you have any comments, please raise your hand and they will try to comment on the questions.

Okay, the first question is, you both have argued that the scholarly approach to understanding the politics of higher education is flawed. Can you discuss why that is? If the field did better understand the politics of higher education, what would be different for scholars, practitioners and institutions?

Brian Pusser: Okay, thank you, Jussi. I'm going to go first on this one. Thank you for bringing us here, and, Taru, for your work in organising this, and to everyone for being here. Jussi has a whole series of cards here that say one minute, five minutes, three minutes. He's like a soccer referee. He has a yellow card and a red card. So, I'm going to tell you my conclusion before I work through this question with the time that I have. Then Imanol will tell me what I did wrong. Fundamentally, the answer to the question about why I feel the approach of politics of education is flawed is twofold, really. The first has to do with a historical story about the way in which the study of higher education developed as a scholarly field. The second is that for a very long time, there has been a lack in many parts of the world of a critical scholarship of higher education. Those two pieces together, I think, begin to explain the dearth of truly political approaches to higher education.

Higher education as a field, I think as we know it, and particularly the study of something like the politics of higher education goes back only to the late 1960s and early 1970s. The study of higher education grew out of other disciplines. Fundamentally from its origin, it drew on sociology, drawing upon people like Weber[1] and Blau, and then later, of course, Burton Clark and a whole school of sociologists. In a very prominent way, it also grew out of the study of organisations. You have people like Cohen and March, and Weick and Pfeffer and Salancik, who were very influential in the 70s and early 80s. We borrowed rational choice economics, from Adam Smith through Gary Becker.

Most importantly for what we'll talk about a little later in the questions, people like Hayek and later, Milton Friedmanx, who have been very, very influential in the development of the field, and there's also a scholarship of students and student affairs, which is very powerfully shaped by psychology and industrial organisational psychology.

In that evolution, there's not much political science. Many of the people who have practiced political science in higher education were not themselves political scientists. I don't mean this as a critique of economics or sociology or psychology or organisations. They're all very useful but they don't lead to the kind of fundamental model of politics that you find in the field of political

KEYNOTE CONVERSATION 109

science and in some other areas scholarship. It's also the case that the political science that came to higher education was a particular form of political science. In the early 1960s in political science, there's a schism. As Terry Moe has noted, one area of the field goes into research on things like agency theory and models of the executive branch and political action and so forth, people like Skowronek and Kingdon, agenda control scholars, those who study interest groups and median voters, and that sort of thing.

The other branch of political science went into what we think of today as public administration. That's people like Selznik and Lindblom, who are really working more on institutional function and systemic institutional function. It's the latter group that influenced higher education the most, and in combination with organisation studies, we got something you might call the politics of functional institutions. We didn't get a politics of power and higher education, or interest groups or state political authority and institutions. We adopted isomorphism and iron cages. We adopted the sociology of organisations, but not really the political theory of either institutions of higher education, or, systems of higher education. What we really lacked was state theory. When I talk about political theory, we're talking about state theoretical approaches to power. Thinking about contest in the Gramscian sense.

There are some exceptions to how this unfolds. There is some interesting critical work from people like John Meyer and Paulo Freire on marginalisation and the state. A very strong feminist and critical theory and theoretical approaches, Nancy Fraser and Foucault and Bourdieu and Derrida, all of who've had huge influence on critical scholarship in higher education, but not particularly political scholarship. It's really in the late 1970s and early 80s, in elementary and secondary education where people like Martin Carnoy and Hank Levin, and Bowles and Gintis, Giroux, Michael Apple. They really begin critical political studies of education. It's not really for another decade or so when people like Sheila Slaughter, Gary Rhoades, Cynthia Hardy, Imanol, others come and begin to bring the state back in, to borrow a phrase from Theda Skocpol.

Now let me just say a couple things about what we would understand differently if from the beginning we had a stronger approach to politics. I think we would have been much better positioned to understand the rise of markets in higher education from a political perspective as opposed to the classic, rational choice, economic perspective. The critical scholarly approach to markets in higher education was very slow in building. Slaughter's work, Simon Marginson's early work on markets and education, doesn't come out really until the late 1990s, which is long after the rise of Ronald Reagan and Margaret Thatcher and broad neoliberal policies. We were seeing the effects of neoliberalism on institutions long before as a field we had a strong scholarly understanding and response to that.

I think that it's also the case that we would have been alerted to what I would call today a kind of a growing crisis of human capital theory. The economic wing of the study of higher education, it's founded, essentially, in human capital theory. It's the foundation of policy arguments for higher education and for education everywhere and all the time, both for individual returns on social mobility, but the sort of collective community returns to human capital. Yet today we see a stagnation of wages for college-educated people in many parts of the world. We have an international crisis of student loan debt in which students are not accepting, going forward, the idea that this investment is worthy of the level of debt that they're carrying. The relationship between the state, students' debt, and their economic and educational futures are not accepted and understood within the classic models of human capital theory. We aren't doing enough to challenge the model and ways in which we teach students to think about different forms of capital. I think it's a big issue that, again, lacking that political, that strong political frame, we've been very, very slow in coming to that.

I also think we were slow to come to international and comparative political work. Had we earlier had a stronger sense, certainly in the US, had we had a stronger sense of state theory and the way to apply that, we would have had a better comparative approach to the politics of higher education. Particularly, so much of our focus has been on institutions, institutional function, institutional life, institutions in their national context. That's really that public administration history, that's the organisations history. It lacks the nuance of higher education institutions as sites of contest, as instruments in broader contest. It doesn't situate them as political institutions in the way that I think we would have if we had a stronger sense of the political narrative from the start of the field of higher education. Maybe I'll pause there and let Imanol take over.

Imanol Ordorika: Brian has just presented a great summary of political approaches to higher education. I recall that 12 years ago, there was a meeting here in Jyväskylä, a CHER meeting. I was invited as a keynote speaker to try to convince the audience that universities were among the most important political institutions in society. Maurice Kogan, by the way, was sitting two rows into the crowd. He was the 'owner' of the political perspective as you may recall. In 1987 he participated in the book, *Eight Perspectives on Higher Education*, edited by Burton Clark, with a chapter called the "Political

KEYNOTE CONVERSATION   111

Perspective". Kogan's political perspective was nowhere
close to politics, in my view. I was younger, dressed up in a
Finnair t-shirt, because my luggage didn't arrive, as it didn't
arrive this time. Now I have Jussi's shirt.

My argument then was that, especially in the context of what was called and
is still called 'the knowledge society', universities that had historically been a
site of political struggle for nation building and economic development, were
so amazingly political and still were always depicted and described as non-
political institutions. Instead of arguing it from a political, from a theoretical
perspective, let us think a little bit about the presentation we just saw with
the particularities and very interesting views about the University of Jyväskylä.
This is the opening presentation of any administrator all over the world in
their universities, in our universities.

This is a lovely city and a beautiful campus. I used to say that Jyväskylä is
how the world used to look before we humans destroyed it. It must be great
to be here. Still, we can't forget that our world, if we open the newspapers, is
populated by poverty, inequality, violence, migrations and now the crisis of
international and national political institutions. The previous presentation
shows how many times we say nothing about all this in connection to our universities. We are geared toward knowledge development, and towards having
good campus life, and to being very inclusive, and to bringing people from all
over the place. We always seem to be so capable, in our institutions, to just
shut out the real problems of the world, away from our auditoriums and our
classrooms and our meeting places.

I think that's the original flaw, if we could call it that. Like, the original sin or
the original accumulation of capital. We can use Marx or the Catholic Church,
or the Christian view, whatever. There is something out there in the way in
which we have internalised our understanding of universities and higher education, that we always keep the political components away. Only when we are
faced with issues of access – in my country, something like 91% of the students
that demand access to public higher education institutions are not admitted.
They have to go to these horrible 'garage' privates, if they can make it. You
know?

Sometimes we have to discuss the issue of financing. We have talked about
the public funding becoming less and how governments have been privatising
our institutions, but it has been in some ways a marginal debate, or discussion, in higher education. Instead of that, we talk about high tuition-high aid
models or we talk about the ways in which businesses and universities can collaborate. The last time I came here, Nokia shared a building with the university

and really developed a lot of exchange. Even financial exchange; they bring a lot of funding for the institution. But we have discussed the uses of knowledge a lot less.

There are three aspects of political contestation, permanent aspects of political contestation. Not all of the projects, research projects that we pull forward are funded. Many times, you go out on a limb if you are trying to address issues of narco violence and higher education institutions in Latin America, or many other places. We have been very successful at criticising the ivory tower while maintaining ourselves within the ivory tower. This has impacted theory, of course.

Suddenly, some crazy wacko from somewhere else comes and says, "Oh, no, no, no. This is an absolutely political institution. Decisions are being made all the time that are essentially political. We are connected to some economic development models, not even projects. Broader models. We are connected to a discourse of economisation of societal life at every level". We do cost benefit analysis for buying novels, no? Should I really benefit from buying this or this other one? We have bought into this new public philosophy that philosophers were talking about in the late 1980s with the coming of Thatcher and Reagan that Brian was mentioning. We have totally bought into the idea that we can think about the world in economic terms and that economics is really the most serious and formal of the social sciences. We can do positive political theory based on economic models, and rational models and all of this stuff.

We have essentially left out of the picture the fact that the universities are defined by power. That they are established with a mission and that this was probably much more in the open in earlier days. It was either the church or the crown putting together universities, at least in my part of the world. They fulfilled two purposes. One was to expand the Catholic religion in the Americas. (By the way, just to clarify, America is not only the *United States*. America is a whole continent.) The second was to build local elites in order to fulfil colonial projects. That was the purpose of the university. What are the purposes of universities now? Are they really geared to the idea of giving people fine campus experiences? Is this the motive why so many states in the world provide funding, maybe less than before, but still a vast amount of funding to institutions?

The core argument here is that universities, like other levels of education, are sites of political struggle, where there are tensions between the idea of expanding access versus the meritocratic idea of selection of students. There are competitions or contests or political battles for what should be studied and debated, and what should be kept away from universities. There are discussions about resources, not only if we get them from the government or not. If we have to increase tuition: that's a big political debate almost everywhere

KEYNOTE CONVERSATION 113

in the world and, obviously, of political mobilisation. Also, of resource allocation within institutions. May be there are some political struggles within the
bureaucracy, within the collegial organisations, until maybe a presidential
election comes about in Spain or in South America or some of the universities
where there actually are elections. (Not in the US universities or most of the
Anglo-Saxon world.)

I will try to close this first round. I think that, politics is all about relations
of forces, political forces. Forces for what? What are we going to try to build
coalitions for? I think, to generate a coalition of forces in order to provide a
theoretical understanding of how universities really work, but also in order to
build an alternative political agenda, vis-à-vis, the established political agenda
that we sometimes cannot even figure out. It has to be discussed in terms of
these issues of access, the uses of knowledge and resource allocation. Coalition
building and political force building, which defines politics in the end, has to
be built with ideas, programmes, and a very strong awareness about constitu-
encies and social groups that might be willing to be connected to the university. In that sense, we have also made a lot of headway in isolating ourselves
from the public, from the rest of the world outside of our universities. A lot
of people don't give a damn about what we do here. There's kind of a schizo-
phrenic discourse where people value our universities and still do not have
any connection to our universities. I think this is, in a very broad sense, the
scenario in which we try to build up theory and a political understanding of
an institution that, most of the time, appears as non-political. In many, many
cases, even government authorities, or university authorities, or even faculty,
argue in favour of the university not being a political institution and saying
that politics is something pathological within higher education. Thank you.

Jussi Välimaa: Thank you very much. Do you (directed to the audience)
           have any comments or some debate?

Georg Krücken: Yes. Many thanks Jussi, and I have a comment on Brian's
           take on the role of political science in higher education.
           First of all, I fully agree with what you say with role of dis-
           ciplines as a necessity to link higher education research to
           disciplinary research and that maybe political science did
           not play the role that it should have played. I'm wonder-
           ing, though, about your broader claim that the discussion
           about state and market is simply not there. I think maybe
           you answered this in the states but I think in Europe, it is
           not the case. In Europe, it's about two decades we have a

very vivid comparative, theoretically oriented, empirical, methodological and fast debate on government. Government mechanisms, obviously includes the state and the market. It has a strong comparative aspect. We will have an entire session on that in the afternoon. I was wondering, obviously it's the state and the market but publicly also the community. Its competition for me is analytically distinct from the market as governance mechanisms.

My question is, rather, because I do that kind of research too. Here I see a huge cleavage between Europe and the US because here with all my kind of US orientation, I don't find a US American counterpart. My question is why is this the case? Why is, and my guess is maybe it has become so institutionalised, so much taken for granted, that maybe the US is no longer discussed. I think in Europe we have a long current vivid discussion on market creation, higher education and so on. Maybe you can reflect on this difference between US American debate and European debate. Thank you.

Brian Pusser: It's a really good point. I don't disagree with you. It's also the case, there's a much stronger theory of the state in higher education developed in the US over the last couple of decades. Sheila Slaughter wrote *Academic Capitalism* with Larry Leslie in 1997. It's having its twentieth anniversary now. I think if we go back to the origin of the field, 50 years ago, I don't think it's so different in Europe than it is in the US.

The other point I would make, too, is it is not abundantly clear to me and you all can help me in the audience that the study of governance of higher education globally is the study of the state. It may be in some cases, but it is not uniformly the study of states, theories, power, politics and context. The study of governance globally is leadership, organisations, systems, network theory, you know, some political sociology. We can discuss in some more detail. I'll just say one other quick thing if I can about one of the problems with the origin I think certainly in the US and maybe to a lesser degree in Latin America and in Europe, one reason the politics of higher education has been so under developed in the US is that we can't even account for the political support that higher education had originally. The support for higher education in the political sense, certainly in the US, is beyond the ken of most scholars and people in the institutions. The political dynamics, that special space that the university has occupied historically is politically, it has a political origin and politically

KEYNOTE CONVERSATION 115

mediated. We have been so, so separate from that political scholarship and contest that we don't even know our own political power is eroding and don't know the origin of those powers.

Jussi Välimaa: Any other comments? Questions? Imanol, would you like to comment on that?

Imanol Ordorika: Yeah, I'd like to say that I agree with Brian that talking about governance, and nowadays governability, is a way of depriving theoretical understandings of university organisation and ruling of all their political content. It becomes very technical. In the 1970s, we were debating about the state: Was it a pluralistic state? Was it a common interest state? We were debating Poulantzas and Althusser, and the notion of state apparatuses and institutions. Are universities state apparatuses? Are they state institutions? Have we abandoned all the discussion about what is a connection between the university and the state? The emphasis on globalisation brought a trend of thought around the notion that the state was withering. It was disappearing, virtually and none of that has happened.

The state has strengthened itself. It has become leaner, but it has become much more incisive in terms of establishing a lot of policies, economic policies, amongst them. Still, now we don't connect our universities with the state, except for arguments about steering at a distance and stuff like that. No, what is the ideological and political purpose of an institution in a class society? We have even abandoned these concepts. Should we use some different ones in this heavily stratified socio-economic state, in our contemporary societies, so that we don't use 'bad words', because people become uncomfortable when we talk about class?

Higher education specialists are not talking about the state and the university anymore. We're talking about government and the university. We're talking about government *in* the university. When we talk about governability – this has become one of the major topics today – in the allegedly more or less political understanding of higher education institutions, we're talking about government techniques in order to become legitimate, more or less participative and to have stable governments within institutions.

To show how disconnected we are as universities all over the world, from state and international issues, is the fact that last year a lot of things happened all over the world of which we were almost totally unaware. The vote about Brexit came by and all the polls said that it was not going to pass. Our universities were very comfortable arguing, "No, this is not a major issue. It's not going to pass". It passed. Then everybody was saying, and the universities were not deeply committed to preventing Trump from getting the nomination of the Republican Party. It was not going to happen. Then it happened. He was not going to become a president. He became the president. The day after the elections we had the opening meeting of the Association for the Study of Higher Education (ASHE) Conference in the US, and people were in awe. At nine in the morning, I had to deliver the opening speech. I changed it completely. What had happened here? We never thought this could happen. We were going to talk about public goods, but the world had changed. As it changed so intensively in Colombia: there was a negotiation between a 50-year-old guerrilla group called the FARC[2] and the government. They established a peace agreement, and it was put out on a referendum and everybody thought it was going to pass, and it didn't pass. The universities were totally out of it. They didn't play a role in campaigning in favour of it. There was no debate about it in the universities. Totally unaware, totally uncommitted, totally separated from the political process.

In Brazil, the universities were challenged by the government in the midst of a 'legal' coup d'état against elected president, Dilma Rousseff. And the incoming government issued a statement saying that public universities were not allowed to debate about the removal of the president. The federal universities had to go to the Supreme Court in order to open a debate that had not happened. It was only when they were told that they couldn't debate, that the universities started saying, "Oh we have something to say about this. At least we should be able to debate about it".

Are there more issues? What about Barcelona and the struggle for independence from Spain? What about 30,000 missing people in Mexico? Lots of clandestine burial sites full of missing people. Killings all over the place. What about the expanding conflict between the Arab world and the rest of the world, in spite of a sixteen-year-old occupation in Afghanistan? That is, we should have been debating about the connections between the state and the university at the broad international, the national and at the local level. From the university we should try to clarify an understanding of what the world really looks like. How it is expressed through institutions, and how universities connect to that. That is what universities used to do in the 70s. But we seem to have forgotten all about it.

I'm not saying that we have to recycle the same arguments and theories that we used in the 70s, but we have to develop something of that magnitude in

KEYNOTE CONVERSATION

order to understand where we are sitting now. Otherwise we can discuss a lot about financing, about how much of the private sector comes into the university. I have even criticised Brian, and Sheila Slaughter (although it is very difficult to criticise Sheila because we love her so much) but I think some of the analytical frames we have suggested are still limited in our understanding of the state, because you really don't go very far with path dependency theories to really challenge state theory, but we're not there. At least we have to be clear on what we're lacking in order to fill a void that needs to be filled today.

Jussi Välimaa: Hugo?

Hugo Horta: My name is Hugo Horta. I might have very naive perspectives on this, but I would like to have your input on two things. To what extent, and I have to say I totally agree with what you're saying, but I wonder to what extent this relates to the training that we're receiving, and that we're giving to our own graduate students? We have policy, we have politics, and I wonder if our training has led us to simply stay in our comfort zone and choose the policy side?

Because we have become very good at analysing what's going on, but we have become really terrible at proposing something else. In my university, what was it, three months ago, we had quite a prominent scholar come to present to us. He did a wonderful keynote, but at the end we were like, okay, so what? What is the alternative to this? The presenter's answer was, "it's not up to me to really propose alternatives". So what are we doing then? Do we already know the answers? We're saying the same thing over and over. Some things are bad, some other things are happening. What is the alternative? This I think relates back to the training that we had, and that we're providing to our students.

A second question on this point is, how does this relate to careers? Because it may be we are doing this because we are in a comfort zone, or because we are already hugely stretched in terms of time constraints and the things our careers demand of us. We do research, we do teaching, we do service. If now we engage in this more political component, what about our family life? What about our personal time? We can't do everything. So either this somehow becomes part of our careers, and our careers change at the universities, or some of the things we have been doing are not going to happen.

I'm from a territory where the government presents the new leadership. The first thing the new leader of the council said was, "You guys at the faculty of Hong Kong are all a bunch of lazy people. Stop writing articles for newspapers and start doing your job. And your job is not giving opinions that can influence public opinion. It's to do research, it's to do teaching. That is what you're there for". So how do we deal with this? That is what I'd really like to hear from you. Thank you so much.

Jussi Välimaa: I think that Don has a question about that. Then I think we will need to go forward here.

Don Westerheijden: Thanks. I'd like to give the green light also to our discussants. It's a great way of opening a conference.

Two remarks and a question, if I may. First about higher education and its role in the state. We shouldn't over estimate ourselves. We talk about political debates about education, usually it's about what the Americans call K-12. Primary and secondary education. Universities are not politically interesting. Perhaps because parliamentarians or politicians don't think that you can get many votes there. Which is strange, because students are the ones who can start voting, and primary and secondary school children can't.

At the same time, higher education has become very much instrumentalised in the governmental debates. The ivory tower could be allowed to exist in the times when higher education was an elite thing, and it was really small enough to benefit from benign neglect. Nowadays it's instrumentalised for, let's say workforce planning, good old communism in effect gaining all over the world, even though we call it neoliberalism. What do you think about that? This type of paradoxical development?

And then your reaction to what Imanol was saying about our role as universities as a critical element in the society. Is that a role for a university as a whole? Should we ask our presidents, our rectors to do this or is this an individual task? As Hugo was just saying, I mean what are we doing with our time? How are we teaching our own students? What are we doing with our own pieces for the newspapers? Which we're not allowed to write anymore, at least not there in Hong Kong. So is it individual role of the intellectual or is it really an institutional role?

Jussi Välimaa: Excellent questions. Could you give short comments?

Imanol Ordorika: Yeah.

Brian Pusser: You're looking at him when you say that, right?

KEYNOTE CONVERSATION   119

Imanol Ordorika: I've never made a short comment in my life.

Brian Pusser: Just so we're clear. Just so we're clear on that. Let me make
a very short reply to Hugo, and then Imanol maybe can tie
some of this in. So, I'm very sympathetic to what you have
laid out. I think it mirrors the experience that many of us
have in universities around the world.

With regard to graduate training and so forth, you can't train people with tools
that you don't use yourself. And I think one of the things we probably should've
said at the outset also is, we're doing what we always do here. Which we're talking about higher education like it's one thing, and we're talking about the faculty like it's one thing. Frankly, there is a lot of action research, a lot of research
translating into practice. I would say right now much more effectively, if you
will, politically on the right than on the left.

So Imanol and I were at Stanford together. There's a very powerful Hoover
Institution. I'm close to Washington DC today. You have things like Brookings,
and Cato and American Enterprise Institute and they work closely with faculty.
They have people moving in and out of academe, and into the policy arena, and
many of the things we have talked about, the rise of neoliberalism, the shrinking of the state. Some were very powerfully driven by academics and academic
ideas. There's funding there for that and so forth. So people are getting it done,
and there's very, very good critical and action research coming from different
perspectives, different models. Political action particularly driven by students.
Again, a lot of the energy there is coming from there.

Just quickly on Don's point. The universities are moving much more to the
centre, I think, of some of these political debates now. I think the competition globally around economic development, tech transfer innovation and so
forth. You're absolutely right, traditionally the political battle has been about
elementary and secondary, certainly in the US, but I think clearly the attention
to the university as a site of high value-added education is pushing the political
debate further and further to even professional education, higher education
and so forth.

Imanol Ordorika: Well, I think that we have historical evidence in the 1960s of
how universities changed the world. There can be no argu-
ment against the idea that students from within the universities, but not only the students, the universities themselves
challenged the state of things and they brought, or they

strengthened, an alternative culture. And they strengthened ideas about gender equality, and about the environment, and about democracy and about the war in Vietnam or Algeria. So the universities have been there before.

I'm not saying that we have to be there in the same fashion, and I'm not saying that this is a matter of volunteerism, Hugo. But this is where agency comes about, where we can try to bring something onto the table that may be different.

But I am also sensing...And this was going to be my closing argument. I don't know if I should put it in there now.

Brian Pusser: You could do it twice.

Imanol Ordorika: We are living in the context of the collapse of political institutions in many countries in the world, as has been seen by some of the examples that I put forward. I could put many more of them forward. This collapse of political institutions is putting universities in very uncomfortable positions.

Trump is putting the universities in the US in a very uncomfortable situation. So, either you can have university administrations trying to float around and not commit in any direction, or we can start pushing for stronger political stances. When the white supremacists come to campus, you have to position the university in one direction or another, and it's starting to happen. I just think that we – I'm going to talk more about it if there's a chance – that we should be ready for that and thinking about that in order to make it happen from within. Not wait until we're in a very, very anguished and difficult situation.

Jussi Välimaa: Pedro, did you have a comment?

Pedro Texeira: Good morning. Thank you so much for the very stimulating start of our conference. Just a few quick comments, or questions, or provocations! The first one refers to the fact that I think, at a certain point, we were starting to have what I thought was very much a macro discussion of the political dimension of universities. However, I appreciated very much some of the subsequent comments, because they focused our attention more into the micro political dimension of universities. This appreciation may be biased because of the fact in recent years I have had institutional responsibilities and am more sensitive to them.

One of the first lessons that I draw from that experience was how much of the personal issues explains institutional decisions. (Other people here that have that kind of responsibility may also share this view.) The moment you start questioning why were things organised this way you realise that the reasons refer to difficulties between some persons and the degree of power and institutional influence of some of them.

In a more sophisticated way, Imanol, you raised the issue about competition and power battles inside institutions. Being an economist, I tend to regard a lot of what is an institution as a space for competition for resources between individuals, between groups, between disciplines. I think that this has been to a large extent disregarded by our research. I think we tend to focus very much in terms of the grand discussion about the political dimension of universities, but much less about the internal politics in universities.

This competitive battle within universities has in some ways a more noble dimension about different views of what an institution is about, but some fewer noble ones. I think that those battles also explain a lot of institutional and organisational dynamics.

Just as an example. We talk very much about the public mission of universities, but we talk far less about the public mission of individual academics. I think very often what we have is a ex post reconstruction of what we've done vis-à-vis certain principles, or certain missions where we try to make some cogent argument about what people have been doing. Though, in fact, it's actually the sum of largely individual or group strategies.

The other aspect that I think would be interesting to discuss is that we focus quite often in terms of system-level policies, for example, regarding the impact of funding changes, quality assessment, internationalisation and so on. However, we don't discuss so much how uneven the impact of these changes can be inside institutions. As you said in terms of the broader social level, internationalisation, globalisation may be an opportunity for some people, but it's certainly a challenge for others. This is also the case within universities. You can have age gaps where for some people it's too late to catch up with some of those trends. You can have disciplinary differences as well, but the same could be applied to research and research assessment, to the way quality assessment is perceived, implemented, so on and so forth.

Regarding the issue in terms of careers. A lot of the issues that we've been having in higher education in recent years, tend to promote what Hugo was

122   PUSSER AND ORDORIKA

highlighting, that is, safe careers, effective careers. I don't think much of that relates to a lot of what we've been discussing in terms of the mission of university. It tends to place an enormous stress in terms of individual returns, and not so much in terms of the social returns of academics' contributions. I think that also links to the complacency that Imanol was alluding to.

Brian Pusser: So let me just say something quickly. That's a wonderful comment, but to the competition for resources and the mission of the university, those are driven by external forces. The competition for resources, at least in elite research universities, is state funding. In the US the National Institutes for Health, National Science Foundation and foundations are driving the research agenda in universities. Not the other way around.

So that competition for resources that we're seeing is directly linked to the political legitimacy of various forms of research and funding. To your point, I don't disagree at all that the mission is increasingly, that people are looking for safe careers, but that's because foundations and national funders are pushing them in safe directions, and that's where the resources come from. And this is only going to accelerate. This is going to get worse before it gets better.

So I think all the instincts are right, but essentially this is always, I think, an intermingling of external political pressures, internal alignment structures and political pressures. It's not one or the other, but certainly in the US, increasingly the institutional life is driven by external funding. Universities generate very little funding. There isn't any funding in the university, other than philanthropy, we can argue that, in a public university in the US that doesn't come from some kind of external mandate or charter for the rate of tuition, or the sources of research funding. That is essentially inherently a political process.

Jussi Välimaa: Amy, did you have a comment?

Amy Metcalfe: I'm Amy Metcalfe from the University of British Columbia. Friends, I do not think you are pushing yourself far enough. I think you aren't being critical. I think you're being critical-ist. You're being like critical, meta-critical. I know both of you have a lot more in you.

One of the things that Imanol very casually, quietly slipped in there was the concept of colonialism, and the history of our institutions, but as historical

KEYNOTE CONVERSATION 123

object and not as a conditional presence that we are continuously being colonial in our activities, and in many ways that is a political act. It's a political act of a particular type. We may not see it within a state framework. It's a supernational framework of imperialism, new imperialisms. So, I think we can continue to speak about that as a politics.

Imanol, also when speaking about the conditions of 1968, students were protesting the university itself for those very same histories and complicities. So, it's not so much to say that in the 60s the institutions themselves were critical. It's that people within in the institutions, not all of them, some of them, were calling into question and calling those institutions to host a different set of conversations with different bodies and different peoples with different outcomes.

Brian, in working with you on the book *Critical Approaches to the Study of Higher Education*, I don't know if you remember this but, you asked me do you really want to use a particular word in my chapter? And that word was "genocide". I said, "Yes. We need to speak these words". Your concern was very collegial, and trying to protect me as a researcher from people's perception of what I'm saying about my use of that word, but we need to do that. We need to use these words. We need to say we are supporting, in this field to many extents, a colonial, imperialist, genocidal, organisational and institutional space. So please continue.

Brian Pusser: Thank you.

Imanol Ordorika: Well, let me tackle several of the things that have been said. I'll start with you, Amy. I do think there's a new colonialism, and it's the colonialism of a dominant university model. The notion of the elite research university model from the US is a new colonial project that, amongst others, is imposed upon all of our universities. We all have to be measured with a sort of Harvard-ometer. That is a ranking, of any type, that says how much a university is fulfilling the role of highly-ranked (RU-1) private research university in the US. That's a new colonial project and we have adopted it fully, and we adopt it, for example, in our own research journals. We adopt it everywhere in the ways in which we are performing our individual careers everywhere, and we're not challenging that at all.

We're not even arguing how our university might want to develop – not even if they can fulfil that role or not, if we want them to do that or should they focus on a totally different project. I don't think that the 60s were about essentially challenging the institutions. It was the Vietnam War, it was civil rights in the US, it was against the authoritarian political regime in Mexico, and Czechoslovakia and Hungary. It was against the dictatorship in Spain. It was maybe in a few places, or some of the issues were local, maybe free speech, but what about the loyalty oath that the faculty stopped adopting in the US in the 1960s? And challenging McCarthyism as a whole.

Faculty have done that, and they didn't stop publishing, or writing sociology or biochemistry papers. They came out in the open and challenged a state of things that was unacceptable at the time. If we look elsewhere, we can see the streets in Buenos Aires full of hard science researchers, and teachers and faculty in the streets challenging the government, because there is no funding for science. The people are out there, and at the same time they are demanding that marijuana be legalised. This is a really strange coalition, and it makes sense. These are people that are well informed.

So, I do think that the times they are changing, I would say and not necessarily in our favour. Somebody mentioned, I think it was Jussi, that once there are alternative facts, and that the most powerful government on earth can argue that everything that we do in our institutions is a biased fact that they can challenge just by political discourse. We have been thoroughly challenged, and the politically correct discourse that stemmed essentially from universities and university thinkers and intellectuals within universities, like gender equality, and anti-racism, and human and civil rights, and stuff like that, has been challenged from the topmost level of power.

It's happening in other countries too. Well, the Le Pen party in France came relatively close to winning the national election. So, that's a very strong racist political discourse. Are we going to say anything about that? Do we have anything to do? That's the way in which colonialism is expressed in each country. There is no colonial layer that is exactly the same everywhere. In South Africa students were bringing down the last Rhodes statues within campuses last year, or the year before that. University authorities were not sure how to react. In some places they were in favour of the students, in others they were like, "What do we do now?" The ANC,[3] well they had disappointed everybody around, so we didn't know exactly what the position was.

Basically, we are seeing a lot of local and international political processes that are putting the universities in the cross hairs, really. It's gone way beyond funding. It's challenging the nature of higher education itself. In the vast majority of the world, it's not like this nice campus in Finland. When Jussi went to Puerto Rico a few years ago and put forward the problems of higher education in Finland, everybody from Latin America said, "We want Finland's problems. Can we have them here?"

KEYNOTE CONVERSATION   125

Well, most of the students never get to higher education in Latin America, and that exclusion is increasing. Not the reverse. We are on the verge of big political and social outbreaks – and I'm doing a little bit of what may be looking at the crystal ball or something. I do think that we are facing strong political battles in society, and that universities are necessarily in the centre of that. Independent of our careers and our willingness to be a participant of that, but we, in some ways, those who became the strongest part or who promoted the movements in other times, because it was not only the 60s, where the people that were prepared for that were discussing the issues that had to be brought to the front, and were able to generate the alternative ideas that we had to put forward.

Yes. Well, very simple alternative ideas like universal enrolments and others like that can be brought to the fore, but we are still lacking clarity and commitment in that direction. I agree with you, Pedro.

Jussi Välimaa: I think I want to give a Brian a chance this time.

Imanol Ordorika: He spoke in all of them.

Brian Pusser: There's a new question?

Jussi: I'm exercising power now.

Brian Pusser: Good.

Jussi Välimaa: I think what we have been discussing so far is somehow related to the role of higher education in civil society. Also to the ways, the social role of higher education in societies and in states. I would like to change the focus to what actually Imanol was speaking to in his last note. On the inequalities, and inequalities of and around higher education. My question to you would be, from the political and theoretical perspective, is higher education part of the problem of social and economic inequality in national and global context, or the solution for reducing inequality? Brian?

Brian Pusser: In the time-honoured tradition, I would say both. And I say both *because* this is really where we confront that problem of talking about higher education in monolithic terms. This is very contextual, depending on whether we're talking about an emerging higher education system, or we're talking about a very old and established system, or an old system with a few very powerful institutions, like Chile. The degree to which people are able to access higher education and the degree to which higher education in different contexts is linked to reducing inequality is very different in different places. So let me just talk a little bit conceptually by using the US as an example, and clearly I would say the US is not doing nearly enough to reduce inequality, and this is happening on two levels. It's happening very distinctly in the ways in which income distributions track levels of educational success. I think also it's happening in the ways in which we're training people in higher education to think about inequality and to go back out into the broader society to address, in the civil society and in other ways, the problem of inequality.

As many people know, the higher education system in the US is probably the best funded system overall in the world, very powerful and diverse system of higher education, but let's look a little bit at what's happening with inequality in the US and with higher education. So between 1975 and 2010, if you think about that, that's some 35 years, maybe you can think of that almost as two generations, family income in the US increased by an average of about 40% over those 35 years and, in that same period, family income for the poorest American families and children actually declined, over a 35-year period the average income of those families declined. Children who were in the top five percent of families in terms of income saw their family's income double over the same 35 years from 1975 to 2010. A child in the US born to parents in the lowest income quintile has about a 43% of chance of becoming an adult with income in the lowest income quintile. If you're born in the lowest income quintile in the US, there's a significant likelihood that you're going to stay in that lowest income quintile throughout your life. The chances of you starting in the lowest income quintile in the US and reaching the highest income quintile over your lifetime are very low.

This is not social mobility in the sense that we like to talk about it and think about it, but a child born into a family in the highest quintile has about a 40% chance, has about double the chance that you would predict of staying in that highest quintile. So if you're born in the highest income quintile in the US your chances of landing in the bottom quintile over your lifetime are somewhere around six or seven percent, it's not likely to happen. It's a highly stratified

KEYNOTE CONVERSATION

127

system, which is not entirely due to higher education, of course, but higher education is a big part of that story.

Let's just take a minute and think about graduation rates. If we think about college graduation rates for people who were born between 1961 and 1964, and then compare them to people born between 1979 and 1982, so you have two different cohorts, again roughly two generations, the graduation rate for those in the lowest income quintile increased four percent from one generation to the next. So it hardly changed at all. For those born in the highest income quintile the graduation rate increased by 20%. So over those 20 years we did a much better job of graduating wealthy people than of increasing the graduation rates of people who were in that lowest income quintile. But when children from the lowest income quintiles or young people from the lowest income groups in the US do get college degrees they tend to advance pretty quickly in the income quintiles.[4] So there's an effect in higher education but we haven't done a very good job of getting people access and success in college. The degree to which people graduate and complete higher education is distinctly related to income and wealth, to a rather astonishing degree. Around the world, high income inequality is associated with low social mobility and the US, Brazil, Chile, Peru, they're places with low social mobility. Denmark, Finland, Canada, they have low income inequality and they have higher social mobility.

So, although institutions of higher education don't fully control the preparation of people who try to access higher education, we could do a lot more than we're doing now, I think, to prepare people for college education and moving into the higher ranks of the society, professions and income. This is really shaped by what happens within the institutions around curriculum, around mentoring, around civic engagement, around a sense of collective action, but not enough apparently in higher education or in our education system to change the approach to inequality in the US. We're not teaching people to address the problem and make changes through the civil society or the political system, and the system itself in place is credentialing and educating people in ways that are increasing inequality, moving the best prepared and best educated away from the least prepared and least educated, and it's actually accelerating as we speak.

We should talk more about what it would look like around the globe if we had a more strongly enforced right to a good education, what it would mean if there was something like a right to a good education that could be enforced globally. There's no such right in the US, incidentally. You don't have a right to a higher education, and I think that it gets into a conversation we might have a little bit later about the public interest or the public good, but fundamentally, without some kind of rights-based claim, this is going to require action in the civil society and political society that right now just isn't there. So, as we speak, in the US the higher education system is part of a system that is increasing inequality; it's not reducing inequality.

Imanol Ordorika: Well, I agree that it is both, but I would approach it differently. I don't disagree with Brian. I would approach it from a different perspective. It has been argued strongly from different perspectives – Bourdieu, and Althusser – that education at every level is always reproducing the stratified nature of society. There, Don, is where I don't necessarily agree with you that universities are uninteresting to the political systems. Probably not about numbers, but they are very strongly linked to the meritocracy of explaining social stratification in places where there is more or less broad higher education enrolment.

I'd say that against the deterministic view that Bourdieu put forward at one point there's the idea that precisely that is one of the issues for political contestation, and it goes in one, in a very basic direction, once again, about access. The US can be the most highly funded system in the world but it still only enrols 40% of the age group. Many countries are above that, even in Latin America (not Mexico by the way). That doesn't necessarily mean that there's equality in access immediately, and the notion that was put forward by the California Master Plan by Kerr in the 70s and later by Burton Clark in this diversification of institutions agenda all over the world that was – I don't know, maybe Burton Clark just rationalised what the World Bank and other international agencies were pushing or driving for – this stratification between universities and vocational institutions and other types of higher education, where it's obvious that students do not have access to the same levels of income and socio-economic status if you come from one institution or the other.

So, basically what Simon Marginson's work on universalisation – it's interesting that we call universal enrolment systems those that are more or less around 60% of enrolment – would that work for a basic elementary education if we said, "Oh we have a universal system, we only enrol 60%?" Of course it doesn't work and it's only a hundred years ago that universal enrolment for elementary education was put forward. I do think that we have to move towards an agenda of true universal enrolment in a much more homogenous setting of institutions in different countries. Obviously that is a big, big, big political battle and it comes surrounded with a lot of issues of how the contemporary

KEYNOTE CONVERSATION

society is built and how inequality is explained, but because, well, we all know this discourse about how our performance in the educational system essentially explains how well we're doing in society, and that gives a lot of leverage and legitimacy to social systems. It has been doing it for ages.

So, I do think that instead of saying that universities are basically driving inequality, I'd say that it depends on the state of the political battles at the time. In moments in which social groups in society are capable of expanding enrolments and access to more homogenous institutions in terms of quality and opportunity, then universities can perform a role to overcome or to diminish inequality. As we are right now, in the state that universities in most of the world are in right now, essentially we are not only reproducing, but increasing inequality everywhere. Just that would be my response to your question, Jussi.

Jussi Välimaa: Yes, any comments, questions?

Tiffany Viggiano: Hello, my name is Tiffany Viggiano, I'm here from the University of California at Riverside, and I am here on a Fulbright Finland grant so I'm interested in studying global equity in Finland and so I'm really interested in this conversation because also to Amy's point I think that it's just not critical enough, because I don't think that you can talk about global equity without talking about international education and the way that many systems of higher education across the world are contributing to global inequity. So I'm interested to hear your thoughts on that.

Imanol Ordorika: Well, I probably haven't come across clearly enough. I'm not talking about global equality. I'm talking about equality, trying to address it from an international perspective, bringing cases from different places in the world. There is global inequality, there is inequality between countries and within countries and between regions and all of that we all know, but I'm trying to bring some cases forward, just to show how inequality in education in higher education is expressed in different ways.

For example in the US, you have this 40% coverage where more or less 60% of enrolment is in community colleges and special-focus institutions, not in the RU-1 and the master's degree-granting institutions and all of that, that's one type of inequality. When you have like eight million young people, between

18 and 24 years old, that have no education at all and no jobs, that's a different type of inequality, so there's no unique global form of inequality, at least in my view. We can say that globally there is inequality, but it is expressed in very different ways and in the ways in which they have developed in our countries, and we need to have this broad international understanding but we also have to be grounded in the realities of our systems everywhere, our countries and even our regions, and the even the types of institutions within our countries because sometimes, as we were saying before, we are a very privileged crowd.

We come from the research universities from everywhere, but most of the faculty in the world don't even come to conferences like this. They live in a different world and, talk about the students, that's a different type of setting and dialogue.

Brian Pusser: To your point, which I think is a really, really important one. As I'm sitting here, if you were to think about the ebb and flow of this conversation, at times we argue that we're powerless, increasingly powerless, and other times we're powerful and I think we have to take a stand on that and I think that universities are enormously powerful because they're institutions of the state. And to Amy's point, they reflect the missions and values of the state and we're not very comfortable with that. We simply don't want to confront the idea that, as institutions of states that are attempting to dominate others, universities are trying to impose a kind of hegemony globally, this is a very old story. Universities play a very powerful role in that. They're centres of instantiating and reinforcing norms through scholarship and through the construction of discourse, through alliances with the political sector. That doesn't mean at the same time that they can't be forces for various kinds of protest, contests, liberation. They're conflicted, they're contested in their own right, they're enormously complicated institutions. But I think it's important. There's enough romanticising of them to go around, and it's really important for us to call ourselves out. I don't think we can argue for state theory and that political institutions of the state play an instrumentally important role, and then assume that somehow universities are not going to incorporate and reflect some of the primary missions of the state that are not aligned with social justice, that are not the kinds of things that we might

KEYNOTE CONVERSATION

advocate in some other setting or some other context, that's what we are.

Jussi Välimaa: Well, part of the reasons why I wanted to focus on inequality is that one of the promises of higher education when the massification of higher education started was the promise or assumption that when there were more students in the higher education there will be more equality. So, more equality because of the increasing number of students. Simon Marginson has edited, with Brendan Cantwell and Anna Smolentsova, a book on high-participation systems where they argue, and we have a chapter in there, that what has happened is really that, instead of increasing equality, inequality has maintained. There's been a strong stratification of the systems, the stratification of the higher education institutions, where the elite go to the best universities and we rest go to those less good higher education institutions. The only exception to this rule seems to be Nordic institutions. My point is mainly, state integration really matters. But what kind of state integration, do you have an opinion about that?

Imanol Ordorika: What kind of state integration?

Jussi Välimaa: Yeah.

Imanol Ordorika: Oh, I think that the state in itself, and there we address state theory itself and it's a site of political contestation. This is an old debate: Is the state instrumental to capitalist accumulation? Is the state relatively autonomous? Is a state a site of contestation? Gramsci wrote a lot about this and also Poulantzas in his later work, about the fact that there are certain state institutions within which contestation is taking place.

One of them is a political system. But what we're seeing is that many political systems are in crisis. Bobbio has said you can see that you have trouble in a political system when there is not much difference between the political parties that you're voting for. Yeah, it's not the same to vote for Hillary or for Trump, but in terms of state project itself and economic development, it's not such a big, different story. Now probably that's the most extreme case in all of the countries, or in many of the countries, but what is the role of higher education in that condition? Are we only reproducing? I don't think so, I think that we have been in a long stage of reproduction with this idea that the universities are connected to the knowledge economy and that we are producers of knowledge to be exchanged in the market.

And one of the products of universities are graduates of higher education, it's for the job market. We have been doing that historically. That has been the role of institutions. But there's always, sometimes it's a weak battle, other times it's a stronger confrontation, to establish at least some equilibrium between the creation of goods to be exchanged in the market and the creation of other types of knowledge and understandings of society, other types of value related to higher education and to expand it to a broader set of the population.

So, I'd say that the confrontations that take place inside and around higher education are part of confrontations that are taking place in terms of trying to redirect nation-states. It's very difficult to think about it after 30 or 35 years of neoliberalism, where nothing seems to move, and everything seems to be set in stone, and all the discourse of possible transformations and changes in society has been in some ways overwhelmed by the notions that the market and the economy define everything in society. Now, that is part of the intellectual challenges of universities to try to develop new ways of thinking about transformations in a broader arena that goes outside of the university itself. But I do think that this is happening, and it's happening because we have all of these demographic changes, migrations that are shifting the political balance everywhere.

We have all of these human rights crises everywhere, we have a very unstable international political condition that allows for at least starting to think that things can be different in a broader sense than some of the battles that we have taken in the last years, where we are trying to establish small equality projects, community connections between universities and small local businesses or local communities and stuff like that, which was like kind of a small resistance space that we have taken. We need to be thinking in a much broader scope in order to make these challenges to the state in general and to its institutions and in particular to higher education.

Brian Pusser: So, one quick comment on that. If we're going to talk about higher education as a product of contest between the state, the civil society, actors who are marginalised by both the state and the civil society, we're going to have to do more on inequality in the civil society. So the differences in wealth are something we talk about all the time and I talked about it today. But there are also differences in political access, in access to discourse, gender inequalities, historical racism, any number of historical and contemporary structures and standpoints in the civil society that are in turn driving the contest over higher education. Or at least attempting to drive the contest, the relationship between inequalities in the civil society and inequalities that are driven by state policy are very similar to conversations about inequality in higher education and the role of higher education institutions. To the point about, your point about Scandinavia, Nordic states I would say that the attitude in the civil society towards collective action, towards shared institutions and responsibilities is different than in other contexts. It's reflected in all the institutions of these societies and it's reflected in the state role, but no one of these is driving that or reflecting the other. Again, it gets back to this idea that this is a contest, so to argue for a more robust and emancipatory higher education system probably argues the same has to happen in the civil society and in another debate a few years from now we could have the same structure where we'd be talking about the civil society and higher education and ask the same questions and march through where we stand and where we sit with regard to that.

Imanol Ordorika: Just a very brief comment because we don't need to think that *everything* is moving backwards or in the wrong direction, just look at female enrolments almost everywhere in the world. There are some regions that are really in very difficult conditions, but in a lot of countries, female enrolments are above male enrolments now. This is a change that has happened in 20 years. Now, feminist discourse has two explanations for this. One is that higher education has become uninteresting for males and they are withering or they're moving away from higher education. I don't think there is evidence to support that argument. I would think that one of the groups, or one of the social movements that almost all over the world has been pushing more strongly to attain certain levels of equality, especially in education, has been women's movements. And there have been very important results and these are relevant contests. These are some of the things that have been gained and that have happened because there has been social action around it, and there are numbers to show it which is something in favour, and that also shows that things can be done when there is social action and organisation.

Jussi Välimaa: Thank you very much. I think we are reaching the end of our session. We have been discussing about higher education and the politics in higher education, looking at higher education from a micro and a macro perspective, about academic careers, the role of higher education in society, so actually my question to you would be, do you think that academics should be politically active? Just to make it more serious, I'd like to ask all of you who think that academics should be politically active to raise their hands. Thank you very much. This is a very personal but also academic question, where we commit these tools to our careers, to our society, to our higher education institutions. I don't think that there are right or wrong answers, but I think that all of us need to have a personal relationship to the question.

So I think my colleagues, my friends, would have many more things to say, but I'm very sorry, we have to stop now.

Acknowledgements

Brian Pusser and Imanol Ordorika were asked to collaborate on this keynote panel at a time of increasing contest in a wide array of national contexts over the purposes and organisation of higher education. Individually and in collaboration, these scholars have produced scholarly works that have advanced a conceptual model based upon theories of the state and contest that conceptualises universities as political institutions of the state, and as sites and instruments of broader political contest. They are grateful to the organisers of the 2017 CHER and its participants, with particular gratitude to Dr Jussi Välimaa for the invitation to discuss the politics of higher education with the conference attendees and through these conference proceedings.

Notes

1 Works by scholars mentioned in this conversation can be found in the References at the end of the chapter.
2 Revolutionary Armed Forces of Colombia – People's Army (Spanish: Fuerzas Armadas Revolucionarias de Colombia – Ejército del Pueblo.
3 African National Congress.
4 For statistics and examples of research and analyses of inequality and social mobility in higher education that informed this conversation, see the work of Professor Raj Chetty, Harvard University, Professor Emanuel Saez, UC Berkeley, cited in the References.

References

Althusser, L. (1977). *For Marx*. London: New Left Books.

Apple, M. (1982). *Education and power*. Boston, MA: Routledge and Keegan Paul.

Becker, G. S. (1964). *Human capital: A theoretical and empirical analysis: With special reference to education*. Chicago, IL: University of Chicago Press.

Blau, P. M. (1955). *The dynamics of bureaucracy*. Chicago, IL: University of Chicago Press.

Bobbio, N., Pontara, G., & Veca, S. (1985). *Crisis de la Democracia*. Barcelona: Editorial Ariel.

Bourdieu, P., & Passeron, J. (1977). *Reproduction in education, society and culture*. Beverly Hills, CA: Sage.

Bowles, S., & Gintis, H. (1976). *Schooling in capitalist America*. New York, NY: Basic Books.

Cantwell, B., Marginson, S., & Smolentseva, A. (Eds.). *High participation systems of higher education*. Oxford: Oxford University Press.

Cantwell, B., & Kauppinen, I. (Eds.). (2014). *Academic capitalism in the age of globalization*. Baltimore, MD: Johns Hopkins University Press.

Carnoy, M., & Levin, H. M. (1985). *Schooling and work in the democratic state*. Stanford, CA: Stanford University Press.

Chetty, R., Friedman, J. N., Saez, E., Turner, N., & Yagan, D. (2017, July). *Mobility report cards: The role of colleges in intergenerational mobility*. National Bureau of Economic Research (NBER) Working Paper 23618.

Chetty, R., Hendren, N., Kline, P., Saez, E., & Turner, N. (2014). Is the United States still a land of opportunity? Recent trends in intergenerational mobility. *American Economic Review, 104*(5), 141–147.

Clark, B. R. (1983). *The higher education system: Academic organization in cross-national perspective*. Berkeley, CA: University of California Press.

Cohen, M. D., March, J. G., & Olsen, J. P. (1972). A garbage can model of organizational choice. *Administrative Science Quarterly, 17*(1), 1–25.

Foucault, M. (1980). *Power/Knowledge*. Brighton: The Harvester Press LTD.

Fraser, N. (1992). Rethinking the public sphere: A contribution to the critique of actually existing democracy. In C. Calhoun (Ed.), *Habermas and the public sphere* (pp. 109–142). Cambridge, MA: MIT Press.

Freire, P. (1985). *The politics of education*. South Hadley, MA: Bergin and Garvey.

Friedman, M. F. (2002). *Capitalism and freedom* (40th anniversary ed.). Chicago, IL: The University of Chicago Press.

Giroux, H. A. (1983). *Critical theory and educational practice*. Victoria: Deakin University.

Gramsci, A. (1971). *Selections from prison notebooks*. New York, NY: International Publishers.

Hardy, C. P. (1990). Putting power into university governance. In J. C. Smart (Ed.), *Higher education handbook of theory and research* (Vol. 6). New York, NY: Agathon Press.

Hayek, F. (1960). *The constitution of liberty*. London: Routledge and Kegan Paul.

Kerr, C. (2001). *The uses of the university* (5th ed.). Cambridge, MA: Harvard University Press.

Kingdon, J. W. (1984). *Agendas, alternatives and public policies*. Boston, MA: Little Brown.

Kogan, M. (1984). The political view. In B. R. Clark (Ed.), *Perspectives on higher education* (pp. 56–78). Berkeley, CA: University of California Press.

Lindblom, C. E. (1959, Spring). The science of 'muddling through'. *Public Administration Review, 19*(2), 79–88.

Marginson, S. (1997). *Markets in education*. Melbourne: Allen and Unwin.

Meyer, J. W., & Rowan, B. (1977). Institutionalized organizations: Formal structure as myth and ceremony. *American Journal of Sociology, 83*, 340–363.

Moe, T. (1996). *The positive theory of public bureaucracy*. New York, NY: Cambridge University Press.

Ordorika, I. (2003). *Power and politics in university governance: Organization and change at the Universidad Nacional Autonoma de Mexico*. New York, NY: Routledge Falmer.

Ordorika, I., & Pusser, B. (2007). La máxima casa de estudios: The Universidad Nacional Autónoma de México as a state-building university. In P. G. Altbach & J. Balan (Eds.), *World class worldwide: Transforming research universities in Asia and Latin America* (pp. 189–215). Baltimore, MD: Johns Hopkins Press.

Pfeffer, J., & Salancik, G. R. (1978). *The external control of organizations: A resource dependence perspective*. New York, NY: Harper and Row.

Poulantzas, N. A. (1978). *State, power, socialism*. London: NLB.

Pusser, B. (2015). A critical approach to power in higher education. In A. M. Martinez-Aleman, B. Pusser, & E. M. Bensimon (Eds.), *Critical approaches to the study of higher education*. Baltimore, MD: Johns Hopkins University Press.

Pusser, B., Kempner, K., Marginson, S., & Ordorika, I. (Eds.). (2012). *Universities and the public sphere: Knowledge creation and state building in the era of globalization*. New York, NY: Routledge.

Pusser, B., & Marginson, S. (2013). University rankings in critical perspective. *Journal of Higher Education, 84*(4), 544–568.

Rhoades, G. L. (1992). Beyond "the state": Interorganizational relations and state apparatus in post-secondary education. In J. C. Smart (Ed.), *Higher education: Handbook of theory and research* (Vol. 8). New York, NY: Agathon.

Skocpol, T. (1992). *Protecting soldiers and mothers: The political origins of social policy in the United States*. Cambridge, MA: Harvard University Press.

Skocpol, T., Evans, P., & Rueschemeyer, D. (Eds.). (1985). *Bringing the state back in*. Cambridge University Press.

Selznick, P. (1949). *TVA and the grass roots*. Berkeley, CA: University of California Press.

Skowronek, S. (1997). *The politics presidents make: Leadership from John Adams to Bill Clinton*. Cambridge, MA: Belknap Press.

Slaughter, S. (1990). *The higher learning and high technology: Dynamics of higher education policy formation*. Albany, NY: State University of New York Press.

Slaughter, S., & Leslie, L. L. (1997). *Academic capitalism*. Baltimore, MD: Johns Hopkins University Press.

Smith, A. (1776). *An inquiry into the wealth of nations* (1979). Harmondsworth: Penguin.

Välimaa, J. (2012). The corporatization of national universities in Finland. In B. Pusser, K. Kempner, S. Marginson, & I. Ordorika (Eds.), *Universities and the public sphere: Knowledge creation and state building in the era of globalization*. New York, NY: Routledge.

Weber, M. (1947). *The theory of social and economic organization*. Glencoe, IL: Free Press.

Weick, K. E. (1976). Educational organizations as loosely coupled systems. *Administrative Science Quarterly, 21*, 1–19.

CHAPTER 6

Universitas Reformata Semper Reformanda: A Political Parallelogram of Continual University Reform

Susanne Lohmann

[Managing a university is like] trying to herd cats.
GERHARD CASPER[1] (in Cohn & Robinson, 1999)

• • •

Changing a college curriculum is like moving a cemetery.
MANY A UNIVERSITY PRESIDENT[2] (Kerr, 2001, p. 396; Logue, 2017, p. 54; and Summers, 2012, p. ED26)

• • •

Changing the direction of [a university] while it continues its day-to-day operations [is like] performing surgery on a man while he hauls a trunk upstairs.
J. B. LON HEFFERLIN CHANNELLING ARTHUR SCHLESINGER, JR.[3]
(Hefferlin, 1972, p. 1)

•••

Abstract

Universitates semper reformandae sunt (Latin: universities are continually in need of reform).[4] They are naturally and inherently antithetical to change. The politics of university reform resemble a tug of war between foot-dragging university faculties and their whip-cracking political principals. The former win for the most part, the latter every now and then, which is why university history features the punctuated equilibrium pattern, to wit: long periods of institutional stasis punctuated by occasional bursts of university reform.

© KONINKLIJKE BRILL NV, LEIDEN, 2020 | DOI: 10.1163/9789004422582_007

This facile narrative deserves to die.

With this essay I seek to complexify our thinking about the politics of university reform. Properly configured, the university is naturally and inherently dynamist. It constitutes the point of attraction in a political parallelogram of forces, with the net resultant force representing the forward movement of science and society. If the resultant goes awry, would-be university reformers can tweak the force field, by modifying one or the other component force in the parallelogram, or by adding or subtracting a force.

The prescription is to proceed conservatively, however. The university's defects are complexly entangled with its defences. A brute force attempt to repair the university's defects can inadvertently ruin its defences. Chances are that the cure is worse than the disease, in which case the principle 'do no harm' calls for a policy of 'do nothing'. University reform properly understood is about defending the inherited idea of the university as it manifests itself in the form of the political parallelogram.

I examine two cases of university reform politics, one that played out wastefully in the United States, the other, destructively in the United Kingdom. I demonstrate that my bottom-up complex systems approach, as epitomised by the political parallelogram, gives us a better handle on the politics of university reform than does top-down principal-agent reasoning, as evidenced in the facile narrative.

Keywords

universitas reformata semper reformanda – political parallelogram – politics of university reform – isomorphic cross – defects vs. defences – punctuated equilibrium theory

1   Introduction

The history of university reform is about as old as the history of the university (Kittelson & Transue, 1984; Rudersdorf, 2016). Ringing down the centuries are twin complaints to the effect that universities are – at once – shot through with rot and dead set against change. University reform is conceptualised as corrective action imposed upon the university by the outside world:

> [L]ight flashes from the college to the community, and life streams back again from the community to the college, so that while the college

redeems the community from the curse of ignorance, the community preserves the college from an undue tendency to monkish corruption and scholastic unprofitableness. (Tyler, 1857, p. 10)

In modern-day liberal democracies the politics of university reform plays out as a deadlocked dance between foot-dragging academics and reform-minded elected politicians. The former win for the most part, the latter every now and then, which is why university history features the punctuated equilibrium pattern, to wit: long periods of institutional stasis punctuated by occasional bursts of university reform (Eldredge & Gould, 1972; Lohmann, 2019a).

This facile narrative deserves to die. It is loaded with partial truths, which is why it is readily believable. Its top-down principal-agent take on university politics is wrongheaded, however, for it promotes brute force university reform, which is wasteful at best and destructive at worst.

I illustrate the intellectual bankruptcy of the facile narrative with reference to two cases of university reform politics, one that played out wastefully in the United States, the other, destructively in the United Kingdom.

In place of the facile narrative, I take a bottom-up complex systems approach to the politics of university reform (Birnbaum, 1988; Lohmann, 2006). Properly configured, the university is naturally and inherently dynamist. It is "closed in an open sort of way" (Persaud, 2009/4), that is, individual universities are operationally closed, and yet their internal decision making is receptive to pressures emanating from science, society and other universities. Conceptually, the university constitutes the point of attraction in a political parallelogram of forces (Fraenkel, 1964/2011), with the net resultant force representing scientific progress and societal change.

If the resultant goes awry, would-be university reformers can tweak the force field, by modifying one or the other component force in the parallelogram, or by adding or subtracting a force. The prescription is to proceed conservatively, however. The university's defects are complexly entangled with its defences. A brute force attempt to repair the university's defects can inadvertently ruin its defences (Lohmann, 2004b). Chances are that the cure is worse than the disease, in which case the principle 'do no harm' calls for a policy of 'do nothing'. University reform properly understood is about defending the inherited idea of the university as it manifests itself in the form of the political parallelogram.

I employ the parallelogram concept to examine the truth content of the facile narrative and its three claims about the university, namely, *semper reformanda*; antithetical to change; and punctuated equilibrium.

In conclusion, I return to my two cases, the United States and the United Kingdom, to argue that my bottom-up complex systems approach, as

UNIVERSITAS REFORMATA SEMPER REFORMANDA

epitomised by the political parallelogram, yields a better handle on the politics of university reform than does top-down principal-agent reasoning, as evidenced in the facile narrative.

Before I proceed with my argument, two caveats are in order. First, my discussion of the politics of university reform is restricted to developed countries and liberal democracies. Every country must grapple with the problem of getting its universities right, but the nature of the problem differs across countries. In developing countries, the issue is not the reform of a mature university system in a fully modernised society but the development to maturity of an embryonic university system as part and parcel of the process of modernisation. In a non-democracy, the issue is whether and how the university system will co-evolve with the political system as university-led modernisation creates pressures for liberal democracy. These are important issues to address, but they are not the focus of this essay.

Second, there is an American parochialism to the way I describe the institution of the university and liberal democracy. The idea of the university is universal but it is instantiated concretely in locally grounded universities and nationally grounded university systems, which differ in their historical paths, collective memories, organisational cultures, governance structures, political cultures, funding sources, positions in the reputational pecking order, and what not. In the same vein, liberal democracy is a universal, and yet each nation state pursues its own path-dependent and place-dependent version of it. No doubt my argument would be stronger if I based it in history and rendered it locally and nationally specific, but there is only so much ground you can cover in one essay.

Without further ado, let me turn to two cases that show evidence of top-down principal-agent reasoning about university reform, first in the United States, then in the United Kingdom.

2 Brute-Force University Reform

My starting point is the global 'can't the university be more like business' reform movement (Lohmann, 2004a). In the United States, James Carlin's 1999 *Chronicle of Higher Education* essay, titled "Restoring Sanity to an Academic World Gone Mad", served as the opening salvo:

> I have been a businessman for over 35 years, and I was a trustee of the University of Massachusetts and chairman of the Massachusetts Board of Higher Education for a total of 12 years. I am, or have been, a director

of eight public corporations, and was chief executive officer of a transit system with an annual budget of $1 billion. I have also founded four businesses, in separate fields, that were recognised by *Inc.* magazine for their rapid growth and success. I think I've learned something about management and controlling costs. Never have I observed anything as unfocused or mismanaged as higher education. Clearly the reason tuition is high is that college costs are high. Why are costs high? Nobody is in charge. (Carlin, 1999, p. A76)

In the United States the movement peaked in 2006 with the publication of the Spellings Report titled "A Test of Leadership: Charting the Future of U.S. Higher Education" (Spellings Commission, 2006). One year earlier, Secretary of Education Margaret Spellings had tasked a blue-ribbon commission with studying access, affordability and instructional quality as well as institutional accountability to students, families, taxpayers, and investors in for-profit higher education enterprises. Her conceit was to compel US universities to address the educational needs of the twenty-first century globalised workplace.

The person tapped to lead this ambitious effort was Charles Miller, a prominent businessman in Houston, Texas, who had a history of taking on one educational leadership role after another: Chairman of the Texas Education Policy Center, which designed the public school accountability system for Texas; Chairman of the Education Committee of the Governor's Business Council; Chairman of the Board of Regents of the University of Texas System; and is now Chairman of the Spellings Commission, tasked with turning upside-down the American university system. Miller's ideas about higher education echoed Carlin's, as if the two businessmen were twins separated at birth. Here are Miller's musings as they were recorded by one of his colleagues on the Spellings Commission:

> What was wrong with higher education, he observed, was that no one was really in charge. Rather than making colleges more disciplined, the pursuit of new revenues was making higher education just plain wasteful. "Where's the accountability"? he asked. "Who are the change agents? Why is it taking the academy so long to recognize the need for systemic change"? (Zemsky, 2007, p. B6)

The Spellings Report was consequential in one respect, namely, that it promoted for-profit higher education in the United States, to the detriment of students, families, and the taxpayers, and to the benefit of investors in for-profit higher education enterprises. For the most part, however, the report sank like a

UNIVERSITAS REFORMATA SEMPER REFORMANDA

143

stone never to be heard of again. America's public universities and their private non-profit counterparts emerged largely unscathed.

The English universities were not so lucky. (Why English and not British? The Scottish system is distinctly different and independently run, and Wales and Northern Ireland are peculiar in ways I do not wish to pursue in this essay.) Public sector reform started out in the Thatcher era, taking on transportation, health, welfare and – eventually – higher education. The universities were subjected to quality assurance mechanisms, research assessment exercises and academic audits. The reach of the state extended beyond university finances to areas – research and teaching – previously considered sacrosanct.

In his 2013 *London Review of Books* essay titled "Sold Out" Stefan Collini, a professor of intellectual history and English literature at the University of Cambridge, ruminated:

> Future historians, pondering changes in British society from the 1980s onwards, will struggle to account for the following curious fact. Although British business enterprises have an extremely mixed record (frequently posting gigantic losses, mostly failing to match overseas competitors, scarcely benefiting the weaker groups in society), and although such arm's length public institutions as museums and galleries, the BBC, and the universities have by and large a very good record (universally acknowledged creativity, streets ahead of most of their international peers, positive forces for human development and social cohesion), nonetheless over the past three decades politicians have repeatedly attempted to force the second set of institutions to change so that they more closely resemble the first. Some of those historians may even wonder why at the time there was so little concerted protest at this deeply implausible programme. But they will at least record that, alongside its many other achievements, the coalition government took the decisive steps in helping to turn some first-rate universities into third-rate companies. (Collini, 2013, p.12)

The United States and the United Kingdom both fell prey to New Public Management ideas emanating from American business schools and management consulting firms (Hood, 1991). Whence the opposite outcomes – why were the American universities able to fend off the attack, and what rendered the English universities vulnerable? Three factors made the difference between the two cases, I would argue.

First, in the United States the two political parties – Democrats and Republicans – split over higher education reform. Neither party is particularly fond of universities: Democrats favour community colleges on social justice grounds, and Republicans support the for-profit higher education industry for reasons of market ideology and campaign contributions. The Republicans have a special chip on their shoulders, however, on account of the left-wing slant of the professoriate. The Presidential Commission that produced the Spelling Report was nominally non-partisan, but Margaret Spellings was Secretary of Education at a time when the Republicans controlled the presidency and both houses of Congress, and the Spellings Report consequently reflected Republican priorities. Mere months after the report was published, the Democrats regained control of Congress, and they promptly ignored the Spellings Report. Two years later, the Democrats won the White House, and the Department of Education reversed course on for-profit higher education, seeking to reign in the industry's worst excesses.

By way of contrast, in the United Kingdom the Conservatives and Labour had long degenerated into 'cartel parties' (Katz & Mair, 1995) in the matter of public sector reform. (The cartel-party hypothesis asserts that political parties in advanced democracies no longer offer voters a real choice between ideologically distinct party platforms; instead, the polity is managed technocratically by self-serving party-political professionals.) On the face of it the two parties hold diametrically opposed philosophies, with Conservatives favouring market competition, Labour, state intervention. The higher education sector is not a natural fit for market competition, however, and so the New Public Management settled for quasi-markets in place of the traditional collegial and bureaucratic delivery systems. Quasi-markets call for quantitative performance standards and bureaucratic management practices, which is to say: heavy-handed state intervention. Under the motto 'more markets, less state', the state imposed controls. To contain public sector bloat, the state mandated a bloated audit regime. The New Public Management's quasi-markets appeal to marketeers (the Conservatives starting in the Thatcher era); its heavy-handed state intervention, to technocrats (New Labour).

Second, the US political system is highly decentralised; the same holds for the university system. The federal government controls federal student loans and federal research funding, but it is not a unitary actor, and for the most part it is gridlocked as a consequence of party-political disagreement between all the various separate powers. Public universities are controlled by the regional states, and private non-profit universities are autonomous corporations. On top of that, universities are city-based 'anchor institutions' (Birch, Perry, & Taylor, 2013). In the event that a university is threatened by regional or national political actors, chances are its city government will go to bat for it.

By way of contrast, the English political system is highly centralised. The government is generally supported by a majority in Parliament. The House of Lords, nominally a check on power, is a peripheral player. England has no

UNIVERSITAS REFORMATA SEMPER REFORMANDA

regional states that might serve as a counterweight to the central government. Outside of all-dominant London, the municipal councils are politically feeble.

Third, in the United States the boundaries between the professions are well-defined and well-respected. In a given university, shared governance pits the university administration against the academic senate, and each side knows to stay in their own lane. Academic administrators are as prone to "management fads in higher education" (Birnbaum, 2000, title) as their brethren in other parts of the world, but the contagion tends not to extend to matters of research and teaching. Academic senates famously "do not work but will not go away" (Birnbaum, 1989), but if their only function is to prevent the university administration from disturbing the professoriate's circles, they have earned their keep.

The professionalisation of the university administration further strengthens the boundary between the university's internal affairs and its external political environment. Academic administrators serve a bureaucratic buffer function vis-à-vis the outside world. Think of a concentric castle with two curtain walls (Beaumaris Castle in Wales comes to mind). Any policymaker seeking to intrude into the academic affairs of a university has to fight their way through a layer of bureaucracy before they reach the faculty defences. Good luck with that.

True, academic administrators (former university presidents and the like) and academics (higher education scholars and the like) served on the Spellings Commission alongside representatives of the for-profit higher education industry. But the Spelling Commission's reach never extended into any actual university; all of its energies were expended chattering away in the marketplace of ideas. Significantly, one of the former university presidents who served on the commission, David Ward, refused to sign the final report. One academic, Robert Zemsky, signed hesitantly only to publish a tell-all in *The Chronicle of Higher Education*, titled "The Rise and Fall of the Spellings Commission" (Zemsky, 2007).

By way of contrast, in England the boundaries between academics, academic administrators, and politicians are fuzzy. The state-sponsored quasi-markets of the New Public Management create high-powered incentives shaping personnel and programmes in the research and teaching enterprises. At the heart of the quasi-markets lie peer-driven evaluations and discretionary management decisions, with potentially devastating financial consequences for academics, academic departments and universities deemed to be underperforming. Academics are actively complicit, with academic administrators playing an enabling role, in the state-sponsored violation of university autonomy and academic freedom.

The core failure of university reform à la New Public Management is a narrative that reduces the politics of university reform to a binary clash between a political principal and an academic agent. In its stead, I offer a complex systems narrative which turns on the concept of a parallelogram, to which I turn next.

3 A Political Parallelogram of Forces

The parallelogram concept originates in the physics discipline and is commonly taught in engineering school. Two or more component forces acting on a common point differ in their magnitude and direction. They are summarised by, or can be replaced with, a resultant force. The parallelogram of forces serves as a visual aid for the geometric construction of the resultant force (see Figure 6.1).

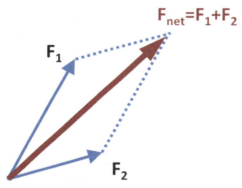

FIGURE 6.1 A parallelogram of forces consisting of a point of origin, two component forces, and a net resultant force (Source: Brews ohare, https://en.wikipedia.org/wiki/Parallelogram_of_force, under license CC BY-SA 3.0, https://creativecommons.org/licenses/by-sa/3.0/deed.en)

The parallelogram of forces is educationally valuable. It encourages the engineering student to run two kinds of simulations in their mind or on the computer. First, the student can examine how a change in the magnitude or direction of one of the component forces yields a change in the magnitude and direction of the resultant force. To this end, the student can drag around the tip of one of the component arrows. They thereby tug systematically at the whole system of arrows, and the magnitude and direction of the resultant arrow changes accordingly. Second, the student can explore how a given resultant arrow can be generated by different component arrow combinations.

UNIVERSITAS REFORMATA SEMPER REFORMANDA   147

To this end, the student can keep fixed the resultant arrow. They can then drag around the tips of the component arrows in a coordinated fashion so as to preserve the form of the parallelogram.

Because of its powerful hold on the student imagination the parallelogram of forces migrated into political science, where it serves as a metaphor for political pluralism in a competitive democracy (Fraenkel, 1964/2011). Each and every political force – no matter its strength, no matter its direction – has the power to tug at the entire political force field and influence the political outcome. The political parallelogram conveys two messages to the political science student.

First, the resultant force is generated by component forces *that look nothing like it*, in terms of their magnitude and direction. In a competitive democracy, political actors pursuing different ends can bring about a political outcome that is not desired by any one political actor. Thus, the observation of a political outcome does not necessarily imply the existence of a political actor who willed that outcome. Conversely, a policymaker seeking to bring about a particular political outcome need not impose it brute force. Instead, they can tweak the constellation of political forces so as to achieve the desired outcome indirectly.

The second message follows from one easily overlooked aspect of the parallelogram law: two or more component forces *acting on a common point* are summarised by, or can be replaced with, a resultant force. The political parallelogram can work its magic only if the political force field is properly configured. Political forces must engage one another productively for them to bring about a political outcome that is an improvement on the default outcome. Absent a focal point to their disagreement, they will bombinate in a void, and their political energy will dissipate unproductively.

By virtue of applying the parallelogram concept in my study of the university, I invoke the above two messages. The university serves as the focal point for a complex array of forces emanating from science and society. The result is scientific progress and societal change. Let me spell out the political parallelogram for the university.

4   The Isomorphic Cross

A university system is made up of individual universities, each of which stands at the centre of an isomorphic cross consisting of a vertical axis (science-university-society) and a horizontal axis (university-university-university) (see Figure 6.2). The autopoiesis icon at the centre of the isomorphic cross signifies that the individual university at once operationally closed and environmentally open. The university's internal decision making processes are protected by university autonomy even as its internal decision makers (academics, students and academic administrators) are receptive to influences emanating from the university's environment (science, society and other universities).

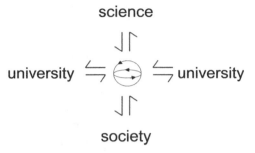

FIGURE 6.2 The individual university at the centre of the isomorphic cross

Science, the individual universities, and society are vertically isomorphic in that the constellation of the scientific disciplines matches the organisation of the faculties and the structure of the curriculum, which in turn mirrors the system of the professions (see Figure 6.3). Universities are horizontally isomorphic in that faculty organisation and curriculum structure are similar across universities.

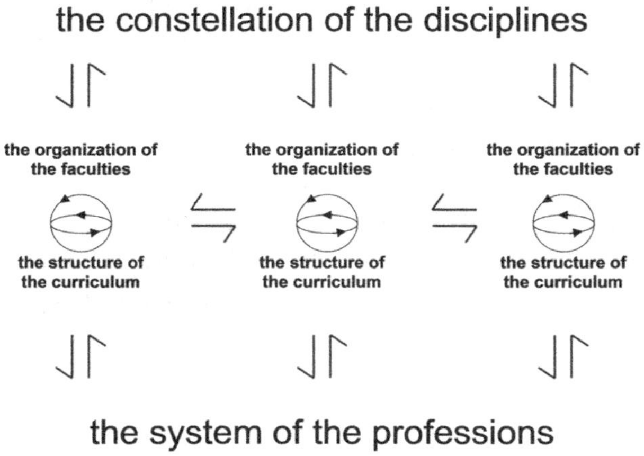

the constellation of the disciplines

the organization of the faculties	the organization of the faculties	the organization of the faculties
the structure of the curriculum	the structure of the curriculum	the structure of the curriculum

the system of the professions

FIGURE 6.3 Vertical and horizontal isomorphism

(Before I continue with my argument, let me defend my conception of science for its consistence with the medieval and German heritage of the university [Latin: *scientia*, German: *Wissenschaft*]. A discipline is defined as a science

UNIVERSITAS REFORMATA SEMPER REFORMANDA

by virtue of the fact that it has a university basis. The discipline of chemistry is represented in the university, in the form of chemistry departments; the discipline of alchemy is not. Hence chemistry is a science, and alchemy is not. Alchemy may, of course, be the subject of research or teaching in the university. For example, it is generally covered in the history of science. In this example, however, the underlying science is not alchemy but history. By my definition, physics is as much a science as theology, and when a new area of inquiry emerges, such as communications studies, once it gains a university basis, it thereby becomes a science. My conception of science contrasts with the English-language practice of treating the natural sciences as science, the humanities as not-science and the social sciences as a halfway house.[5])

Key to the university's dynamism is the individual university's position at the intersection point of two dynamic pathways, the science-university-society axis and the university-university-university axis. Let me describe the two pathways in turn, starting with the vertical axis.

Science continually generates novel ideas about the way the world works. Academics pass on these ideas – in the form of higher education – to students who, upon graduation, spill out into society. The resulting changes in societal mind-set and functioning upset the citizenry and the professions. Calls for new kinds of higher education feed into the university, which consequently reorganises itself. Science reconfigures itself to match the university's reorganisation, and it subsequently generates different kinds of novel ideas about the way the world works.

In the feedback loop described above, society pressures the university to change. In a separate feedback loop, it is science that triggers the change. The global scientific networks consist of disciplinary, sub-disciplinary and interdisciplinary clusters that are continually jostling with each other for influence and resources. Academics who are research-active in up-and-coming clusters pressure their home universities to strengthen their clusters with the creation of departments, subfields within departments, and interdisciplinary centres.

The communications between science and society run through the university. They take the form of a massively multiplayer multilogue involving academics, students and academic administrators.

Academics carry out three kinds of activities: research, teaching and governance. As scientists they generate novel ideas about the way the world works. As teachers, they pass their knowledge on to their students. As citizens of the university, they deliberate and vote on the kinds of faculty that should be hired and promoted, and they thereby influence what kinds of research and teaching will be carried out in the future. They set the curriculum, which shapes the worldview of the student body.

University organisation further serves to differentiate the faculties. For example, in the United States the pure science faculty are typically housed in the undergraduate liberal arts college, the applied science faculty, in the professional schools. Pure science academics care about internal scientific progress, that is, they solve basic puzzles that emerge out of the internal logic of science. Individually they are deeply specialised. Collectively they offer a unified liberal arts education. They thereby serve to refresh society's collective belief system. Applied science academics promote external scientific progress, that is, they apply science to solve puzzles of practical relevance to the external society. The specialisation of the academics in a given kind of professional school, such as a school of dentistry, mirrors the specialisation of the matching profession, such as dentistry. Applied science academics translate abstract understanding into concrete applications. They thereby refresh the various professional belief systems.[6]

Some academics connect directly with the citizenry and the professions. For example, a political science professor might survey voters as part of their election research, and an engineering professor might serve as a consultant on a tunnel project. As a by-product of studying society and interacting with societal actors, academics gain an understanding about society's needs and wants, and that understanding enters into research, teaching and governance.

Students serve as the primary conduit for the dissemination of ideas into the citizenry and the various professions. They further contribute to the reorganisation of the university via three mechanisms: exit, voice, and loyalty (Hirschman, 1970). (The customers of a company can respond to a decline in performance in three ways: they can exit to another company; they can voice their complaints; and they can remain loyal to the company so as to strengthen it from within.) Students choose which university to attend and decide which major to pursue. They participate in student governance and join student movements. Student alumni attend college football games and donate money to their alma mater. Students' individual choices and collective action shape the relative flourishing of the individual university's compartments and the competitive balance between the individual universities.

There are two types of administrators, academic and functional. Academic administrators, who like to call themselves university leaders, are recruited from the professoriate. They are organised as a bureaucratic hierarchy. The university president is positioned at the top; the academic deans, in the middle; and the department chairs, at the bottom. This hierarchy connects the university's political principals to the university's academics. External pressures enter at the top and filter down until they reach the academics in starkly diluted form. Academic administrators do not directly interfere with the research and teaching enterprises, but by virtue of holding the power of the purse they have a say in the reorganisation of the university, and they thereby influence what kinds of academics will be hired and promoted in the future, which foretells what will be researched and taught.

Functional administrators take on roles such as university lawyer, student mental health practitioner and information technology expert. They pick up signals from the outside world such as affirmative action lawsuits, suicide trends among young adults, and cybersecurity threats.

Now that I have covered the vertical axis linking science to society via the university let me describe the horizontal axis linking the individual universities to one another.

The higher education literature on the horizontal isomorphism of universities bifurcates into two extreme positions. World society theory emphasises global institutional convergence (Frank & Gabler, 2006; Meyer, Ramirez, Frank, & Schofer, 2007). Comparative higher education accentuates the persistence of local and national differences in higher education institutions (Schriewer, 2000). Jointly the two sides describe a dialectical tension between the forces that promote institutional convergence and the counterforces that preserve institutional diversity.

The sociology literature identifies three drivers of institutional convergence: normative, mimetic, and coercive (DiMaggio & Powell, 1983). Let me describe each of the three in turn.

Academics and academic administrators impose their professional norms on their home institutions by virtue of ensuring that their university's faculty organisation and curriculum structure mirror the constellation of disciplines in science, the system of the professions in society, and other universities' faculty organisation and curriculum structure.

Universities mimic each others' faculty organisation and curriculum structure by virtue of benchmarking their own performance against the performance of similar institutions; competing for academics, students and academic administrators; and seeking to move up in university rankings.

Universities respond similarly to common coercive forces such as cost pressures, demographic trends and management fads.

The three drivers of institutional convergence – normative, mimetic and coercive – run up against three drivers of institutional diversity. First and foremost, universities exist in places, and they differ by their locations (the city they are located in), and their national affiliations (the nation state they belong to) (Lohmann, 2019a). Second and third, they are vertically and horizontally differentiated (Clark, 1983; Sørensen, 1970; Teichler, 2007).

Science is universal, but the faculty organisation and curriculum structure in any given university reflect local and national agendas. The University of California, Los Angeles features aerospace engineering and Chicana/o studies;

the University of Alaska, Fairbanks, mining engineering and Eskimo studies. Scottish and British history loom large at the University of Edinburgh; Taiwanese and Chinese history, at National Taiwan University.

Individual universities, for local and national reasons, experiment with faculty organisation and curriculum structure. Some of these experiments spread to other universities, and some are adopted universally.[7] For example, women's studies emerged out of nowhere to become a global juggernaut (Wotipka & Ramirez, 2008). For starters, individual faculty at scattered universities offered courses. Then a couple of universities launched formal programmes. The movement gradually gained momentum, and all of a sudden there was a stampede. Today no self-respecting university can afford *not* to have a women's studies programme.

A national university system is vertically differentiated if its universities are ordered on a better-worse scale according to some criterion such as faculty research productivity or the competitiveness of the student admissions process. Vertical differentiation does not inherently imply differences in faculty organisation and curriculum structure. Universities positioned differently in the institutional pecking order may differ, however, in their willingness to innovate. For example, highly ranked universities seeking to reinforce their position may embrace emerging disciplines, and lowly ranked universities seeking to improve their position may follow the example of their betters. Then again, at the top of the food chain the competitive pressures may be too intense for controversial new disciplines to gain a toehold, in which case innovation may be nurtured in the protective niches provided by the merely very good universities.

A national university system is horizontally differentiated if it houses a variety of higher education institutions such as research universities, specialised teaching institutions, liberal arts colleges and community colleges. Horizontal differentiation implies differences in faculty organisation and curriculum structure. Such institutional diversity promotes local experimentation, but it can undercut the dissemination of successful experiments, simply because the various kinds of institutions are too dissimilar for them to attend to each others' experiments. With the right kinds of connections between the various institutions, however, innovations can ricochet around the higher education system.

For example, in the United States the commitment to a liberal arts education, which is strong in the liberal arts colleges, extends to the community colleges even though the two kinds of institutions pay little if any attention to each other. They are indirectly connected, however, through the private non-profit and public universities. In the private non-profit sector, liberal arts colleges compete for students with universities, and hence the two kinds of institutions attend to each others' course and programme offerings. Meanwhile, world-class research universities – private non-profit and public alike – are subject to global pressures encouraging institutional convergence in faculty organisation and curriculum structure. Finally, in the public sector, state governments promote student transfers between universities and community colleges, and the two types of institutions are consequently forced to coordinate their course and programme offerings. It is thus that the circle is closed, enabling the liberal arts colleges to exercise an influence on the community colleges.

Let me now revisit the facile university reform narrative to assess the truth content of its three claims about the university: *semper reformanda*; antithetical to change; and punctuated equilibrium.

4.1   *Semper Reformanda*

The institution of the university is naturally and inherently dynamist as a result of the dynamic interplay between science, the university, and society, on the one hand, and the dialectical tension between the forces promoting institutional convergence and the counterforces preserving institutional diversity, on the other hand.

The individual university's position at the centre of the isomorphic cross implies that science, society and other universities are constantly prodding it to modify its faculty organisation and curriculum structure. Each university responds somewhat idiosyncratically to the prodding. Some of these idiosyncratic innovations take off. Upon their universal adoption, they force systematic reconfigurations of science and society. The changes that upset science and society inspire the next round of university prodding. *Universitates reformatae semper reformandae sunt* (Latin: the reformed universities continue to be in need of reform).

Individual universities are continually in need of reform precisely because they are change agents. The *semper reformanda* property of the universitity is a consequence of the university's institutional dynamism, and hence cannot be read as evidence that universities are change-resistant.

5   Antithetical to Change

The complaint about the change-resistance of universities is not so much a complaint about academics being slow to generate novel ideas in their research, nor is it a complaint about academics failing to pass on novel ideas in their teaching (though there is some of that). Instead, the complaint is centrally geared towards the one activity academics undertake collectively, namely, governance.

The glacial pace of faculty deliberations is one irritant. Laypeople (i.e. people with no political science expertise) generally underestimate how long it takes for people who disagree with one another to come to an agreement. Politics is "a strong and slow boring of hard boards" (Weber, 1919/2009, p. 128). It takes time for arguments to be heard and for people to be persuaded. If this is true for legislatures, it is true for universities with a vengeance. Unlike legislators, academics are deeply and diversely specialised. Faculty disagree within subfields within departments, they disagree across subfields within departments, they disagree across departments, and they disagree across the divisions of the university. There are all sorts of other lines of disagreement. Young Turks disagree with the Old Guard. Academics who favour quantitative methods disagree with faculty who favour qualitative methods. Lumpers (who emphasise commonalities) disagree with splitters (who accentuate distinctions). I could go on forever.

The problem of disagreement extends beyond the individual university, for universities need to coordinate the changes to their faculty organisation and curriculum structure with one another. It is not enough for academics at one university, or even a couple of universities, to be willing to embrace change. It has to be common knowledge that the academics at close-to-all universities are willing to embrace change. Creating common knowledge when everybody involved is assembled together in one room, such as a courtroom or a legislative chamber, is easy (Chwe, 2001). Creating common knowledge when the academics involved are scattered around the world is hard, and it takes time. At the end of the day, even if all academics are in agreement, the coordination process still has ways to go, for the changes in the university must be matched by corresponding changes in science and society.

Academic tenure is another irritant. (Not all national university systems feature academic tenure, but mature systems generally have some institution in place by which academics enjoy security of employment and are subject to low-powered incentives.) An academic, at the time they appointed to an initial university position, is on the cutting edge of their discipline. Thirty years later, at the time of the academic's retirement, their knowledge is obsolete. Hence the common quip that science can advance no faster than one funeral at a time (Planck, 1948, p. 22).

One solution would be for universities to hire young academics on the cutting edge and then fire them five years later in order to replace them with the next batch of young academics on the cutting edge. Such a hire-and-fire regime would be counterproductive, however. Academics carry out tasks – research, teaching and governance – that require them to hold certain attitudes and values, including curiosity about the way the world works, love for students and feelings of loyalty towards their home institution. Attitudes and values of this kind can flourish only in an environment with security of employment.

Academic tenure comes with downsides such as academics shirking their duties. One solution would be for universities to set high-powered incentives for their academics. Such a carrot-and-stick regime would be counterproductive, however, for two reasons. First, the tasks academics carry out are complex. Second, because of deep specialisation academic performance is unobservable or unverifiable by outsiders (or, equivalently, observation and verification are prohibitively costly). Hence, any high-powered incentive scheme is necessarily simplistic and incomplete. If a university were to impose and enforce some simplistic and incomplete measure of faculty performance, some academics would stop carrying out their complex tasks and instead play to the measure, and they would be rewarded. Other academics would continue to carry out the complex tasks, they would fail to measure up, and they would consequently be punished. Let this regime run on for a while, and it will result in unfortunate selection effects. The kind of academics who play to the measure will flourish, and the kind of academics who carry out the complex tasks no matter what will fall by the wayside. The university will end up a hollow shell, with its academics merely going through the motions of researching and teaching.

The downsides of academic tenure are readily apparent, but the solution is not to get rid of academic tenure altogether. Instead, the solution is to improve professorial functioning at the margin. For example, a university can embed its academics in departments featuring overlapping generations, thereby forcing young, middle-aged and old faculty to interact with one another in matters of university governance. In this setting, ambitious researchers, dedicated teachers and committed administrators complement each other. Academics can switch gears productively in the course of their life cycle as their research declines, their teaching experience expands and their institutional loyalty cumulates.

University autonomy is yet another source of irritation. A university's political principal orders it to change, and the university disregards the order. Implicit in this complaint is the flawed principal-agent model. A university is not supposed to follow the orders of its political principal. It is meant to juggle, and ultimately integrate, the cross-cutting pressures emanating from its entire environment, which includes science, society and other universities. University autonomy protects the juggling act and the integration function.

University autonomy comes with downsides such as democratically elected politicians being unable to impose their legitimate will on their universities. Once again the solution is not to get rid of university autonomy altogether, but to manage the downsides at the margin. For example, it helps to profession-alise the university administration and to have academic administrators run the university in shared governance with academics. The result is to improve the university's responsiveness to political pressures without destroying the institution.

Academic tenure and university autonomy are not defects; they are defences (Lohmann, 2004b). Defects are unambiguously counterproductive. The policy prescription for a defect is to eliminate it. Defences are productive, but they come with costly trade-offs. The policy prescription for a defence is to tweak the system with the goal of improving the benefit-cost trade-off at the margin.

The university is a complex system, and it can be difficult to distinguish between the university's defects and its defences. It takes a deep understanding of the institution of the university and detailed knowledge of a particular university to surgically eliminate a defect without inadvertantly destroying a defence. If the political surgeon lacks the requisite knowledge, the policy prescription is to do nothing.

6 Punctuated Equilibrium

Paleobiologists studying the fossil record found that new species appear suddenly rather than emerging gradually. Punctuated equilibrium theory explains this finding (Eldredge & Gould, 1972). In compactly connected large populations there is too much interbreeding for a new species to emerge. If some members of the species split off to lead a niche existence, the changes they undergo will create a survival advantage, and their geographical isolation will ensure that the changes have a chance to stick so that a new non-interbreeding species can arise.

This paleobiological theory has implications for university studies if we substitute animal species with scientific disciplines. Novel clusters in the global scientific networks have a hard time breaking free of the established disciplines to form new disciplines. After all, a discipline is called a discipline for good reason: it disciplines its followers to stay within the confines of what the discipline considers acceptable methodologically and substantively. Institutional diversity is the solution to this conundrum. Universities, for local and national reasons, provide protective niches for emerging disciplines.

There is one critical difference between paleobiology and university studies, however. In paleobiology a new species can emerge in a niche and stay put in that niche. In university studies, after a promising candidate for a new discipline has found a departmental home in a couple of universities, for a

UNIVERSITAS REFORMATA SEMPER REFORMANDA

prospective discipline to become an actual discipline, universities worldwide must establish supporting departments. The process by which universities worldwide adopt innovations is subject to revolutionary bandwagons and information cascades (Lohmann, 2019b).[8]

A revolutionary bandwagon results when the costs and benefits of adopting an innovation, from the perspective of the individual university, depend on the number of universities that have adopted the innovation. Adopting an innovation is costly if the individual university is an early adopter. As the number of adopters increases, the costs of adoption decrease and the benefits of adoption increase. Once the innovation is close-to-universally adopted, not only has it become beneficial to adopt the innovation; now it is costly *not* to adopt the innovation. With this cost-benefit structure in place, universities can be trapped in a change-resistant equilibrium where no university has incentives to make the first move. Institutional diversity solves this collective action problem. Some universities, for local or national reasons, adopt the innovation. As a result of their adoptions, other universities join the club. All of a sudden a critical mass of adoptions is reached, and there is a global stampede.

An information cascade is similar to the revolutionary bandwagon, except that the underlying mechanism is informational. A university experiments with an innovation. The success or failure of the experiment serves as a signal to other universities as to whether the innovation is universally beneficial. Experimentation is costly. A couple of universities, for local or national reasons, are willing to bear the cost of experimenting, and to the extent that their experiments are mostly successful, they encourage a couple more universities to pile on with experiments of their own. All of a sudden a critical mass of successes is reached, and there is a global stampede.

Revolutionary bandwagons and information cascades give rise to the punctuated equilibrium pattern: nothing much happens for the longest time, and then all of a sudden there is a stampede. The pattern does not by itself constitute evidence that universities are change-resistant. Instead, the pattern can emerge as a result of the collective action problem faced by universities worldwide. It is consistent with university dynamism.

The political science literature picked up on punctuated equilibrium theory to explain why policy is often stable for long periods of time and then all of a sudden there is a major policy change (Baumgartner & Jones, 1993). Paleobiology and political science share in common the punctuated equilibrium pattern, but the political mechanisms are distinctly different.

One such mechanism is bounded rationality. Bureaucratic subsystems engage in parallel processing of routine political demands, but big ticket items must be decided by elected politicians, such as the US president or members of the US Congress, who engage in serial processing. Here, the limited attention span of human beings kicks in, and the decision makers must prioritise which policy issue to address. Hence we observe no reaction for the longest time and then all of a sudden, when the issue makes it onto the presidential or Congressional agenda, we observe a reaction.

Another mechanism consists of political and bureaucratic institutions having friction built into them so that signals favouring action must cumulate before the leadership will spring into action. Hence the system underreacts for the longest time, and then all of a sudden, once the signals have sufficiently cumulated, the system springs into action.

Yet another such mechanism ties in with the concept of a policy window (Kingdon, 1984). Just the right constellation of political actors has to be in place for legislation to pass. Policy ideas develop gradually, but policy windows open only occasionally. The result is the punctuated equilibrium pattern.

Individually or collectively these three mechanisms explain why universities change in fits and bursts. The punctuated equilibrium pattern does not, however, originate with the universities themselves, but with the political principals tasked with regulating the universities. Once again, the punctuated equilibrium pattern does not constitute evidence that universities are change-resistant.

The facile narrative about universities is flawed. It does not follow, however, that there is no such thing as university failure. Let me return to my two cases – the United States and the United Kingdom – to lay out what university failure looks like and to spell out what follows for university reform.

7 The Machine Never Stops

In the year 2016 the United Kingdom and the United States were shocked to the core. On 23 June the British electorate unexpectedly supported the withdrawal of the United Kingdom from the European Union. On 8 November, the American electorate unexpectedly elevated Donald Trump to the presidency.

The votes were geographically distinctive. Scotland and Northern Ireland elected to remain in the European Union, and England and Wales voted to leave. Within England, London favoured Remain, and the rest of England (the 'London hinterland' if you so will) cast its lot with Brexit. In the United States, the East and West Coasts (the so-called 'coastal elites') rejected Trump, and the nation's interior (also known as 'flyover country') supported Trump.

Brexit and Trump revealed toxic cleavages in the United Kingdom (once again England is the problem child) and the United States that go beyond

UNIVERSITAS REFORMATA SEMPER REFORMANDA

geography. The cleavages are highly correlated, which gives rise to a polarisation into two tribal camps (see Table 6.1).

TABLE 6.1   Societal polarisation in the age of Trump and Brexit

ANTI BREXIT	PRO BREXIT
London	London hinterland
ANTI TRUMP	PRO TRUMP
coastal elites	flyover country
the educated	the uneducated
experts	laypeople
the professional class	the working class
people with prospects	the left behind
women	men
people of color	white people
young people	old people
the people from anywhere	the people from somewhere
urbanites	ruralites
cosmopolitans	nativists
progressives	conservatives
liberals	authoritarians
PRO UNIVERSITY	ANTI UNIVERSITY

The universities in England and the United States are hardly neutral bystanders in this conflict. They support the anti-Brexit-anti-Trump side and reject the pro-Brexit-pro-Trump side. Their stance is reciprocated. Universities are tolerated by the anti-Brexit-anti-Trump side and resented by the pro-Brexit-pro-Trump side.

This, I contend, is what university failure looks like. One central purpose of a national university system is to integrate a people in the form of an "imagined political community" (Anderson, 1983, p. 7; see also Gellner, 1983; Lohmann, 2019a). Amidst all of the university reform flurries of the preceding decades, the two university systems – English and American – failed in this most basic task.

Over the years, as the societal divide built up, the universities were not passive vessels that happened to agree with one side, but change agents who actively implanted a worldview – let us call it neoliberalism for short – in the minds of the citizenry and the professions. Now society is upset with the results, and it is pushing back. The ball is in the court of the universities: as much as they are part and parcel of the problem, they are key to the solution, which entails replacing the old worldview with a new worldview.

The neoliberal view of research celebrates cosmopolitanism, world-class university rankings and the vertical differentiation of national university systems. In the future, the pendulum needs to swing back to provincialism, nationalism and egalitarianism. Universities must take responsibility for the well-being of the cities and nation states that harbour them, and they must address the plight of the rural hinterlands. For a nation state to flourish it is arguably more important for every part of the country to have access to a decent university than for some parts to have excellent universities even as other parts are university deserts.

The neoliberal view of teaching favours the natural sciences, technology transfer and human capital development. In the future, the pendulum needs to swing back to the social sciences and the humanities. Universities must revive the idea of the liberal arts and strengthen their capacities for offering civic education. The teaching of history is central to this effort.

The neoliberal view of governance relies on academic administrators, quantitative performance standards, contingent faculty and political intrusion into academic affairs. In the future, the pendulum needs to swing back to shared governance, with academic administrators and academics jointly modifying the faculty organisation and curriculum structure even as academics – and academics alone – call the shots in matters of research and teaching. Academic tenure, which combines security of employment with low-powered incentives, must be revived. University autonomy is a non-negotiable feature of the university.

I advance these proposals in the spirit of 'and' rather than 'either-or'. For example, when I push for more provincialism and nationalism, I am not thereby arguing that we should give up on cosmopolitanism. A university needs to be provincial, national, and cosmopolitan. There is nothing wrong with cosmopolitanism per se; what is wrong at this moment in time is an excessive cosmopolitanism that is insufficiently balanced by provincialism and nationalism. Once universities correct the excess, no doubt sometime in the future provincialism and nationalism will develop excesses of their own, and at that point in time, the universities will have to strengthen their cosmopolitanism. The university is, after all, *semper reformanda*.

Indeed, the neoliberal worldview itself was a course correction relative to what came before, and now it in turn is due for a course correction. The university is the vehicle by which such course corrections occur.

In conclusion, let me draw a distinction between university reform at the surface level and university reform deep down. The surface consists of the

UNIVERSITAS REFORMATA SEMPER REFORMANDA

university's faculty organisation and curriculum structure. It is at this level that the individual universities are *reformatae semper reformandae*. Deep down, the institution of the university is constant. It is this constancy that powers the university's dynamism at the surface level. Deep down university reform is about defending the inherited idea of the university as it manifests itself in the form of the political parallelogram.

Notes

1   Casper is a former president of Stanford University.
2   This saying, in various formulations, has been attributed to – among others – Woodrow Wilson, who served as president of Princeton University before he took on the position of US president; Robert Hutchins, a former president of the University of Chicago; and Derek Bok, a former president of Harvard University (Kerr, 2001, p. 396; Logue, 2017, p. 54; Summers, 2012, p. ED26).
3   Hefferlin was Co-Director of the Academic Administration Project at the Ellis H. Phillips Foundation. Schlesinger's original quote reads: "Changing the direction of an agency while it continues its day-to-day operations is one of the hardest tricks in government; it has been likened to performing surgery on a man while he hauls a trunk upstairs" (Schlesinger, 1965, p. 595).
4   Popularised by Karl Barth, the saying *ecclesia semper reformanda est* (Latin: the church is continually in need of reform) and its longer version *ecclesia reformata semper reformanda est* (Latin: the reformed church continues to be in need of reform) is popular in Reformed and Presbyterian churches. It allegedly originates with Augustine (Mahlmann, 2010).
5   In the English-language world, C. P. Snow popularised the idea of the two cultures, namely, science (by which he means the natural sciences) and the humanities (Snow, 1959).
6   This line of reasoning is inspired by Immanuel Kant's argument in *The Conflict of the Faculties* (Kant, 1798/1979).
7   This line of reasoning is inspired by the 'states as policy experiments' argument, which is routinely invoked in the United States (Volden, 2006).
8   Susanne Lohmann's review essay juxtaposes Timur Kuran's revolutionary bandwagons with Lohmann's information cascades (Kuran, 1989, 1995; Lohmann, 1994).

References

Anderson, B. (1983). *Imagined communities: Reflections on the origin and spread of nationalism*. London: Verso.

Baumgartner, F., & Jones, B. D. (1993). *Agendas and instability in American politics.* Chicago, IL: University of Chicago Press.

Birch, E., Perry, D. C., & Taylor Jr., H. L. (2013). Universities as anchor institutions. *Journal of Higher Education Outreach and Engagement, 17*(3), 7–15.

Birnbaum, R. (1988). *How colleges work: The cybernetics of academic organization and leadership.* San Francisco, CA: Jossey-Bass.

Birnbaum, R. (1989). The latent organizational functions of the academic senate: Why faculty senates do not work but will not go away. *Journal of Higher Education, 60*(4), 423–443.

Birnbaum, R. (2000). *Management fads in higher education: Where they come from, what they do, why they fail.* San Francisco, CA: Jossey-Bass.

Carlin, J. F. (1999, November 5). Restoring sanity to an academic world gone mad. *The Chronicle of Higher Education,* p. A76.

Chwe, M. (2001). *Rational ritual: Culture, coordination and common knowledge.* Princeton, NJ: Princeton University Press.

Clark, B. (1983). *The higher education system: Academic organization in cross-national perspective.* Berkeley, CA: University of California Press.

Cohn, B., & Robinson, M. (1999, November/December). What he did. *Stanford Alumni Magazine.* Retrieved September 28, 2018, from https://alumni.stanford.edu/get/page/magazine/article/?article_id=40312

Collini, S. (2013, October 24). Sold out. *London Review of Books,* 3–12.

DiMaggio, P. J., & Powell, W. W. (1983). The iron cage revisited: Institutional isomorphism and collective rationality. In P. J. DiMaggio & W. W. Powell (Eds.), *The new institutionalism in organizational analysis* (pp. 147–160). Chicago, IL: University of Chicago Press.

Eldredge, N., & Gould, S. J. (1972). *Punctuated equilibria: An alternative to phyletic gradualism.* In T. J. M. Schopf (Ed.), *Models in paleobiology* (pp. 82–115). San Francisco, CA: Freeman.

Fraenkel, E. (2011). Strukturdefekte der Demokratie und deren Überwindung. In E. Fraenkel (Eds.), *Deutschland und die westlichen Demokratien* (9th expanded ed., pp. 91–113). Baden-Baden, Germany: Nomos. (Original published 1964)

Frank, D. J., & Gabler, J. (2006). *Reconstructing the university: Worldwide shifts in academia in the 20th century.* Stanford, CA: Stanford University Press.

Gellner, E. (1983). *Nations and nationalism.* Ithaca, NY: Cornell University Press.

Hanau, A. (1928). Die Prognose der Schweinepreise. *Vierteljahrshefte zur Konjunkturforschung, 7*(special issue), 5–41.

Hefferlin, J. B. L. (1972). Hauling academic trunks. In C. U. Walker (Ed.), *Elements involved in academic change* (pp. 1–10). Washington, DC: Association of Academic Colleges.

Hirschman, A. O. (1970). *Exit, voice, and loyalty: Responses to decline in firms, organizations, and states.* Cambridge, MA: Harvard University Press.

UNIVERSITAS REFORMATA SEMPER REFORMANDA

Hood, C. (1991). A public management for all seasons? *Public Administration, 69*(1), 3–19.

Kant, I. (1979). *Der Streit der Fakultäten* [*The conflict of the faculties*]. New York, NY: Abaris Books. (Original published 1798)

Katz, R. S., & Mair, P. (1995). Changing models of party organization and party democracy. *Party Politics, 1*(1), 5–31.

Kerr, C. (2001). *The gold and the blue: A personal memoir of the University of California, 1949–1967: Academic triumphs* (Vol. 1). Berkeley, CA: University of California Press.

Kingdon, J. W. (1984). *Agendas, alternatives, and public policies.* Boston, MA: Little, Brown.

Kittelson, J. M., & Transue, P. J. (1984). *Rebirth, reform, and resilience: Universities in transition 1300–1700.* Columbus, OH: Ohio State University Press.

Kuran, T. (1989). Sparks and prarie fires: A theory of unanticipated political revolution. *Public Choice, 61*(1), 41–74.

Kuran, T. (1995). *Private truths, public lies: The social consequences of preference falsification.* Cambridge, MA: Harvard University Press.

Logue, A. W. (2017). *Credits and conflict at the City University of New York: Pathways to reform.* Princeton, NJ: Princeton University Press.

Lohmann, S. (1994). Dynamics of informational cascades: The Monday demonstrations in Leipzig, East Germany, 1989–1991. *World Politics, 47*(1), 42–101.

Lohmann, S. (2004a). Can't the university be more like business. *Economics of Governance, 5*(1), 9–27.

Lohmann, S. (2004b). Darwinian medicine for the university. In R. G. Ehrenberg (Ed.), *Governing academia* (pp. 71–90). Ithaca, NY: Cornell University Press.

Lohmann, S. (2006, September 25–29). *The public research university as a complex adaptive system.* Paper presented at the European Conference on Complex Systems, University of Oxford. Retrieved September 28, 2018, from http://www.cabdyn.ox.ac.uk/complexity_PDFs/ECCS06/Conference_Proceedings/PDF/p88.pdf

Lohmann, S. (2019a). *Genius of place: Universities and the fate of nations* (Unpublished manuscript). University of California, Los Angeles, CA.

Lohmann, S. (2019b). Bandwagon effects, information cascades, and the power in numbers. In L. Suhay, B. Grofman, & A. Trechsel (Eds.), *The Oxford handbook of electoral persuasion.* Oxford: Oxford University Press.

Mahlmann, T. (2010). 'Ecclesia semper reformanda'. Eine historische Aufklärung. Neue Bearbeitung. In T. Johansson, R. Kolb, & J. A. Steiger (Eds.), *Hermeneutica Sacra. Studien zur Auslegung der Heiligen Schrift im 16. und 17. Jahrhundert* (pp. 381–442). Berlin, Germany: Walter De Gruyter.

Meyer, J. W., Ramirez, F. O., Frank, D. J., & Schofer, E. (2007). Higher education as an institution. In P. J. Gumport (Ed.), *Sociology of higher education: Contributions and their contexts* (pp. 187–221). Baltimore, MD: Johns Hopkins University Press.

Persaud, S. (2009/4). *"Closed in an open sort of way": Luhmann's autopoiesis and the border control of law*. The Westminster International Law & Theory Centre Online Working Papers. Retrieved December 12, 2018, from https://www.westminster.ac.uk/file/12936/download?token=mMsenimz

Planck, M. (1948). *Wissenschaftliche Selbstbiographie*. Leipzig, Germany: Johann Ambrosius Barth Verlag.

Rudersdorf, M. (2016). *Universitas semper reformanda. Die beharrende Kraft des Humanismus. Zu einem Grundkonflikt neuzeitlicher Universitätsgeschichte im Jahrhundert der Reformation*. Stuttgart, Germany: S. Hirzel Verlag.

Schlesinger Jr., A. (1965). *A thousand days: John F. Kennedy in the White House*. Boston, MA: Houghton Mifflin.

Schriewer, J. (2003). Multiple internationalities: The emergence of a world-level educational ideology and the persistence of indigenous world-views. In C. Charle, J. Schriewer, & P. Wagner (Eds.), *Transnational intellectual networks: Forms of academic knowledge and the search for cultural identities* (pp. 473–533). New York, NY: Campus.

Snow, C. P. (1959). *The two cultures and the scientific revolution*. New York, NY: Cambridge University Press.

Sørensen, A. B. (1970). Organizational differentiation of students and educational opportunity. *Sociology of Education, 43*(4), 355–376.

Spellings Commission. (2006, September). *A test of leadership: Charting the future of U.S. higher education: A report of the commission appointed by Secretary of Education Margaret Spellings*. Washington, DC: US Department of Education.

Summers, L. (2012, January 22). The 21st century education. *The New York Times*, Section Education Life, p. ED26.

Teichler, U. (2007). *Higher education systems: Conceptual frameworks, comparative perspectives, and empirical findings*. Rotterdam, The Netherlands: Sense Publishers.

Tyler, W. S. (1857, February). Colleges: Their place among American institutions. An address before the society for the promotion of collegiate and theological education at the West, delivered in Bridgeport, CT, on November 12, 1856. (Reprinted from the *American Journal of Education and College Review* 1867. New York, NY: Calkins & Stiles)

Volden, C. (2006). States as policy laboratories: Emulating success in the children's health insurance program. *American Journal of Political Science, 50*(2), 294–312.

Weber, M. (2009). *Essays in sociology*. London: Routledge. (Original published 1919)

Wotipka, C. M., & Ramirez, F. O. (2008). Women's studies as a global innovation. In D. P. Baker & A. W. Wiseman (Eds.), *The worldwide transformation of higher education* (pp. 89–110). Bingley: Emerald Group Publishing.

Zemsky, R. (2007, January 26). The rise and fall of the Spellings Commission. *The Chronicle of Higher Education, 53*(21), B6–B9.

CHAPTER 7

Student Protests and Higher Education Transformation: A South African Case Study

Magda Fourie-Malherbe and Anneke Müller

Abstract

In 2015 and 2016 South African higher education was shaken by countrywide student protests that became known as the #FeesMustFall student movement. Against a backdrop of the history of student protests in the country, this chapter outlines the main issues that drove the protest movement with a view to highlighting the intersectionality and complexity of the issues. The focus is then narrowed to how #FeesMustFall played out at one particular university, demonstrating the similarities and differences within the broader movement. In addition, the authors employed document analysis to highlight the university management's responses to six issues raised by the students. Although there were some wins in terms of 'free' higher education and amendments to the university's language policy, the lasting effects of #FeesMustFall on institutional transformation could not conclusively be shown. The analysis also shows that, in turbulent times, the interface between external and internal contexts of higher education institutions can become very disruptive.

Keywords

student protests – institutional transformation – social justice – financial need – language policy – institutional culture – power relations – decolonisation

1   Introduction

Higher education cannot be seen separately or in isolation from global geopolitical events and national socio-economic conditions. This was vividly illustrated by widespread student protests, known as the #FeesMustFall movement (FMF) that rocked South African society in 2015 and 2016.

© KONINKLIJKE BRILL NV, LEIDEN, 2020 | DOI: 10.1163/9789004422582_008

Contemplating the development of higher education over the past century, it is clear that major changes have occurred because of, among other things, social changes (exemplified by the massification of higher education that followed on the democratisation of societies), changes in the labour market (resulting in growing attention to the development of graduate attributes), the shift to a knowledge economy (leading to increased emphasis on postgraduate studies), and technological advances (with a concomitant rise in blended learning and Massive Online Open Courses – so-called MOOCs). All of these factors have led to regions and countries globally seeing a boom in their uptake of higher education.

Yet, the potential positive effect of this growing uptake of higher education globally is marred by dissent in and dissatisfaction with higher education. Some malcontents still regard higher education as being in an 'elitist ivory tower' (Dlamini, 2018; Sekulich, 2017). Increasingly the 'consumers' of higher education are raising questions about the 'value for money' that higher education affords (Giroux, 2002). In addition, in many higher education institutions across the world both staff and students are feeling progressively alienated from their institutions, with their voices not being heard, and a growing conviction that the academic project is being sacrificed in the interest of 'balancing the books' (Case, 2008; Macfarlane, 2005; Mann, 2001). Many of the above views were evidenced in protests over the past few years on university campuses in Chile (Bellei, Cabalin, & Orellana, 2014), the United States (Cooke, 2018), and the Netherlands (Gray, 2015), to name but a few. In South Africa, during 2015 and 2016, university campuses became political battlegrounds, when the higher education system came virtually to a standstill due to countrywide student protests for free higher education (Badat, 2016; Booysen, 2016; CSVR, 2016).

Since the country became a democracy in 1994, many changes in South African higher education have occurred at the systemic level. The number of higher education institutions has been reduced from 36 to 26 through a process of mergers and incorporations, the number of students in the public system has virtually doubled from 495,356 in 1994 to 975,836 in 2016 (CHE, 2018; Mathebula & Calitz, 2018), and the participation rate of African students, who were the most underrepresented in higher education under apartheid, has grown from 9% in 1993 (Bunting, 2002) to 16% in 2016 (CHE, 2018). At the institutional level, however, transformation has been uneven and more difficult to achieve.

Fourie (1999) points out that transition, referring to changes in the political, economic, social, cultural and educational structures of society, often leads to institutional transformation. "This implies profound and dramatic changes in institutions, sometimes occurring as a result of turbulence inside institutions or, more frequently, resulting from changes in their external environment" (Fourie, 1999, p. 276). In South Africa, following the country's transition to a democratic society, the transformation of, among others, higher education institutions has been an ongoing process. Yet, at many South African universities transformation has not been easy, nor has it satisfied the criteria of being not only "a comprehensive (i.e. encompassing) process, but also a radical one (i.e. going to the roots)" (Fourie, 1999, p. 276). Drawing on this conceptualisation of institutional transformation, the main research question for this study is: what were the implications of the FMF movement, as a manifestation of turbulence both inside and outside institutions, for institutional transformation of South African universities?

We argue that the issues raised by students as part of the FMF campaign should be regarded as vital areas of institutional transformation. What we sought to investigate was whether and how these issues in the case university were addressed at the institutional level as part of transformation, with a view to developing a better understanding of institutional transformation, particularly in a climate of external and internal political turbulence. From the research question above, the following sub-questions were derived:

- What were the implications of FMF for Stellenbosch University at the time?
- How did the institution respond to the issues raised in FMF?
- How was institutional transformation at the time being enacted and how was it planned for the future?
- What did this contribute to our understanding of institutional transformation in higher education?

To answer the research question and sub-questions we first present a brief overview of student protests in South Africa, followed by a more detailed account of the FMF protests. Secondly, we narrow our focus to one institution, presented in the form of a case study, and we explain how FMF played out at this institution, with a particular focus on six crucial issues highlighted by the protests. Subsequently we analyse management responses to the issues raised by student protesters by means of a document analysis of institutional policies and speeches of the current vice-chancellor (president) of the university. This analysis illuminates the power struggles occurring within a politicised higher education environment and the intersectionality of the transformation issues South African higher education institutions are grappling with. This research sheds light on one of the major upheavals in South African post-apartheid higher education, with particular emphasis on the implications for a future transformative journey for the case institution and its stakeholders.

2 Student Protests in South Africa as a Manifestation of an Ongoing Struggle for Social Justice

Even though the FMF student movement of 2015 and 2016 was not the first or only student protest that South Africans witnessed after the demise of apartheid, the wide-spread and sustained nature of the protests characterised them as "especially dramatic and distinctive" (Badat, 2016, p. 1). Whereas ostensibly the main concern of the movement was the escalation of student fees, we posit that the student protests were primarily a manifestation of an ongoing struggle for social justice in post-apartheid South African society. This is also argued by Mathebula and Calitz (2018, p. 185): "In our analysis, the #FeesMustFall movement is part of the post-apartheid class struggle in which black youth across the socio-economic spectrum are resisting institutions and policies that fail to adequately address the widening gap between socio-economic elites, the middle class and the poor". February (2018) relates the student protests more directly to the government of the day by contending that "the #FeesMustFall movement was a form of rebellion against the ANC government itself" (p. 119).

From literature, newspaper articles, social media postings and personal conversations with students, it has become clear that the current student generation is disillusioned with the 1994 political settlement and its failure to deliver on its promises of equality for all. In addition, the lack of profound change in the structure and culture of universities, including the core area of the curriculum, has deepened the sense of alienation that particularly black students experience. Issues such as established institutional traditions and patriarchal practices that inhibit student agency have also been highlighted.

Student unrest has a long history in South Africa. In apartheid South Africa student protests were evidently about opposing a political system more than about educational issues per se (Badat, 2016; Ndlovu, 2016). FMF has often been compared with the 1976 Soweto student uprising, and not without reason. This was the biggest student protest during apartheid, and contrary to FMF, involved not university students, but mainly schoolchildren. When Afrikaans alongside English was made compulsory as the medium of instruction in schools, it constituted "the tipping point in a long line of education reforms introduced by the apartheid government that disadvantaged African youth" (Cooke, 2018), and black schoolchildren mobilised in all earnest (Mkhabela, 2016). In Soweto, schoolchildren began marching peacefully on 16 June 1976, but were met by a strong police presence. The news of the police opening fire on a group of unarmed young people in Soweto soon spread and protest actions flared up elsewhere in the country. As a result, many student leaders were detained. This incident fuelled the liberation movement and students became even more politicised. Cooke (2018) describes this as "an important step toward the dismantling of apartheid".

The end of apartheid did not mean the end of student protests. Post 1994 student protests still sporadically occurred, mainly at poorer or historically disadvantaged universities, and often in reaction to financial and/or academic exclusions (Davids & Waghid, 2016). Student accommodation was another contentious issue at these mainly rural and often under-resourced institutions. These protests were much more localised and related primarily to institutional issues, characterised by students as the poor quality of education received at the historically disadvantaged institutions and the lack of effort or ability of university managements to bring about improvements. The protests on those campuses were, however, barely noticed and received scant attention in the media (CSVR, 2016). This changed dramatically in 2015.

3 #FeesMustFall Student Protest Movement, 2015 and Beyond

In January 2015 tension started building up at the University of Witwatersrand (WITS) when students could not register because they had not yet received financial aid. #TransformWits was launched.

On 9 March 2015 Chumani Maxwele, a Political Science student at the University of Cape Town (UCT) set off a wave of student protests (Ndlovu, 2016) when he threw a bucket of human faeces into the face of a statue of Cecil John Rhodes[1] on the campus. Three days later more than a thousand students of all races gathered on the campus demanding that the statue be removed. The first Facebook post of the RhodesMustFall movement appeared. In the weeks that followed students began protesting at several other universities. At Rhodes University students demanded that the university change its name, and at Stellenbosch University (SU) student demands included that Afrikaans, as the medium of instruction, be removed.

In October 2015, the Minister of Higher Education and Training called the Second National Higher Education Summit for a broad representation of stakeholders to reflect on changes in higher education over the past five years and to discuss the way forward. Student representatives from all the public higher education institutions attended the Summit, and dominated the discussions. Transformation of higher education was high on the agenda, but the crucial question for student representatives was whether real change was possible without adequate student funding.

Whereas the universities were accused of turning their backs on poor students, the Minister on the other hand urged the institutions to identify the "cost-drivers pushing up the cost of higher education" (Nzimande, 2015). Shortly after the Summit student uprisings exploded across South Africa when it became clear that student fees would increase in 2016 by an average of 10.5%. The student protests on different campuses were soon actively linked nationally, and became known as the FMF movement.

Naidoo (2016) and Peterson (2016) argue that comparing these uprisings to those of the 1960s and 1970s seems appropriate as 'blackness' was once again at the centre of the debate, while 'whiteness' and privilege were criticised. These were protests for more than affordable higher education; they were protests for social justice in the broader South African society. As in 1976, the issue of Afrikaans as the medium of instruction was one of the issues (mainly at historically Afrikaans universities). At the same time the plight of outsourced workers (representing the parents of under-privileged students) was high on the agenda at many institutions.

The following demands and concerns were raised by students during the FMF movement (CSVR, 2016; Luister video[2]; Naidoo, 2016; Philips, 2015):

— Free education or more financial support so that more students from poor and working-class families can access higher education;
— A lack of quality, affordable accommodation on campuses;
— Students feeling unwelcome and uncomfortable at historically white institutions due to heritage symbols and institutional racism;
— Decolonising higher education;
— Language policy and other academic policies leading to forms of exclusion;
— Transformation of staff demographics;
— Patriarchy;
— Class, language and gender;
— Homophobia;
— Interpersonal racism; and
— Outsourcing of workers.

Whereas some of the issues were related to access to higher education (financial support, language of instruction, academic policies), or overt lack of transformation (student and staff demographics), others spoke to more covert forms of discrimination (unwelcoming institutional culture, prevalence of race and gender stereotyping, 'Western' curriculum).

In a bid to avoid more protests at the beginning of the 2016 academic year, former President Zuma announced a zero percent increase in student fees for 2016 and an addition of R6.8 bn (€0.4 bn) to the higher education budget to cover the funding shortfall of universities and to bolster the resources of the National Student Financial Aid Scheme, that provides loans and bursaries to poor and working-class students. A commission of inquiry into the feasibility of free higher education was also appointed (the so-called 'Fees Commission').

STUDENT PROTESTS AND HIGHER EDUCATION TRANSFORMATION 171

In mid-August 2016, the announcement of the fees for the 2017 academic year was expected with anticipation. A fee increase not beyond 8% was announced. This led to a revival of the campaign under the hashtag #FeesMustFall2016, which, however, soon waned. The support amongst students was much less – many of the previous year's leaders were not on campuses anymore or did not want to get involved again. Some of them were trying to finish their studies to be able to graduate at the end of 2016.

The Fees Commission submitted their report on the feasibility of free higher education in June 2017. Eventually, "(i)n what many saw as a cynical and populist move, President Zuma announced 'free tertiary education' during the ANC conference...on 16 December 2017" (February, 2018, p. 120).

4 Institutional Case Study: #FeesMustFall at Stellenbosch University

Stellenbosch University (SU) occupies a very specific place in South African history. It is often referred to as the birthplace of apartheid and the 'bastion of Afrikaans' – the very language of instruction the students protested against in 1976. At the time this research commenced, Afrikaans was still the predominant language of communication on campus and one of the languages of instruction (together with English) (Philips, 2015; Lourens, 2013; Luister video).

Hendrik Verwoerd, the so-called "architect of apartheid" (Leonard, 2010, p. 1661), was first a student and, between 1928 and 1936, a professor of Sociology and Psychology at SU. Many of the ministers who served in the National Party government since 1948 as well as a number of prominent white business leaders, studied at SU. The fact that the Verwoerd commemorative plaque on one of the buildings on campus, known as the H.F. Verwoerd Building, was taken down only in May 2015, and the building officially renamed, illustrates the close connection between the university and the apartheid regime, but also the slow pace of institutional transformation.

Shortly after the RhodesMustFall movement started in Cape Town, a group called Open Stellenbosch, consisting of predominantly black students and staff members of the university, was formed. On their Facebook page (first entry on 15 April 2015) they described themselves as "a collective, an anti-racist, anti-sexist, non-partisan movement working in a space of deeply entrenched structural and institutional racism and patriarchy...working to purge the oppressive remnants of apartheid in pursuit of a truly African university" . Particularly students of colour experienced the institutional culture as not welcoming (Lourens, 2013). On 28 April 2015 in an article in the Daily Maverick, the Open Stellenbosch Movement wrote: "Although our institution claims that continuous transformation is part of the core being of the University, this could not be further from our everyday reality at Stellenbosch" (Open Stellenbosch Collective, 2015). In their "Open Stellenbosch Memorandum of Demands" they stated: "We want to see an end to Afrikaans-only classes. We want our University to represent our cultures as well. We want to be taught by more black faculty". These demands highlighted the language policy, the institutional culture, and the lack of demographic transformation as the most important issues.

Open Stellenbosch was not the only dissenting voice on campus. On 20 August 2015, a group of Stellenbosch students released a video, called Luister, which they described as "a film about a group of students whose stories have been ignored" (Contraband, 2015). In a series of interviews students recount instances of racial prejudice that they continued to experience in the divided society of the town of Stellenbosch and on the university campus. As in the case of Open Stellenbosch, they also voiced the challenges that they faced due to the use of Afrikaans as a language of teaching at the university, and about their continuing experiences of racism.

The weeks that followed saw student protests escalating on the Stellenbosch campus. Students from all populations and socio-economic groups participated and demanded an opportunity to interact with university management. A group of staff members also held a poster demonstration in solidarity with the students in front of the main administration building, highlighting staff demographics and power relations on campus as issues that needed to be addressed.

Tension built up on campus when, on 20 October 2015, a group of 60 students were forcibly removed by the police from the main administration building. They occupied the building after Open Stellenbosch in vain tried to get the university management to meet with them and hear their demands. The university management called in the police to remove the students from the building and issued them with interdicts. In practice, this meant that they were temporarily banned from campus.

As at other institutions, Stellenbosch University was uncertain of what the 2016 academic year would bring. Publicly, nothing much happened until August 2016 when the Minister announced an 8% cap on fee increases for 2017. Although not with the same intensity, student protests commenced again.

During this time, a small group of students tried to block the entrance to the Stellenbosch University library and demanded to engage in discussions with management. This was a nonviolent, sit-in event.[3] Other students, who demanded to enter the library, reacted violently and became abusive. Lectures and tests were disrupted in the days that followed, but no classes were suspended for more than a day. However, the university employed a private security company – soon known as the 'Men in Black' because of their apparel – to

STUDENT PROTESTS AND HIGHER EDUCATION TRANSFORMATION   173

monitor the situation closely with the police. The campus atmosphere was tense with them around and this unfortunately strengthened the students' perceptions that the university management was heavy-handed and unwilling to engage.

The unresolved issues, such as language, accommodation, the lack of funding, the position of the interdicted students (among others, the chairperson of the Student Representative Council), decolonisation of the curriculum, gender, sexual abuse issues, were discussed by students and staff members on several platforms on campus.

The most burning issues at SU in January 2017 were the interdicts against some of the students and the fact that, because most students were still awaiting the outcomes of their National Student Financial Aid Scheme (referred to as NSFAS) applications for funding, they could not register for the year. At a meeting where students voiced their frustration, the registrar immediately conceded to postpone the final date of registration to resolve this issue. This was a positive step taken by management to accommodate students and was welcomed by them.

In May 2017, according to an article in a local newspaper (Die Burger, 17 May 2017) the SU vice-chancellor reported to Parliament that the University was on track with institutional transformation. In the same paper, in another article, however, the vice-president of the Student Representative Council was quoted saying that the slow pace of transformation at the institution was a huge frustration to students. This is but one illustration of the different perspectives held by two major institutional stakeholders about the nature and pace of transformation. This will be further illustrated in the next section of the chapter.

5   Research Methodology

The previous section provided a synopsis of how FMF played out at Stellenbosch University, highlighting both similarities and differences with the national student movement. The following section focuses on management responses to FMF incidents and issues by presenting a narrative record of management actions and the results of a document analysis. For this part of the chapter we drew primarily on the following documents:
- Stellenbosch University Transformation Plan, March 2017;
- Stellenbosch University Language Policy, June 2016;
- Stellenbosch University Institutional Intent and Strategy, 2013–2018;
- Presentation to Parliament's Portfolio Committee on Higher Education and Training on 31 May 2017;

- Media statements and articles by the vice-chancellor of Stellenbosch University, Professor Wim de Villiers, from 2015 to 2017.

The documents were subjected to a systematic document analysis that is consonant with a case study research design. The exploratory case study pertains to transformation at a single higher education institution, which limits the generalisability of the research. What this part of the chapter intends to achieve is to "generate an understanding of an insight into a particular instance by providing a thick, rich description of the case and illuminating its relations to its broader contexts" (Rule & Vaughn, 2011, p. 7), i.e. developing a deeper understanding of a particular institution's transformation in a complex and challenging context.

Bowen (2009, pp. 29–30) defines document analysis as "a systematic procedure for reviewing or evaluating documents", and goes on to highlight five functions of documentary material:
- To provide data on the context;
- To suggest questions that should be asked;
- To provide supplementary research data;
- To track change and development;
- To verify findings or corroborate evidence from other sources.

In this case study of FMF and subsequent transformation at Stellenbosch University, documents are used in virtually all of these ways. First, we used mainly media reports to sketch the context of FMF, how it played out at Stellenbosch University (the case), and how this differed from what happened at other universities.

In selecting the documents for the document analysis, we considered the following: the documents should be either formal institutional policies and/ or plans adopted during or after FMF, or they should be written or oral communication from the institutional leadership (in this case the vice-chancellor himself) released during or after FMF. This, we believe, would point to the institutional response to FMF, as envisioned by the institutional leadership.

In analysing the documents, we first made use of content analysis, i.e. organising the information into categories related to the research questions, in order to identify the sections of the texts that are relevant. Subsequently we did thematic analysis where we coded the data according to predetermined categories to uncover the institutional response to the highlighted issues in the relevant sections of the set of documents (Bowen, 2009, p. 32). Finally, we interpreted the institutional response in terms of theoretical perspectives on institutional transformation, reflecting on what new perspectives have been generated by our research.

STUDENT PROTESTS AND HIGHER EDUCATION TRANSFORMATION

6   Management Responses to FMF Incidents and Issues

For purposes of this study, the issues highlighted above in the discussion of the institutional case study were categorised as follows:
- Financial need (free education, financial support, accommodation);
- Language policy and implementation;
- Institutional culture;
- Student and staff demographics;
- Power relations and discrimination against minorities;
- Transforming the curriculum.

Coding revealed the institutional responses to the above categories of issues. Our analysis commenced with the SU Transformation Plan (TP),[4] seeing that this is the primary documented directive for transformation at the institution. This was then supplemented by an analysis of the other documents and media articles by the current vice-chancellor.

6.1   *Financial Need*

One of the differences between FMF at SU and at other universities, was the lower level of prominence given to students' financial need. Although this matter was not irrelevant to student protest at SU, it was overridden by other burning issues. Yet, SU students demonstrated their solidarity with students countrywide with protest action on campus. When the national increase of 10% in student fees for 2016 was announced in October 2015, students nationally united and mobilised to close all campuses. As elsewhere in the country, student activists at Stellenbosch University went from class to class convincing students to take part in the protest.

Eventually a crowd of staff and students gathered at the intersection of two busy streets on campus and demanded that the vice-chancellor address them. It was his first public appearance since the beginning of the protests. The discussion was led by a female student leader, publicly known as part of the LGBQTI (lesbian, gay, bisexual, queer, transgender, intersex) group. At that meeting, the vice-chancellor announced that SU would not increase its fees in 2016, just before President Zuma announced that there would be a zero percent increase in fees nationally in 2016. Students rejoiced as they had achieved what they were campaigning for.

As explained above, student financial need was not seen as the first priority in terms of institutional transformation at SU. The TP (SU, 2017a) does not devote much attention to financial support for students. Section 4.2.5.2 of the TP states: "Strengthening and expanding initiatives...to address the growing need for adequate socio-economic support and alternative funding models for students" (SU, 2017a, p. 10). In the list of "Transformation Policies" in the TP, the purpose of which is to "advance the transformation priorities of SU more explicitly" (SU, 2017a, p. 11), a 'Transformative Student Funding Model' is listed. However, no further documented information on what this entails could be found. In addition, *Student financial support* is listed as one of the process indicators of "Transformation support programmes aimed at student and staff success", whereas *Provide cost-effective student support to improve module and graduation success rates* is listed as a practice indicator. What is noticeable from this formulation is the close connection drawn between financial support and student success.

The vice-chancellor mentioned financial issues in several of his media articles: student bursaries (De Villiers, 2015a; De Villiers, 2016b), student fees and financial sustainability (De Villiers, 2016a). In the institutional presentation to Parliament's Portfolio Committee on Higher Education and Training (31 May 2017) the institutional representatives explicitly stated that there would be "no financial exclusion where there is academic merit" (SU, 2017b).

It is noteworthy that the main driver of the FMF movement, namely financial need, receives rather scant attention in the transformation initiatives of SU. Two factors may account for this: first, a large proportion of students at SU are from middle-class or well-to-do families for whom financial need is not a daily reality. A report on trends in admission, enrolments and enrolment rates that served at the SU Senate in August 2018, illustrated that only 12% of first-year enrolments in 2016 were from medium to high socio-economically disadvantaged groups (Kistner, 2018). This relates strongly to the population distribution at the institution, as the first-year enrolment rates for black African students, who are overall the most disadvantaged population group in South Africa, were significantly lower (28%) than those of white students (54%) who are overall socio-economically more privileged. Second, SU has devoted a growing percentage of its annual budget to student bursaries. This percentage has grown from 15.6% in 2011 to 17.7% in 2015. The total amount for bursaries paid by SU in 2015 amounted to R658.7 million (€42 million), 24% of all students received bursaries, and 78% on average of all student fees were covered by bursaries. In 2017 the vice-chancellor reported to Senate that the institution assists all students with family incomes of less than R 240,000 (€16,000) per year with bursaries from the National Student Financial Aid System and from institutional funding. Financial need therefore does not seem to have similar priority among institutional challenges as at other higher education institutions (HEIs).

6.2 Language Policy and Implementation

As pointed out above, SU is somewhat of an anomaly in the South African higher education context. Another way in which this is demonstrated, is the issue around language policy and implementation or the medium of instruction. Open Stellenbosch, for one, focused their campaign quite strongly on Afrikaans as the medium of instruction; this was also one of the main issues highlighted in the Luister video (Contraband, 2015).

Language policy and planning has been an ongoing institutional concern for many years. As part of this process, the university's Language Task Team released a 10-point plan in September 2015. Among other things, they recommended that the institutional language policy be changed to afford equal status to Afrikaans and English and put forward a proposal to Senate that English would, from 2016, become the default institutional language, with accommodation of Afrikaans and isiXhosa[5] where possible.

In spite of widespread support for this proposal among academics, the stipulations of the language policy prohibited this proposal from being implemented without the sanction of the university Council. As a result, confusion reigned, with some faculties implementing the management proposal in 2016, and others sticking to the requirements of the language policy at that time. Court cases ensued, and management was forced to retract their proposal and follow the prescribed procedure to effect the necessary changes to the language policy and plan.

The complexity of the matter is illustrated by various pronouncements by the vice-chancellor. In 2015 he referred to language practices at the institution in terms of the Constitution that provides for the right of everyone to receive education in the official language of their choice in public education institutions (De Villiers, 2015b). Subsequently he justified the continued use of Afrikaans as the medium of instruction as a constitutional right, and pointed out the advantages of multilingualism (De Villiers, 2016a), while acknowledging that language should never be a barrier for student access or success.

The revision of the language policy of SU, although not officially in reaction to Open Stellenbosch and FMF, was certainly precipitated by events on campus. The revised policy that was approved in 2016 and implemented in 2017 stipulates the teaching of all undergraduate modules in English. However, summaries are also given in Afrikaans, and students can ask questions in either Afrikaans or English. In addition, parallel-medium instruction[6] (English and Afrikaans) is given where student numbers necessitate more than one class group, and in first-year modules simultaneous interpretation services are also available (either from Afrikaans to English or vice versa), depending on the language proficiency of the lecturer (SU, 2016). It seems as if the revised language policy has addressed the needs of English-speaking students; however, legal action by Afrikaans pressure groups to reinstate 'equal status' for the two languages are ongoing.

6.3 *Institutional Culture*

Open Stellenbosch characterised the institutional culture at SU as oppressive to the extent that students of colour cannot breathe. On their Facebook page, posted on 3 March 2016, Open Stellenbosch highlights some of the issues: "The presence of the J.H. Marais statue is one that represents the prevailing nature of white supremacist and racist institutional culture at Stellenbosch University. Join us as we unpack the meaning and necessity of the statue's presence on our campus as well as the structural and institutional violence that it represents". The dispute around statues on campuses, that started with the removal of the statue of Cecil John Rhodes from the UCT campus, has been ongoing, pointing to the importance of creating spaces that welcome a diverse study body, as part of transforming the institutional culture.

The TP prioritises "a welcoming institutional culture" that "facilitates a sense of belonging among students and staff" (SU, 2017a, p. 7). The TP goes on to argue that the "place", i.e. the institution should promote "social inclusion that facilitates belonging and that is rooted in Africa" (SU, 2017a, p. 8). The purpose of the renewal of the institutional culture is "to ensure that it is free of all forms of overt and, especially, covert discrimination, including (but not limited to) racism, classism, sexism, patriarchies, misogyny, homophobia, heteronormativity, ableism and ageism" (SU, 2017a, p. 9). A welcoming institutional culture requires "facilities that validate diverse identities and needs and a visual redress strategy that is aligned with a new African university" (SU, 2017a, p. 8). This relates to the renewal of "public semiotics, i.e. the public meaning and symbolism of the physical infrastructure of SU (buildings, signage, statues, pictures, etc.) in a resolute, intentional, coordinated way" (SU, 2017a, p. 8). Mention is also made of "best practice guidelines for a welcoming culture in student communities" (SU, 2017a, p. 13), but no detailed proposals are made in this regard.

In April 2016, the vice-chancellor prioritised "building greater social cohesion on our campuses" and expresses his disappointment "that we are still struggling with racism, sexism, gender violence and other forms of discrimination and abuse" (De Villiers, 2016b, p. 9). In 2017 he again drew the attention to the institutional culture by saying the following: "Stellenbosch University certainly needs to be a welcoming home to all, and in getting there we have to ask some difficult questions and confront hard realities" (De Villiers, 2017, p. 30).

STUDENT PROTESTS AND HIGHER EDUCATION TRANSFORMATION 179

A close reading of the texts, however, does not reveal specific, practical steps that will be taken to achieve this welcoming institutional culture, apart from the visual redress strategy. Institutional culture, defined in the TP as "the subtle and subconscious pictures, expectations, perceptions, perspectives, prejudices, attitudes and intellectual frameworks with which people live and which determine the visions, values, ideals, communal identity and collective character of an institution" (SU, 2017a, p. 6) is an amorphous, complex and intractable phenomenon that takes time to change. In this respect, the importance of role models and leadership at all levels of the institution cannot be overemphasised.

6.4 *Student and Staff Demographics*

Student and staff demographics at SU have been slow to change. Earlier reference was made to the small percentage of black students at the university. Hence, this was one of the vital issues that the FMF student movement focused on. Open Stellenbosch remained critical of steps taken by university management to address this matter. Their scepticism was clear when, on 7 August 2015, the university management announced it would be investing R68.8 million (€4.5 million) in the diversification of its staff and their response was that although they welcomed attempts to transform SU, they refused "to be taken in by easy victories, measured out in quantitative compromised positions" (Shabangu, 2015).

The TP distinguishes between 'quantitative' and 'qualitative' transformation. As to the former, the TP includes, amongst others, "the statistical diversity of the staff corps and student body" (SU, 2017a, p. 6), and goes on to specify that student and staff numbers should "reflect the diversity of the broader South African and African society" (SU, 2017a, p. 7). For both staff and students, the intention is to set clear, appropriate, and challenging yet achievable targets. The 'transformation policies' listed in the TP include the Employment Equity Policy, the Employment Equity Plan, the Admissions Policy, the Residence Placement Policy and the Policy regarding Student with Special Learning Needs or Disabilities.

Some of the process indicators related to the objective of increasing student and staff diversity with a specific focus on the increase of the percentage of black, coloured and Indian students and staff, include the annual monitoring, analysis and communication of progress with regard to student enrolments and staff diversity.

Shortly after being inaugurated as the new vice-chancellor of SU, De Villiers (2015a) made the connection between social justice, equitable access and quality education, in an opinion piece that he wrote for *The Conversation*. He again made the link between diversity and quality later in the same year: "Diversity is an absolute requirement for excellence, because it exposes us to a variety of people and ideas, which broadens the mind and enriches us" (De Villiers, 2015b, p. 10). This was reiterated in an article by him in 2016 (De Villiers, 2016a), and in reflecting on his first year in office, De Villiers (2016b, p. 9) lists a number of institutional achievements, amongst others growing numbers of black, coloured and Indian graduates, and student success rates that surpass the national average, and makes specific mention of the "pursuance of the twin goals of greater access and student success". In 2017, the vice-chancellor highlighted the fact that the diversity of the student body is promoted by the new admissions policy that "expands Stellenbosch University's admission criteria beyond applicants' academic achievement and racial classification to include their socio economic status" (De Villiers, 2017, p. 30). This statement embodies an interesting juxtaposition of quality, race and poverty (social justice), and is an expression of the competing challenges that South African universities are grappling with.

6.5   *Power Relations and Discrimination against Minorities*

After the release of the Luister video (Contraband, 2015) the vice-chancellor issued a statement negating the impression created by the video that he and his team did not listen to students, declaring it 'disingenuous'. The official statement ended with the declaration that the management of SU remains committed to open discussions with all stakeholders and to transformation. This commitment was also expressed in the Institutional Intent and Strategy of 2013 and in 2018 in the Vision 2040 and Strategic Framework 2019–2024 (SU, 2018).

In the account of the FMF protests given above, issues of power and power relations surface repeatedly. Reading the accounts of how the protests were experienced by such divergent groupings as vice-chancellors (Jansen, 2017; Habib, 2016), and the participating students and student leaders (CSVR, 2016; Philips, 2015), it becomes clear that power relations (or rather power struggles) played an important role in the events. At SU, this was certainly no different. In addition, the diverse minorities that struggled to make their voices heard, proliferated as the events unfolded, with gender and sexual preference being high on the agenda. Female students came out particularly strongly against the 'rape culture' on campuses, while students identifying with the LGBTI cause also became more vocal.

The TP makes specific mention of discrimination in terms of, amongst others, gender and sexual orientation, with an equally strong focus on students with disabilities. The transformation of 'place' at the university would, for example, require the following: "4.1.6 Advance gender justice and renew university access amenities, such as bathrooms" and "4.1.7 Alter buildings to ensure universal access to and justice for people with disabilities" (SU, 2017a, p. 8). As far as power in formal institutional structures is concerned, more inclusive and more representative representation in governance structures is an important objective of the TP, so "that stakeholders can participate with ease in the governance structures of Stellenbosch University" (SU, 2017a, p. 7). For this purpose, "a process of monitoring and analysing longitudinal diversity trends within institutional governance structures" will be undertaken in order to "inform future strategies and interventions" (SU, 2017a, p. 11).

In his media articles, the vice-chancellor's underlying message seems to be inviting stakeholders to participate in open discussion – within certain parameters:

> But neither am I going to tolerate the unacceptable – the disruption of classes, hate speech, violence, destruction of property, by whomever. Because these things are also wrong, however, we are not victimising any-one, and I am certainly not silencing protest. Students should be critical – that is the nature of the open discussion. (De Villiers, 2015b, p. 10)

This standpoint is reiterated the following year (De Villiers, 2016a; De Villiers, 2016b) with an emphasis on 'open conversation', critical and robust debate and the constitutional right to lawful and peaceful protest, while not disrupting institutional activities and respecting everyone's rights. The difficult balancing act of respecting individual rights while protecting the collective within a turbulent political environment is certainly one of the major challenges all South African vice-chancellors face.

6.6   *Transforming the Curriculum*

Even though not evident in the beginning, the call for 'decolonising the curriculum' or 'decolonising science' became stronger as the FMF movement progressed. This struck at the heart of academic life and universities' core business – the 'what' of teaching and learning. The TP (SU, 2017a, p. 9) speaks of "transformative learning and teaching programmes" and the objective to "prioritise, expand and develop curriculum renewal and teaching method-ologies to ensure the relevance of teaching and learning programmes to the societal transformation needs in the contexts of Africanisation, decolonisation and global relevance". It needs to be noted that various initiatives in this regard are ongoing on campus, such as a programme renewal project in which all faculties are participating, and a Decolonising STEM Focused Interest Group that engages in ongoing discourse on what decolonisation in STEM (Science, Technology, Engineering and Mathematics) entails and how it can be achieved.

At the behest of the university Council a Decolonisation Task Team (DTT) with the overall purpose of making recommendations to the management of SU on the Decolonisation of the Curriculum, was appointed in 2017. Their draft report explicitly rejects the defining of decolonisation by the Task Team itself, or by any of the major institutional stakeholders in isolation, but argues that "decoloniality in curricula and pedagogy must result from a shared process of dialogue, meaningful engagement and shared meaning-making with those who continue to suffer colonial exclusion" (DTT, 2017, p. 1). The draft report furthermore clearly links decolonisation to institutional transformation:

> It is recommended that the university includes Decolonisation as a core aspect of its transformation strategy and that all transformational work needs to embrace principles of Decolonisation. It is further recommended that systemic institutional transformation and its related themes of Place; Programmes; and People cannot assume that decolonisation will automatically be present. Decolonisation and the process thereof needs to be deliberately written into all future processes and practices relating to Institutional Transformation. (DTT, 2017, p. 3)

In a 2017 media article, the vice-chancellor explicates his interpretation of decolonising (or transforming) the curriculum. He identifies the elements of

> putting Africa at the centre of knowledge production, not at the periphery…That means rejecting the notion of Africa as a mere extension of the West, that the Western intellectual tradition is the only valid paradigm, that African thinkers cannot be thought leaders, that we have to mimic Europe or North America. (De Villiers, 2017, p. 30)

He goes on to argue that this does not imply a rejection of the Western model of knowledge,

> (b)ut it does mean placing Africa at the centre of our thoughts, words and deeds. We have to acknowledge the perspectives of our immediate environment and use them to enrich our insights and outputs, it is not either/or, one or the other, but and/and, using all models and perspectives. (De Villiers, 2017, p. 30)

The vice-chancellor subsequently explains how various elements of transformation such as broadening access, partnering with other African universities in research and postgraduate study, and addressing the institutional culture, all work together towards 'putting Africa back' into SU. The article also points to the fact that the complexity and interconnectedness of all the factors involved require further investigation.

7 Institutional Transformation Revisited

In our introduction we referred to some of the actors and stakeholders responsible for making or resisting decisions in universities, to the multiple and complex relations and relationships internal and external to universities, and how these contribute to higher levels of political turbulence in universities. Ever since Baldridge in 1971 added his political model of the university to the then existing models of the bureaucracy and the collegium, and Birnbaum (1988) explicated this idea further, many views on the political nature of universities have been advanced. In the South African context, for example, Fourie (2009) identified the following four prerequisites for overcoming destructive political power-play in HEIs:

- An acknowledgement and tolerance of the incommensurability of and lack of perfect solutions for all challenges in higher education by all stakeholders;
- The importance of stakeholders sharing the same vision for the institution, and an understanding of the distinctive roles and responsibilities of the different stakeholders in attaining that vision;
- A well-established sense of trust among all stakeholders and
- Open and honest communication among all stakeholders.

These prerequisites seem to have been absent during FMF. The movement occurred in a macro-environment characterised by dissent, lack of resources, and profound distrust among stakeholders: the government and university management, the government and students, university management and students. These perceptions and attitudes were transposed into the micro-environments of the HEIs, leading to the perfect storm in South African higher education. What we have learned is how fragile the social fabric of our society and our HEIs is, and how deeply the fault-lines of historical distrust are still running. We have also learned that external politics and internal politics are often deeply entwined, and that political opportunism needs to be counteracted in the best interest of higher education. Lastly, we have learned that superficial change will not last and that true transformation requires an honest, thoughtful, holistic, and multifaceted approach.

Our analysis of documentary evidence did not produce conclusive evidence of FMF having had deep and lasting effects on transformation at SU, although changes to, for example, the language policy and campus spaces (the renaming of buildings, for example) did address some of the issues raised by the students. In June 2018 a new institutional vision and strategic framework: Vision 2040 and Strategic Framework 2019–2024 was adopted. This new directive for SU pays scant attention to transformation. One of the strategic themes is "a transformative student experience" to be achieved by, among other things, providing "a unique, personalised student experience that serves as a catalyst for transformational change amidst opportunities for engagement and development through a first-class academic offering, which prepares graduates to lead and excel in a diverse world" (SU, 2018, p. 20). Whether these measures will succeed in making SU 'home' for a diversity of students remains to be seen.

The institutional values espoused in Vision 2040 and Strategic Framework 2019–2024 resonate more strongly with what we experienced during, and hopefully learned from FMF: excellence, compassion, equity, respect, accountability. The following definitions are particularly powerful:

– Compassion: Recognition of, and care for, the well-being of all our students and staff;
– Equity: Restitution in response to our past legacy and fairness in our aspirations
– Respect: Civility in our mutual and public discourse, due regard for the freedom, equality and dignity of all, and respect for the environment and
– Accountability: Accepting the highest level of responsibility for our actions (SU, 2018, p. 16).

The challenge to all the stakeholders in SU is living these values on a daily basis.

8 Conclusion

The chapter is not only of interest to South African or African scholars. Higher education systems and universities worldwide face growing levels of disillusionment of their primary stakeholders because of a perceived inability to deliver on their core functions in an inclusive and affordable manner. Many of the issues raised by South African students resonate with what has been highlighted in research in other systems. Presenting these issues in their complexity and interconnectedness and attempting to clarify and deepen our understanding of these issues through analysis and synthesis, makes this an original contribution of interest to a wider international audience.

STUDENT PROTESTS AND HIGHER EDUCATION TRANSFORMATION

Notes

1 The campus of the University of Cape Town was developed on a piece of land donated by the controversial imperialist, Cecil John Rhodes, and his statue occupied a central place on the campus until its removal on 9 April 2015.
2 Luister is the Afrikaans word for 'listen'. The video contains a series of interviews with Stellenbosch University students who recounted their experiences of racism and prejudice on campus and in the town of Stellenbosch (Contraband, 2015). The video can be downloaded from https://www.youtube.com/watch?v=sF3rTBQTQk4
3 One of the authors of this chapter was present at this and some of the other events.
4 The Transformation Plan was developed by the Institutional Transformation Committee. After campus wide consultation the plan was subsequently amended and approved in March 2017 by the institution's senior management team and Senate.
5 Two indigenous languages are spoken by the majority of people in the Western Cape Province, the area in South Africa where Stellenbosch University is located.
6 When large student numbers necessitate more than one class group, lectures are given separately in English and in Afrikaans. Students make a choice according to their own language preferences.

References

Badat, S. (2016). *Deciphering the meanings, and explaining the South African higher education student protests of 2015–2016*. Unpublished manuscript.

Baldridge, J. (1971). *Models of university governance: Bureaucratic, collegial, and political*. Washington, DC: ERIC.

Bellei, C., Cabalin, C., & Orellan, V. (2014). The 2011 chilean student movement against neoliberal educational policies. *Studies in Higher Education, 39*(3), 426–440.

Birnbaum, R. (1988). *How colleges work*. London: Jossey-Bass.

Booysen, S. (2016). *Fees must fall. Student revolt, decolonisation and governance in South Africa*. Johannesburg: Wits University Press.

Bowen, G. A. (2009). Document analysis as a qualitative research method. *Qualitative Research Journal, 9*(2), 27–40.

Bunting, I. (2002). Students Transformation in higher education. In N. Cloete, R. Fehnel, P. Maassen, T. Moja, H. Perold, & T. Gibbon (Eds.), *Global pressures and local realities in South Africa* (pp. 147–173). Cape Town: Centre for Higher Education Transformation.

Case, J. M. (2008). Alienation and engagement: Development of an alternative theoretical framework for understanding student learning. *Higher Education, 55*, 321–332.

CHE (Council on Higher Education). (2018). *VitalStats. Public higher education 2016.* Pretoria: Council on Higher Education.

Cooke, C. (2018, March 13). #NeverAgain: Do student protests work? History tells us why they can. *The Conversation.* Retrieved January 10, 2019, from https://www.theconversation.com

Contraband. (2015). *Luister.* Released on YouTube Retrieved August 20, 2015, from https://www.youtube.com/watch?v=sF3rTBQTQk4

CSVR (Centre for the Study of Violence and Reconciliation). (2016). *#Hashtag. An analysis of the #FeesMustFall movement at South African universities* (M. Langa, Ed.). Johannesburg: CSVR.

Davids, N., & Waghid, Y. (2016, October 10). #FeesMustFall: History of South African student protests reflects inequality's grip. *Mail & Guardian.* Retrieved February 10, 2019, from https://mg.co.za/article/2016-10-10-feesmustfall-history-of-southafrican-student-protests-reflects-inequalitys-grip

De Villiers, W. (2015a, July 17). Mandela's belief that education can change the world is still a dream. *The Conversation.* Retrieved December 7, 2016, from https://www.theconversation.com

De Villiers, W. (2015b, August 31). We are all 100% responsible to be the change we want to see. *Cape Times,* p. 10.

De Villiers, W. (2015c, September 8). Maties is serious about fostering transformation. *Cape Argus,* p. 13.

De Villiers, W. (2016a, February 2). Verandering vereis aanpassing [Change requires adjustment]. *Die Burger,* p. 11. [in Afrikaans]

De Villiers, W. (2016b, April 13). Stellies committed to achieving greater inclusivity, equality. *Cape Times,* p. 9.

De Villiers, W. (2017, March 3). Put Africa back in our universities. *Mail & Guardian,* p. 30.

Dlamini, R. (2018). Corporatisation of universities deepens inequalities by ignoring social injustces and restricting access to higher education. *South African Journal of Higher Education, 32*(5), 54–65.

February, J. (2018). *Turning and turning. Exploring the Complexities of South Africa's Democracy.* Johannesburg: Picador Africa.

Fourie, M. (1999). Institutional transformation at South African universities: Implications for academic staff. *Higher Education, 38,* 275–290.

Fourie, M. (2009). Institutional governance in South African higher education: For the common good or political power-play? In E. Bitzer (Ed.), *Higher education in South Africa: A scholarly look behind the scenes* (pp. 349–366). Stellenbosch: SUN MeDIA.

Giroux, H. A. (2002). Neoliberalism, corporate culture, and the promise of higher education: The university as a democratic public sphere. *Harvard Educational Review, 72*(4), 425–463.

STUDENT PROTESTS AND HIGHER EDUCATION TRANSFORMATION 187

Gray, J. (2015, March 17). Dutch student protests ignite movement against management of universities. *The Guardian*. Retrieved January 10, 2019, from https://www.theguardian.com

Habib, A. (2016, December 5). Op-Ed: The politics of spectacle – Reflections on the 2016 student protests. *Daily Maverick*. Retrieved December 5, 2016, from https://www.dailymaverick.co.za

Jansen, J. (2017). *As by fire. The end of the South African university*. Cape Town: Tafelberg.

Leonard, T. M. (2010). *Encyclopedia of the developing world*. New York, NY: Routledge/ Taylor & Francis.

Lourens, E. (2013). *Understanding the experiences of educationally disadvantaged students at Stellenbosch University* (Unpublished master's thesis). Stellenbosch University, Stellenbosch, South Africa.

Kistner, L. (2018). *Trends in admissions, enrolments and enrolment rates, 2016 to 2018 newcomer first-years. Full Report* [Unpublished report]. Stellenbosch: Stellenbosch University Centre for Business Intelligence, Division for Information Governance.

Macfarlane, B. (2005). The disengaged academic: The retreat from citizenship. *Higher Education Quarterly, 59*(4), 296–312.

Mann, S. J. (2001). Alternative perspectives on the student experience: Alienation and engagement. *Studies in Higher Education, 26*(1), 7–19.

Mathebula, M., & Calitz, T. (2018). #FeesMustFall: A media analysis of students' voices on access to universities in South Africa. In P. Ashwin & J. Case (Eds.), *Higher education pathways. South African undergraduate education and the public good* (pp. 177–191). Cape Town: African Minds.

Mkhabela, S. (2016). Action and fire in Soweto, June 1976. In A. Hefferman & N. Nieftagodien (Eds.), *Students must rise* (pp. 55–64). Johannesburg: Wits University Press.

Naidoo, L. A. (2016). Contemporary student politics in South Africa. In A. Hefferman & N. Nieftagodien (Eds.), *Students must rise* (pp. 180–190). Johannesburg: Wits University Press.

Ndlovu, S. M. (2016). A brief history of the African students' association. In A. Hefferman & N. Nieftagodien (Eds.), *Students must rise* (pp. 6–15). Johannesburg: Wits University Press.

Nzimande, B. (2015, October 15). *Speech by minister Blade Nzimande at the higher education summit held.* Inkosi Albert Luthuli ICC, Durban. Retrieved December 5, 2016, from http://www.gov.za/

Open Stellenbosch Collective. (2015, April 28). Op-Ed: Open Stellenbosch – Tackling language and exclusion at Stellenbosch University. *Daily Maverick*. Retrieved December 5, 2016, from https://www.dailymaverick.co.za

Peterson, B. (2016). Youth and student culture: Riding resistance and imagining the future. In A. Heffernan & N. Nieftagodien (Eds.), *Students must rise* (pp. 16–23). Johannesburg: Wits University Press.

Philips, A. (2016). *Formation of identity under political flux: The lived experiences of student activists at Stellenbosch University* (Unpublished thesis). Submitted in the fulfilment of the BA Hons degree in the Department of Sociology & Social Anthropology, Stellenbosch University, Stellenbosch, South Africa.

Rule, P., & Vaughn, J. (2011). *Your guide to case study research.* Pretoria: Van Schaik Publishers.

Sekulich, D. (2017, April, 7). Rise of populism is a wake-up call for universities. *University World News Global Edition*, p. 454. Retrieved January 10, 2019, from https://www.universityworldnews.com

Shabangu, M. (2015, August 28). Not open, says open Stellenbosch. *Mail & Guardian.* Retrieved December 6, 2016, from https://www.mg.co.za/section/education

SU (Stellenbosch University). (2016, June). *Language policy of Stellenbosch University.* Unpublished document.

SU (Stellenbosch University). (2017a, March). *Transformation plan.* Unpublished document.

SU (Stellenbosch University). (2017b, May 31). *Presentation to parliament's Portfolio committee on higher education and training.* Unpublished Powerpoint presentation.

SU (Stellenbosch University). (2018, June). *Vision 2040 and strategic framework 2019–2024.* Unpublished document.

CHAPTER 8

University Third Mission as an Organisational and Political Field: Evidence from Three Case Studies in Italy

Giacomo Balduzzi and Massimiliano Vaira

Abstract

This chapter is an empirical analysis of University Third Mission (UTM), using a combination of organisational field concept drawn from new institutionalism, along with Bourdieu's social field. Its aim is to understand UTM not just as a set of activities, but as an emerging area of institutional life structured by organisations, institutions, actors, relationships, activities, agendas as well as struggles. Moving from a multiple case study on three public universities located in Northern Italy, our analysis focuses on different degrees of structuration and institutionalisation of UTM. Further, for each case it considers the tensions arising among actors in the field (internal/external dimension) and inside the university setting (internal dimension).

Keywords

University Third Mission – Italian university – organisational field – social/political field – structuration process – institutionalisation process

1 Introduction

In the last 25 years University Third Mission (UTM) has become widespread as a (relatively) new activity (Pinheiro, Benneworth, & Jones, 2012b), carried out by universities and academics pushed by public policies that directly and indirectly promote it (Laredo, 2007; Pinheiro, Benneworth, & Jones, 2012a; Zomer & Benneworth, 2011). These policies are rooted in the global neoliberal agenda linked to cost-cutting programmes of state funding and policies pressuring universities to produce and transfer knowledge useful for social and, above all, economic needs and purposes. Italian universities have gone

© KONINKLIJKE BRILL NV, LEIDEN, 2020 | DOI: 10.1163/9789004422582_009

through such changes too, although more recently: policies for UTM originated less a decade ago, along with the institution of the National Agency for University and Research Evaluation (ANVUR). Nonetheless, UTM has become an increasingly relevant part of university activities formally evaluated for their public funding allocation.

Policies for UTM exert pressures on universities and academics to find and retrieve external economic resources in order to compensate for public financial cuts, especially for research activities and, more generally, to open up to the societal environment. Both pressures find legitimacy in the discourse of the social utility and exploitability of universities and scientific knowledge for different purposes (economic, cultural, political, social, etc.).

Research and literature on the subject has grown over time, focusing on how institutions, their organisational articulations and academics carry out third mission activities. Such studies have largely followed the seminal works since the late 1990s of Gibbons and colleagues (1994), Etzkowitz and Leyesdorff (1997), Slaughter and Leslie (1997), Clark (1998), Etzkowitz (2001), Slaughter, and Rhoades (2004). They highlight the changes as well as the contradictions and tensions produced on institutions and academics' work by the enactment of mainly economic relationships with external organisations and actors. More recently, and with a different analytical-empirical focus, Pinheiro, Benneworth and Jones (2012a) and Kitagawa, Barrioluengo, and Uyarra (2016) have stressed tensions arising from third mission activities.

Although such analyses are relevant, our paper will not follow that line of reasoning to account for our cases; we will focus on third mission not (only) as a complex of activities, but above all as a *field* where those activities take place, shape and orientation. The concept of field opens the way to consider UTM as a fabric of organisations, institutions, actors, relationships, activities, agendas and struggles that structure an area of institutional life. This, in turn, makes it possible to shed light on the main constitutive aspects of UTM: how it emerges, tends to institutionalise as an academic activity and how, in such a structuring process, it becomes a ground of struggle for its definitions, goals and means to achieve them. Those aspects attract attention to the political dimension, in which UTM and its institutionalisation are embedded. In turn, such embeddedness is not only concerned with public policies, but also, and above all, it is related to a complex of political dynamics and actions, constructing UTM itself, enacted by university institutions, their organisational articulation, academics and organisations and institutions populating the societal environment.

In this regard, UTM is one of the most privileged aspects for analysing universities as political institutions. In this framework, universities respond to

UNIVERSITY THIRD MISSION

changes in their environment, while simultaneously they change both their internal organisation and the environment itself.

Overall, our analysis aims at showing how UTM neither can be taken-for-granted as a mechanical/deterministic effect of public policies supporting and imposing it to universities, nor can it be treated as a quantum leap change in university structures and functions. On the contrary, it is an institutional, organisational and, above all, political construct produced by actors' actions and interactions within definite structural conditions.

Following this line, the paper analyses this kind of structuring dynamics, by using data drawn from three in-depth case studies carried out in three universities in Northern Italy and from external organisational and institutional actors of their surrounding environment. The three case studies are part of wider research on the university's role in the development of local economies ('Universities, innovation and regional economies') carried out at the national level and funded by the Ministry of Education University and Research (Rostan, Ceravolo, & Vaira, 2013).

The structure of this essay is as follows. First, we sketch the theoretical and methodological framework used for our analysis. Second, we provide a brief reconstruction of the general context and the conditions established by policies promoting/imposing the third mission as a new activity of institutions and academics. Third, we deal with the three investigated case studies adopting the field approach analysis. In particular, we account for the activities, and relational structure between universities, their administrative and research articulations and external organisations and institutions. Finally, we present and analyse the tensions emerging in the UTM field at both the internal academic level and between the academic and the economic sectors in their relations.

2   Theoretical Background

A large number of studies on UTM address five main points. The first is seeing UTM as an *activity* undertaken by universities and/or academics (e.g. Laredo, 2007; Thune, Rymert, Gulbrandsen, & Aamodt, 2016). The second is concerned with *knowledge transfer* from universities to businesses and society (e.g. Bekkers & Bodas Freitas, 2008; Geuna & Muscio, 2009; Mowery, Nelson, Sampat, & Ziedonis, 2004). The third treats the *social/economic impact* of UTM activities (e.g. Bornmann, 2012, 2013). The fourth deals with *collaborative and exchange relations* between universities and, in particular, industry (e.g. Abreu, Grinevich, Hughes, & Kitson, 2011; Callaert, Landoni, Van Looy, & Verganti, 2015; Thune & Gulbrandsen, 2011). The fifth concentrates on *organisational effects and consequences* of UTM as part of the process of organisational complexification of universities (Musselin, 2007; Scott, 2006). Related to this last point, Nedeva (2007), suggests looking at UTM's effects on universities' organisational structures not only in functional terms, but also, above all, in relational ones. That is, UTM does not simply add new activities/functions but entails a deeper organisational change in university structures and operational logics.

Our work takes a relational perspective but considers relations not only as a matter of exchange and collaboration. Actually, actors are engaged in political struggles (i.e. conflict relations), with definite stakes, by which UTM is constructed. Consequently, we analyse UTM in terms of the new institutionalism concept of the organisational field (DiMaggio & Powell, 1991; DiMaggio, 1991), combined with Bourdieu's concept of the social field (1993).

The organisational field concept highlights how the structuration of a given field takes place through actions and relations at different levels among multiple heterogeneous organisational actors having different roles, functions and logics of action. All this occurs through different kinds of relational dynamics, e.g. competition, collaboration and authority (DiMaggio & Powell, 1991). Those dynamics are constitutive of a field's structuring process. Such a process gives rise to a particular area of institutional life and to its structural configuration (DiMaggio & Powell, 1991). This, in turn, is at the core of the institutionalisation of organisational structures, functions (DiMaggio, 1991), as well as activities and practices in the field. In other words, according to organisational field theory, organisations and organisational arrangements are institutional constructs, defined by the complex of social, political and economic relations at a given time. To summarise: 'structuring' means that collective and individual actors are engaged in constructing a field and in defining its logics, functioning, goals and the means to achieve them. This process gives rise to a dense texture of political relations concerning the construction of the field and the legitimated activities within it, which are at the basis of the institutionalisation process of the field, of the activities and relational patterns within it. 'Process of institutionalisation' means that a given cultural construct (in our case UTM activities) tends to diffuse in a given field and in organisations populating it and to become growingly taken-for-grated by actors as a set of enough stable and stabilising organisational activities, practices, actions and relations.

Bourdieu's social field concept highlights the structure of relations among actors. This perspective was already implicitly contained in Weber's concept of *Lebensordnungen* and in his theory of social action, from which Bourdieu's notion derives. Those relations stem from the different positions of actors in the field and from their different dispositions (i.e. representations, points of view, definitions and logics of action), which are related to the different kinds, quantities and qualities of capital owned by them. In any given field, a dominant form of capital emerges from the struggles among groups. The dominant group, as owner of the dominant form of capital, defines how the field is structured and how it operates. Hence, this second concept focuses on the political dimension, including power, hierarchical structures, established as well as contended definitions, and the different forms of valuable capital and stakes. All these aspects become the objects and stakes of the struggles among actors in the field.

The two concepts combined shed light on UTM as a product of both organisational/institutional dynamics and political conflict relations involved in its structuration, and hence in its process of institutionalisation. In other words, this theoretical framework allows for seeing UTM as a political construct as well as a product of relations and interactions enacted by individual and collective actors having different positions within the field. Such interactions in the field produce different representations and definitions of what UTM should be, what goals it should achieve, and how it should achieve them.

One of the seminal studies in this perspective is DiMaggio's analysis on the construction of the art museum field (1991), drawn from both organisational field analysis and Bourdieu's concept of social field. While his analysis concentrates on the structural macro-level dynamics, we use it to explore dynamics at the meso-level and micro-levels, including macro-structural aspects as well. From this perspective, Bourdieu's social field concept is suitable for embodying in the analysis representations, orientations and actions of actors, largely constituted and derived – although not determined – by their structural position within the field. In a very similar perspective, Powell, White, Koput, and Owen-Smith (2005) analysed the structure and dynamics of interorganisational relations in biotechnology as a field.

Recently Thornton, Ocasio, and Lounsbury (2012) have elaborated this kind of perspective, labelling it *institutional logics approach*. This approach – rooted in the organisational new institutionalism perspective and largely in line with the Weber and Bourdieu's theories – signals that there is a growing theoretical and heuristic interest in linking various levels of structural conditions to the agents' positions and actions. Finally, and more related to our theoretical approach, Hamadache (2015) has recently stressed the importance of a more systematic integration of the new institutionalist approach and Bourdieu's approach in analysing organisational fields.

3   Research Design and Methods

Our research is a qualitative case study (Yin, 2014). We consider three universities in Northern Italy, namely Ferrara, Padua and Pavia, where the research team carried out 50 in-depth interviews with academics, university administrative staff, entrepreneurs and members of business associations. Official documents are also included in the empirical field research, designed as a multiple level case study. Each case involves three levels of analysis: the context, the embedded case and one sub-unit of analysis (Yin, 2014, pp. 49–50). As regards the context, we draw attention to the different local systems in which the single university institution is located, taking into account the main features of their economic activity. The analysis of the embedded case concerns the university institution itself, with particular attention to its governance and to the organisational divisions and roles specifically dedicated to UTM (deputy rectors and delegates, offices of technology transfer, university incubators and so on). The third level of analysis considers four significant departments in each university. The analysis of the departments aims at exploring heterogeneous processes and organisational implications at the micro-level, where individuals make operational decisions directly affecting external/internal relations and tensions within the UTM field.

In order to compare the findings, it seems relevant that the three universities operate in Northern Italy, a macro-region traditionally considered as the most developed and productive part of the country. On closer examination, the area seems anything but homogeneous. The cases considered in our study belong to the three different types of local systems, classified according to the Italian National Institute of Statistics (ISTAT, 2015, pp. 44–47): *città diffusa*, or urban sprawl (Padova); *cuore verde*, or the green core (Ferrara); *le città del Centro-Nord* or the Centre-Northern urban systems (Pavia). We will see later more in detail further elements inherent to the institutions, their history and their economic, political, social and territorial context that indicate the three cases as interesting and meaningful in a comparative perspective (Section 5).

Although such a research methodology cannot provide and produce a statistical generalisation, it is useful for exploring, in a thick description fashion (Geertz, 1973), how the structuring of UTM as a field occurs. Further studies replicated in other contexts could gather more evidence on this topic.

4 The Macro-Structural Context: The Italian University System and Public Policies for UTM

The next subsections provide the structural framework guiding our research. First, we briefly depict the Italian university system in order to supply some basic information about the system itself and its changes in the last 25 years. Second, we deal with public policies for UTM in Italy.

4.1   *The Italian University System*

Italian universities are among the oldest institutions in the Western world: the foundation of many of them goes back to the Middle Ages and the Renaissance (21 Italian institutions out of the current 91 were founded before the sixteenth century; those 21 institutions are also part of the 48 oldest European universities). Yet, the institution of a national university system took place only in 1859, along with the process of national unification, which modelled the system after the Napoleonic institutional archetype and the German Humboldtian one.

Those two basic features largely reproduced for 130 years, in spite of economic, political and social changes. Only between the early 1990s and 2010 did the university system and institutions undergo major changes through multiple waves of reform. The main changes introduced are as follows:

- Wider institutional autonomy, along with narrower state regulative intervention (at least until 2008);
- The introduction of lump sum budget as system's funding mechanisms;
- New study programmes and degrees following the Bologna Process;
- Institutional, research and study programme assessment;
- The decentralisation of academic recruitment, followed later by its partial recentralisation.

In many cases reforms were also meant to push universities to open themselves to the societal environment and, particularly, to the economy.

Reforms and innovations that occurred during the first decade of the 2000s, clearly inspired by a neoliberal agenda, are of particular interest. In 2008, the centre-right government dramatically cut university public funding, while a new form of recentralisation and control over institutions and bureaucratisation took place through evaluations by ANVUR, instituted in 2008 after a reform of the previous evaluation system infrastructure). Further, public funding based on institutional performance evaluations have gained increasing importance.

As far as the system's structure is concerned, there are 91 university institutions, 61 of which are public. Among these, there are three institutions specialised in engineering and architecture called Polytechnics.[1] Public institutions are supplemented by 30 non-state institutions (largely private, only three of them supported by public authorities different from the state), formally recognised and accredited by the state as universities. Of those institutions, 11 are distant teaching universities providing on-line study courses with no, or negligible, research activities. The other 19 institutions are rather small and specialised in particular disciplinary fields (such as economics and medicine) except for one, the Catholic University, a large institution with a complete educational supply.

4.2 Public Policies for UTM

In Italy the UTM as a formally structured and, moreover, required activity is rather a novelty, since it was introduced, along with the last university reform, in 2011 as a part of the institutions' activities to be evaluated by ANVUR. In this general policy framework, ANVUR defines all research exercise and evaluation aspects, from timetables to specific contents and goals. For all practical purposes, the Agency acts as a regulatory and policy-making actor, substituting the Ministry in elaborating and addressing evaluation policies related to teaching, research, UTM and academic recruitment/career matters.

Currently Departments have to account, on a three-year basis, for teaching, research and third mission activities, and their evaluation is important for allocating part of the ordinary funding to universities, as well as, since 2018, for the special funding for the best performing departments. Besides, every five years a research exercise evaluation is undertaken to assess the scientific productivity of departments through their members' publications, on which, again, funding allocation partly depends.

Aside from the controversies on evaluation criteria, aims, practices and results, these policies are exerting pressure on institutions, departments and academics to undertake and valuate third mission activities. To be more precise, policies produce a chain of coercive pressures: The state on university institutions, institutions on departments, departments on their members. This is true for UTM too.

Actually, UTM policies have formally opened a field of activity for universities and academics. It must be noted that they are based on a twofold assumption: first, that universities have to open up to the economic and societal environment; second that the environment is ready to welcome their opening up, to take advantage of the universities' knowledge production, and is willing to collaborate with them. This last premise is much more problematic than is commonly assumed, as we will show in the case studies analysis. In this last regard, third mission policies have largely neglected the private sector side and have directed few efforts to incentive and/or support businesses and private organisations to engage and commit themselves to business-university relationships. Thus, third mission, supposedly structured by a collaboration between universities and external stakeholders, is more an affair of the former, while the stakeholders seem quite reluctant or passive about constructing collaborative relations and partnerships.

Overall, policy makers still place the burden of activating the environment on the shoulders of the universities. This is due also to a double constraint that universities face: first, since part of their income comes from UTM activity

UNIVERSITY THIRD MISSION

evaluations, they are pressed to enact such activities; the second is, because of public funding cuts, institutions are pressed to seek economic resources from the private sector.

5 Setting the Scene: The Three Cases Investigated

As case studies, we examined three public universities: Ferrara, Padua and Pavia. The three institutions considered have both similarities and differences, making them interesting comparative cases (Table 8.1).

TABLE 8.1 Case study main features

		University of Ferrara	University of Padua	University of Pavia
		SIMILARITIES		
Founding year		Historical (1391)	Historical (1222)	Historical (1361)
Educational supply		STEM, HSS, Medicine undergraduate, graduate, postgraduate, doctoral programs	STEM, HSS, Medicine undergraduate, graduate, postgraduate, doctoral programs	STEM, HSS, Medicine undergraduate, graduate, postgraduate, doctoral programs
		DIFFERENCES		
Size	n. enrolled students	15,000	58,000	21,000
	n. staffed academics	575	1,972	876
Economic-industrial context		Low industrialised Agricultural and food SMES	Industrialised Mechanical SMES and large enterprises	De-industrialised Engineering, chemical SMES

At the three institutions, we interviewed qualified informants at the central level, such as provosts for third mission, executives and administrative staff responsible for the Technological Transfer Office and the Research Office.

In order to compare how disciplinary differences may affect UTM activities, we selected in each institution two STEM departments and two HSS departments (Table 8.2).

TABLE 8.2   Case study departments at the three institutions

University	Ferrara	Padua	Pavia
Departments	Economics (HSS)	Cultural and Artistic Heritage (HSS)	Economics (HSS)
	Architecture (STEM)	Engineering (STEM)	Engineering (STEM)
	Humanistic studies (HSS)	*Psychology* (HSS)	Arts (HSS)
	Chemistry and Pharmacy (STEM)	Chemistry (STEM)	*Pharmacy* (STEM)

At the departmental level, we interviewed Heads of departments (or the Head's deputies) and one scholar of each department selected as particularly active in UTM activities. The three departments highlighted in italics are the most active and best performing in third mission activities in each institution, although each department presents a decent level of engagement and commitment in those activities.

To account for the business/entrepreneurial side of the third mission we interviewed members of business associations and entrepreneurs or managers of local firms.

TABLE 8.3   People interviewed for each case study and institution of membership

	Ferrara	Padua	Pavia
Academics and university managers	10	10	9
Entrepreneurs/firms' managers	2	8	3
Entrepreneurial associations' representatives	3	2	3

6   Main Research Findings

The following three subsections present the main findings of our research. Section 6.1 is about third mission activities at the institutional and departmental

UNIVERSITY THIRD MISSION

levels; Section 6.2 deals with the structuration of UTM as an organisational field; Section 6.3 depicts UTM as a social field characterised by tensions, contradictions and struggles.

6.1   Third Mission Activities

At the three institutions and the departments examined, UTM activities show a remarkable degree of structuration. As mentioned in Section 4.2, this is largely due both to the cuts in public spending on research and to policies enhancing the interactions of universities with their environment.

At the individual institution level, UTM has at different times been politically enacted, promoted, supported and pushed by rectors: in the early 2000s, in Padua and Ferrara's cases, some years later in Pavia. Although conditions pushing towards UTM are important, the rectors' leadership role is crucial for incorporating UTM in the organisational structure and culture of institutions. Actually, the rectors' commitment has manifested itself through organisational innovations at the institutional level. In all three institutions, we can observe that: (1) there is a UTM provost; (2) the Technology Transfer Office (TTO) is widening its tasks to include the whole range of UTM activities; (3) the Research Office and the provost for research have incorporated UTM in their respective tasks. Further, internal policies and regulations addressed the promotion of UTM's departmental and academic activities, especially those producing economic value and revenues.

All these changes and innovations signal not only the activism in UTM of the investigated institutions, but are also and above all indicators of the ongoing institutionalisation process. Along with their internal institutionalisation process, the activism of institutions has grown as well, in terms of academic capitalism and entrepreneurialism, public/social engagement, efforts to communicate with and inform external public and private organisations and construction of linkages, relationships, networks and partnerships with them.

At the departmental level, where the UTM activities concretely take place, the 12 investigated structures show a rather high level of engagement. Yet, it must be stressed that at this organisational level UTM activities are neither mediated nor organised by the departments: rather, they are the product of research group initiatives and, even more often, of those of individual academics. Thus, departmental third mission is more an aggregate by-product of the initiatives and actions of individuals based on personal knowledge, contacts, ties and bargaining between the individual academic and other external actors.

For more complex pursuits, such as spin-off creation or patenting from applied research results, the institutions' central offices are involved in administrative, regulative and infrastructural (physical spaces, facilities and the like) matters, while, again, the activities are promoted, undertaken and pursued by research groups and individuals.

Most third mission activities pursued by academics in all departments relate to commissions, contracted research, consultancies and public/social engagement activities. Academics generally use the remunerated activities to fund their lines of research and research-related aspects, such as study grants and laboratory/office equipment. Academics pay a percentage of the revenues to the department, which, in turn, partly rewards the institution in order to contribute and support the funding of departmental and institutions' wider research activities.

6.2   *The Relational Structure: UTM as an Organisational Field*

Policies promoting UTM not only create conditions pushing universities towards it, but also, necessarily, for constructing an organisational field where UTM activities take – or should take – form, orientation and substance. The degree of structuration of an organisational field is also an indicator of its institutionalisation, which, in turn, the institutionalisation of organisational forms and also of relations and activities within it depend on (Di Maggio, 1991, p. 267). Structuration entails a process by which organisations increasingly engage in mutual interactions and relations, exchange of information and various kinds of influences, to create an awareness of being part of a common enterprise (DiMaggio & Powell, 1991, p. 65).

In this respect, our case studies show that UTM's organisational field is sufficiently developed and it has reached a significant degree of structuration. In particular, Ferrara and Padua show the highest degree of structuring, while Pavia is the least structured.

Although the University of Ferrara is located in a less industrialised environment (prevalence of agriculture and food industry and small firms in traditional sectors), since 2004 it has given rise to a dense entwining of relations, especially with local public authorities (at the provincial and municipal level), a local bank foundation and representative business institutions. Those institutions join in the Committee of Ferrara University Supporters, which is part of the university's governance body. Further, the regional authority has created a public-private consortium, Emilia Romagna Network for High Technologies (ASTER) whose task is to fund collaborative research among regional universities, firms and research institutions.

An important interorganisational structure is the Technopole, which is part of ASTER, supported by the municipalities of Ferrara's territory, and is a structure devoted to technological transfer to firms. Technopole finds economic support in the Region via the European Fund for Regional Development.

UNIVERSITY THIRD MISSION

Technopole operates through four advanced laboratories in medicine and biotechnologies applied to the fields of medicine, advanced mechanics, urban and architectural requalification and cultural heritage, and environment soil and water. More recently, the university, local actors and stakeholders instituted a consortium named Future in Research, in order to create contacts between firms and the university's research structure. Finally, the university has instituted (in collaboration with the Provincial Agency for Development) the Research Portal, a physical space where firms can find information, services and resources to build collaborative research opportunities with the university.

The case of Padua is similar to Ferrara's, showing a relevant degree of structuration of the UTM field. The Galileo Science and Technology Park (PST) is an association joined by the Chambers of Commerce of Padua, Treviso, Vicenza and Belluno, the University, Province and Municipality of Padua, a bank foundation, Rovigo Consortium and Veneto Innovazione (a regional company for applied research, innovation and technology transfer). The mission of the technology park is to strengthen the competitive capacity of businesses by spreading technology and applied research results. The PST excels in the areas of innovation and research (a meeting point between the demand for and supply of technological innovation), design and new materials (creativity for product innovation), quality and certification (interface between businesses and laboratories) and start-ups (an incubator of new businesses).

Since 2010, the University of Padua has had a Territorial Council, which is a new internal governance body made up entirely of representatives of external social, cultural and economic institutions. The body has consultative tasks representing the interests of the major local stakeholders. Furthermore, the Council appoints the external members of the University of Padua to the board of directors.

Finally, in 2016, the University of Padua launched a company in charge of managing the consulting activities of technology transfer and innovation, else through collaboration with companies, industrial associations, professionals, investors, banks, and other public and private bodies, on a local, national and international scale. This new, wholly owned private subsidiary organisation, named Smart Unipd, aims at leveraging on the competences and networks of the university and systematically exploiting the most promising multidisciplinary research results and intellectual property.

The case of Pavia, as mentioned, is where UTM's organisational field appears less structured, largely because, in this case, only in recent years has UTM become an important issue in the university's governance and policy. In order to promote and support technology transfer and innovation, two technology parks operate in Pavia. The first one is a public-funded initiative named Polo Tecnologico Servizi. The University, Municipality, Province and Chamber of Commerce of Pavia jointly established the technology park in 2007. It focuses exclusively on life sciences projects, generally characterised by longer time-to-market and high development costs. The other organisation, named Polo Tecnologico di Pavia, is a private innovation hub owned by Durabo, a locally based real estate company. Started in 2011, the number of its firms and operators has rapidly increased within few years. Nowadays, 46 companies and 320 employees have settled in the technology park. Most of the technology park companies operate in IT related business, while the rest of them are almost equally divided between biotechnology and advanced services.

The description of the relational structure characterising each case suggests three considerations related to the construction and structuration processes of UTM's organisational field.

First, this process seems rather independent, at least to some extent, from the economic-industrial structure features. Padua's dynamism is largely due to its industrial structure, while conversely Pavia's lesser structuration relates to its de-industrialisation process. Yet, the economic context is not everything, although undoubtedly university's action takes advantage of favourable economic conditions. This is most evident in the case of Ferrara, where the relatively less industrialised context has not prevented the construction of a broad and dense organisational field, if institutional actors have the interest and willingness to undertake such a process. The same institutional activism characterises Padua's case, although the more developed industrial structure of its territory has surely played a crucial role in developing relational networks among institutions and organisations.

Second, the organisational field does not coincide with the geographical space of the universities' territories; rather, its network structure spreads to the regional area, gathering and connecting institutions in the political, administrative and representative business sectors, mediatory bodies (public or public-private) and economic actors. In some cases, the field encompasses collaborative national and even international linkages, especially with the largest companies operating in more technologically advanced sectors, whose innovation interests and needs match more easily, than small-medium enterprises, with the research and knowledge supply of the universities.

Third, from our case studies it emerges that universities take a pivotal role in the enactment of the structuring process. Even if external actors and stakeholders take part in the enterprise, universities take the first step. This is especially true for Ferrara, but it is also for the most recent dynamics characterising Pavia. Overall, this corroborates what we noted at the end of Section 4: the creation

UNIVERSITY THIRD MISSION   203

and construction of relations, networks and partnerships is mostly an affair of
the university institutions. In other words, the socio-economic environment
does not often solicit the university to collaborate, but largely the contrary. In
this context, an exception are the proposals for collaboration by companies,
mainly addressed to the STEM departments. It is noticeable, however, that
scholars often reject proposals of collaboration, especially if they come from
small local companies. Actually, scholars and university departments select
collaborations with large firms, on long-term and highly knowledge-intensive
projects. This last remark introduces us to the next section, related to tensions
in the UTM field.

6.3   *UTM as Social Field: Tensions, Contradictions and Struggles*

UTM underwent, or is undergoing, a growing process of structuration, which
indicates that it is gaining a certain degree of institutionalisation. Yet, what we
have presented so far is only part of its structuration process. That is, it is not
enough to analyse and account for the quantity and density of relationships
among actors, because those relations bring on tensions, contradictions and
conflicts. This remark calls for attention to consider UTM as a social field where
actors are involved in a political dimension and action to which they bring
their dispositions, definitions, interests, representations, logics and strategies.
What is at stake is how the field should work, for what purposes, and under
what principles and logics.

We now turn to those aspects, considering two crucial relational dimensions in which this political view of the field takes place: the tensions among
actors in the field (the *internal/external dimension*) and those that arise inside
the university setting (*internal dimension*).

As far as the internal/external dimension is concerned, we previously
showed how UTM as a field is constructed by heterogeneous institutions
belonging to other social/organisational fields (university, business, the polit-
ical-administrative sector); thus agents, entering the third mission relational
space bring with them the main logics, definitions, dispositions, representations and expectations of the respective fields they belong to. In this regard,
Bourdieu in his many empirical works (in particular, 1993) and DiMaggio (1991)
showed that the process of constructing a social/organisational field is characterised by tensions, conflicts and struggles among the actors involved in it.

The UTM field presents such dynamics, especially as related to its main players: the university and the business worlds.

On the university's side, both the academics and the administrative staff
involved in third mission activities highlight difficulties and problems in relating with the economic actors. First, it is lamented that there is scant interest

from the business sector in university research, so that universities' academic and administrative personnel often have to "knock on the enterprises' doors like door-to-door salesmen". These words, taken from an interview with the responsible of TTO of the University of Ferrara, epitomise a common view expressed by other interviewees. Although a huge amount of information is available on universities' websites and at businesses associations and various intermediary bodies, the economic world appears largely indifferent or passive. Further, universities are making huge efforts to communicate their supply of personnel, infrastructures, services and research products available to enterprises, while in some cases nothing or very little comes back to the universities from the economy's side in terms of demands for scientific advanced knowledge. Some interviewees stated that entrepreneurs think universities have to provide their services free, since they receive public funding. Others highlight that since most firms are rather small and operate in traditional and mature market sectors, or as subcontractors of larger firms, they have no interest in investing in advanced technologies and knowledge. A further cultural problem is that most entrepreneurs, especially those who run small-medium enterprises have a low educational attainment, perceive the university and science as distant, alien objects. They have no idea of how universities work and often consider them as an educational institution (more in terms of the social prestige granted by a university degree than as a source of advanced knowledge), and they are infused with the culture of doing (practical knowledge) as opposed to that of studying (theoretical knowledge).

Another line of tension arises from the contradictory conceptions of time linked, respectively, to scientific and business activities and by different expectations. While scientific activities and achievements need relatively long time and are open to a relevant degree of uncertainty related to results, the timeline of businesses is short and market-dictated, and business people expect things to work rapidly and efficiently for their purposes. These respective concepts and expectations inevitably clash with each other.

Other problems relate to the requests that firms make to academics. Many interviewees complain that collaboration proposals are excessively specific and/or piecemeal. Firms present to universities problems whose solutions are largely available in the marketplace. Scholars of high scientific and academic reputation criticise their colleagues who carry out measurements, tests, small consultancies and other forms of collaboration with industry without a strong scientific impact factor. "The university should not look like a place where firms get low-cost services and consultancy", one interviewed professor said, suggesting that universities and departments should phase out collaborations considered scientifically non-prestigious and/or fruitless. In many cases

UNIVERSITY THIRD MISSION

academics refuse such requests because their monetary returns are useless for research purposes (e.g. funding research bursaries or lines of research), as well as for the achievement of advanced knowledge results.

Various interviewees on the university side highlighted how the economic actors are indifferent, rather uninterested, distrustful and to some extent arrogant. In this regard, we quote an emblematic passage of an interview with a university researcher engaged in a spin-off hosted in Pavia's technology park:

> I hold a two-sided business card: one side as an academic, the other as an entrepreneur. However, I also have just a businessman's card: actually I don't want to tell a customer that I'm a university scholar because I know that it would damage my reputation with them.

On the economic-entrepreneurial side, critics toward the university are largely mirror-like. Universities are still too distant from the needs of firms and entrepreneurs. Academics have little or no entrepreneurial mentality. The university is unable to communicate and inform the business world, so it is very difficult to know what a university or an academic can do for entrepreneurs. The university bureaucracy is cumbersome and time-consuming. Very often what academics want is to carry on their research and not solve practical problems. Academics are haughty and, in some cases, they just want to get money from business for their own interests and goals.

Overall, entrepreneurs judge the university rather negatively. Universities and academics keep on reasoning and acting in a self-referential fashion. In this regard, an interviewee from Ferrara's business association used a blunt expression to label academics, calling them *ermines*.[2] Such a label refers, at the same time, to the distance of the academic world, its closure (ermine is a symbol of an aristocratic and, at the same time, hieratic position detached from the ordinary world) and a certain dose of disdain toward that world. Subsequently, the interviewee expresses his thought in this way: "You [academics] study how to send missiles to Mars, but I [entrepreneur] have to produce a piece of metal to fit into part of a ship...I'm trivialising...but...".

Those different dispositions, representations and critical remarks that each side addresses to the other one represent, in euphemised form, the struggle occurring in the UTM field. This struggle is based on the different positions of the actors involved, determined, to say it with Bourdieu, by the different forms of capital they own. Academics own scientific knowledge capital, while entrepreneurs own the economic kind. What is at stake is the definition of the most strategic kind of capital inside the UTM field and, according to it, how the field should operate. On the university side, UTM should enhance innovation and scientific progress. In this view, economic capital is only the means to create exploitable advanced knowledge. Entrepreneurs, conversely, think that academics must adapt their activity to their firms' demands, since the academics need economic capital to fund their scientific research.

Each side involved is interested in being the main player (that is, the one who monopolises the strategic form of capital) in the UTM field, in order to occupy the dominant position inside it, dictating the logics and rules of the field. This, in turn, means being relatively autonomous from other actors in term of power relations.

Now let us focus on the internal dimension. UTM as a field involves tension, struggles and contradictions inside the academic world too. Those aspects have emerged more or less explicitly during the interviews with Heads of departments and academics engaged in the third mission.

An initial tension, produced at the macro level of the university system, takes place at the intersection of UTM policies, university assessment schemes and the academic recruitment and career system. On the one hand, as we explained in Section 4, policies have instituted UTM, operationalising it through its incorporation in the assessment schemes set out to detect and evaluate third mission activities for institutions' funding purposes. Third mission activities serve mainly applied and practical purposes and often of an interdisciplinary kind. On the other hand, recruitment/career system rests on quality-quantity assessments of individual academic's scientific publications, especially scientific books and articles published in highly reputed referred journals, based on scientific-disciplinary sectors. Further, the possibility of getting an academic position depends on the evaluation of a candidate's scientific productivity, assessed by a disciplinary-based panel of academics in specific disciplinary fields.

Those two arrangements generate a dualism at the system level, producing contradictory pressures on academics: policies, evaluations and economic shortages call on academics to make more intense commitments to third mission activities, but those activities and results, for their particular features, are not suitable for academics' recruitment and career advancement assessment. This contradiction produces three kinds of strategic responses by academics. Those who are most active in third mission in some cases tend to give up career aspirations for economic advantages (third mission activities are remunerative for them and for their research groups) and/or for expressive reasons (they feel fulfilled by serving the economy and society). A different strategy, less based on a trade-off logic, enacted by engaged academics is being highly selective in the choice of third mission activities, preferring those which have positive effects on their disciplinary-based research and thus for their career advancement opportunities. Finally, other academics may prefer to devote themselves only to traditional research work, largely giving up third mission activities, with a view of achieving career advancement.

A second line of tension relates to the revenues of third mission activities. As noted in Section 6.1, institutions have issued policies and regulations about UTM activities, which state that academics are required to pay a portion of their revenues (between 10 and 20%) to their department, which in turn allocates a portion of this withdrawal to the institution. Some interviewees consider it as an iniquitous tax, since in most case such revenues barely cover expenses. After this 'taxation' and the refunding of activity costs, the amount of money may not be enough for academics to pay for the most expensive items linked to their research activities (for example, research bursaries for young researchers, consumables and tools, equipment, etc.) and to undertake new research projects. Other interviewees, such as a director of a STEM department at the University of Pavia, have an opposite view: "Although scholars do not like to pay operating costs to the university, this is a just compensation for using university facilities and equipment". Hence, in his opinion, the university should implement policies to reinvest the revenues with a redistributive logic. An appropriate reinvestment strategy is supposed to enhance the quality of the whole institution's research, equipment and services.

A third and very important tension is the one that opposes academics favourable to third mission and those who are not. Academics more willing to undertake third mission consider not only those who reject it, but also those who are highly selective in choosing which activities to accept, as old-style academics unable or unwilling to change the traditional and deep-rooted academic cultural and cognitive schemes. They state that any academic has a lot to learn from relations with firms and entrepreneurs, even from piecemeal collaborations, in order to innovate and change the way university institutions work and the way academics relate to the external world. On the other hand, those who have a more traditional view of university and academic work stress that third mission is not part of (true) scientific work, so that scholars must reject it as a kind of commercial prostitution, or use it instrumentally to fund 'real' scientific research work. It is worth mentioning that these opposing views are not disciplinary-dependent mirroring the HSS/STEM dichotomy: they are present in both of those disciplinary macro-fields. Thus, these different dispositions and positions toward UTM are ascribable to different academic habitus.

Embracing UTM, or refusing it, or using it in a utilitarian fashion, gives rise to subtle, sometimes barely visible forms of struggles among academics, whose stake is the academic consecration or, conversely, desecration of UTM activities in the university and thus its possibility of institutionalisation as a legitimated and recognised field.

7 Conclusions

Although based on contextual and limited case studies, our analysis highlights some important points.

First, we cannot solely consider UTM as an activity carried out by academics. It is a structured field, albeit to different degrees, where universities, societal institutions and organisations, and individuals are involved in a relational network in which third mission activities are embedded, conditioned and possible. While the macro-structural context, represented by state policies promoting/imposing UTM, is an important condition, many others play a key role, especially those related to the enactment of UTM's relational structure and activities by institutional, organisational and individual actors.

A second point is that differences regarding territorial industrial-economic structure are certainly important but, again, by themselves are not enough to construct UTM as a field of activities. Our three case studies are rather different in terms of their respective economic-industrial structures. Nonetheless, those differences have not prevented the construction and structuration of the organisational field and activities linked to third mission, albeit with some peculiarities. The territorial economic-industrial structure, yet, is more relevant for the kind, quantity and quality of third mission activities carried out in each context.

Thirdly, UTM is gaining a significant degree of institutionalisation, at least at the university's organisational level, measurable by the following indicators: (1) the issuing of dedicated policies and regulations; (2) the institution of specialised functions that manage the activities politically and administratively; (3) the growth of communication with the social environment; (4) the efforts to link external actors and academics. At the societal level, the number of local public authorities, mediatory bodies and representative business organisations actively involved in UTM contribute significantly to structuring and thus to the institutionalisation process. Lesser activism and contribution stem from entrepreneurs and firms, but those who are involved in UTM play a significant role in this institutionalisation process. Overall, the UTM field is still in the stage of semi-institutionalisation (Tolbert & Zucker, 1996) for which it is sufficiently widespread but not completely accepted, practiced and taken-for-granted by all the main actors.

Fourth, linked to the previous point, university institutions enact the societal environment, especially the economic one, while the converse is more of an exception. This higher activism is due both to state policies pressing universities toward third mission and to their need to find and retrieve economic resources in order to compensate for public funding cuts. On the economic side, the scant activism in enacting relations with university is due to a complex of cultural representation of the academic world that leads entrepreneurs to distrust it. Further, the different timeline and expectations of entrepreneurs in relation to scientific and research production carried out in the universities make them rather sceptical and critical.

From this latter point derives the fifth issue, concerning tensions all across the UTM field. Such tensions characterise both relations between the academic and the entrepreneurial worlds and the academic world itself. The complex of tensions shows that the UTM field is a contested terrain of struggles among actors with different positions, dispositions, interests and goals. The issues at stake are the following: (1) how the field should operate and function; (2) who are the dominant players within it; (3) how economic profits generated by the activities are to be distributed; (4) whether and to what extent UTM is legitimated inside the university. All these issues are the object of more or less visible and euphemised struggles among the actors involved. These struggles, in turn, show that the construction of a field is not only a matter of networking among institutions and organisations, albeit of great importance but, above all, that networking is a political and conflict construct which the network configuration, its structure of relations (power relations included) and its functioning depend on. This last remark has consequences on the way the UTM institutionalisation process takes place, form, content and orientation.

Finally, we would like to point out two issues related to policy-making, drawn from our analysis.

First, UTM policies, especially those promoting economic oriented activities, should pay much more attention to the business side. A proper policy intervention should include actions that stimulate enterprises to engage collaborative projects with universities, beyond short-term incentives and tax relief.

Second, the basic assumption of national evaluation schemes is that institutions are accountable for third mission activities but that individuals are not. Scholars perceive UTM as irrelevant for their career advancement opportunities. The assessment system should include UTM activities carried out individually by academics, for example considering results from the collaboration between scholars and external partners as products recognisable in academic applications for recruitment and career advancement. Currently, since the evaluation system operates substantially within the boundaries of the scientific-disciplinary sectors, it tends to exclude products deriving from a multi/trans/interdisciplinary perspective and applied research. In order to evaluate UTM activities, the assessment system needs to open up much more to the variety of products generated by collaborative, multifaceted and applied research.

Acknowledgement

Although this chapter is the result of the joint efforts of the two authors, Sections 3, 4.2, 5, 6.1 and 6.2 are written by Giacomo Balduzzi, while the author of Sections 2, 4.1 and 6.3 is Massimiliano Vaira. The Introduction (Section 1) and Conclusions (Section 7) are written by both authors.

Notes

1 The Italian Polytechnics are different from the UK's former ones, being part of the university system and following the same rules as the university institutions.
2 The interviewee refers to the ermine fur cape worn on the gown in occasion of official ceremonies by the highest ranks of the university and of magistracy.

References

Abreu, M., Grinevich, V., Hughes, A., & Kitson M. (2011). *Knowledge exchange between academics and the business, public and third sector.* University of Cambridge; Imperial College London.

Bekkers, R., & Bodas Freitas, I. M. (2008). Analysing knowledge transfer channels between universities and industry: To what degree do sectors also matter? *Research Policy, 37*(10), 1837–1853.

Bornmann, L. (2012). Measuring the societal impact of research. *EMBO Reports, 13*(8), 673–676.

Bornmann, L. (2013). What is societal impact of research and how can it be assessed? A literature survey. *Journal of the American Society for Information Science and Technology, 64*(2), 217–233.

Bourdieu, P. (1993). *The field of cultural production.* Oxford/Cambridge: Polity Press and Blackwell Publishing.

Callaert, J., Landoni, P., Van Looy, B., & Verganti, R. (2015). Scientific yield from collaboration with industry: The relevance of researchers' strategic approaches. *Research Policy, 44*(4), 990–998.

Clark, B. R. (1998). *Creating entrepreneurial universities: Organizational pathways of transformation.* New York, NY: Pergamon.

DiMaggio, P. J. (1991). Constructing an organizational field as a professional project: US art museums, 1920–1940. In W. W. Powell & P. J. DiMaggio (Eds.), *The new institutionalism of organizational analysis.* Chicago, IL: University of Chicago Press.

DiMaggio, P. J., & Powell, W. W. (1991). The iron cage revisited. institutional isomorphism and collective rationality. In W. W. Powell & P. J. DiMaggio (Eds.), *The new institutionalism of organizational analysis*. Chicago, IL: University of Chicago Press.

Etzkowitz, H. (2001). The second academic revolution and the rise of entrepreneurial science. *IEEE Technology and Society Magazine, 20*(2), 18–29.

Etzkowitz, H., & Leydesdorff, L. (1997). *Universities in the global knowledge economy: A co-evolution of university–industry–government relations*. London: Cassel Academic.

Geertz, C. (1973). *The interpretation of culture*. New York, NY: Basic Books.

Geuna, A., & Muscio, A. (2009). The governance of university knowledge transfer: A critical review of the literature. *Minerva, 47*(1), 93–114.

Gibbons, M., Limoges, C., Nowotny, H., Schwartzman, S., Scott, P., & Trow, M. (1994). *The new production of knowledge: The dynamics of science and research in contemporary societies*. London: Sage.

Hamadache, K. (2015). Reintroducing power and struggles within organisational fields. In A. Tatli, M. Ozbilgin, & M. Karatas-Ozkan (Eds.), *Pierre Bourdieu, organization, and management*. New York, NY: Routledge.

Istat. (2015). *Rapporto annuale 2015. La situazione del paese*. Rome: Istituto Nazionale di Statistica.

Kitagawa, F., Barrioluengo, M. B., & Uyarra, E. (2016). Third mission as institutional strategies: Between isomorphic forces and heterogeneous pathways. *Science and Public Policy, 43*(6), 736–750.

Laredo, P. (2007). Revisiting the third mission of universities: Toward a renewed categorization of university activities? *Higher Education Policy, 20*(4), 441–456.

Mowery, D. C., Nelson, R. R., Sampat, B. N., & Ziedonis, A. A. (2004). Ivory tower and industrial innovation. In *University-industry technology transfer before and after the Bayh-Dole Act*. Stanford, CA: Stanford Business Books.

Musselin, C. (2007). Are universities specific organizations? In G. Krücken, A. Kosmützky, & M. Torka (Eds.), *Towards a multiversity? Universities between global trends and national traditions*. Bielefeld: Transaction Publishers.

Nedeva, M. (2007). New tricks and old dogs? The 'third mission' and the re-production of the university. In D. Epstein. R. Boden, R. Deem, F. Rizvi, & S. Wright (Eds.), *World yearbook of education 2008: Geographies of knowledge, geometries of power: Framing the future of higher education*. New York, NY: Routledge.

Pinheiro, R., Benneworth, P., & Jones, G. A. (Eds.). (2012a). University and regional development. *A Critical Assessment of Tensions and Contradictions*. London: Routledge.

Pinheiro, R., Benneworth, P., & Jones, G. A. (2012b). Introduction university and regional development. In R. Pinheiro, P. Benneworth, & G. A. Jones (Eds.), *A critical assessment of tensions and contradictions*. London: Routledge.

Powell, W. W., White D. R., Koput, K. W., & Owen-Smith, J. (2005). Network dynamics and field evolution: The growth of interorganizational collaboration in the life sciences. *American Journal of Sociology, 110*(4), 1132–1205.

Rostan, M., Ceravolo, F. A., & Vaira, M. (2013, September 9–11). *Universities, innovation and regional economies in Italy.* Paper presented at the 26th CHER Conference, The Roles of Higher Education and Research in the Fabric of Societies, Lausanne.

Scott, J. (2006). The mission of the university: Medieval to postmodern transformations. *The Journal of Higher Education, 77*(1), 1–39.

Slaughter, S., & Leslie, L. (1997). *Academic capitalism: Politics, policies, and the entrepreneurial university.* Baltimore, MD: The Johns Hopkins University Press.

Slaughter, S., & Rhoades, G. (2004). *Academic capitalism and the new economy.* Baltimore, MD: John Hopkins University Press.

Thornton, P. H., Ocasio, W., & Lounsbury, M. (2012). *The institutional logics perspective: A new approach to culture, structure and process.* Oxford: Oxford University Press.

Thune, T., & Gulbrandsen, M. (2011). Institutionalization of university-industry interaction: An empirical study of the impact of formal structures on collaboration pattern. *Science and Public Policy, 38*(2), 99–107.

Thune, T., Reymert, I., Gulbrandsen, M., & Aamodt, P. O. (2016). Universities and external engagement activities: Particular profiles for particular universities? *Science and Public Policy, 43*(6), 774–786.

Tolbert, P. S., & Zucker, L. G. (1996). The institutionalization of institutional theory. In S. R. Clegg & C. Hardy (Eds.), *Studying organizations.* London: Sage.

Yin, R. K. (2014). Case study research. In *Design and methods.* Los Angeles, CA: Sage.

Zomer, A., & Benneworth, P. (2011). The rise of the university's third mission. In J. Enders, H. de Boer, & D. Westerheijden (Eds.), *Reform of higher education in Europe.* Rotterdam, The Netherlands: Sense Publishers.

CHAPTER 9

Teaching Staff in Non-University Higher Education in Japan: Career Experience, Competencies and Identities

Yuki Inenaga and Keiichi Yoshimoto

Abstract

The non-university higher education sector in most countries conveys vocational education. In Japan, both junior colleges and professional training colleges also provide vocational education at Level 5 of the International Standard Classifications of Education (2011). However, the historical origins of these two types of institutions differ and there is ambiguity concerning their objectives and legal requirements for their educational programmes and teaching staff. We argue that there is a need to develop a convergent research framework to assess the career experience and competencies of the teaching staff of such institutions to improve the quality of vocational education. This study investigates the career experience, competencies and identities of teaching staff in the non-university higher education sector to understand how various types of academic qualifications and work experience are related to their careers through the analysis of nationwide empirical survey data in Japan. The results identified four model types of teaching staff members' career experience: 'dual', 'academic', 'vocational', and 'other'. While most junior college teaching staff were classified as 'academic', there was a conflict between the identities of junior college teachers and institutional demands. 'Academic' teaching staff reported conflicting demands when their academic experience did not meet the professional demands made of them by junior college students. Both junior colleges and professional training colleges revealed similar demands; to strengthen teachers' professional/vocational orientations. However, the historical origins and inertia of such institutions have not supported the improvement of education and training quality offered to students.

© KONINKLIJKE BRILL NV, LEIDEN, 2020 | DOI: 10.1163/9789004422582_010

Keywords

non-university higher education – vocational education and training – teaching staff – career – competency – identity

1 Introduction

The demand for vocational education is increasing along with the expansion and diversification of higher education in Japan as well as most advanced countries. In Europe, employability and professional relevance have been discussed in depth due to the development of the European Area of Higher Education (Teichler, 2009). Even though universities comprise the largest group of higher education institutions, universities cannot continue to simply pursue their traditional educational model of disseminating academic knowledge without any relation to the professional world. Several concepts, such as a change in what is considered 'valid knowledge' in university caused by new and vocationally oriented student demands (Williams, 2007) and new 'academic' disciplines, including nursing in post-1992 universities in the UK (Findlow, 2011), have already been discussed. However, this trend has not been well considered in discussions concerning non-university higher education and its teaching staff.

The traditional university sector has commonly fostered the concept of its professors possessing integrated competencies of research and pedagogical skills developed through the Humboldtian model of higher education. Boyer's (1990) four scholastic competencies – discovery, integration, application and education – cover the third mission of service and related activities; however, they are still in line with the Humboldtian university model. Tigelaar and colleagues (2004) summarised a common framework of teaching competencies in higher education studies: competency in content knowledge, didactic competency, organisational competency and scientific competency. They attempted to define new competencies in response to the shift towards student-centred pedagogical approaches, which represents a new challenge in university education. However, this discussion remains within the limits of the Humboldtian model, as the knowledge contents that are disseminated by universities have not been questioned. Furthermore, the convergent concept of the 'teaching professional' as a common model both in higher education and further education in terms of andragogy (Robson, 2009) also does not consider the increasing demand for vocational education in either sector.

Vocationally oriented education was traditionally provided by the non-university sector rather than the university sector. As Teichler (2008) notes, new types of non-university higher education institutions began appearing worldwide in the 1960s and 1970s alongside the expansion of university enrolment. However, by the 1990s, some of these first generation non-university higher education institutions began asserting that they provided education equal to that of universities and that the qualifications they awarded were equivalent to bachelor's and master's degrees; some non-university institutions even succeeded in 'raising their rank' by having their higher education accreditation level according to the International Standard Classification of Education (ISCED, 2011) stepped up from 5 to 6, without effecting any major changes in the educational content that they offered. This phenomenon has been referred to as 'academic drift' (Dunkel, le Mouillor, & Teichler, 2009). The resulting gap in ISCED 5 education was filled by the appearance of a new sector of advanced vocational education and training. This sector, which placed greater emphasis on vocational education, developed on a separate track, side by side with the academic sector of tertiary education (Teichler, 2008).

The teaching staff of non-university higher education institutions are also pressured to ensure the vocational relevance of the educational contents that they provide. However, the research framework for understanding vocational institute teaching staff is less discussed than that used to investigate university teaching staff. The first generation of non-university higher education teachers has adhered to the university model of academics with some emphasis on applied education. However, Levin, Kater, and Wagoner (2006) found that in the case of community colleges in the United States, the identity of affiliated institutions is quite important, whereas the staff's own disciplinary emphasis adhered to the four-year university degree model.

The second generation of non-university higher education institutions has different origins from those of vocational education and training institutes; accordingly, teacher competencies also emphasise relevant occupational experience. Regarding vocational education and training, many countries have set requirements concerning years of vocational experience and academic qualifications for applicants seeking employment as teachers, although requirements concerning career experience differ from country to country (Clayton, 2015; Inenaga, 2018).[1] Improvement in non-university and vocational higher education calls for – at the minimum – a revision of the institutes' requirements to ensure higher teaching standards and that professional expertise is properly incorporated into this framework.

Using two separate models – the academic profession model as the dominant standard in the university sector, and the vocational education and training teacher model in the vocational sector – may help us to better understand non-university teaching staff. However, to increase the permeability of higher education and vocational education and training (Dunkel et al., 2009), a convergent model with both academic and vocational dimensions may be more appropriate to understand non-university teachers' career experience, competencies and identities. In such a convergent model, it is necessary to define the measures of teachers' vocational experience and competency apart from academic experience and research competency related to their areas of specialisation.[2] Furthermore, the dilemma involving academic and vocational identities based on both backgrounds may apply at the institutional and individual levels. At an institutional level, institutions demonstrating inertia towards the academic world may face some difficulties caused by vocational missions in higher education. At an individual teacher level, some teachers may face dilemmas concerning institutional identity versus individual identity.

Who is responsible for non-university higher education? It is a significant question concerning the assurance of quality teaching, and a response to the expansion, diversification and increasing social pressures of higher education. However, when the purpose of each sector is ambiguous institutionally and the requirements of teachers are also legally ambiguous due to the sector's ambiguity (such as in the case of non-university higher education in Japan), there is a need to develop a convergent research framework to investigate the career experience, competencies and identities of teaching staff in higher education to improve its quality; this includes vocational education.

2 Literature Review: Non-University Higher Education in the Japanese Context

2.1 *The System*

In Japan, non-university higher education programmes are offered through junior colleges (*Tanki Daigaku*), professional training colleges (*Senmon Gakkō*, a type of specialised training college (*Senshū Gakkō*) offering post-secondary courses), and colleges of technology (*Kōtō-Senmon-Gakkō*). Junior colleges offer two- or three-year education programmes leading to associate degrees (*Tanki Daigaku Shi*) as a certain type of degree in the Japanese legal setting. Professional training colleges offer post-secondary education programmes of which the study duration ranges from one to four years, leading to a diploma (*Senmon Shi*) following the completion of a two-year programme and an advanced diploma (*Koudo Senmon Shi*) following the completion of a four-year programme. Colleges of technology are unique institutions that provide five-year education programmes combining three years of upper secondary education and two years of higher education. This educational programme also leads to associate certificates (*Jun Gakushi*).

In the legal context, the non-university higher education institutions, in contrast to universities, are typically grouped within a category of schools with a strongly vocational or professional orientation. The School Education Act mentions the "cultivation of competencies necessary for vocational occupations" as a purpose of the establishment of junior colleges (Article 108), colleges of technology (Article 118), and professional training colleges (Article 124). These chapters are different from the stated purpose of universities (Article 83). However, junior colleges and professional training colleges include other elements of non-vocational education: 'life skills' in the case of junior college, and 'life skills' as well as 'liberal education' in the case of professional training colleges. In the cases of both types of institutions, the ambiguity of the legal purpose of the institution can lead to difficulty in setting requirements for teaching staff from the perspective of vocational/professional education.

The expansion of the higher education sector in Japan is supported by the expansion of the university sector – particularly the private university sector – as well as the increase in enrolment in professional training colleges founded after 1976. On the other hand, the junior college sector established in 1964 is currently shrinking with regard to the increase in the enrolment ratio of female students in the university sector. In 2015, the enrolment ratio of non-university higher education institutions was 28%, whereas that of universities was 52%; the professional training college sector is the second largest sector in the higher education system, next to the university sector. However, the number of fourth-year students in colleges of technology comprise less than 1% of the total higher education enrolment (Table 9.1).

TABLE 9.1   Basic data of tertiary education system in Japan (2015)

	Universities	Junior colleges	Professional training colleges	Colleges of technology
Number of institutions	779	346	3,201	57
Number of students	28,60,210[a]	1,32,681	5,88,183[b]	57,611
Enrollement ratio for age 18 cohort (%)	51.5	5.1	22.4	0.9
Number of teaching staff (full-time)	1,82,723	8,266	37,063	4,354
Part-time academic staff/ full-time academic staff ratio	*1.08*	*2.24*	*2.80*	*0.49*

a Including graduate students. The total number of bachelor level student is 2,556,062.
b Including 1st to 3rd year students.

SOURCE: SCHOOL BASIC SURVEY (MEXT)

Junior college represents the first generation of the non-university sector of higher education, as reported by Teichler (2008). It is defined as one type of university under the law with permanent status. Junior college became associated with women's education, and offered programmes primarily in the fields of humanities and arts, secretarial school, child care and home economics. With the popularisation of higher education, junior colleges also spread rapidly. The number of junior colleges reached a peak of 598 in 1996; however, this number decreased to 341 in 2016. Most of the former junior colleges were converted to four-year universities, especially in the fields of humanities and arts, secretarial training and nursing, which are among the fields of education classified for junior college in statistics. The remaining junior colleges should adapt and strengthen their vocational or professional orientations due to recent social changes, such as The Equal Employment Opportunity Act of 1985 (amended in 1997)[3] and the wave of office automation affecting secretarial and office assistant work.

Professional training colleges can be seen as the second generation of non-university higher education institutions. Their main roots are in the conventional 'miscellaneous schools' (*Kakushu Gakkou*), which had many different education and training categories: dress sewing, calculations on abacus, culinary seminars and cram school, among others. In Japan, despite several revisions of the International Standard Classification of Occupations, technical occupations are not well recognised and classified. Following the era of rapid economic growth in Japan in the 1960s and early 1970s, the industrial structure has been continuously transformed into the service and soft economy sectors. Therefore, there are more jobs in non-manual occupations and workers' skills in this sector need continual upgrading. When the system of professional training colleges was founded, most miscellaneous schools were also upgraded. This is because the regulations concerning the establishment of specialised training colleges are not strict – but rather flexible like that of the miscellaneous schools – in terms of requirements for institutional conditions, learning hours, class sizes and teaching staff. Now, around 3,000 professional training colleges have been established under this laissez-faire policy and receive negligible support as compared with national universities that are heavily invested in as the top of the institutional hierarchy, even though they provide overlapping training in many fields, such as nursing. However, as Teichler (2008) reported, it is difficult for the second generation of non-university higher education institutions to upgrade to universities due to their origins. Professional training colleges face the same difficulty. Current challenges in this sector are to develop a clear identity of vocational education and to receive social recognition and support within a well-defined, quality assurance framework.

2.2   *Requirements for Teaching Staff*

Japan does not have a set of national qualifications or requirements that apply to all teaching staff in vocationally oriented education institutions, although there are certain fields that have their own teaching qualifications and training obligations, such as in the nursing profession. These requirements, in turn, vary according to the type of institution. Furthermore, there is no standard requirement pertaining to the number of years of work experience and other such matters across all institution types.

In the case of junior college, the legal requirement is similar to that in universities. However, this requirement applies to areas in which acquisition of practical techniques is necessary. In this case, only expertise in practical techniques is recognised: neither academic expertise, such as university degrees, nor the number of years of necessary work experience are defined. Furthermore, the requirements for teaching staff are flexible at specialised training colleges, where one may become a teacher provided one has graduated from secondary school and has at least six years of experience either in academic pursuits or a relevant occupation (Inenaga & Yoshimoto, 2018). This is partly caused by the legal ambiguity of the purpose of such institutions.

Existing research on the teaching staff of vocationally oriented education institutions in Japan is lacking, and studies on teaching staff of higher education institutions are almost entirely based on the academic model (Arimoto, Cummings, Huang & Cheol Shin, 2015).

3   Research Questions

How do the career experiences, competencies and identities of teaching staff of non-university higher education institutions differ or what do they resemble? Following the above discussion, three research questions were formulated concerning the contrast and combination of vocational expertise and academic research.

1. What are the similarities and differences in the career experience of teaching staff of the two types of vocational education institutions regarding professional experiences and academic qualifications?
2. How are the competencies required and possessed at the time of recruitment explained by both types of affiliated institutions and career experiences? The competencies required and possessed are analysed separately and then considered with regard to any competency gap and matching between institutional types and career experiences.

3. Do teaching staff with different career patterns and competencies in two institutional types form common or different identities and satisfactions as teachers in the non-university higher education sector? Due to the differences in career experience profiles of the two types of institutions supposed by the first research question, these patterns of identity and satisfaction may be considered differently in the two sectors, which is statistically examined as the interactional effects.

4 Methods

4.1 *Data*

The survey data analysed in this paper were obtained from the Survey of Teaching Staff and Educational Organisations in Higher Education (EQ1-TSS) conducted in 2011 by the authors and their colleagues in the Research Group on Higher Education and Qualifications at Kyushu University. This survey is the first nationwide scientific survey of junior college and professional training college teaching staff, whereas Japanese official statistics only contain limited information pertaining to the academic backgrounds of teaching staff.

The data were collected by an internet survey sent to the staff with the support of their affiliated institutions. A total of 1,051 full-time staff from 158 junior colleges and 1,754 from 414 professional training colleges responded to the survey (response rate 23.7% for junior colleges and 31.1% for professional training colleges).[4] From these effective responses, this study selected 1,672 samples[5] with no missing values for this analysis (651 for junior colleges and 1,021 for professional training colleges). It was also found that the profile analysed here is common with the national representative sample based on the School Teacher Statistical Survey conducted by the Ministry of Education, Culture, Sports, Science and Technology (MEXT) in 2010, at least concerning academic credentials (54.9% of teaching staff with a master's degree or higher for junior college and 9.5% for professional training college, whereas 59.0% and 12.2% respectively in this study, as shown in Table 9.3).

The following variables were analysed (Table 9.2): institutional-level variables (Group A), pertaining to the institution and training field; and experience and career variables (Group B). For the analysis of career experience, two operational indicators were developed. The indicator of academic research expertise was supposed metric, using the cutting point as possessing higher education experience equal to a master's degree or higher. It is also considered the formal requirement of teaching staff of professional training college with six years of academic or professional experiences after completing upper secondary education. A masters' degree is enough for this criterion without any professional experiences. The indicator of professional expertise was metric one, using the cutting point as possessing five years or more of professional work experience directly related to the training field. Then, four professional expertise categories were developed and labelled: 'dual', 'academic', 'vocational', and 'other'. Teaching staff who had both academic and professional expertise were categorised as 'dual'. Those with only academic expertise were categorised as 'academic' and those with only vocational expertise were categorised as 'vocational'. The remaining teaching staff who did not possess either type of expertise was categorised as 'other'. This means that they had an academic background equal to a bachelor's degree or lower and work experience of less than five years.

This stage was followed along with temporal order by two phases of causal analysis based on the following variables: required and possessed competencies (Group C variable) at the time of recruitment and identity and job satisfaction (Group D variable) at the time of this study. Regarding competencies, this survey originally set ten items on a 5-point scale, including those of teaching and management dimensions. The most highly required among the ten original competencies was 'teaching and coaching'. This had consensus and no variation. Thus, this study focused instead on the other two leading teaching competencies: 'research' and 'vocationally practical'. The respondents were asked about both types of competencies required by their affiliated institution and those that they possessed at the time of recruitment. Four dependent required and possessed competency variables were supposed as independent but correlated with each other and therefore analysed through a multivariate analysis of variance (MANOVA).

On identity and satisfaction during analysis of Group D variables, two types of identity and satisfaction were distinguished. The first was the identity of the work of the affiliated college and the other was individual work and career. The former two variables were (1) the mission of the college, and (2) the roles of its staff; devotion to research activities and professional practical experiences were compared with daily teaching practice using a 4-point scale. The latter individual level was work satisfaction and future career plans. For the discussion of identity in the non-university sector, a table from the appendix in Boyer (1984) showed the identity towards the affiliated college to be stronger in two-year institutions (non-university sector) than in four-year institutions (the university sector). Two variables were used: (1) the conflict between education and research, and (2) that between professional practice and specialised knowledge.

222 INENAGA AND YOSHIMOTO

TABLE 9.2   List of variables and categories analysed

Variable name   Value ranges and categories

A) Institution level variables
  Institution
   1   junior college
   2   professional training college
  Training field Field of education and training
   1   humanities and arts
   2   business
   3   education
   4   engineering and agriculture
   5   co-medical
   6   service

B) Experience and career before recruitment
  E1 Education (highest credentials)
   1   high school
   2   professional training college, junior college or college of technology
   3   bachelor
   4   master
   5   doctoral degree or course completion
  E2 Vocational experiences before recruitment
  0–43 (years of work)
  Career type   (combination of E1 and E2)
   1   dual: E1 >= 4 and E2 >= 5
   2   academic: E1 >= 4 and E2 <= 4
   3   vocational: E1 <= 3 and E2 >= 5
   4   other: E1 <= 3 and E2 <= 4

C) Competency required and possessed at recruitment
  CR1 Scholastic competency required
  CR2 Vocational competency required
  1–5   1 = most highly required, 1 = least required
  CP1 Scholastic competency possessed
  CP2 Vocational competency possessed
  1–5   5 = possessed more above requirement, 3 = possessed as equal as
           requirement, 1 = possessed less below requirement

(cont.)

TEACHING STAFF IN NON-UNIVERSITY HIGHER EDUCATION IN JAPAN

TABLE 9.2   List of variables and categories analysed (*cont.*)

Variable name	Value ranges and categories

CP_1C and CP_2C (converted from CP1 and CP2)

1	lower than requirement :	CP1 (or CP2) <= 2
2	enough to or higher than requirement :	CP1 (or CP2) >= 3

D) Identity and satisfaction during work

I_1 Staff development: research v.s. teaching[a]

1–4   4 = external research presentation to be encouraged, 1 = concentration on daily teaching preferred

I_2 Staff development: practical expertise v.s. specialty[a]

1–4   4 = vocationally practical expertise to be improved, 1 = specialty recommended irrespective to practical expertise

I_3 Job satisfaction at college

1–5   5 = most satisfied, 1 = least satisfied

I_4 Desires to move to another type of HEI

1–5   5 = considered most feasible, 1 = least considered

a Values of category of I_1 and I_2 are reversely ordered on the original questionnaire, and converted for this analysis.

Concerning the statistical tools of two phases of causal analysis on the competencies at recruitment and identity during work, MANOVA with a generalised linear model (GLM) of SPSS Version 23 were used to analyse the main and interactional effects of multiple independent variables of this survey data, as well as the examination of the significance of multiple dependent variables by MANOVA. In the second phase of analysis on identity and satisfaction, competency variables (Group C) were added by recoding them into the binary categories as independent variables.

5   Results

5.1   *Career Experience and Academic Qualifications Prior to Employment*

Due to the ambiguity of the requirements for teaching staff of non-university higher education institutions, the experiences and careers of the respondents were dependent on the historical background of their affiliated institutions.

Junior colleges recruited their staff with higher academic qualifications than first-generation institutions, and in contrast, professional training colleges did not pursue higher academic qualifications as second-generation institutions.

As Table 9.3 shows, there was a significant difference in career experience at the time of recruitment between junior college and professional training college teaching staff. Teaching staff categorised as 'dual' comprised 22% of junior college teachers but only 4% of professional training college teachers. The second biggest category was 'academic' (38%) among junior college teachers and 'vocational' (32%) among professional training college teachers. In junior colleges, 28% of teachers were PhD holders, with one respondent having completed doctorate course work. In contrast, more than half of professional training college staff (56%) were categorised as 'other'. It should also be pointed out that the number of teaching staff with professional expertise was low in both colleges. This trend seemed to be partly reflected in the historical roots of each type of institution.

TABLE 9.3   The type of academic and vocational experiences

	Junior college (%)	Professional training college (%)
'Dual' (academic and vocational)	21.5	4.1
'Academic'	37.3	8.1
'Vocational'	17.7	32.0
'Other'	23.5	55.7
Total	100.0	100.0
"N"	651	1,021

5.2   *Competencies Required and Possessed at the Time of Recruitment*

Both sectors emphasised vocational education and the vocationally practical competency of staff was more important to the professional training colleges (77.9% as assessment of 4 or 5 on a 5-point scale) than to junior colleges (57.6% as assessment of 4 or 5). However, in both sectors, research competency was required less than vocational competency, with 43.2% in junior colleges and 39.4% in professional training colleges. In summary, the teaching staff of junior colleges and professional training colleges had overlapping training fields at the same education level – ISCED 5 – and therefore, they have certain levels of

TEACHING STAFF IN NON-UNIVERSITY HIGHER EDUCATION IN JAPAN   225

consensus concerning their approaches to college education. That is, most considered that research competency was not necessarily relevant to teaching vocational classes. Vocationally practical competency was found to be valued more than research competency by professional training colleges and junior colleges.

Next, a causal model on the competencies required and possessed at the time of recruitment was analysed with independent variables of teachers' career patterns as well as the affiliated institution and training field. Table 9.4 shows the results of MANOVA (and GLM) and the estimated means by the career pattern and institution after examining and deleting interaction effects for institutions and careers.

As Table 9.4 shows, the required competencies (CR1 and CR2) were relatively less explained by these independent variables as compared with possessed competencies. However, the vocational requirement of CR2 is influenced by the institution, more for professional training colleges than junior colleges. In other words, there is more consensus – they are both more vocational-oriented rather than research-oriented – than conflict concerning the priorities of junior colleges and professional training colleges, despite different career patterns between the two sectors. Even staff with 'academic' careers did not emphasise the importance of research competency as compared with vocational competency.

On the contrary, the competencies possessed (CP1 and CP2) correspond clearly with each teacher's career experience pattern. This indicates that 'dual' and 'academic' staff have self-confidence related to research competency, even though it is not highly required by their institutions. 'Dual' and 'vocational' staff have vocational competency, which is highly valued by both types of their institutions. The former gap pattern was observed more among junior college teachers and the latter consensus pattern among professional training college teachers.

5.3   Identity and Work Satisfaction

Concerning the identities of teaching staff in junior colleges, if they have higher educational backgrounds but poor professional expertise due to their lack of practical work experience, such staff may face problems in their own identity formation, as suggested in the previous section. Junior college as a sector shows a certain level of vocational orientation in its education contents, although the requirements of teaching staff in junior colleges rather follow those of universities, as the first generation of non-university sectors. In contrast, many teaching staff in professional training colleges may lose their confidence if they do not excel in vocational experience, regardless of the flexibility of their institution's requirements.

TABLE 9.4   Determinants of competencies required and possessed at recruitment

		Dependent variables						
		CR1 (research)		CR2 (vocational)		CP1 (research)		CP2 (vocational)	
Independent variables		estimated mean	(S.E.)	estimated mean	(S.E.)	estimated mean	(S.E.)	estimated mean	(S.E.)
Junior college	'dual'	3.29	(.09)	3.59	(.07)	3.25	(.08)	3.20	(.07)
	'academic'	3.07	(.07)	3.41	(.05)	3.22	(.06)	2.82	(.06)
	'vocational'	3.44	(.07)	3.86	(.06)	2.68	(.06)	3.19	(.06)
	'other'	3.40	(.07)	3.74	(.06)	2.49	(.06)	2.63	(.06)
Professional training college	'dual'	3.22	(.10)	3.96	(.08)	3.12	(.09)	3.09	(.08)
	'academic'	3.00	(.08)	3.78	(.07)	3.10	(.07)	2.72	(.07)
	'vocational'	3.37	(.06)	4.23	(.05)	2.56	(.05)	3.08	(.05)
	'Other'	3.33	(.05)	4.10	(.04)	2.36	(.04)	2.52	(.04)
		F	Eta square (partial and adjusted)	F	Eta square (partial and adjusted)	F	Eta square (partial and adjusted)	F	Eta square (partial and adjusted)
Main effects	Institution	1.01	.00	42.84**	.03	4.43*	.00	3.31	.00
	Career type	6.84**	.01	13.74**	.02	44.54**	.07	38.49**	.06
	Training field	7.78**	.03	3.70**	.01	3.76**	.01	3.89**	.01
	Modified Model	6.73**	.04	19.48**	.10	26.20**	.14	14.98**	.08
Adjusted R square		0.03		0.10		0.13		0.08	

*p < 0.05, **p < 0.01

TEACHING STAFF IN NON-UNIVERSITY HIGHER EDUCATION IN JAPAN 227

5.4 Roles of Teaching Staff Concerning Research and Vocational Experience Versus Education

Concerning vocational teachers' job satisfaction, it was found that the variable I_1 (publishing research papers and delivering presentations) was more desired in junior colleges (27%) than in professional training colleges (20%). On the other hand, the variable of I_2 (possessing related vocational experience) was more emphasised in professional training colleges (38%) than in junior colleges (21%). The previous section on required competencies implied a rather common area of education and training to be pursued: greater emphasis on vocational qualifications than on academic qualifications. However, this section shows divergent directions. There is more evidence of differentiation that 10% of junior college staff had acquired higher level of academic qualifications and that no substantial upgrades were detected in professional training college staff.

5.5 Job Satisfaction and Career Plans

On an individual level, current job satisfaction and future career plans were examined. Current job satisfaction (variable I_3) was slightly higher among junior college teachers (50% as 4 or 5 of the 5-point scale) than among professional training college teachers (43%). This result seems to indicate a more positive attachment towards the sector that they belonged to, both in junior colleges and professional training colleges. However, the last variable, future career plans (I_4), requires further speculation: more junior college teachers had plans to change to other higher education institutions (59% as 3 or higher on a 5-point scale) than teachers in professional training colleges (37%). Most full-time staff sign work contracts with indefinite durations, as is the custom in other occupations in Japan. Therefore, in principle, they do not necessarily need to have a plan beyond working for their current affiliated college. It was found that both junior college and professional training college teachers were satisfied with their work but did not deny the possibility that they might work for other higher education institutions in the future.

5.6 Identity and Institutional Drivers

Table 9.5 shows the results of MANOVA (and GLM) concerning the effects of the independent variables on teachers' identity and job satisfaction by examining the interaction effect of institution and career type as well as relationships among four dependent variables. It also shows the estimated means according to institution and career type.

The roles of research (I_1) and vocational experience (I_2) are well explained by career pattern and relevant competencies possessed. Vocationally practical

TABLE 9.5   Determinants of identity and satisfaction during work

		Dependent Variables							
		I1 (emphasis on research)		I2 (emphasis on practical expertise)		I3 (job satisfaction)		I4 (desires to move out to other HEI)	
Independent variables		estimated mean	(S.E.)	estimated mean	(S.E.)	estimated mean	(S.E.)	estimated mean	(S.E.)
Junior college	'dual'	2.98	(.07)	2.83	(.07)	3.32	(.09)	2.99	(.11)
	'academic'	3.06	(.06)	2.62	(.05)	3.24	(.07)	3.17	(.08)
	'vocational'	2.73	(.08)	3.14	(.07)	3.51	(.10)	2.05	(.12)
	'other'	2.96	(.07)	2.89	(.06)	3.30	(.08)	2.17	(.10)
Professional training college	'dual'	2.93	(.13)	3.28	(.12)	3.00	(.16)	2.76	(.19)
	'academic'	2.79	(.09)	2.91	(.08)	2.98	(.11)	2.90	(.13)
	'vocational'	2.70	(.05)	3.18	(.05)	3.35	(.06)	2.17	(.08)
	'other'	2.77	(.04)	3.12	(.04)	3.32	(.05)	2.03	(.06)

(*cont.*)

TABLE 9.5 Determinants of identity and satisfaction during work (*cont.*)

		I1 (emphasis on research)		I2 (emphasis on practical expertise)		I3 (job satisfaction)		I4 (desires to move out to other HEI)	
		F	Eta square (partial and adjusted)	F	Eta square (partial and adjusted)	F	Eta square (partial and adjusted)	F	Eta square (partial and adjusted)
Main effects	Institution	5.66*	.00	23.95**	.01	6.80**	.00	2.37	.00
	Career type	4.35**	.01	12.87**	.02	5.61**	.01	43.61**	.07
	Traing field	6.18**	.02	5.26**	.02	2.64*	.01	2.26*	.01
	CP1C	19.16**	.01	5.64	.00	2.03	.00	11.89**	.01
	CP2C	1.09	.00	17.34**	.01	0.00	.00	0.06*	.00
Interaction	Institution x Career Type	1.43	.00	2.74*	.00	1.69	.00	1.56	.00
Modified model		8.05**	.07	15.79**	.13	2.43**	.02	21.45**	.16
Adjusted R square			0.06		0.12		0.01		0.16

*p < 0.05, **p < 0.01

experiences were less necessary than good daily teaching practices in professional training colleges, even if the sector is considered to be vocational education. Staff roles related to the institutional mission were differentiated on the matter of professional practical experience among junior college teachers, by both career type and the competencies possessed.

Regarding individual job satisfaction (I3), most staff felt satisfied with their jobs (81% of junior college teachers and 80% of professional training college teachers rated their satisfaction as 3 or higher on the 5-point satisfaction scale). It was found that there were no strong explanatory factors for this dependent variable.

On the contrary, there were many strong explanatory factors – including 'career type' – for the desire to change jobs (I4), as shown in Table 9.5. Many 'academic' type staff expressed a desire to change to another higher education sector. In particular, junior college 'academic' teachers, although not generally quite unsatisfied, expressed plans to change to other sectors. In total, the percentage of staff who wanted to change to another higher education sector amounted to 57% (3 or higher on the 5-point scale). Although many of the 'academic' type of professional training college staff reported a desire to change jobs in the future, they were relatively less represented in such institutions, so that those wanting to change sectors was only 37% (corresponding percentage) among professional training college staff.

6   Conclusions and Future Directions

Career experience, competencies and identities of teaching staff in two types of non-university higher education institutions were investigated using data from a Japanese national representative sample survey. The results of the study were as follows: First, it was found that despite similar target training areas and levels of talent training, the career patterns of first-generation junior college and second-generation professional training college teachers differed, with the former possessing less professional expertise and the latter less academic expertise.

The targeted area of the ISCED 5 education model is not the same as that of university bachelor level, ISCED 6, where the Humboldtian idea of integration of teaching and research dominates. The ISCED 5 sector may require both academic and professional expertise of its teachers; however, in Japan, due to historically different patterns of institutional inauguration and development, different education and learning models co-exist and are not moving towards forming a convergent model. Rather, each model would prefer to remain distinct from the other.

Second, this diversification of ISCED 5 is associated with the competencies and orientations of teaching staff. The 'academic' (and non-professional) type of junior college staff represents the majority of junior college teachers and will thus lead the opinions and directions of this sector. They value professional practical competencies and less experiences, which are held in esteem by other types of colleges. They are happy with these circumstances, but if they would sincerely pursue this direction, they may change sectors. This 'academic' group is relatively young (47.4 years old on average, as compared with the other group average of 52.4); however, the duration of working years in the same college did not significantly differ in this dataset. In the era of upgrading of junior colleges into four-year universities around the turn of the century, more academically ambiguous junior colleges may have to leave the sector.

Third, in professional training colleges, practical vocational experience and competencies are highly valued among teaching staff. However, as the regulation and requirements for teaching staff are rather flexible, the improvement of teaching staff quality is not an easy matter. Half of professional training college staff was classified into the 'other' group. This means that while they may possess the minimum required educational qualifications and work experience, they may not possess the desired academic expertise levels nor related professional experience. In this sector, 'other' and 'professional' types of staff are the largest group, while 'academic' staff may have fewer opportunities and resources to continue to improve their competency. Some of them expressed job dissatisfaction and planned to change to other higher educational sectors.

One direction for future research includes applying this convergent model to the university sector and conducting an analysis that utilises the data of university faculty members. Additionally, although this convergent model may serve to clarify the career experience, competencies and identities of teaching staff, whether it is valuable to their affiliated institution depends on the orientation and mission of the institution itself. Further analyses that consider the mission of institutions and how this affects teaching staff are needed to further develop and improve the quality of higher education.

Acknowledgement

This research was supported in part by grants from Japan Promoting Scientific Research (JSPS) Grant-in-aid for Scientific Research A (No. 21243400) and C (No. 16K04599).

Notes

1 Inenaga (2015) discussed four requirements of teaching staff in non-university higher education: vocational performance, academic research, teaching and educational management. In this study, the dimensions of vocational performance and academic research are targeted as these are the aspects that are focused on at the time of recruitment.

2 Even in the case of typical academic professors and researchers, this convergent model may apply, because the individual academic dimension is synonymous with the vocational dimension. Educational background and academic research accomplishments are used as representative indicators of both dimensions. Nevertheless, it is appropriate to assume that even teaching staff involved in vocational education will be expected to have a certain amount of research competency in addition to practical vocational competency. Concerning the academic dimension of research competency and drawing on the implications provided in the specialist model, which is discussed in the form of the 'reflective practitioner' model (Schön 1983), vocational teaching staff are expected to possess the competency of reflection, both as professionals and teachers.

3 These laws opened the door for women's career paths and women-specific programmes in junior college, and many women's colleges lost their attractiveness.

4 See the explanation of the outline of the survey (https://eq.kyushu-u.ac.jp/formoutline.html) and Inenaga and Yoshimoto (2018) for further information on this survey.

5 This analysis selected samples with full detailed information on career experiences, such as all periods of occupational titles other than their current teaching occupation.

References

Arimoto, A., Cummings, W. K., Huang, F., & Cheol Shin, J. (Eds.). (2015). *Henbou suru Nihon no Daigaku Kyoujyu Syoku* [*The changing academic profession in Japan*]. Springer.

Boyer, E. L. (1990). *Scholarship reconsidered: Priorities of the professoriate.* The Carnegie Foundation for the Advancement of Teaching.

Clayton, B. (2015). Developing the capacities of VET teachers: Opportunities and challenges. In K. Yoshimoto (Ed.), *Quality assurance of tertiary education and teaching staff: Comparative approaches from Germany, Australia and Japan* (pp. 23–33). Fukuoka: Kyushu University. Retrieved from http://rteq.kyushu-u.ac.jp/en/etc/document_vol.7.pdf

TEACHING STAFF IN NON-UNIVERSITY HIGHER EDUCATION IN JAPAN   233

Cummings, W. K. (2014). The conditions of continuity and the drivers of change. In W. K. Cummings & U. Teichler (Eds.), *The relevance of academic work in comparative perspective* (pp. 17–39). Cham: Springer.

Dunkel, T., & le Mouillour, I., in cooperation with Teichler, U. (2009). 'Through the looking-glass': Diversification and differentiation in vocational education and training and higher education. In *CEDEFOP, modernising vocational education and training* (Fourth report on vocational education and training research in Europe: Background report, Vol. 2, pp. 239–268). Luxembourg: Office for Official Publications of the European Communities.

Findlow, S. (2012). Higher education change and professional-academic identity in newly 'academic' disciplines: The case of nurse education. *Higher Education, 63*(1), 117–133.

Galaz-Fontes, J., Arimoto, A., Teichler, U., & Brennan, J. (Eds.). (2016). *Biographies and careers throughout academic life*. Cham: Springer.

Grubb, W. N., & Associates. (Eds.). (1999). *Honored but invisible: An inside look at teaching in community colleges*. London: Routledge.

Inenaga, Y. (2015). Quality assurance of tertiary education through teaching staffs: Current situation and issues in Japan, from the point of international comparisons. In K. Yoshimoto (Ed.), *Quality assurance of tertiary education and teaching staff: Comparative approaches from Germany, Australia and Japan* (pp. 59–69). Fukuoka: Kyushu University. Retrieved from http://rteq.kyushu-u.ac.jp/en/etc/document_vol.7.pdf

Inenaga, Y. (2018). Dai San Dankai Kyouiku ni okeru Syokugyou Kyouiku Kyouin [Teaching staff in charge of professional/vocational education in tertiary education: Research question and issues]. In Y. Inenaga & K. Yoshimoto (Eds.), *Teaching staff and organization in two sectors of non-university higher education in Japan [Hi Daigaku gata Koutou Kyouiku wo ninau Kyouin to Kyouiku Soshiki]* (pp. 1–14). Hiroshima: RIHE, Hiroshima University.

Inenaga, Y., & Yoshimoto, K. (Eds.). (2018). *Teaching staff and organization in two sectors of non-university higher education in Japan [Hi Daigaku gata Koutou Kyouiku wo ninau Kyouin to Kyouiku Soshiki]*. Hiroshima: RIHE, Hiroshima University.

Kyushu University 'Higher Education and Qualification Research Group'. (2012). Koutou Kyouiku ni okeru Kyouin to Kyouiku-sosiki ni kansuru Chousa [Overview: The survey of teaching staff and educational organization in higher education]. Retrieved from http://eq.kyushu-u.ac.jp/pdf/chousagaiyou.pdf

Levin, J., Kater, S., & Wagoner, R. L. (2006). *Community college faculty: At work in the new economy*. New York, NY: Palgrave McMillan.

MEXT. (2011). Syogaikoku ni okeru Kouki Chuto Kyouiku go no Kyouiku Kikan ni okeru Shokugyou Kyouiku no Genjyou ni Kansuru Chosa Kenkyu (Houkoku sho) [Research report on the present situation of vocational education in educational institutions after senior secondary education in foreign countries].

OECD. (2009). *OECD thematic review of tertiary education: Japan.*

Robson, J. (2006). *Teacher professionalism in further and higher education: Challenges to culture and practice.* Abingdon: Routledge.

Schön, D. A. (1983). *The reflective practitioner.* Basic Books Inc.

Teichler, U. (2008). The end of alternatives to universities or new opportunities? In J. S. Taylor et al. (Eds.), *Non-university higher education in Europe* (pp. 1–13). Dordrecht: Springer.

Teichler, U. (2009). Professionally relevant academic learning. In U. Teichler (Ed.), *Higher education and the world of work: Conceptual frameworks, comparative perspectives, empirical findings* (pp. 295–308). Rotterdam, The Netherlands: Sense Publishers.

Teichler, U. (2015). The teachers in higher education and tertiary education in Germany in comparative perspective. In K. Yoshimoto (Ed.), *Quality assurance of tertiary education and teaching staff: Comparative approaches from Germany, Australia and Japan* (pp. 35–48). Fukuoka: Kyushu University. Retrieved from http://rteq.kyushu-u.ac.jp/en/etc/document_vol.7.pdf

Tigelaar, D. E., Dolmans, D. H., Wolfhagen, I. H., et al. (2004). The development and validation of a framework for teaching competencies in higher education. *Higher Education, 48*(2), 253–268.

Williams, P. J. (2007). Valid knowledge: The economy and the academy. *Higher Education, 54*(4), 511–523.

Yonezawa, A., & Inenaga, Y. (2017). The consequences of market-based mass post-secondary education: Japan's challenges. In P. G. Altbach, L. Reisberg, & H. de Wit (Eds.), *Responding to massification: Differentiation in postsecondary education worldwide* (pp. 89–100). Rotterdam, The Netherlands: Sense Publishers.

Yoshimoto, K. (2009). Koutou Syokugyo Kyoiku no Taikei-ka to Senmon gakko [Special training colleges and the higher vocational education system]. *Research in Higher Education [Daigaku Ronshu]*, 40, 201–215.

Yoshimoto, K. (Ed.). (2015). *Quality assurance of tertiary education and teaching staff: Comparative approaches from Germany, Australia and Japan.* Fukuoka: Kyushu University. Retrieved from http://rteq.kyushu-u.ac.jp/en/etc/document_vol.7.pdf

PART 3

Societal Values, National Regimes and Higher Education

∵

CHAPTER 10

Inclusion and Fairness in Access to Higher Education: Theoretical Distinctions, Measurement and Patterns of Interaction

Pepka Boyadjieva and Petya Ilieva-Trichkova

Abstract

The article aims at exploring access to higher education as a complex and multidimensional phenomenon by distinguishing two of its aspects: inclusion and fairness, as well as at outlining the policy relevance of a social justice perspective on higher education. At the theoretical level, it bridges two of the most influential theories of justice: the Rawlsian perspective of 'justice as fairness' (1971) and Amartya Sen's idea of justice (2009). At the methodological level, it develops two indices, of inclusion and fairness and uses data from the European Social Survey, Labour Force Survey, and EUROSTUDENT Survey to calculate them for two social groups: of low and high social background. Based on two criteria which account for the correspondence between the directions of change in the two indices over time, the article identifies different relationship patterns between inclusion and fairness for both social groups across Europe, assessing them as logical or contradictory.

Keywords

inclusion – fairness – access – social justice – higher education – indices

1 Equity in Access to Higher Education as a Contested Issue

The issue of access to higher education occupies a central position in every higher education system. The established access policies in a given country reflect the social value of higher education and the way it is perceived as a public or private good. Behind and through these policies, the way social justice is understood can be decoded, as well as how the social right to education is interpreted, what social equality means, etc. That is why access to higher

© KONINKLIJKE BRILL NV, LEIDEN, 2020 | DOI: 10.1163/9789004422582_011

education is a contested issue and is an arena of struggle between different actors, many of them external to higher education systems. A recent report, prepared for the European Commission, clearly demonstrates that the nature and extent of autonomy which higher education institutions have over how they select their students vary considerably across countries and that admission process is subjected to constant policy interventions (Orr, Usher, Haj, Atherton, & Geanta, 2017).

The last several decades have been marked by the expansion of higher education as a worldwide trend which is expected to continue (Schofer & Meyer, 2005). A huge number of studies have been published which develop theories and hypotheses relating overall educational expansion to the dynamics of inequalities in access to higher education. Thus, for example, acknowledging that "there is a worldwide tendency to high-participation systems in higher education, systems that enrol more than 50% of the school-leaver age cohort," Marginson (2016, p. 34) claims that higher education "is becoming more socially inclusive at a rapid rate and on a worldwide scale." However, he also states that "[e]quality of opportunity in the full sense is unrealisable, because of the persistence of irreducible differences between families in economic, social and cultural resources" (p. 69). Indeed, several studies suggest the stable and persistent effect of socio-economic status on school success and access to higher education (Mare, 1981; Blossfeld & Shavit, 1993; Raftery & Hout, 1993; Lucas, 2001; Pfeffer, 2008; Ilieva-Trichkova & Boyadjieva, 2014).

Previous literature also highlights that equity in access to higher education "is becoming an international standard" (Goastellec, 2008, p. 72) due to the interwoven influence of demographic, economic and political factors. Goastellec's study explores the gradual change in admissions policies from a principle of 'inherited merit' through the norm of equality of rights (formal equality) to a principle of equality of opportunity. This tendency has been accompanied by "a growing appreciation of the complexity of social identities" and "by significant national specificity in respect of the social categories which are used to define social diversity" (Clancy & Goastellec, 2007, p. 137).

Recent debates about equity in higher education have received a strong new impetus. Social justice has become a constituent part of the European Higher Education Area through the social dimension in higher education, which has been firmly emphasised within the Bologna Process since 2003 (Berlin Communiqué). This understanding of the social dimension in higher education, as for the first time defined by the London Communiqué in 2007, sets the very ambitious aim that "the student body entering, participating in and completing higher education at all levels should reflect the diversity of our populations" (p. 5). This goal clearly points to a specific notion of social equity in

INCLUSION AND FAIRNESS IN ACCESS TO HIGHER EDUCATION

higher education: not one confined to increasing enrolment rates in higher education, but which insists on fairness in student body representativeness with regard to the general population. However, notwithstanding efforts so far made within the Bologna Process, there are concerns that widening access to and participation in higher education is but only one step towards guaranteeing equal opportunities to all (Elias & Brennan, 2012).

Against this background, the present article claims that a social justice perspective is indispensable to both research and policy-making in the sphere of higher education. It aims to rethink the way social justice in access to higher education can be conceptualised and measured. More specifically, the aim of the article is twofold: (1) to explore access to higher education as a complex and multidimensional phenomenon by distinguishing two interwoven but irreducible aspects, inclusion and fairness, and (2) to outline the policy sensitivity of the social justice perspective to higher education.

The article proceeds as follows. First we discuss social justice in higher education and, relying on Sen's and Rawls' ideas, we outline two different dimensions of social equity in access to higher education – inclusion and fairness. This is followed by a description of the data, methodology and explanation of the composition of two indices we developed to measure social equity in higher education – Index of inclusion in higher education (IincluHE) and Index of fairness in higher education (IfairHE). Our study shows that most of the countries studied differ considerably with respect to the extent to which the development of access to higher education is inclusive and fair, and that inclusion in access to higher education is not always associated with fairness in higher education. We further identify different patterns of interaction between inclusion and fairness in higher education. In the discussion section, we argue that the widened access to higher education, brought about by the massification and expansion of higher education, was not enough to reduce inequalities in access to higher education over time. The article concludes with some remarks about the possibility that the presented understanding and measurement of social justice in higher education as a complex phenomenon be used as a basis for developing strategies and concrete policies regarding access to higher education at institutional, national and European level.

2 Rethinking Social Justice in Access to Higher Education

It is stated that "like 'equality of opportunity' or 'choice', 'social justice' is one of those politically malleable and essentially contested phrases which can mean all things to all people" and that it tends to suffer from "vagueness and oversimplification" (Thrupp & Tomlinson, 2005, p. 549). There are different views about what is meant by social justice in (access to) higher education, how justice in higher education changes over time and the models used to measure it. To a great extent, differences in understanding social justice in higher education reflect a variety of views on the very essence of social justice and how it can, and should, be conceptualised. Among different lines of reasoning about justice and the way it may be achieved, two are most prominent – the institutions-centred approach of John Rawls and the human-centred approach of Amartya Sen. The first one is based on the idea of establishing a hypothetical social contract, the aim of which is to contribute towards achieving justice in society. In his theory of "justice as fairness," Rawls (1971) develops an approach which concentrates on identifying perfectly-just institutions and is arrangement-focused in its essence. The metrics of justice in the Rawlsian theory of justice is that of primary goods, which may be rights, liberties, opportunities, income or wealth. Their distribution should be regulated by the principles of equal basic liberties, of fair equality of opportunity, and the difference principle (Rawls, 1971). However, as Robeyns (2008, p. 410) points out, the "[i]deal theory sharpens our thinking on justice and serves as a guide that is indispensable in many cases, but it does not tell us how to reach that ideal of justice."

In contrast to this line of reasoning, the humanistic perspective adheres to the idea that justice may be achieved on the basis of making comparisons between different ways in which people's lives may be led, thus ascertaining which are more or less just. This approach focuses on ranking alternative social arrangements, instead of concentrating exclusively on the identification of a fully-just society. As Robeyns (2008, p. 411) notices, Sen has developed a "non-ideal theory on justice, with greater *direct* relevance for pressing issues of injustice."

As a theoretical background against which our attempts to rethink social justice in higher education are placed, we argue for the mutual enrichment of these two approaches and propose to bridge them, as both provide value when conceptualising social justice in higher education and trying to achieve it. Unlike the Rawlsian understanding of justice as fairness, in Sen's view, justice is a "momentous concept" (Sen, 2009, p. 401) and the comparative questions are inescapable for any theory of justice that intends to give some kind of guidance to public policy or personal behaviour. Sen, who has expressed many times that, although he criticises Rawls, he is enormously intellectually indebted to him, has a more realistic vision of how justice can be enhanced. He acknowledges that there is a possibility, even with 'just institutions', for injustices to be observed at the individual level and in people's everyday lives. Sen (2009) also claims that primary goods cannot adequately account for the differences in people's abilities to convert these primary goods into what they

INCLUSION AND FAIRNESS IN ACCESS TO HIGHER EDUCATION 241

are able to be and to do in their lives. He argues that we should focus directly on people's beings and doings, that is, on their capabilities to function. Therefore, the informational basis of Sen's theory of justice is human capability. This capability is understood as a special kind of freedom, which refers to the alternative combinations that are feasible for a person to achieve. It is determined by the space of possibilities open to an individual – not in terms of some prior end, such as utility, or initial conditions like equality of primary goods, resources or utilities. This capability is also constrained by so-called conversion factors (personal, social and environmental, see Robeyns, 2017 for more details) which determine the capacity of people to convert the resources they have into a good living. These factors may vary greatly and can explain why people with the same resources available to them are not able to achieve the same outcomes as others. The variety of conversion factors shows that it is not sufficient to know how many goods a person owns or can use in order to assess the well-being that he or she can achieve; rather, we need "to scrutinise the context in which economic production and social interactions take place, and whether the circumstances in which people choose from their opportunity sets are enabling and just" (Robeyns, 2005, p. 99).

By taking into account these conversion factors, the capability approach allows us to consider not only individual-level characteristics in evaluating inequalities but also the institutional and macro-level features of the contexts in which these inequalities are analysed. Given this, by emphasising the role of conversion factors, the capability approach offers a bridge between agency and structure. In Sen's words, "the freedom of agency that we individually have is inescapably qualified and constrained by the social, political and economic opportunities that are available to us. There is a deep complementarity between individual agency and social arrangements" (1999, pp. xi–xii).

Previous research shows that both theories can be applied to the issue of access to higher education. Thus, in her review of key theories of social justice and their implications for higher education, Wilson-Strydom (2015) outlines some aspects of Rawls' theory that are useful for understanding access and social justice. Among them are Rawls' critique of unfair advantage and the related concept of meritocracy, as well as the idea that policy decisions should be made so that the worst-off benefit most. The capability approach, in contrast, could bring to the fore the unequal conversion of higher education opportunities that arguably perpetuate everyday injustices that work against the development of a more just higher education environment. Marginson (2011, 2016) argues that the two understandings of justice described above resonate in two perspectives through which social equity in higher education has already been conceptualised: equity as social inclusion and equity as the equal access of students from all social groups to opportunities, i.e., fairness.

The inclusion perspective refers "to the significance of improvement in participation of any particular group, irrespective of how other groups have fared" (Clancy & Goastellec, 2007, p. 146). The fairness perspective "implies ensuring that personal and social circumstances – for example gender, socio-economic status or ethnic origin – should not be an obstacle to achieving educational potential" (Santiago, Tremblay, Basri, & Arnal, 2008, pp. 13–14). Thus, whereas the first approach "focuses on growth in the absolute number of people from hitherto under-represented socio-economic groups, as defined in terms of income measures or social or occupational status," the second one concentrates on the proportional distribution of study places between different social groups (Marginson, 2011, pp. 23–24). Marginson is in favour of the inclusion aspect of equity, as it provides a clear and feasible basis for improvement. When inclusion is pursued as a goal, each advance in the participation of persons from under-represented groups represents a move forward, while achieving better fairness is more difficult and less visible; it requires structural improvement of representation in higher education from different social groups, i.e. changes in the composition of the student body so that it better represents the diversity of the general population.

However, we think that both aspects are important, as they capture different dimensions of social justice in access to higher education. Moreover, they are irreducible, and that is why neither of them should be neglected. Our understanding is in line with the idea of bridging Rawls' and Sen's approaches, instead of looking at them as rival reasonings about justice (Robeyns, 2008; Brighouse & Unterhalter, 2010; Maffettone, 2011).

Based on the above theoretical considerations, the article aims to answer the following research questions (RQ):

RQ1: Do countries differ with respect to the development of access to higher education as inclusive and fair over time?

RQ2: Is inclusion in access to higher education associated with fairness in higher education at country level?

RQ3: What kind of patterns of interaction between inclusion and fairness in access to higher education can be identified across European countries?

3   Research Methodology

Having outlined the theoretical background and the main research questions of the present study, we proceed with a presentation of the data and the indices which will be used to answer these research questions.

INCLUSION AND FAIRNESS IN ACCESS TO HIGHER EDUCATION

3.1   *Data and Research Strategy*

The research strategy is a secondary data analysis, as the empirical basis for the calculation of these indices comes from EUROSTUDENT Surveys IV (2008–2011) and V (2012–2015), the European Social Survey (ESS)[1] – rounds 4, 5, 6 and 7, implemented respectively in 2008/2009, 2010/2011, 2012/13 and 2014/2015 – and the Eurostat statistics on the Labour Force Survey (LFS) as of 2009 and 2013. These data allowed us to adopt a wide comparative perspective, since they were conducted in many European countries. These surveys are representative and provide cross-national, rather than panel-data and there are no overlaps of people who were interviewed, as for each wave a new sample from the population is drawn.[2] In the present article we use data from countries for which there were data at two points in time. We need data at two points in time in order to be able to answer our first research question about differences between countries with respect to the development of access to higher education as inclusive and fair over time.[3] This is important as it allows us to see not only how the massification of higher education unfolds in different countries but also how this process influences on inequalities in access to higher education. Thus, we used data from the EUROSTUDENT Survey for 18 countries and from the ESS for 18 countries, as well.

We use two different types of measures in order to assess inclusion and fairness aspects of social equity in higher education – participation rates of groups with different social background in higher education (based on data about students in higher education) and indices of social equity (based on data about graduates of higher education) – and apply them to students and graduates of low and high social background.

3.2.1   Participation Rates in Higher Education

Social groups could be defined based on many different characteristics, such as completed level of education, occupation status, social background (defined according to parental education, income or occupation), place of residence, gender or age. We only focused on social groups with respect to their social background according to paternal education, because previous studies have shown that parents' education is a key factor for determining children's educational outcomes (e.g. Ianelli, 2002; Pfeffer, 2008). More specifically, we used the data for the father's educational level as a measure of social background,[4] in both rounds of the EUROSTUDENT Survey collected by question Q6.1: What is the highest level of education your father and mother have obtained? (Indicated separately). The two groups are: students with fathers with low educational levels according to the International Standard Classification of Education (ISCED 0–2) and students with fathers with high educational levels (ISCED 5–6).[5] However, our indices allow their calculation with any of the above-mentioned characteristics of the social groups.

Participation rates are widely used measures which show the percentage of students with a specific characteristic (in our case with different social background in terms of father's education) within the student population. This gives a general picture of the inclusion of different social groups in higher education. However, the participation rates of groups with different social background do not tell us enough: 1) about the probability of people having low or high social background studying in higher education institutions, regardless of their gender or age; and 2) to what extent the representation of groups is fair with regard to the overall population in a given country. That is why, for our analysis, we rely on more complex measures, such as indices.

3.2.2   Indices of Social Equity in Higher Education

There are two well-established indices of social equity in higher education. The first one is the Educational Equity Index (EEI). It was developed by Usher (2004) and has been used for the construction of accessibility rankings among 14 countries (Usher & Medow, 2010). The EEI is calculated as a ratio between the percentage of males aged 45–64 with a higher education degree in the general population of a country and the percentage of the student body whose fathers have a higher education degree. The index ranges between 0 and 1. A high score on this index indicates that the student body is very similar in socio-demographic characteristics to the overall population, whereas a low EEI score indicates less equity. However, the EEI only takes into account the representation of one social group – made up of those holding a higher education degree – thus neglecting disadvantaged groups with lower levels of education.

The typology of social inclusiveness within European higher education systems proposed in the EUROSTUDENT IV report (Orr, Gwość, & Netz, 2011, pp. 50–51) goes beyond this simple measure and includes information from two indices: 1) the share of students' fathers with low educational levels (ISCED 0–2), divided by the share of men from the corresponding age group (40–60) in the national population with the same level of education; and 2) the share of students' fathers with higher educational levels (ISCED 5–6), divided by the share of men from the same corresponding age group in the national population with the same level of education. Thus, the social inclusiveness of a given higher education system reflects the degree of underrepresentation among students of low social background and of overrepresentation among students of high social background. However, there are two drawbacks to these indices. First, the values of measurement go from below 1 to above 1 and have different interpretations. Thus, for students of low social background, the value is below 1 and the higher it is, the greater the degree of fairness, i.e., this group of students is getting better represented within the student population, whereas for

INCLUSION AND FAIRNESS IN ACCESS TO HIGHER EDUCATION   245

students with high social statuses, the value is usually above 1 and the higher it is, the lesser the degree of fairness, i.e., this group of students is getting more overrepresented within the student population. Second, the indices do not reveal how the inclusiveness of a given higher education system changes over time.

In order to overcome the above-described drawbacks of the measures available, we have introduced two indices – IincluHE and IfairHE – to measure how the inclusion and fairness aspects of social justice in access to higher education change over time for two social groups. More specifically, we calculated these indices for those with a low level of father's education, ISCED 1997 0 to 2, and those with a high level of father's of education, ISCED 1997 5 to 6 or ISCED 2011 5–8.[6] We selected these two extreme categories in order to more clearly account for the educational inequalities.

The IincluHE measures the trends towards more or less inclusion of a given social group in higher education. For the calculation of IincluHE, we estimated binomial logistic regression models separately for all 18 countries. The dependent variable which we use distinguishes whether or not people aged 20–34 had a tertiary education degree. The main independent variable is father's educational attainment level, which was divided into three categories: low (ISCED 0–2), medium (ISCED 3–4), and high (ISCED 5–6). We included gender and age as control variables in the models. These were also calculated for two temporal points. First, they were calculated using data from the ESS rounds 4 and 5, and then using data from the ESS rounds 6 and 7. This calculation was made in order for both indexes to refer to relatively the same period of time.[7] Aiming to account for the time difference, we also included the ESS round as an additional control variable in our models. Based on these logistic regression models, we derived their so-called marginal effects – which indicate the predicted probabilities of people with low and high social background to have a tertiary degree. These probabilities range between 0 and 1. The higher the value, the higher the probability for a given social group to have a tertiary degree. Then we calculated the ratio between these probabilities for the time period falling within the two selected temporal points. This ratio ranges from 0 to infinity. Thus, an IincluHE index above 1 indicates the increased inclusion of a given social group within one and the same country within the above-described period of time, whereas an index below 1 shows a tendency towards exclusion of this group over time. An index value of 1 indicates that no change was made regarding the inclusion of this group.

The IfairHE is built upon Usher and Medow's equity index (2010) and measures how the fairness of representation by a given social group in higher education within a given country for a given year has changed over time. It is calculated as the ratio between fairness indicators of representation by a given social group at two temporal points, in our case – 2013 and 2009. More specifically, for the high social background group, the IfairHE measures the ratio between the percentage of all males aged 45–65 with a high level of education in the overall population and the percentage of all students whose fathers have completed higher education, calculated for two temporal points. As for the social group with lower father's education, this formula is reversed. For the levels of education in a given country's general population, we used data from Eurostat (LFS) for males aged 45–64 with low and respectively high levels of education as of 2009 and 2013. The data for the student father's educational level were taken from EUROSTUDENT IV and V. As for given temporal points, the ratios vary between 0 and 1. The closer the ratio is to 1, the fairer the system; and vice versa. For the IfairHE, we calculated the ratio between these ratios for two temporal points. A value above 1 indicates increased fairness of representation for a given social group within one and the same country within the above-described period of time, whereas an index below 1 shows a tendency towards less fairness for this group over time. An index value of 1 indicates that no change was made regarding fairness for this group.

3.3 *Research Limitations*

Our research has some limitations that stem from the fact that we were only able to calculate both indices for 11 of the 18 countries. For the inclusion aspect, we used information available about people, aged 20–34, who had already graduated as a proxy for the student populations with low and high social background.

4 Results

4.1 *Participation of People with Low and High Social Background in Higher Education*

First, we present a general picture of the inclusion of students (regardless of their age) with low and high social background in higher education and how it changes over time. That is why we first looked at participation rates for these two groups. The social make-up of students of low and high social background is evident from data from the EUROSTUDENT Survey (see Figures 10.1 and 10.2).

Figures 10.1 and 10.2 show that in all countries, except Ireland, Italy and Malta, students of high social background (i.e. whose fathers had reached

INCLUSION AND FAIRNESS IN ACCESS TO HIGHER EDUCATION 247

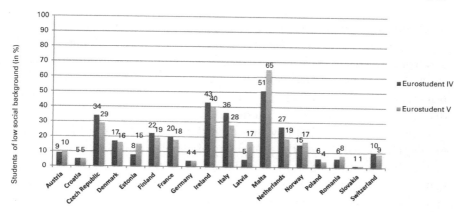

FIGURE 10.1 Students of low social background (in %) in two waves of EUROSTUDENT (IV and V). Source: EUROSTUDENT IV 2008–2011 (Orr, Gwość, & Netz, 2011, p. 47) and EUROSTUDENT V 2012–2015 (Hauschildt, Gwość, Netz, & Mishra, 2015, p. 56)

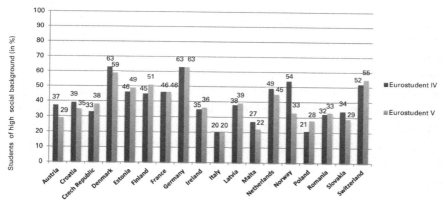

FIGURE 10.2 Students of high social background (in %) in two waves of EUROSTUDENT (IV and V). Source: EUROSTUDENT IV 2008–2011 (Orr, Gwość, & Netz, 2011, p. 47) and EUROSTUDENT V 2012–2015 (Hauschildt, Gwość, Netz, & Mishra, 2015, p. 56)

ISCED 5–6) considerably outnumber students of low social background (i.e. whose fathers had reached ISCED 0–2) for both waves; in the Czech Republic, this was only the case for the wave in 2008–2011. They also reveal that countries differ with regard to changes in student composition between 2008–2011 and 2012–2015. These differences refer to both the direction of change and its amount. Thus, in some countries we can observe an increase in the number of students from high social background and a decrease in the number of students from low social background (e.g. the Czech Republic, Finland, Poland, and Switzerland), whereas in others there was an increase in the number of students from low social background and a decrease in the number of students from high social background (e.g. Malta and Norway), or even an increase (or decrease) for both groups (e.g. Estonia, Latvia and the Netherlands).

In order to go beyond simply registering the general trends, in the next step of our analysis we analyse the probability of people having low or high social background of studying in higher education institutions, regardless of their gender or age, and the fairness of the representation of the two groups with regard to the overall population in a given country.

4.2 Inclusion and Fairness in Access to Higher Education

Next we present the results from our calculations of both indices with regard to inclusion and fairness.

We found that in half of the studied countries we observe inclusion over time with regard to both social groups. This inclusion is particularly prominent in the Czech Republic for both social groups and in Poland and Switzerland with regard to the low social group. In four out of all 18 European countries (Belgium, Finland, Hungary, and Ireland) the low social background group became more excluded from higher education, whereas the high social status group became more excluded in five out of 18 countries (Denmark, Great Britain, Ireland, Norway, and Portugal, see Figure 10.3).

Regarding the fairness aspect, we first present the scores for fairness of representation by people of low and high social background as of 2009. Figure 10.4 shows that, in 2009, among the fairest systems with regard to both social

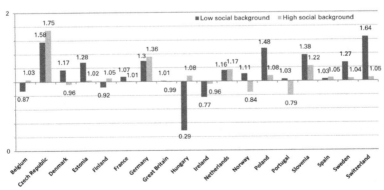

FIGURE 10.3   Index of inclusion in participation in higher education for people of low and high social background for the period 2009 and 2013, by country. (Source: ESS 2008–2010 and ESS 2012–2014)

groups were the Netherlands, Switzerland and Ireland. At the same time, the least fair systems as regards to people with low social background were mainly in post-socialist countries: Slovakia, Croatia and Romania. In these countries there is a considerable underrepresentation of students with low social background (i.e. the share of students with fathers with low level of education/ social background within the student population is much lower that the share of men from the corresponding age group (45–64) in the national population with the same (low) level of education/social background). For the high social background group, the Romanian and Maltese systems were the least fair, as in these countries we observe the highest levels of overrepresentation of students with high social background (i.e. the share of students with fathers with high level of education/social background within the student population is much higher than the share of men from the corresponding age group (45–64) in the national population with the same (high) level of education/ social background).

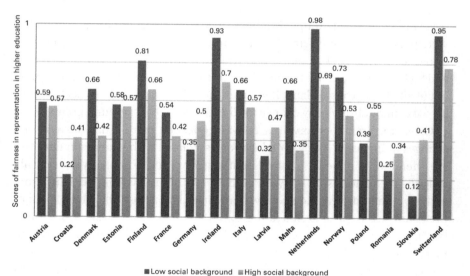

FIGURE 10.4 Scores for fairness of representation in higher education by people of low and high social background as of 2009, by country. (Source: EUROSTUDENT IV, 2008–2011 and Eurostat, LFS data for 2009 extracted on 14.03.2018, code: edat_lfse_03). Note: The Czech Republic was excluded from the figure as an outlier with regard to the low social background group with low social background. The value is 5.23. For the high social background one, it is 0.46

Figure 10.5 presents the values for the index of fairness in participation in higher education by people of low and high social background for the period 2009 and 2013. In most of the countries, we can observe increased fairness with

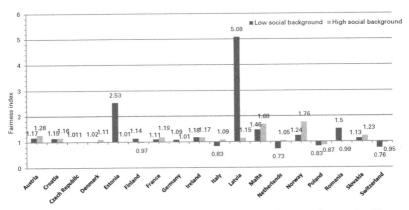

FIGURE 10.5   Index of fairness in participation in higher education for people of low and high social background for the period 2009 and 2013, by country. (Source: EUROSTUDENT IV 2008–2011 and EUROSTUDENT V 2012–2015 and Eurostat, LFS data for 2009 and 2013 extracted on 14.03.2018, code: edat_lfse_03)

regard to both social groups. The figure also shows that the higher education system has become less fair in five out of the 18 countries studied with regard to the low social background group (Italy, Finland, the Netherlands, Poland, and Switzerland) and has become less fair for the higher-status group in three out of all 18 countries (Poland, Romania and Switzerland). In the Czech Republic, we cannot observe any change for the high social background group.

Given the trends observed, a relevant question can be drawn: were the changes in inclusion in higher education associated with changes in fairness? We therefore conducted a correlation test in order to more systematically describe the relationship between both aspects of justice in higher education: inclusion and fairness. However, we only had data across all indices for 11 of the countries. We also excluded the Czech Republic as an outlier from these, leaving just 10 countries to work with. We found no evidence that increased inclusion of people of low social background during the studied period was associated with better fairness with regard to this group in higher education (Pearson's r = −0.128, not significant at $p < 0.05$). However, we found evidence (see Figure 10.6) for a negative correlation between the inclusion of more people of high social background and the increase of fairness in higher education with regard to this group (Pearson's r = −0.60, significant at $p < 0.10$). This means that in countries with higher inclusion of people of high social background, the increase in fairness with regard to this group is lower, i.e., the process of achieving similarity between the representation of this group within the student body and the whole population is slower.

INCLUSION AND FAIRNESS IN ACCESS TO HIGHER EDUCATION

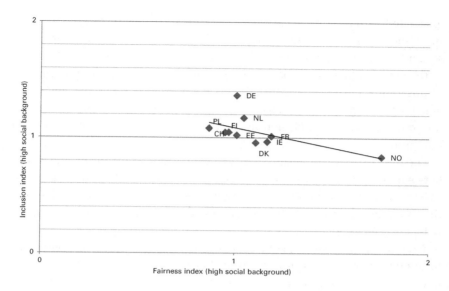

FIGURE 10.6   Indices of inclusion and fairness for people of high social background
(Source: EUROSTUDENT IV 2008–2011 and EUROSTUDENT V 2012–2015 and Eurostat, LFS data for 2009 and 2013 extracted on 14.03.2018, code: edat_lfse_03 and ESS 2008–2010 and ESS 2012–2014)

4.3   Patterns of Interaction between Inclusion and Fairness in Access to Higher Education

Based on our theoretical considerations, we suggest two criteria for identifying patterns of interaction between inclusion and fairness in access to higher education. The criteria account *for the correspondence between directions of change in the indices over time*: 1) between the two aspects of social justice – inclusion and fairness; and 2) for both social groups – of low and high social background. The correspondence between directions of change in both indices for the two social groups over time could take the form of synergy (increased inclusion and fairness for both social groups), and/or diversion (different tendencies regarding inclusion and fairness for both groups).

Taking into account discussions about and the data supporting the underrepresentation of people of low social background and the overrepresentation of those of social background in higher education (see Figures 10.1 and 10.2; Orr, Gwość, & Netz, 2011, pp. 47–50), we could assess changes in the indices for a given country as either logical or contradictory. Logical changes, it follows, are those in which more inclusion is associated with more fairness for both groups or in which more inclusion for the low social background group is associated with more fairness; whereas for the high social background group, more inclusion is associated with less fairness, i.e., the composition of the student body has become less similar to the society as a whole with regard to the group of high social background, which shows that overrepresentation of this group continues. As contradictory changes we define those tendencies which are hardly explicable regarding inclusion and fairness for both groups, for example decreased inclusion and increased fairness for people of low social background.

On the basis of our results and the trends observed during the period between 2009 and 2013 in the 10 countries we have data concerning both aspects of fairness for both social groups (see Table 10.1), we have identified the following patterns of interaction between inclusion and fairness in access to higher education:

Logical synergy (Estonia, France and Germany) refers to full and logical correspondence between the directions of change in the indices of inclusion and fairness over time for both social groups. In other words, more people from both groups access higher education, and children of both groups are better represented in higher education.

Logical diversion (Denmark and Norway) – this is the case when for people of low social background there is an increase in both inclusion and fairness, whereas for people of high social background there is a decrease in inclusion and an increase in fairness. This means that more people from low social background are involved in higher education and this group is becoming better represented while fewer people of high social background are included in higher education, which decreases the level of their overrepresentation.

Contradictory synergy (Poland and Switzerland) – in this case the change is the same for both social groups, but runs in a different direction for inclusion and fairness: both groups see an increase in inclusion and a decrease in fairness. Thus, more people from both groups are involved in higher education, but the composition of the student body has become less similar to the society as a whole with regard to these two social groups, which shows that underrepresentation of people with low social background and overrepresentation of those with high social background are not overcome. Obviously, the pace of expanding inclusion for students of low social background is not enough in order to result in better fairness for this group. There is a different type of contradictory synergy in Ireland, where both groups see a decrease in inclusion and an increase in fairness.

Contradictory diversion (Finland) – under this pattern there is a decreased inclusion and increased fairness for people of low social background (i.e. fewer students of low social background in higher education and better

INCLUSION AND FAIRNESS IN ACCESS TO HIGHER EDUCATION

representation of this group) and increased inclusion for people of high social background with decreased fairness over time (i.e. more students of high social background enter higher education, but the representation of this group in higher education does not improve due to its continuing overrepresentation). In the Netherlands we observe an increased inclusion for social groups, increased fairness for the high social background group, and decreased fairness for the group with low social background group.

TABLE 10.1   Tendencies of interaction between inclusion and fairness in higher education for people of low and high social background in the period between 2009 and 2013

Countries	People of low social background		People of high social background	
	Inclusion	Fairness	Inclusion	Fairness
Estonia	↗	↗	↗	↗
France	↗	↗	↗	↗
Germany	↗	↗	↗	↗
Denmark	↗	↗	↙	↗
Norway	↗	↗	↙	↗
Ireland	↙	↗	↙	↗
Poland	↗	↙	↗	↙
Switzerland	↗	↙	↗	↙
Finland	↙	↗	↗	↙
The Netherlands	↗	↙	↗	↗

Legend: ↗ Increase   ↙ Decrease

   Logical synergy   Logical diversion

   Contradictory synergy   Contradictory diversion

5   Understanding Social Justice in (Access to) Higher Education as a Complex Phenomenon: Steps Taken and Beyond

The article demonstrated that social justice is an indispensable and independent perspective for assessing widening access to higher education for both research and policy-making. The bridging of the Sen's and Rawlsian understanding of justice provides a basis for differentiation and takes into account two important aspects of equity in access to higher education – inclusion and fairness. The inclusion aspect emphasises the significance of improvement in participation in higher education of a given group of people, independently of the achievements of the other groups (for example, the growth in absolute numbers of people from low social background), whereas the fairness perspective focuses on the proportional representation of students from different social groups within the student population (for example, the overrepresentation of students from high social background). The analysis undertaken allowed us to answer the three formulated research questions. We found that most of the countries studied differ considerably with respect to the extent to which the development of access to higher education is inclusive and fair over time (RQ1). However, in three of the studied countries we observed identical trends in the development of inclusive and fair access to higher education. The results showed that inclusion in access to higher education is not always associated with fairness in higher education at country level (RQ2). As for finding any patterns of interaction between inclusion and fairness in access to higher education (RQ3), we identified several patterns which were designated as logical synergy, contradictory synergy, logical diversion and contradictory diversion. Our analysis demonstrates that a) a higher education system could be fair without being inclusive – small share of students accessing, but representing the social diversity; b) a higher education system could be inclusive but unfair – large number of students entering higher education but mainly from the same (high social background) social group.

We have contributed to the literature on social justice in higher education in three ways.

First, this study gave a comprehensive account of how social justice in higher education can be conceptualised and measured. In defining social justice in (access to) higher education, the article bridged two of the main contemporary lines of reasoning about justice, i.e., institutions-centred one and the human-centred one, and considered their application to higher education by Marginson (2011). We argued that social justice in higher education is a complex phenomenon which is context and time-specific. The article differentiates between the inclusion and fairness aspects of social equity in higher education and claims that both aspects of equity should be studied separately for different social groups. This analysis demonstrates that the widened access to higher education brought about by the massification and expansion of higher education was not enough to reduce inequalities in access to higher education over time.

Second, building on the understanding of social justice in higher education as a complex phenomenon, the article developed and applied two indices –

IincluHE and IfairHE – for measuring how the inclusion and fairness aspects of social justice in access to higher education change over time. The IincluHE and IfairHE reveal specific features of participation in higher education which have not yet been captured through previously-existing measures and indicators. This is evident from the fact that some countries which have relatively low participation rates in higher education among low and high social background groups are more inclusive and fairer in comparison with countries where such rates are high (for example Switzerland and Austria have relatively low participation rates for people with low social background but are among the fairest countries with regard to this group). It is also evident from our findings that, during the studied period, in most of the countries studied, increased inclusion of people of low social background was not associated with better fairness in higher education. This means that the pace of expanding inclusion for students of lower social background should grow significantly faster in order to result in better fairness for this group.

Third, based on two criteria, we have suggested that any correspondence between the directions of change in the two indices over time could take the form of both synergy and diversion. The analysis undertaken allowed us to identify different relationship patterns between inclusion and fairness regarding low and high social status groups across 10 European countries and to assess them as logical or contradictory.

Our analysis and the obtained findings outlined some possible routes worth pursuing in *future research*. It is very important to continue the theoretical reflection on the understanding of social justice in higher education and how it relates to other issues in higher education, e.g. quality and effectiveness. There is a need to develop a comprehensive understanding of social justice in access to higher education which – applying, for example, the capability approach – recognises the vital importance of freedom and opportunity to human life. In that vein, another study has outlined the importance of widened participation in higher education going hand-in-hand with widened capability as a mechanism for reducing inequalities in the distribution of knowledge and skills (Walker, 2008). Thus, achieving greater justice at the entry to higher education should not be seen as an end in itself, but should rather also be linked to reducing inequalities in participation and outcomes of higher education, i.e., with consideration of what both retention and completion of higher education look like through the lens of social justice.

A fruitful and very important direction for future study would investigate factors at the macro as well as the micro level, helping to explain differences between countries as far as the inclusion and fairness aspects of social justice in higher education are concerned. At the macro level, for example, it is worth investigating how different types of welfare regimes, social cohesion regimes and education systems influence social justice in higher education. It is plausible to expect that the arrows of change in our indices of inclusion and fairness reflect the magnitude of changes for each of them and for both of the social groups. That is why it is worth trying to take into consideration both the direction and magnitude of changes in the indices. In all countries, students from high social background are overrepresented. In almost all of the countries we also observe inclusion with regard to people with low social background, although the level of fairness for this group does not increase considerably. In order to understand the levels of inclusiveness and fairness of a given system of higher education, and how they evolve over time, we need to consider the specificity of this system in terms of its history, structure and major developments. That is why the meaning of tendencies (either increase or decrease in inclusion and fairness) is different in different countries. Thus, for instance, the fact that the inclusion is particularly prominent in the Czech Republic for both social groups can be described as a catch-up phenomenon as the pace of massification of higher education in this country is a relatively recent phenomenon in comparison to other countries, for example Ireland. In order to understand the observed trends, we should also pay attention to the specificity of the structure of higher education institutions in a given country. For example, in some countries (e.g. Malta and Norway), in which there is an increase in the number of students from low social background and a decrease in the number of students from high social background, the massification and expansion of higher education are probably reached through development of professional higher education institutions or other higher education institutions which are not regarded as very prestigious by people with high social background.

Our analysis does not take into account the stratified nature of contemporary higher education systems. Still, it could be viewed as the basis for a very important line of future research. Due to the differences in prestige and quality of education offered at different higher education institutions, the number and diversity of students in higher education cannot be taken for granted as an indicator of greater 'equality': "unevenness persists as regards to who studies what and where" (Archer, 2007, p. 637). According to Marginson, too many countries' higher education systems "are so stratified as to reduce sharply – sometimes empty out – the value of participation for the majority of students" (Marginson, 2016, p. 77). That is why further research should pay special attention to the quality aspect of higher education and see how the two indices (IincluHE and IfairHE) stack up when applied to different higher education institutions and programmes (differentiated by type of degree – bachelor's, master's or PhD – and field of study).

INCLUSION AND FAIRNESS IN ACCESS TO HIGHER EDUCATION

The present analysis has both *policy implications* and *social implications*. A comparative analysis of different admission systems shows that although "higher education can perpetuate inequality across generations if social inclusion is not explicitly targeted," "social inclusion is rarely a central goal for higher education institutions" (Orr et al., 2017, p. 64). At the European level, the Europe 2020 strategy set the goal for all EU member states, by 2020, to increase the share of the population aged 30–34 having completed tertiary education to at least 40%. The achievement of this target will ensure a significant increase in the number of people with higher education and thus will stimulate social inclusion in higher education. However, the extent to which it will enhance fairness in access to higher education remains unclear. By revealing that social justice in higher education is a complex phenomenon with two different aspects – inclusion and fairness – the present paper can provide a reliable conceptual basis for developing strategies and concrete policies regarding access to higher education at the institutional, national and European level.

The analysis demonstrates that the institutions-centred approach of John Rawls and the human-centred approach of Amartya Sen can be used as theoretical lenses for understanding the specificity of social equity in higher education. The finding that the pace of expanding inclusion for students of low social background should be much higher in order to result in better fairness for this group resonates with Rawls' idea that policy decisions should be made so that the worst-off benefit most. In turn, viewed from the capability approach perspective, our result that people with high social background continue to be unfairly represented in higher education, clearly shows that this group has higher capabilities to convert available educational opportunities into real achievements and thus to perpetuate already exiting inequalities. The developed indices for measuring social equity in (access to) higher education can be calculated for other social groups based on other characteristics, such as gender, place of residence or ethnic origin, and using different time periods. The results of these indices can be used to monitor social justice in higher education. In this regard, regular collection of such data is crucial for this process. As such, these indices can be applied as a tool by policy-makers in their design of adequate and justified policies on access to higher education.

6 Data

This article used data for rounds 4, 5, 6 and 7 from the cumulative dataset ESS 1–7 (2002–2014). European Social Survey Data. Data file edition 1.0. NSD – Norwegian Centre for Research Data, Norway – Data Archive and distributor of ESS data for ESS ERIC.

Acknowledgements

This research was undertaken within the ENLIVEN project and received funding from the European Union (EU), Horizon 2020 research and innovation program under [grant number 693989], the project 'Current State and the Opportunities to Optimize Information Flows in the Russian Education System' funded by Russian Science Foundation under Grant No. 18-18-00047, and within the the National Research Programme 'Young scientists and postdoctoral students' (grant number DCM # 577/17.08.2018) funded by the Bulgarian Ministry of Education.

We would like to thank the anonymous reviewer and the editors of the book for their valuable comments on earlier versions of this chapter.

The authors contributed equally to this chapter and their names are listed in alphabetical order.

Notes

1 We have to bear in mind that data in the ESS are available only for graduates and this information is used as a proxy for access to higher education.
2 More information about both surveys is available at http://www.eurostudent.eu/ and https://www.europeansocialsurvey.org/
3 However, as we work with data on a macro level, it is not possible to establish whether the change for a given country is statistically significant or not.
4 We choose father's education following Usher (2004, p. 6) who argues that "since males aged 45–64 are more likely to possess a university education than women aged 45–64, it was felt that fathers made slightly more sense as a measurement."
5 According to ISCED 1997, ISCED 0–2 corresponds to primary and lower secondary education, while ISCED 5–6 to short-cycle tertiary education and bachelor's or equivalent level (UNESCO, 2006).
6 ISCED 2011 5–8 corresponds to short-cycle tertiary education, bachelor's or equivalent level, Master's and doctoral degree or equivalent levels (UNESCO, 2012).
7 We accumulated data from two rounds of the ESS (2008/2009 and 2010/2011) because the EUROSTUDENT IV Survey refers to the period 2008–2011. Furthermore, as we focus only on the age group 20–34, but not to the entire population, in this way have a solid number of cases for analytical use. Respectively, the same was made for the rounds 6 and 7 (2012/2013 and 2014/2015) in order to correspond to EUROSTUDENT V Survey which refers to the period 2012–2015. However, it is still possible to observe some dynamic between waves over time; this is why we included the round as a control variable in the logistic regression models.

References

Archer, L. (2007). Diversity, equality and higher education: A critical reflection on the ab/uses of equity discourse within widening participation. *Teaching in Higher Education, 12*(5–6), 633–653.

Blossfeld, H.-P., & Shavit, Y. (1993). Persisting barriers: Changes in educational opportunity in thirteen countries. In Y. Shavit & H. P. Blossfeld (Eds.), *Persistent inequality: Educational attainment in thirteen countries* (pp. 1–23). Boulder, CO: Westview Press.

Brighouse, H., & Unterhalter, E. (2010). Education for primary goods or for capabilities?" In H. Brighouse & I. Robeyns (Eds.), *Measuring justice. Primary goods and capabilities* (pp. 193–214). Cambridge: Cambridge University Press.

Clancy, P., & Goastellec, G. (2007). Exploring access and equity in higher education: Policy and performance in a comparative perspective. *Higher Education Quarterly, 61*(2), 136–154.

Elias, M., & Brennan, J. (2012). Implications of the Bologna process for equity in European higher education. In A. Curaj, P. Scott, L. Vlasceanu, & L. Wilson (Eds.), *European higher education at the crossroads: Between the Bologna process and national reforms* (pp. 101–118). Dordrecht: Springer.

Goastellec, G. (2008). Globalization and implementation of an equity norm in higher education: Admission processes and funding framework under scrutiny. *Peabody Journal of Education, 83*(1), 71–85.

Hauschildt, K., Gwość, Ch., Netz, N., & Mishra, S. (2015). *Social and economic conditions of student life in Europe. Synopsis of Indicators | EUROSTUDENT V 2012–2015.* Bielefeld: W. Bertelsmann Verlag.

Iannelli, C. (2002). *Parental education and young people's educational and labour market outcomes: A comparison across Europe.* Mannheim: MZES.

Ilieva-Trichkova, P., & Boyadjieva, P. (2014). Dynamics of inequalities in access to higher education: Bulgaria in a comparative perspective. *European Journal of Higher Education, 4*(2), 97–117.

London Communiqué. (2007). *Towards the european higher education area: Responding to challenges in a globalised world.* Retrieved from https://www.eurashe.eu/library/bologna_2007_london-communique-pdf/

Lucas, S. R. (2001). Effectively maintained inequality: Education transitions, track mobility, and social background effects. *American Journal of Sociology, 106*(6), 1642–1690.

Maffettone, S. (2011). Sen's idea of justice versus Rawls' theory of justice. *Indian Journal of Human Development, 5*(1), 119–132.

Mare, R. D. (1981). Change and stability in educational stratification. *American Sociological Review, 46*(1), 72–87.

Marginson, S. (2011). Equity, status and freedom: A note on higher education. *Cambridge Journal of Education, 41*(1), 23–36.

Marginson, S. (2016). *Higher education and the common good.* Melbourne: Melbourne University Publishing.

Orr, D., Gwość, Ch., & Netz, N. (2011). *Social and economic conditions of student life in Europe. Synopsis of indicators. Final report. Eurostudent IV 2008–2011.* Bielefeld: W. Bertelsmann Verlag.

Orr, D., Usher, A., Haj, C., Atherton, G., & Geanta, I. (2017). *Study on the impact of admission systems on higher education outcomes: Comparative report* (Vol. I). Luxembourg: Publications Office of the European Union.

Pfeffer, F. T. (2008). Persistent inequality in educational attainment and its institutional context. *European Sociological Review, 24*(5), 543–565.

Raftery, A. E., & Hout, M. (1993). Maximally maintained inequality: Expansion, reform, and opportunity in Irish education, 1921–1975. *Sociology of Education, 66,* 41–62.

Rawls, J. (1971). *A theory of justice* (Rev. ed.). Cambridge, MA: Belknap Press. (1999)

Robeyns, I. (2005). The capability approach: A theoretical survey. *Journal of Human Development, 6*(1), 93–114.

Robeyns, I. (2008). Justice as fairness and the capability approach. In K. Basu & R. Kanbu (Eds.), *Arguments for a better world: Essays in honor of Amartya Sen: Ethics, welfare, and measurement* (Vol. 1, pp. 397–413). Oxford: University Press.

Robeyns, I. (2017). *Wellbeing, freedom and social justice. The capability approach re-examined.* Cambridge: Open Book Publishers.

Santiago, P., Tremblay, K., Basri, K., & Arnal, E. (2008). *Tertiary education for the knowledge society: Special features: Equity, innovation, labour market, and internalisation* (Vol. 2). Paris: OECD.

Schofer, E., & Meyer, J. W. (2005). The worldwide expansion of higher education in the twentieth century. *American Sociological Review, 70*(6), 898–920.

Sen, A. (1999). *Development as freedom.* New York, NY: Anchor Books.

Sen, A. (2009). *The idea of justice.* Cambridge, MA: The Belknap Press of Harvard University Press.

Thrupp, M., & Tomlinson, S. (2005). Introduction: Education policy, social justice and 'complex hope'. *British Educational Research Journal, 31,* 549–556.

UNESCO. (2006). *International Standard Classification of Education ISCED 1997.* UNESCO: UNESCO Institute for Statistics.

UNESCO. (2012). *International Standard Classification of Education ISCED 2011.* UNESCO: UNESCO Institute for Statistics.

Usher, A. (2004). *A new measuring stick. Is access to higher education in Canada equitable?* Educational Policy Institute. Retrieved from http://www.educationalpolicy.org/pdf/measuringstick.pdf

Usher, A., & Medow, J. (2010). *Global higher education rankings 2010: Affordability and accessibility in comparative perspective*. Retrieved January 18, 2018. from http://higheredstrategy.com/wp-content/uploads/2011/09/GHER2010_FINAL.pdf

Walker, M. (2008). Widening participation; Widening capability. *London Review of Education, 6*(3), 267–279.

Wilson-Strydom, M. (2015). University access and theories of social justice: Contributions of the capabilities approach. *Higher Education, 69*(1), 143–155.

CHAPTER 11

Academic Career, Mobility and the National Gender Regimes in Switzerland and Finland

Terhi Nokkala, Pierre Bataille, Taru Siekkinen and Gaële Goastellec

Abstract

The probability of reaching a permanent academic position is strongly gendered in most if not all higher education systems. Though a widely studied phenomenon, few studies problematise the way national contexts – both academic and non-academic – that shape employment structures and national gender regimes are interpreted by individual academics, and frame their career strategies and the ways of subjectively coping with the norms of academic careers. Aiming to fill this research gap, this chapter compares the subjective representations of early career academics in terms of career expectation and articulation between professional and private sphere in two contrasted national contexts; Finland and Switzerland. Focusing especially on international mobility, the paper aims to reveal how national polities matter to understand young academics' strategies and how these strategies are shaped – or not – by gender relationships in the era of the so called 'internationalisation' of academic labour markets and the norm of the academic staff mobility.

Keywords

academic career – internationalisation – mobility – gender regime – work-life balance – polities – Switzerland – Finland

1   Introduction

As many scientific research and public reports underline, in most national higher education systems, the probability of reaching a permanent academic position is strongly gendered: women having largely less chances than men to access such positions, even if they represent a growing part of the academic staff at the doctoral and postdoctoral levels (Bozzon, Murgia, & Poggio, 2018).

© KONINKLIJKE BRILL NV, LEIDEN, 2020 | DOI: 10.1163/9789004422582_012

ACADEMIC CAREER, MOBILITY AND THE NATIONAL GENDER REGIMES 263

This 'leaky pipeline' phenomenon is well identified in the literature combining gender and academic career analysis (Goulden, Meison, & Frasch, 2011; Dubois-Shaik, Fusulier, & Vincke, 2018).

While there are many investigations into this topic that mobilise data from different national contexts (see for example Eggins, 2017; Goastellec & Pekari, 2013), few studies really problematise how far national contexts (academic and non-academic) that shape employment structures and national gender regimes also guide the academics' career strategies i.e., how gender inequalities in academia are embedded into national specific contexts (Goastellec & von Roten, 2017). In this chapter, we compare the subjective representations of early career academics in terms of career expectations and articulation between professional and private spheres in two contrasted national contexts (Finland and Switzerland). Our paper aims to unravel how national polities matter to understanding young academics' strategies and how these strategies are shaped – or not – by gender relationships in the era of the so called 'internationalisation' of academic labour markets, where international mobility has increasingly become a norm for academic careers. We investigate how the international norm of academic mobility influences the academic careers for men and women, depending on the national gender regime in which the academic market they try to access is embedded.

We use the concept of gender regime to highlight the gendered aspects of societal structures, policies, norms and customs that enable or constrain the differential participation of men, women and those of other gender identity in society and employment. According to Acker (1994, p. 117), the gender regime concept refers to "the patterning of gender processes in particular social units at particular historical times". Units can be national space, institutions or professional groups for instance. In the context of higher education, the notion of gender regime also highlights the structural and political aspects that are sometimes disguised by the seeming meritocracy of academia (Le Feuvre, 2009). We consciously use the term 'polity' to denote the "set of collective choices linking together parts submitted to the rule of 'compulsory belongings'" (Leca, 2012, p. 62) that are embedded in the national context. Instead of the notion of policies, which refer to the contents and implementation of specific rules, such as gender equality policy, maternity policy or recruitment policy, we use the notion of polities to comprise multiple policies but also the tacit understandings and cultures within the national boundaries that frame the Swiss and Finnish gender regimes. We approach the gender regimes from the perspective of individual academic's perceptions regarding the frameworks that facilitate and constrain their choices. By doing so, we acknowledge that gender regimes participate in the social regulation and thus impinge on the values, norms and roles individuals internalise through the socialisation process, leading individuals to develop dispositions which are 'situated' with regard to their context of 'interiorisation' (Lahire, 1998).

The rest of this chapter is structured as follows: in Section 2, we frame our paper in terms of the varied elements of the leaky pipeline phenomenon; and present our research questions. To better understand the observed diversity of the leaky pipeline, we propose to look closer at how representations and practices of young researchers in terms of academic career and mobility are shaped by the national gender regime and the way academic careers are nationally regulated. In Section 3, we outline the context of internationalisation of academic labour markets and the national gender regimes in Finland and Switzerland, as well as introduce the data and method of the study. Section 4 describes the findings of the study along the four dominant dimensions systematically discussed by the interviewees: internationalisation, career, family and work-life balance. We conclude by discussing the similarities and differences in how the early career academics, in Finland and Switzerland, talk about career, international mobility, family and work-life balance.

2   Varieties of 'Leaky Pipelines'

2.1   *The Gendering of Academic Careers as a Politically 'Embedded' Phenomenon*

Although women represent equal or higher student numbers in undergraduate and graduate education or in the early stages of an academic career, they still face many obstacles in advancing on their career path (Rogers & Molinier, 2016).

Cross-national comparisons show that, depending on the national academic system, the 'flow' of women exiting the higher level of the academic hierarchy strongly vary – as does the way they exit (Le Feuvre, 2009). Thus, if

> it is undoubtedly true that women all over the world are victims of discrimination and of the effects of patriarchal stereotypes and that their academic careers are less 'successful' than those of their male counterparts [...] there are [however] considerable differences, both between countries and [...] between disciplinary fields, and there are also signs of considerable change over time. (Le Feuvre, 2009, p. 15)

Such differences may gain from being investigated in order to contextualise the 'leaky pipeline' phenomenon and – in a way – contribute to further

ACADEMIC CAREER, MOBILITY AND THE NATIONAL GENDER REGIMES

point out the political nature of gender inequalities among academic labour markets.

2.2 Being Employable, Being Mobile: A Global Trend Shaping Academic Employment?

By "provid[ing] evidence of a strong societal embeddedness of academic markets" (Goastellec & von Roten, 2017, p. 227), looking at how national gender regimes shape academic careers points out the political nature of the 'leaky pipeline' phenomenon. The culture and policies related to academic employment, especially the mobility norms vary across given polities, contributing to the same discussion.

For a large number of candidates, having some postdoctoral international mobility reduces the risk of remaining on temporary academic positions (Ortlieb & Weiss, 2018) and thus to the 'leaky pipeline'. While the link between individual mobility and internationalisation of scientific and intellectual production remains tenuous (Ackers, 2008), the mobility norm also manifests itself at institutional level. Universities aiming to cast themselves as international or global institutions (Musselin, 2017) are keen to look towards attracting and recruiting the 'best brains worldwide' and thus ensure their global competitiveness (Tung, 2008). To do this, universities have introduced structured career progression models, such as tenure tracks where the performance of an academic is assessed periodically; and those who have achieved the preset targets will have an opportunity to aspire to the full professor position. International mobility period is often required in these new structured career models (Pietilä, 2015; Siekkinen, Pekkola, & Kivistö, 2016).

In general, at the beginning of 2010's only 16% of European academic staff had experienced international mobility (Goastellec & Pekari, 2013, 2016). As the norm of academic mobility at the institutional and international level is becoming stronger in most national academic contexts, practices and policies framing this norm strongly differ across countries. The mobility norm and its effect are stronger within 'small' countries like Switzerland, Norway, Ireland or Austria, although mobility is often regional rather than strictly international (Goastellec, 2016). There is similarly a disciplinary aspect to the mobility norm: 'being mobile' appears to be a stronger prerequisite for being recruited on a permanent position in physics or molecular biology compared with law or humanities. Finally, the attractiveness of local non-academic markets also impacts mobility practices, and young academics' decision to leave the academia: if the chances of getting a stable job outside academia are high; the human and material cost of mobility can be perceived as a good reason for leaving the academic track (Bataille, Le Feuvre, & Kradolfer Morales, 2017;

Dorenkamp & Weiß, 2017). However, mobility is not only a choice dependent on the individual.

2.3 A Mixed Framework to Better Understand the Making of Young Academics Gendered Practices and Representations

Even if it is well known that national gender regimes and mobility norms contribute to shape the gender of academic careers, their combined effects on the ways men and women consider embracing an academic career and deal with it have rarely been analysed. This 'mixed' framework, combining national gender regimes and academic mobility norms is at the core of the present chapter.

We investigate how the international norm of academic mobility influences the academic careers for men and women, depending on the national gender regime in which the academic market they try to access is embedded. Because the temporality of building a family and an academic career are often simultaneous, we focus on men and women who are junior to mid-career academics with a family. Our main research questions include: How do mid-career academics with children envisage international mobility depending on their gender and the national gender regime characterising their country? Does the development of an international mobility requirement in academic careers generate different tensions for both men and women depending on the national gender regimes?

3 Finland and Switzerland: Two Comparable but Highly Contrasted Polities

3.1 Academic Employment and Internationalisation

As previous comparisons between Finland and Switzerland already show (Goastellec & Välimaa, 2016), these two European countries have much in common: relatively small (Switzerland 8 million and Finland 5.5 million inhabitants) and sparsely populated countries, which both used to be poor and "dominated by their neighbours" (Goastellec & Välimaa, 2016, p. 105) but are now among the richest countries of Europe. Both have high standard of living and advanced education and science infrastructure. For all these reasons, Finnish and Swiss cases are well fitted for comparison. Nevertheless, Finland and Switzerland strongly differ in terms of our two main variables of interest – national gender regimes and academic mobility practices. Figure 11.1 presents the proportion of internationally mobile academics – i.e., academics who received their PhD outside their country of current employment – among junior (A) and senior (B) academic staff in several European countries; with Finland and Switzerland appearing at the opposing ends of the continuum.

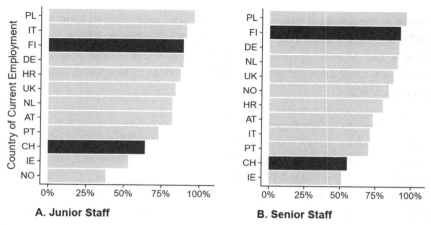

FIGURE 11.1 Doctoral degree obtained in the country of current employment (European academic staff, 2010). (Source: EuroAC)

In Switzerland, people who defended their PhD abroad represent 55% of the senior academic staff and 36% of the junior academic staff. While there are great differences between disciplines, all in all internationalisation of the Swiss higher education institutions' employees is an old phenomenon; albeit one that has varied during the last century (Rossier, Beetschen, Mach, & Bühlmann, 2015). International academic recruitments have nevertheless risen sharply since the end of the 1990s, due to the institutional and national policies and norms aiming to promote Swiss universities in the international rankings (Benninghoff, Goastellec, & Leresche, 2009). The good academic labour market conditions and high salaries can also be strongly appealing for foreign academics, especially those coming from one of the three main neighboured countries, which have experienced a strong precarisation – as in Italy – or a stagnation and a strengthening of internal competition within their own national market since the end of the 1990s.

Conversely, Finland has a relatively small but growing share of international academics, who represent 4% in senior positions and 9% in junior positions; albeit national higher education policies and funding in place to support international mobility. In 2015, the Academy of Finland, the country's most prestigious research funding body, changed the preconditions of personal postdoctoral or senior scholar grants to include a minimum six-month work experience in a university other than where they received their PhD. While this precondition by the Academy of Finland is fulfilled with a stay in another Finnish university, many universities' recruitment policies emphasise mobility periods abroad. Data from 2016, however, shows the disparity between PhD holders who enter the country, and those who exit it: while 495 PhD holders left Finland; only 193 moved to the country (Acatiimi, 2017), sparking concerns of 'brain drain' amongst national media and academic trade unions. The reasons for leaving the university sector as a whole in Finland has been said to be related to the decreasing resources of Finnish universities and poor working conditions with short fixed-term contracts (Siekkinen, Kuoppala, Pekkola, & Välimaa, 2016b).

3.2 National Gender Regimes

Swiss and Finnish States strongly differ in the ways they support childcare, women's employment and non-traditional family. In Switzerland, there is no parental leave at the federal level (Valarino & Gauthier, 2016), fiscal policies are unfavourable to dual-earner households and there is a considerable lack of childcare solutions (Bütler, 2006). Conversely in Finland, parental leave lasts for nine months; three of which are earmarked for the mother and the remaining six can be used by either parent. Additionally, there is an earmarked paternity leave of up to nine weeks. The parental allowance is minimum 70% of the parent's salary. If the child is cared for at home, the parents receive a small sum called the child home care allowance. Also, childcare outside home is heavily subsidised; though the right to full—or part time childcare is dependent on the parents' labour market situation.

These differences between Finland and Switzerland contribute to the observed contrast between the labour market participation of men and women in the two countries (Figure 11.2). While the primary family labour market configuration in Switzerland comprises men working fulltime and women part time; in Finland, families comprising two full time earners are more common than in many other European countries (UNECE, 2018). This 'double full time active' track also seems strong among families with children.

The differences between the two national gender regimes thus comprise both the family labour market arrangements (Switzerland: male breadwinner – female homemaker; Finland: two fulltime earners); and the societal policies that contribute to them – namely the childcare and parental leave policies, and other arrangements that impact on both parents' ability to equally participate in the labour market.

These gender regimes are a significant component that impact, respectively, the gender representation of academia in Finland and Switzerland (Figure 11.3). In Finland, the share of female university students surpassed that of male students already in the 1970s while in Switzerland women remained underrepresented until the 2000s. The makeup of the Swiss and Finnish academic labour markets differs along both the share of male versus female academics, and the share of international versus national academics.

Swiss and Finnish academic markets contrast by their level of feminisation (higher in Finland), their level of internationalisation (much higher in

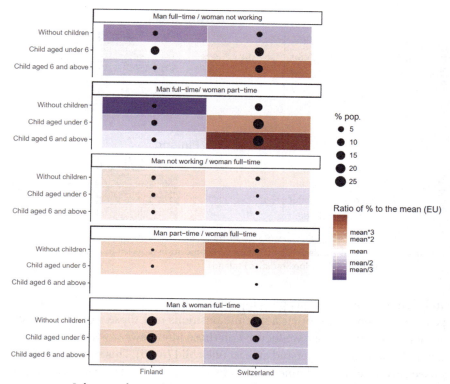

FIGURE 11.2 Labour market participation patterns of couples aged 29–45 years, by family labour market configuration (Finland & Switzerland) 2016. (Source: UNECE)

Switzerland), and across these two dimensions, by a lower share of internationally mobile women academics compared with men in Finland, while it is not the case in Switzerland.

We therefore question whether the challenges of academic career and mobility are perceived differently by women, compared with men, in the gender regimes of Finland and Switzerland; and whether, thus, men and women talk differently about them.

3.3 Data and Methods

The Swiss data was collected in 2015–2016 during the GARCIA Project[1] aimed at investigating gender asymmetries at the early stages of academic careers in Belgium, Iceland, Italy, Netherlands, Slovenia and Switzerland. Altogether 40 interviews were conducted at a major Swiss research university. The interviewees were selected from among a list of all the people hired in a postdoctoral position between 2010 and 2013 by a STEM or HSS department of this university. This selection aimed to represent the broadest range of characteristics possible. The interviewees comprised both males and females, international

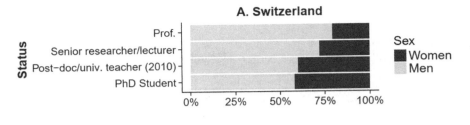
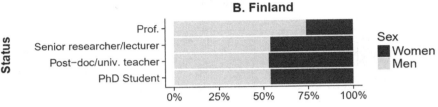

FIGURE 11.3 Swiss and Finnish HE staff gendered composition (2014). (Source: FSO and Vipunen, Education Statistics Finland)

and domestic scholars, people employed at the time of the interviews in postdoctoral positions, other academic positions and those working outside academia. For this paper, we focused on those interviewees who were not yet tenured, and had a partner and at least one child (n=16). This subsample comprised seven women and nine men, 34 to 48 years of age. Six of the interviewees represented social or human sciences, and ten represented STEM fields. Of the interviewees, five were Swiss and 11 foreign nationals.

The Finnish dataset was designed to complement the existing Swiss data. It comprised interviews with altogether 16 respondents, located in a Finnish research university. The authors' personal contacts and a link tracing sampling design were used in identifying the interviewees. The interviewees had to be in an early to mid-career stage; having completed their PhD's, but not yet holding full professor positions. For this paper, only those interviewees were selected who had a partner and at least one child. The sample comprised five men and six women; aged 34 to 47 years old. Two of the selected respondents were international, i.e., not Finnish citizens. Seven of the respondents were in life sciences, four in social sciences. Six had spent a longer or shorter period of their career abroad, while five had no international experience during their careers beyond short-term conference trips. Two of the respondents held permanent positions, while the rest were either tenure-track, fixed-term positions or held personal scholarships.

All the interviews were recoded and transcribed; then analysed by several rounds of reading to identify the key themes and dimensions these themes belonged to.

ACADEMIC CAREER, MOBILITY AND THE NATIONAL GENDER REGIMES

TABLE 11.1 Sample composition

	Finland		Switzerland	
	Male	Female	Male	Female
National	4	5	6	7
International	1	1	5	7
Permanent contract	1	1	5	7
Tenure track/In the process of being made permanent	1	1	2	1
Fixed-term	2	4	2	3
Scholarship	1	–	–	1
Out	–	–	2	2
Period abroad	4	2	11	14
No period abroad	1	4	–	–
Life sciences	3	4	7	6
Social sciences	2	2	4	8
Age	36–40	34–47	–	–
Age of completing PhD	29–32	30–33	–	–

We analysed how interviewees deal – subjectively and objectively – with imperatives about four main topics at the core of our research interest: family, career, work-life balance and internationalisation. We thus interrogate how the interviewees construct internationalisation and international mobility, how they talk about their academic careers; how they describe the relationship between family and career; and finally, how they balance work and family responsibilities, and talk about their routines and coping mechanisms.

4   Analysis

4.1   *Internationalisation*
The first dimension addressed internationalisation as part of academic work and career.

4.1.1   Finland
In the Finnish interviews, internationalisation is primarily constructed as attending international conferences or spending mid-length periods between

a few months to one year abroad in the context of postdoctoral projects funded from Finland. However, the idea of leaving Finland for a longer-term career without the intention of coming back was not common amongst the Finnish-born interviewees. For one of the foreign born academics this was their primary goal, and the time spent in Finland was seen more as an interlude, while for the other one, the primary goal was to stay in Finland although this was made challenging by the partner's labour market situation.

The experiences of the mid-length international mobility periods were, to some extent, gendered in that the male interviewees had more mobility experiences than female interviewees, conducted either alone before children were born or with the whole family travelling along during spouse's parental leave. The scholars in life sciences had more and longer mobility periods than the scholars in social sciences. The two international interviewees who were both married to another academic had spent longer periods of time away from their spouse due to both their own and their spouse's academic career.

The representations of internationalisation in the interviews of the Finnish-born scholars were framed by a critique of the perceived 'compulsory internationalisation'; stemming from the tacit and explicit perception that higher education policy and institutions require scholars to spend certain time abroad as a precondition for academic career progression; or in the case of some of the social science respondents, the critical view of the strengthening norm to publish in English instead of in Finnish. The compulsory mobility was described as being based on a very narrow understanding of internationality as a relatively short period of international mobility after PhD, instead of engaging in international collaborative research while staying at the home institution. The futility of simply 'going abroad' for the sake of going abroad was mentioned in several interviews.

> Internationalisation has become a responsibility for someone working at the university. If you go abroad for 6 months and you are not well prepared or have poor networks, it may all become to nothing. You do the same writing you would have done at home. (Female, soc. sci.)

Similarly, the interviewees perceived that the dominant higher education discourse assumes that everything that is international, i.e., not Finnish/domestic, must inherently be of higher quality, and many interviewees criticised this view.

> Just going abroad will not bring international quality. You have to have the thoughts in your own head already. You don't just go abroad to talk

ACADEMIC CAREER, MOBILITY AND THE NATIONAL GENDER REGIMES 273

nice and suddenly [that way] the quality of science goes up. Instead, something must change in your own head and take [science] forward. [...] I understand that it is difficult to get Finnish people to leave and go abroad, that is a good reason to try and make them go, it does not hurt anyone [to go]. But I don't understand the hype about making structural decisions that you must have a period abroad in your CV. That is a potential indicator for quality of science, but the main indicators are publications and citations. (Male, life sci.)

The negotiations between family obligations and academic work, including for example teaching obligations, influenced the considerations of short-term mobility for both men and women, as attending conferences required interviewees to ensure the other parent, or extended family in some cases, was able to take care of the children during the trip. The representations of the challenges related to this were especially prominent amongst women, although male interviewees also indicated they considered carefully whether a trip was worth making. Amongst women there was a sense that mid-length and longer-term mobility was largely ruled out in the near future, not on the account of lacking interest but on family grounds as it would be impracticable because of children's school or other circumstances, such as the spouse's work. Some also cite their personality, as not having been courageous enough to 'go abroad' before, and now, with family, it is difficult. However, as a longer-term perspective, if no jobs were to be found in Finland or when children were already independent, they considered international mobility to be at least a theoretical, if not actionable, option. The notion of advancing one's career through mobility was not something seen in the interviews. Rather, the representation of mobility is related to the broader frame of talking about academia as simply a job rather than a career in which one should try to advance. If it is simply a job one is doing, then the benefits accrued by mobility, such as networks, collaboration or access to data and previous research can just as well be managed from the location in Finland.

Internationalisation was one of the issues where the respondents in life sciences and social sciences displayed a clear difference, in a sense life science respondents had much more funding available for attending international conferences, and therefore availability of funding did not feature as a factor in their consideration on whether to travel abroad or not. Meanwhile, the social science respondents had to give consideration to whether they had the funds available to attend conferences. This division was even more visible when considering the entire set of interviews, not just the sample of those respondents with families, selected for this paper, illustrating an important disciplinary gap with regard to funding availability and how it impinges on the possibility (and maybe institutional expectations) of short-term mobility.

4.1.2 Switzerland

Most of the postdocs interviewed in Switzerland were not originally from Switzerland and had defended their PhDs in France (17%), the US (8.5%) or Italy (7.9%). Reflecting the global trends of academic mobility, the movers in the Swiss data mostly came from Europe and North America and – above all – are currently working within this geographical area. Thus, North-to-North mobility is the most frequent pattern of migration among the interviewees in Switzerland. Some of the interviewees came from the global South to Switzerland; and few planned to go back to a Southern country. Thus, as many of the interviewees in the Swiss sample came from abroad, they were predisposed to have a good opinion on international mobility.

> [With my wife] we both like...we like to travel a lot. My wife [who is Swiss], she has family in the US, she has family in Germany so...Me too I'm German actually. So, we're pretty international family, so we like to see other cultures and to, to go abroad. So, when she agreed that she would come with me and that she would also like to do a postdoc [...], we went to the US, to look at different place we also thought about ok where are groups where she could work with. And then once we have decided we started to apply also to the different labs in the different departments which were available. (Male, life sci.)

For those interviewees who defended their dissertation in Switzerland and who spent their first postdoctoral years in the same country, going abroad and getting international mobility experience was often presented as necessary for reaching a tenure-track position in a Swiss university. At the same time, the strong internationalisation of the Swiss academic labour markets makes, however, the return to Switzerland after a mobility period a risky strategy:

> If you want a job in Switzerland you are competing with the world in fact, unlike other countries where it is more you are more in competition with local people. Switzerland is a completely open market [...] We are very international so it's not easy to come back to Switzerland at this level. (Male, life sci)

Thus, even some of the Swiss interviewees criticised the mobility norm, which was mostly seen as a necessary ingredient of academic career. This was particularly the case in life sciences, where international mobility period is more

ACADEMIC CAREER, MOBILITY AND THE NATIONAL GENDER REGIMES

often a prerequisite for career advancement than in social sciences. Nevertheless, the Swiss social sciences interviewees also mentioned international mobility during postdoctoral years as a prerequisite to being competitive on the Swiss academic market.

> In Switzerland, therefore, we are obliged to go abroad [...]. When you have a family, it's true that this rule is really hard. And then afterwards, like all that, it's done to promote excellence, to see what is part of the research, to be a bit international, to be aware of what is going on, done elsewhere and well it fit well in the professional academic culture. [Colleagues often say] "It will be very good for you to go elsewhere because you will be able to meet new people and so on". And yeah so in that sense you're still pushed to ask [a postdoc fellowship]. (Female, soc.sci.)

The critical discourse on the mobility norm, prevalent amongst the Finnish interviewees, was also found amongst some, albeit few, of the Swiss interviewees. While such mobility norm had different implications for women and men, the mobility norm seemed to be ingrained in the representation of an academic career.

4.2 *Career*

4.2.1 Finland

The respondents mostly felt optimistic about their future career, despite having been employed on short-term contracts now or in the past. They also recognised that academics often encounter competition in building and maintaining an academic career, and were aware of the general precariousness of academic careers.

While all responders indicated that they were happy being researchers, most nevertheless indicated that this was not the only option for them, and in case it was not possible to pursue further a university career, they could do something else. While the two citations below appear gendered, the data does not allow us to determine this conclusively.

> Somehow I have thought that why would I think about it (precariousness) too much; if this is my dream job, I will do it as long as it works out. (Male, life sci.)

> I think future is not so grim as people paint it. I try to remain positive and believe in my own abilities. Something will always show up. Maybe my future will be elsewhere and I will be in a company rather than university in five years' time. [...] I also see no point in that I would try [to get

funding] for years, as that would certainly lead to desperation. (Female, life sci.)

This notion was typically tied to the family dimension indicating that changing career was preferable to changing geographic location. Two interviewees, one male, one female, further qualified this by stating that their identity was not linked to a given position at the university. Such hedging was also accompanied by the recognition that university careers were precarious and did not easily allow for career breaks.

There were subtle differences between the interviewees in terms of whether they referred research as a career/vocation, or as a job like any other.

My problem is just to figure out what I like more than this. I really love mentoring, you know, I really love doing research. The parts of academia that I hate have to do with things that are very difficult to change you know; the pay, the structure, you know the way that they see woman in science or mothers, you know, in science. Those kinds of things are difficult, the instability, you know, that stuff is hard to change. But everything else about it, you know like doing my research, I love. (Female, life sci.)

Most interviewees indicated they had been lucky in acquiring the posting they currently had, instead of attributing it to their own excellence or hard work. Two men mentioned that they did not think they would be amongst the first people to be let go, if the university was laying off staff.

4.2.2 Switzerland

Amongst the Swiss interviewees as well, there were people who spoke of their future in terms of career building, even if they knew that their chances of reaching a permanent position in Switzerland were low. Those career-oriented people were often men, in a relationship with a partner working outside academia, and holding lower education than themselves.

Going out was pretty straightforward [yeah]. [...] So I did my PhD in [another Swiss university] [...] I stayed almost one complete year as a postdoc in a lab where I did my PhD and during that time. I started to, you know, look at other laboratories, in particular in...in other countries, 'cos I wanted to go somewhere else, and which I'm interested in...Actually, all the laboratories I got really interested in were in the US. So I started to contact them, and then during the summer I went to the US for a road

ACADEMIC CAREER, MOBILITY AND THE NATIONAL GENDER REGIMES   277

trip. We visited different places to see whether we could imagine living there. (Male, life sci.)

While few women spoke similarly of mobility, they were typically either single or in 'atypical' conjugal configuration; such as with a partner who had a lower educational background or an 'egalitarian' way of thinking about gender relationships.

I think I applied for other two places and I didn't know anything about it [salary and so one]. And then I got this one [a postdoctoral position in Germany]. I had to decide. When they took me, they said "yes you have two weeks to decide". And I said "yes"…and then after that I didn't apply anymore. But I'd say at the same time also my husband was applying for other positions. And we were kind of decided: once one of us get first something that is decent, we move. (Female, life sci.)

Swiss interviewees also perceive the international competition to influence academic careers, causing them to experience stress and doubt about their future in academia although some also presented the pressure as normal for academic careers.

I don't suffer but sometimes I think, ok, you know it's normal that you're sometimes stressed and, hum, and that you can't sleep. I talk to other people here and they sometimes have the same problems that you just have lot of responsibilities and a lot of work from different sides. (Male, life sci.)

The level of satisfaction with the employment conditions at the university among Swiss postdocs is lower than among their foreigner counterparts. This low satisfaction may lead some postdocs to leave their academic careers and pursue alternative career paths in the private or public sector (Bataille et al., 2017). The relative precariousness of academic careers was a topic brought up by nearly all interviewees, and included stories about fix-term employment contracts followed by spells of unemployment. The accounts provided by those who left their academic career track were, in particular, shaped by their gendered expectations for the future. The following extract is illustrative of the discourse of those men who viewed the academic career prospects too uncertain compared with opportunities outside academia; and decided to exit the academic labour market. Discussing the reason why he decided to quit academia for a job at an industrial firm, the (male, life sci.)

interviewee said, "I didn't want to end up being over 40 and still with a fixed-term contract".

Since PhDs are highly valued on the non-academic Swiss labour markets, the career-oriented interviewees had a choice of taking a position in a company or in public administration in case their career progression in academia stalled.

4.3 *Family*
4.3.1 Finland

Most interviewees argued that their partner was very supportive in everyday life, though some have more flexibility than others to support the respondent's career or contribute to the family duties, depending on their own work situation. Interestingly, most interviewees argued that they did not think having a family impeded their career; yet having a family was definitely a factor to be taken into account when considering job location or international mobility. Many interviewees stated that they would rather change career than location due to family ties; partner's career cited typically as a reason for not moving abroad or moving to a different city. Stability for children was deemed very important (schools, friends, health care), and consequently, many of the interviewees stated that they were more likely to pursue international mobility when their children were older. This statement was often linked to the critical sentiment expressed towards 'compulsory' internationalisation, which is further discussed under the internationalisation theme. Another popular way to describe potential mobility plans and the role of family was to say that the whole family could go, or indeed has gone, abroad for a short while. Although the sample is too small to draw extensive conclusions about this, it is worth noting that men, rather than women primarily conveyed such experiences; and that such a visit had taken place while their wife had been on parental leave. Similarly, the respondent could be or has been travelling alone for just a few weeks or months. However, long terms plan to relocate the family were on hold due to the consideration of the spouse's employment and aspirations, as illustrated by this quote:

> I could go by myself, if I did not have to think about children's schools and care, and wife's job. I know that my wife will not want to become a housewife abroad, she wants to do something else as well. (Male, soc. sci.)

The international respondents recognised that finding jobs for their partners (in both cases the partner was an academic) might be challenging if the family stayed in Finland. However, the desire to 'put down roots' for the sake of the

ACADEMIC CAREER, MOBILITY AND THE NATIONAL GENDER REGIMES

family, in Finland or elsewhere was a topic addressed also in the international interviews; where the partners had already experienced long periods of staying apart in different countries:

> In the next two-plus years that I have left of my personal grant, I will be applying for jobs to try and get something that will allow us to just lay down roots. [...] I hope that once I apply for jobs in North America, if I get something, many universities there are better with a two-body situation, in that they will do double hires. (Female, life sci.)

There were small differences in the Finnish interviews between men and women with regard to this dimension. One characteristic of the family issue was about treating the family as a unit instead of individuals and their careers.

4.3.2 Switzerland

Since family policies are less favourable for women in Switzerland, the family theme was not prominent, and was primarily negative among Swiss interviewees in general – especially for those who had left Switzerland for a long period. Family was, therefore, more commonly mentioned among people who presented themselves as suffering in the academic system and/or who were thinking leaving the academic career sooner or later.

> I was doing a postdoc in London and my family did stay here. My husband had a fixed position with also responsibilities...so it wasn't possible to leave his job to just spend a year in London. We also had a place in a crèche here. So, finally everything was established and we did not want to just move for a year knowing that uh well this was a postdoc – so not a stable position that I will have. So the family stayed here so it's me who makes the trips. And then uh here I was already exhausted before leaving and this situation really didn't make the things get better. (Female, soc sci.)

While there were some men who shared this discourse, women (and especially Swiss women) were overrepresented among those who put the family at the core of their narratives on work and career.

4.4 Work-Life Balance

4.1.1 Finland

The last dimension addresses questions pertaining to work-life balance, as well as pacing and balancing together the family and career obligations in the daily life. A dualism that was clearly identifiable in the Finnish data was the notion that academic work requires a lot in terms of daily life, and one often has to prioritise work ahead of family; working long hours and during holidays was described as common. At the same time, a majority of the interviewees iterated that academic work also offers a lot of flexibility in everyday life as it does not require one to spend fixed hours in the office, but can instead be done flexibly and in various places, if family obligations require one to leave the office early.

> [I probably work] 7h in the office and it depends a lot on the current work situation how much follows in the in the remaining hours and potentially weekend. [...] It is a luxury to work on something that I also like doing, and difficult to distinguish what is work and what is not. But on the other hand it is also difficult to completely disconnect from work, e.g. go on holiday and not take any papers. (Male, life sci.)

While some social science respondents stated they tried to focus their work on office hours, most also work occasional evenings or weekends. A clear departure from this were those life science respondents who had experimental work or field work, as that kind of work was not tied to conventional working hours, but extended to weekends or, for example, very long working days in the summertime. Perhaps surprising was the ethos represented by the interviewees that they primarily relied on the nuclear family in managing family obligations, instead of making use of wider circles of family, friends or proprietary services. One interviewee even criticised that academic discourse prioritises work, and assumes that family is there to support work, and argued that it would be better to think that the "people close to us should bring something else to our lives than facilitating more work" (Male, soc sci.).

4.4.2 Switzerland

In the Swiss data, the work overflowing into private life was commonly presented as normal. Similar to the Finnish data, the interviewees in life sciences faced this challenge more directly than interviewees in social sciences, as they often reported having to work at the lab during the weekends or in the evenings.

> Personally I try to keep to that work rate 8 a.m.... 8 a.m. to 6 p.m. roughly. I know that a lot of my colleagues come later in the morning and end very late in the evening or work at weekends, etc. In any case it's more than a 100% job [ok] not me though, not in my case. (Male, life sci.)

ACADEMIC CAREER, MOBILITY AND THE NATIONAL GENDER REGIMES

Women, who had to manage between the flexibility of academic daytime work and the lack of affordable childcare, often declared that they suffered from the lack of boundaries between the private and professional spheres.

> To be frank personally I'm not proud of what I've done so far [during her postdoc], so I don't know how much patience he [her supervisor] has, I don't know how reasonable he finds it that I...well I feel terribly handicapped compared to what I, what...what I used to do in the time of the... when I had free use of my time, and well now there are so many constraints in all directions plus the fact that in terms of family all the same it's an enormous sacrifice [yeah] I'm neglecting my little daughter four days a week and also incidentally my bloke. (Female, life sci.)

5   Discussion and Conclusion

Our analysis highlights the similarities and differences in the ways in which male and female academics talk about their careers, mobility and family life and the ways they cope with combining these different spheres in Finland and Switzerland. While the calls for international mobility are present in both polities, the norm seems stronger and less contested in Switzerland than in Finland, where the representations of the mobility norm were more critical. In Finland, there were little differences in terms of how men and women talked about balancing their academic career and family responsibilities. They were also equally critical about the discourse of enforced international mobility, bar that of short-term conferences or visits. In Switzerland, the differences between men and women on these topics were more important. While Swiss men often declared that going abroad before having a tenured position was normal, Swiss women were more critical on this issue – and those who experienced mobility were often pushed to a very difficult situation, especially if they were in partnership with educated Swiss men (Bataille et al., 2017). Similarly, there were differences between Finland and Switzerland in terms of how the interviewees talked of family and work-life balance. Family seemed to be harder to reconcile with an academic career than in the Finnish interviews; and the representations of family were mostly negative.

Previous research show that women are still underrepresented in academia both in terms of institutional leadership higher rungs of the professorial posts or in terms of achieving tenured positions, especially in STEM fields (Goulden et al., 2011) and in full time and permanent positions (Goastellec & Pekari,

2013). Women are also disadvantaged as reviewers, authors and guest editors in scholarly journals (e.g. Nature 2018). Scientific outputs presumed written by men are rated higher than those presumed written by women (Knobloch-Westerwick, Glynn, & Huge, 2013). Women lose out on research funding (van der Lee & Ellemers, 2005); and are at a disadvantage when it comes to forming and benefitting from academic networks (Vázquez-Cupeiro & Elston, 2006), including that they feel uncomfortable forming networks for career advancement purposes (Nokkala, Culum, & Fumasoli, 2016). Minority ethnicity or non-heteronormative identity are also factors that can work to disadvantage academics, cause discrimination, and compromise career advancement (Gutierrez y Muhs, Niemann, Gonzalez, & Harris, 2012). These various aspects of disadvantages play out to greater or lesser degrees in different societal contexts.

In addition to the policies and structures that challenge women's path to senior academic jobs, also the university culture emphasising efficiency, control and strong management (Deem, 1998; Evetts, 2009) as well as the more 'masculine' elements of the university are argued to be inconsistent with the feminine, embodied motherhood (Huopalainen & Satama, 2018). This leads to an ongoing negotiation between being a 'good' academic and a 'good' mother, a process loaded with gendered norms and expectations. Both roles have their ideal that "seems to emphasise full devotion, commitment, professionalisation and high performance" (Huopalainen & Satama, 2018, p. 17). Nikunen (2014, p. 14) also describes how new "meritocratic transparency and entrepreneurialism are difficult to combine with family responsibilities" when flexibility and "individual" means not just academic freedom but responsibility and long working hours. Families are left alone trying to solve their challenges with work-life balance issues and mobility requirement with little social support (Nikunen, 2014).

Our results reflect the different gender regimes in the two countries; which make combining a family with an academic career more difficult in Switzerland than in Finland. The gender regimes are policies-in-action; the extent to which the norm of international mobility has permeated the Swiss discourse also reflects the openness of the Swiss academic labour markets, and respectively, the relative closure of the Finnish ones. However, this may change in the future as Finnish universities also strive to recruit more of their staff internationally.

Illuminating the embeddedness of academic careers in the national gender regimes, our results give rise to a contemplation of policy implications for higher education institutions and national policy-makers alike. Recognising the structures and practices that support or impinge on women's academic careers, such as availability of childcare services and parental

ACADEMIC CAREER, MOBILITY AND THE NATIONAL GENDER REGIMES 283

leave arrangements that facilitate equal division of family responsibilities, is the first step towards more gender equality in academia. Flexible mobility arrangements and financial support for mobility periods that enable the mobility for the entire family may make it easier for women to combine family responsibilities with the requirements for academic mobility. Cultural norms about family division of labour are harder to change, though. The first step is, however recognising that the meritocracy in academia disguise a let of structures and practices, embedded in the academic and societal institutions that impinge on women's careers. These structures and practices also go some way towards illuminating the various reasons behind the leaky pipeline phenomenon, which sees scores of women leaving academic careers or ending up in less prestigious positions in the academic hierarchy. But one might also more largely interrogate the pertinence of international mobility as an absolute constraint to access an academic career, as well as the place allocated to (academic) work in individual's life with regard to family life, i.e., the normative incentives nurturing the multiple social roles people have to articulate. But this is probably a whole other story.

Acknowledgement

We dedicate this chapter to the memory of our colleague and friend Professor Kelly Ward, whose work significantly contributed to a better understanding of gendered academic careers and whose management of the work-family and more generally work-life balance has been and shall long remain a source of inspiration. Kelly participated to the panel in which this paper was presented in the CHER 2017 Jyväskylä conference with her usual enthusiasm and sense of sharing. She will be deeply missed.

Note

1   http://garciaproject.eu/

References

Acatiimi. (2017). Osaamisvaihtotase yhä enemmän miinuksella. *Acatiimi.* Retrieved August, 2017, from http://www.acatiimi.fi/8_2017/3.php

Acker, J. (1994). The gender regime of Swedish banks. *Scandinavian Journal of management, 10*(2), 117–130. https://doi.org/10.1016/0956-5221(94)90015-9

Ackers, L. (2008). Internationalisation, mobility and metrics: A new form of indirect discrimination? *Minerva, 46*(4), 411–435. doi:10.1007/s11024-008-9110-2

Bataille, P., Le Feuvre, N., & Kradolfer Morales, S. (2017). Should I stay or should I go? The effects of precariousness on the gendered career aspirations of postdocs in Switzerland. *European Educational Research Journal, 16*(2–3), 313–331. https://doi.org/10.1177/1474904116673372

Benninghoff, M., Goastellec, G., & Leresche, J. P. (2009). L'international comme ressource cognitive et symbolique: changements dans l'instrumentation de la recherche et de l'enseignement supérieur en Suisse. In J. P. Leresche, P. Larédo, & K. Weber (Eds.), *Recherche et Enseignement Supérieur Face à l'Internationalisation. France, Suisse et Union.* Lausanne: Presses polytechniques et universitaires romandes.

Bozzon, R., Murgia, A., & Poggio, B. (2018). Gender and precarious careers in academia and research. In A. Murgia & B. Poggio (Eds.), *The precarisation of research careers: A comparative gender analysis* (pp. 15–49). London: Routledge. https://doi.org/10.4324_9781315201245-2

Bütler, M. (2006). *Le rendement effectif du travail pour les familles avec des petits enfants.* St Gallen University: Public Economy Department.

Deem, R. (1998). 'New managerialism' and higher education: The management of performances and cultures in universities in the United Kingdom. *International Studies in Sociology of Education, 8*(1), 47–70. https://doi.org/10.1080/0962021980020014

Dorenkamp, I., & Weiß, E. E. (2017). What makes them leave? A path model of postdocs' intentions to leave academia. *Higher Education* (Online publication). https://doi.org/10.1007/s10734-017-0164-7

Dubois-Shaik, F., Fusulier, B., & Vincke, C. (2018). A gendered pipeline typology in academia. In A. Murgia & B. Poggio (Eds.), *The precarisation of research careers: A comparative gender analysis* (pp. 178–205). London: Routledge. https://doi.org/10.4324_9781315201245-7

Eggins, H. (Ed.). (2017). *The changing role of women in higher education: Academic and leadership issues.* Basel: Springer International Publishing.

EuroAC. (2013). *The academic profession in Europe: Responses to societal challenges* (2009–2013). Retrieved September, 2018, from https://www.uni-kassel.de/einrichtungen/incher/forschung/wissenschaftlicher-wandel/euroac-academic-profession-in-europe.html

Evetts, J. (2009). New professionalism and new public management: Changes, continuities and consequences. *Comparative Sociology, 8*(2), 247–266. https://doi.org/10.1163/156913309X421655

FSO. (2016). Personnel des institutions de formation. Edition 2016. Bern: Federal Statistical Office.

GARCIA Project. Retrieved September, 2018, from http://garciaproject.eu/

Goastellec, G. (2016). La mobilité internationale: une qualité des carrières et des marchés académiques en Europe? *Journal of International Mobility, 1*(4), 171–188. https://doi.org/10.3917/jim.004.0171

Goastellec, G., & Pekari, N. (2013). Gender differences and inequalities in academia: Findings in Europe. In U. Teicher & E. E. Höhle (Eds.), *The work situation of the academic profession in Europe: Findings of a survey in twelve countries* (pp. 55–78). Dordrecht: Springer.

Goastellec, G., & von Roten, F. C. (2017). The societal embeddedness of academic markets: From sex to gender in the Swiss context. In M. Machado-Taylor, V. Soares, & U. Teichler (Eds.), *Challenges and options: The academic profession in Europe* (pp. 211–229). Cham: Springer.

Goastellec, G., & Välimaa, J. (2016). Expliquer les inégalités d'accès aux diplômes en Finlande et en Suisse (1950–2004): des structures scolaires aux politiques sociales. *Education et sociétés, 2*(38), 105–121. https://doi.org/10.3917/es.038.0105

Goulden, M., Mason, M. A., & Frasch, K. (2011). Keeping women in the science pipeline. *The Annals of the American Academy of Political and Social Science, 638*(1), 141–162. https://doi.org/10.1177/0002716211416925

Gutierrez y Muhs, G., Niemann, Y. F., Gonzalez, C. G., & Harris, A. P. (Eds.). (2012). *Presumed incompetent: The intersections of race and class for women in academia.* Logan, UT: Utah State University Press.

Huopalainen, A. S., & Satama, S. T. (2018). Mothers and researchers in the making: Negotiating "new" motherhood within the "new" academic. *Human Relations* (Online publication). https://doi.org/10.1177/0018726718764571

Knobloch-Westerwick, S., Glynn, C. J., & Huge, M. (2013). The Matilda effect in science communication: An experiment on gender bias in publication quality perceptions and collaboration interest. *Science Communication, 35*(5), 603–625. https://doi.org/10.1177/1075547012472684

Lahire, B. (1998). *L'Homme Pulriel.* Paris: Nathan.

Leca, J. (2012). L'Etat entre politics, policies et polity. *Gouvernement et action publique, 1*(1), 59–82. https://doi.org/10.3917/gap.121.0059

Le Feuvre, N. (2009). Exploring women's academic careers in cross-national perspective. Lessons for equal opportunity policies. *Equal Opportunities International, 28*(1), 9–23. https://doi.org/10.1108/02610150910933604

Musselin, C. (2017). *La Grande course des universités.* Paris: Presses de Sciences Po.

Nature. (2018). Nature's under-representation of women. *Nature, 558,* 344. Retrieved September, 2018, from https://doi.org/10.1038/d41586-018-05465-7

Nikunen, M. (2014). The entrepreneurial university, family and gender: Changes and demands faced by fixed-term workers. *Gender and Education, 26*(2), 119–134. https://doi.org/10.1080/09540253.2014.888402

Nokkala, T., Ćulum, B., & Fumasoli, T. (2016). Early career women in academia: An exploration of networking perceptions. In H. Eggins (Ed.), *The changing role of women in higher education* (pp. 267–290). Basel: Springer International Publishing.

Ortlieb, R., & Weiss, S. (2018). What makes academic careers less insecure? The role of individual-level antecedents. *Higher Education* (Online publication). Retrieved from https://link.springer.com/article/10.1007/s10734-017-0226-x

Pietilä, M. (2015). Tenure track career system as a strategic instrument for academic leaders. *European Journal of Higher Education, 5*(4), 371–387. https://doi.org/10.1080/21568235.2015.1046466

Rogers, R., & Molinier, P. (Éd.). (2016). *Les femmes dans le monde académique. Perspectives comparatives*. Rennes: Presses universitaires de Rennes.

Rossier, T., Beetschen, M., Mach, A., & Bühlmann, F. (2015). Internationalisation des élites académiques suisses au XXe siècle: convergences et contrastes. *Cahiers de la recherche sur l'éducation et les savoirs, 14*, 119–139.

Siekkinen, T., Pekkola, E., & Kivistö, J. (2016a). Recruitments in Finnish universities: Practicing strategic or pathetic HRM? *Nordic Journal of Studies in Educational Policy*, 2–3 (Online publication). https://doi.org/10.3402/nstep.v2.32316

Siekkinen, T., Kuoppala, K., Pekkola, E., & Välimaa, J. (2016b). Reciprocal commitment in academic careers? Finnish implications and international trends. *European Journal of Higher Education, 7*(2), 120–135. https://doi.org/10.1080/21568235.2016.1248990

Tung, R. L. (2008). Human capital or talent flows: Implications for future directions in research on Asia Pacific. *Asia Pacific Business Review, 14*(4), 469–472. https://doi.org/10.1080/13602380802037714

UNECE (2018). Couples by working patterns: Gender Statistics, UNECE/STAT. Retrieved September 2018, from http://w3.unece.org/PXWeb2015/pxweb/en/STAT/STAT__30-GE__98-GE_LifeBalance

Valarino, I., & Gauthier, J.-A. (2016). Paternity leave implementation in Switzerland: A challenge to gendered representations and practices of fatherhood? *Community, Work & Family, 19*(1), 1–20. https://doi.org/10.1080/13668803.2015.1023263

Välimaa, J., Stenvall, J., Siekkinen, T., Pekkola, E., Kivistö, J., Kuoppala, K., Nokkala, T., Aittola, H., & Ursin, J. (2016). *Neliportaisen tutkijanuramallin arviointihanke: Loppuraportti* (Opetus—ja kulttuuriministeriön julkaisuja 2016:15). Helsinki: OKM.

van der Lee, R., & Ellemers, N. (2005). Gender contributes to personal research funding success in the Netherlands. *Proceedings of the National Academy of Sciences of the United States of America, 112*(40), 12349–12353. https://doi.org/10.1073/pnas.1510159112

Vázquez-Cupeiro, S., & Elston, M. A. (2006). Gender and academic career trajectories in Spain: From gendered passion to consecration in a Sistema Endogámico? *Employee Relations, 28*(6), 588–603. https://doi.org/10.1108/01425450610704515

Vipunen. (2018). *Education statistics Finland*. Retrieved September, 2018, from https://vipunen.fi/en-gb/

CHAPTER 12

The Applicability of Two Graduate Employability Frameworks: How Possession, Position, Integration and Engagement Shape Graduate Employability

Martina Gaisch, Victoria Rammer, Silke Preymann, Stefanie Sterrer and Regina Aichinger

Abstract

The purpose of this article is to enrich the current conceptualisation of graduate employability through the lens of four distinct graduate perspectives, namely possession (of skills and competencies), position (in terms of social capital), integration (with regard to graduate and professional identity) and engagement (related to personal attributes). This contribution attempts to examine the applicability of two frameworks to a specific cross-border region in Austria and the Czech Republic. The findings of this pilot study suggest that current models do not fully cover employability-related factors when investigating the perception of graduate employability. Rather, they can be used as anchor points and need to be adapted with context-sensitive elements. An extended framework is proposed that takes account of additional ingredients for graduate employability found vital in this specific setting.

Keywords

graduate employability – Austria – Czech Republic – higher education institutions – human capital – social capital – identity process – possession – position – integration – engagement

1 Introduction

At the tertiary level, conflicting ideology-driven agendas of governance have been co-existing, leaving universities in the middle of academic, economic and social pressures. While the economy-oriented model puts emphasis on entrepreneurial innovation skills with the aim to increasingly adjust to the needs of private enterprises, the open society approach is driven by today's grand challenges and the conviction that societal needs can only be addressed in an interdisciplinary and democratic way. The third variation in governance ideologies is spurred by national agendas in which political purposes are fore-grounded and funding is based on the expected outcome in terms of effectiveness and efficiency as to the achievement of these political directives. What appears to be a common denominator for all three ideology-driven rationales is the concept of graduate employability, which may build a bridge between the monetary value of skills, fitness of purpose and transversal skills that are transferable and applicable in different social contexts (Suleman, 2017). Yet, the most common argument is that without input from and collaboration with industry, higher education institutions (HEIs) are "hardly able to strengthen their vocational mission of equipping students for the labour market" (Tran, 2016, p. 58).

In this vein, universities are faced with the daunting challenge to prepare future graduates for the needs of the global knowledge society that requires complex thinkers and pattern recognisers that are capable of creating "meaningful narratives and synthesise the seemingly divergent into a cohesive whole" (Gaisch, 2014, p. 74). Hence, an appropriate employability skillset that goes beyond narrow disciplinary boundaries as well as a profound understanding of intercultural aspects have become major drivers for labour market developments (Chydenius & Gaisch, 2016). This contribution sheds light on perceived graduate employability with a particular focus placed on human and social capital, on the integration of academic and professional identity and specific personal attributes – all of which have the potential to further develop career prospects. The study takes two well-established models of graduate employability (Holmes, 2013; Clarke, 2018) as a basis and seeks to establish common ground between them. It identifies a missing link when examining the applicability of these frameworks to one specific cross-border region in Austria and the Czech Republic. This regional focus was taken in view of the close cooperation of two institutions of higher learning within an INTERREG Project. The results of this pilot study leads to an adapted model of graduate employability that has the potential to allow for more informed decisions on curriculum development in these regions.

2 Theoretical References

In view of the dynamics of the conceptual age where "shifting spaces and the need for multiple identities take centre stage" (Gaisch, 2014, p. 50) and in light of the global knowledge economy that requires highly qualified, sophisticated, creative and innovative graduates, increasing attention has been called to lifelong learning opportunities and the development of global competencies (Pegg, Waldock, Hendy-Isaac, & Lowton, 2012; Sin & Amaral, 2016). The necessity to educate students in ways that they can meet the needs for a work-ready mode with an additionally sufficient level of employability has become more prominent than ever (Holmes, 2013; Clarke, 2018). Harvey (2000) states that the economy needs qualified graduates that are endowed with abilities that go beyond mere technical knowledge. In a similar vein, Johnson (2015, p. 10) points out that "employers want highly skilled graduates who are ready to enter the workforce", indicating that fitness of purpose and transferable skills are essential components for the demand-side.

Along these lines, it becomes clear that in terms of supply-side, HEIs need to address learning outcomes that help to improve graduate employability and, if necessary, bridge potential skill gaps between academic theory and practical knowledge (Jackson, 2016). It also becomes evident that major components of today's flexible world of work need to go beyond narrow disciplinary boundaries (Oellinger, Lembke, Gaisch, & Gros Salvat, 2014; Gaisch & Oellinger, 2014) of what is referred to as I-shaped professionals, so to say experts that have a depth of knowledge in one particular area. What is increasingly needed today are T-shaped professionals that draw on a wide portfolio of generic and transversal skills and who have a contextual understanding of how to deal with contemporary complexities (Chydenius & Gaisch, 2016). In other words, while I-shaped professionals are expected to have extensive expertise in one specific field, T-shaped graduates cover a wide breadth of generalist knowledge and interdisciplinary understanding (Gaisch & Aichinger, 2018).

Given the broad range of interpretations to which the concept of employability lends itself, it is only logical that it is used both widely and loosely (Rothwell & Rothwell, 2016; Boden & Nevada, 2010). Consequently, it is scarcely surprising that the concept of graduate employability has been addressed from a variety of angles and through different normative lenses (e.g. Andrews & Higson, 2008; McGrath, 2009; Bridgstock, 2009; Tomlinson, 2012; Holmes, 2013; Sin & Amaral, 2016; Suleman, 2017). In view of the terminological and conceptual inconsistency, Cranmer (2006, p. 172) refers to graduate employability as "a woolly concept" that she considers hard "to pin down" outlining its definitional range from a limited set of threshold skills to a broad range of knowledge, skills and personal attributes. General agreement may only be found on some cognitive, technical and relational skills while it is stated that the supply-side approach tends to broadly overlook economic and social processes that might affect employability (Suleman, 2017, p. 263). Further confusion is created by using different adjectives to describe them, be they 'core', 'common', 'global', 'key', 'generic' or 'transferable' skills which makes this concept even more complex and opaque.

Various debates have focused on the definition of what graduate employability constitutes (van der Heijden, 2002; Knight and Yorke, 2002) while other researchers looked more closely at the measurement and management model of employability (Forrier & Sels, 2003; van der Heijde & van der Heijden, 2006; Clarke & Patrickson, 2008).

One commonly used definition is that employability denotes the ability of an individual to "gain initial employment, maintain employment, move between roles within the same organisation and obtain new employment" (Hillage & Pollard, 1998; McQuaid & Lindsay, 2005, p. 200). Bodea, Dascalu, Velikic, and Stancu (2016) further extend the scope, stating that employability does not only concern the acquirement of a job but also embraces the abilities and competencies of graduates to optimally perform within their positions. In this context, career management competence (CMC) was found to be vital to support an effective transition to the workplace and constructively relate to the complexity of the world of work (Rott, 2015; King, 2004).

Against the background of the pressing requirements of the knowledge economy with its claims for well-educated and highly qualified citizens that can operate as creative knowledge workers, Oliver's (2015) definition of graduate employability seems to embrace the necessity for lifelong learning and continuous re-skilling. For her, employability means that "students and graduates can discern, acquire, adapt and continually enhance the skills, understandings and personal attributes that make them more likely to find and create meaningful paid and unpaid work that benefits themselves, the workforce, the community and the economy" (Oliver, 2015, p. 59). Another angle sheds light on the idea that employability should also contain and reflect the quality of the occupation as well as its range of possibilities for personal growth and satisfaction (Clarke, 2018). Beyond the human capital discourse on employability that foregrounds skills, competencies and work experience, literature revealed that a broader view of management and measurement of employment outcomes may be useful to develop a more holistic understanding of graduate employability (Harré, 1984; Brown & Hesketh, & Williams, 2004; Holmes, 2013).

While most employability research has predominantly focused on the human capital and the acquisition or required skills and competencies, Holmes (2013) identified two further aspects that appear to have substantial influence on graduate employability. In doing so, the narrow lens of human capital and possessing perspective seems to be widened (Gaisch, Rammer, Hrušková, & Krátká, 2017), even more so as he acknowledges that the notion of graduate skills strongly relates to issues of social positioning and societal reproduction (Holmes, 2013, p. 548). He also foregrounds processual interactions by which persons move through their education onto their postgraduate lives, taking account of the variety of possible, always and essentially temporary, positions in which they find themselves (Holmes, 2012, p. 1051). Based on these considerations, Clarke (2018) adapts the concept of Holmes (2013) and brings forward what she calls an 'integrated model of graduate employability' where she includes a number of aspects such as individual attitudes, personal manners and career-related behaviours, labour market variables, current employment status as well as the perceived employability of the graduates. In this model, the author combines different perspectives of graduate employability and points to "the human capital, social capital, and individual behaviours and attributes that underpin an individual's perceived employability" (Clarke, 2018, p. 1931). For her, it is this combination of skills and attitudes that appear to have the greatest impact on employment outcomes. Figure 12.1 compares the concept of graduate employability of Holmes (2013) and the extended model brought forward by Clarke (2018).

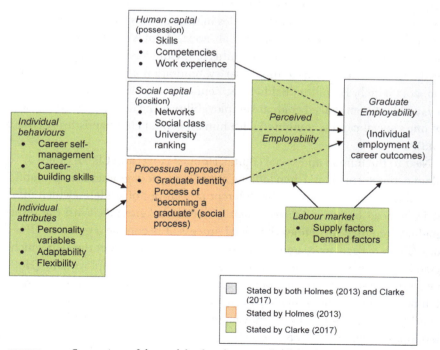

FIGURE 12.1 Comparison of the models of graduate employability by Holmes (2013) and Clarke (2017)

It was found that the possession lens of *human capital* is reflected in almost all studies that deal with graduate employability (Clarke, 2018; Holmes, 2013). Unsurprisingly then, most research looked at a specific skillset needed for accomplishing certain tasks (Schultz, 1971; Cranmer, 2006; Tomlinson, 2012; Delaney & Farren, 2016). In this vein, also Yorke (2006, p. 8) defines graduate employability as "a set of achievements [...] that makes graduates more likely to gain employment". It is argued that human capital is a foundation of graduate identity and hence describes a core component of graduate employability (Clarke, 2018). Holmes (2013) and Clarke (2018) agree that human capital as well as the plethora of frameworks and lists, which includes a multiplicity of skills, competencies and attitudes to develop graduate employability, will not warrant a positive employment outcome.

By using social capital as a further point of reference for graduate employability, Holmes (2013) and Clarke (2018) add an additional perspective. This view foregrounds social class, the type(s) of university attended, the discipline studied as well as the type of degree attained. According to Holmes (2013), social capital heavily influences employment outcome, both directly and indirectly (Blasko, Brennan, Little, & Shah, 2002; Okay-Sommerville & Scholarios, 2017). Arguably, this impact becomes visible when graduates from privileged backgrounds encounter fewer difficulties in their careers than graduates from disadvantaged backgrounds (Blasko et al., 2002, Holmes, 2013). What is more, also the nature of discipline and the status of the university are highly controversial matters that seem to impact salary, reputation and standing (Tomlinson, 2012; Finch, Hamilton, Baldwin, & Zehner, 2013). What is identified as a key enabler for enhanced graduate employability is the use of networks based on one's social capital combined with human capital characteristics (Clarke, 2018).

Next to the human and social capital, Holmes (2013) and Clarke (2018) also adopt a 'processual lens' when looking at the concept of graduate employability. Holmes (2013) focuses on the different trajectories of students which may be influenced by various factors such as social backgrounds. With the term 'graduate identity' he defines the social process of becoming a graduate (Holmes, Green & Egan, 1998) and conceptualises the development through which "graduates achieve a satisfactory and settled position in employment" (Holmes, 2013, p. 549). The concept of identity is considered in terms of the interaction between both the individuals who claim to an identity and the ascribed identity by others as well as the movement through several modalities and the development of various ways of demonstrating the claim on the individuals' identity (Holmes, 2013). In this sense, a richness concerning the language of skills and attributes as well as an appropriate performance of relevant practices are regarded as key ingredients in terms of warranting the identity claims (Holmes, 1995, 2000). The notion of graduate identity has therefore taken a central place within the collective production of social life and social-self positioning of graduates (Holmes, 2013).

In contrast, Clarke (2018) examines the processual approach from another angle and puts the focus on two dimensions, namely *individual attributes* and *individual behaviours*. Appropriate individual attributes such as adaptability and flexibility appear to help future graduates to better deal with work challenges and support individuals in coping with consistent changes within the working environment (Fugate, Kinicki, & Ashforth, 2004; van der Heijde & van der Heijden, 2006; Clarke, 2018). In that respect, Clarke (2018) refers to Holmes' (2013) definition of graduate identity and points to the development of a social position as well as the presentation of the individual identity to gatekeepers (e.g. HR managers) and interlocutors within the occupational area. Individual behaviours, as the second perspective of the processual approach, are understood to be career-relevant behavioural patterns, which were found to play a critical role for enhanced graduate employability (Okay-Sommerville & Scholarios, 2017). To bring further light to this vague concept, Clarke (2018) follows the definition of Bridgstock (2009) who differ between self-management skills (personal awareness in terms of values, interests, abilities, etc.) and career building skills (support individuals to operate and enhance within their working environment). A proactive career self-management process is found to influence subjective and objective employability over and above social and educational backgrounds (Clarke, 2018; Okay-Sommerville & Scholarios, 2017). To this effect, it is necessary to encourage future graduates to reinforce proactive career management and to gain career-related skills (Clarke, 2018).

Clarke (2018) also draws on the aspect of *perceived employability* to show the interaction between internal and external as well as personal and structural factors. Perceived employability refers to the graduate's "individual's perception of his or her possibilities of obtaining and maintaining employment" (Vanhercke, De Cuyper, Peeters, & De Witte, 2014, p. 593). These perceptions are influenced by a multitude of different factors, be they related to human capital, social capital, individual behaviours and attributes as well as to the aptitude of 'knowing how', 'knowing why' and 'knowing whom' (Clarke, 2018; Vanhercke, De Cuyper, Peeters, & De Witte, 2014; Eby, Butts, & Lockwood, 2003). This relates well to the concept of self-efficacy, which is described as self-judgements of capabilities to organise and execute courses of action (see Bandura, 1986). Other factors that influence perceived employability can be found within the current *labour market* (Clarke, 2018) and the economic climate (Jackson, 2013). Unsurprisingly, then, labour market factors including supply and demand within the occupational field have turned out to be a key driver and a measurer of employment success (Clarke, 2018; Jackson, 2013).

Arguably, these approaches may be seen as a fruitful avenue for the provision of a reflective framework for future graduates, which is why it is all the more interesting to find out whether they may serve as an established recipe for achievement or significant condition to guarantee the improvement of employability (Plăiaş, Pop, Dabija, & Băbuţ, 2011). It is for this reason that the two previously discussed models of graduate employability were put to the test in a specific context. For one, graduates from a research university at the Czech Republic were asked about their perceived graduate employability and how they portrayed human capital, social capital, individual behaviours and attributes as well as the social process as an employee asset. At the same time, graduates from one applied and one research university in Austria were asked the same questions and thereby encouraged to bring forward personal narratives of their employment paths and career success. Then context-specific implications for professional development in line with the general themes of the frameworks were analysed.

This focus was of particular interest for two reasons: First, it shed light on two very different socio-economic regions. Deadlocked for some 44 years in between two competing blocks, Austria has become one of the wealthiest and most developed countries in the world with a long-established market economy and impressive industrial strength. In contrast, the Czech Republic, formerly known as Czechoslovakia, once an Eastern Bloc country, only appeared on the map in 1993. It has a strong intention to become an integral part of the West and seeks to "introduce democracy, free capitalist economy, rule of law and all other aspects of developed democracies" (Minařík, 2008, p. 6). Unsurprisingly, then, there are numerous economic links between these countries and many Austrian companies have set up subsidiaries at the Czech side. Second, it was interesting to explore if differences between countries that have a binary (Austria) and non-binary (Czech Republic) higher education system can be identified, and if so, how they might affect perceived employability of technical graduates in this cross-border region. While Austria draws on a binary system with the main division between research universities and universities of applied sciences, the Czech Republic does not have a HE sector that focuses on professionally-oriented higher education. Nevertheless, the proportion of academically and professionally-oriented competencies and knowledge can variegate within the different studies in the Czech Republic (Ministry of Education, Youth & Sports, 2008).

In this sense, the authors of this pilot study seek to examine the applicability of the two chosen graduate employability frameworks (Holmes, 2013;

Clarke 2018) in the cross-border region in Austria and the Czech Republic and identify how the findings may be used for further curriculum development and improved teaching quality in tertiary education.

3   Design, Methodology and Approach

From the variety of potential qualitative approaches, the authors considered narrative analysis best suited to understanding persons' narrative construction and meaning making around events in the context of their own (professional) lives (Chase, 2011). As one model of narrative analysis (Riessman, 1993), thematic analysis lends itself well for this endeavour as it is a flexible method to identify themes in qualitative data, which may allow for both inductive and deductive lenses (Braun & Clarke, 2006). In view of the relatively theoretical flexibility of this analytical method of qualitative research, it can also be utilised across a broad range of theoretical frameworks, "from essentialist to constructionist" (Clarke & Braun, 2013, p. 2).

In the event of this research design, the authors sought to position it as a constructionist approach in which the data was dynamically used to gain in-depth views of the underlying causal mechanisms. Further, a hybrid approach was adopted that incorporates a deductive a priori template of codes with the aim of looking for pre-existing themes and a data-driven inductive approach for emerging themes. This deductive-oriented thematic analysis sought to derive and confirm themes from the framework while at the same time leaving enough space for thematic codes to be constructed and analyse how the narrative links to a broader meaning with "substantive significance" were being enacted (Patton, 2002, p. 467). This balance of deductive and inductive coding has the potential to "reach the second level of interpretive understanding" (Fereday & Muir-Cochrane, 2006, p. 81) and to identify additional determinants of graduate employability. The six stages of thematic analysis were applied recursively.

In this study, an expert is defined as a person with privileged knowledge about the investigated subject (Bogner & Menz, 2009). According to Bogner and Menz (2009) the number of informants can be rather low as long as they were selected carefully to provide extensive insights. Hence, this purposive sampling (Cohen, Manion, & Morrison, 2013, p. 156) consisted of four Austrian and four Czech graduates that have been working at an internationally operating company in this cross-border region for a minimum of six months, but not longer than two years. This range was considered appropriate for a sound evaluation of their academic and professional opportunities and challenges and the perceived ability to obtain and maintain work at a graduate level.

The seven male and one female technical graduates were chosen as informants with the aim to explore personal narratives about their lived work realities and sketch how they translate them into career choices. Three of the interviewees completed their studies in computer science; three in mechanical engineering, one in logistics and one participant had a degree in both civil engineering and mechatronics. These expert interviews (lasting between 26 and 47 minutes) were conducted in German and English between May and July 2017. They started with a narrative section, where the eight participants described their graduate transition into work as well as their values and attitudes towards perceived graduate employability. In a second step, more specific questions were asked by means of a semi-structured interview which were framed along the lines of the key elements outlined in the two models. Prior to the data analysis, all interviews were transcribed verbatim. For the inductive part of our data analysis, we conceptually read the raw data in detail with the aim of gaining further insight into the impact factors of graduate employability while also deductively examining whether the overall data in the transcripts were consistent with prior-identified assumptions (Thomas, 2006). By means of an open coding framework (Boyatzis, 1998), we identified emerging themes and sorted them into underlying determinants related to our coding framework. We then clustered all relevant factors for perceived graduate employability that were identified. All information gathered from the interviews were integrated in the adapted model.

4   Findings

In the following, the adapted frame of graduate employability with its four major categories, namely possession, position, integration and engagement is outlined in more detail.

To illustrate the local specificities of the investigated case each category is described on its own. The empirical findings suggest that in Austria graduates tend to make a clearly pronounced differentiation between academically-oriented and professionally-oriented higher education. This became evident at all investigated levels, namely human capital, social capital, identity process and personal attributes, yet to differing degrees.

As to *human capital* the distinction between vocational and academic education became particularly clear. Austrian graduates from professionally-oriented education systems appeared to be well aware of their lacking

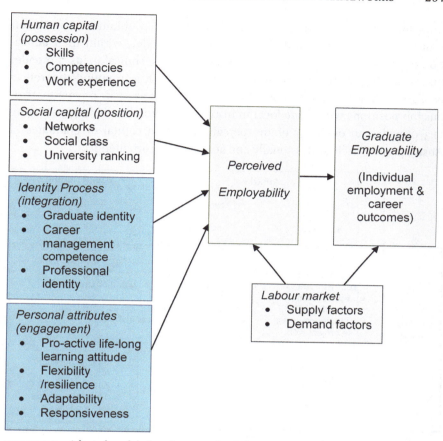

FIGURE 12.2   Adapted model of graduate employability

in-depth theoretical knowledge. At the same time, they take special pride in their real-life professional experiences and their practical knowledge and project management skills. In this vein, the interview participants argued that practice-oriented knowledge, hands-on examples and ready-to-use skills are vital to understand the operating cycles within working environments. Conversely, interviewees of academically-oriented systems in Austria and the Czech Republic stated that a deep theoretical knowledge a scientific mind-set, self-organised learning as well as logical and analytical thinking were essential for understanding complex structures. There was also common understanding that they were best prepared for performing non-routine and highly analytical tasks, given that they had been trained to engage in complex problem solving at very abstract levels. What seems to be missing in Austria is a basic toolkit of soft skills as well as work experience, which was identified as a major asset for a future job.

In contrast, Czech participants highlighted that they obtain some basic soft skills and knowledge of different methods and models within their education of higher learning. However, especially within technical fields, a broader understanding of practical methods combined with a profound theoretical background and the ability to focus on details is seen as a gate opener for various job positions within the local industry in the cross-border region. Figure 12.3 provides an overview of the perceived human capital of graduates of Austrian and Czech professionally and academically oriented HEI.

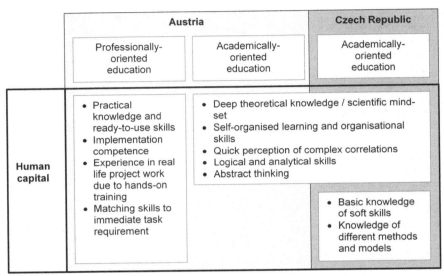

FIGURE 12.3   Human capital of graduates in Austrian and Czech HEI

There was a shared understanding that graduation in a technical field builds the bridge to (interpersonal and monetary) success within the local market, both in Austria and the Czech Republic. In this sense, a technical discipline was equated with *social capital* (Figure 12.4) and identified as a crucial enabler for finding a job because having earned a technical degree was seen as a sense of status, which makes graduates at both countries immensely proud. Especially in the investigated cross-border region, technical study programmes are perceived as a 'supreme discipline' that leads to immediate employment and a good salary. When looking more closely at social capital factors such as university ranking or elite group membership, it was stated that neither the type nor the status of universities plays a significant role when seeking employment in the technical fields. This is explained by the fact that the local industries are in desperate need for engineers, which is why no perceived difference could be identified in terms of gender, ethnicity, social class, network or university ranking.

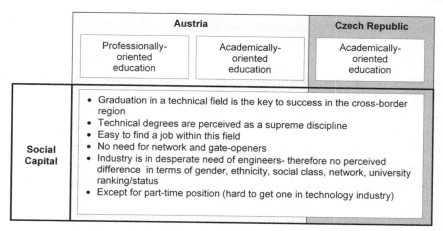

FIGURE 12.4 Social capital of graduates in Austrian and Czech HEI

As to the *identity process* (integration) a disparity between Austria and the Czech Republic in the sense of graduate and professional identity was identified (Figure 12.5). For Austrian participants the quality of the degree as well as a high-class competence played a major role to present themselves and their identity to others. This fact leads to the concept of graduate identity in which graduates claim their own identity to achieve an appropriate employment (Holmes, 2013). In contrast, Czech interviewees rather took on a professional identity by referring to their knowledge, beliefs and practices as well as their professional roles within the company (see Chreim, Williams, & Hinings, 2007). This is even more interesting since Czechs draw on an academically-oriented education that does not have, in contrast to the vocational orientation, strong ties to the industry with a compulsory internship integrated in the curricula. Further, CMC, so to say the capacity to relate constructively to the complexities of the world of work, was considered crucial by all informants. CMC was regarded as a life theme, a never-ending process that helps to contextualise acquired knowledge and transfer it to differing contexts, be they academic or professional. Hence, it was found to be an integral part of the identity process in which social or professional identities are (co- and de-) constructed in multiple ways but also expressed differently according to what educational and occupational values and attitudes are foregrounded.

In this context, Austrian informants from both professionally and academically oriented educations pointed to the German title of *Diplom-Ingenieur*, which has been gradually abandoned for the sake of Master of Science due to the Bologna process. They agreed that the title of *Diplom-Ingenieur* enjoys high national and international acclaim and is highly appreciated within the German-speaking labour market. Due to this, all Austrian informants found it to be a logical step that the title, which is seen as a quality criterion of high-class engineering competence, has been reintroduced by some Austrian institutions of higher learning despite the general Bologna trend of harmonisation. Furthermore, the Austrian informants from professionally oriented HEIs highlighted that a safety net within the working environment including mentors and structures is essential for them as well as a high service orientation whereas Austrian graduates from academically-oriented systems were found to have a sink-or-swim and do-it-yourself attitude with a strong willingness to improve their existing skillset. In other words, Austrian participants that graduated from an academically-oriented institution generally seemed to be proud of their capability of performing highly complex non-routine tasks with abstract and analytical content matter. In contrast, respondents of professionally-oriented systems pointed to their expertise in the application of standardised schemes and their great repertoire of tools as well as sound process knowledge.

As opposed to the Austrian graduates, Czech participants were found to be more focused on their occupational field and professional roles. Almost all interviewees highlighted that they take pride in being employed at an international company. In this context, the Czech informants' dedication of meeting corporate expectation was striking. Their willingness to learn the required codes of significations and the local conventions of appropriateness came particularly to the fore. In addition to that, it was identified that for graduates of Czech academically-oriented educational systems both team cohesion and effective cross-border teamwork are key. Further, it was found that Czech graduates appreciate it when they can assume a certain degree of responsibility and gain trust of their counterparts within the working environment. Here, it is interesting to note that graduates of Czech academically-oriented HEIs take a similar view concerning the need of a safety net as participants of professionally-oriented systems in Austria do. In this context, both perceive the service of mentors and trainers as helpful and important for the work in international companies while participants of academically-oriented HEIs in Austria stated that they do not need any mentors in view of their 'can-do'-attitude and proactive behaviour.

As to individual attributes and personality traits referred to in this paper as *personal attributes* and capitalised under the umbrella term 'engagement' (Figure 12.6), it can be stated that common ground was achieved in a sound understanding that further trainings and lifelong learning are necessary to deal with the complexities of the global knowledge society. Here, the necessity to continuously adapt one's skills and develop transversal competencies was explicitly foregrounded. Apart from Clarke's model, individual attributes have

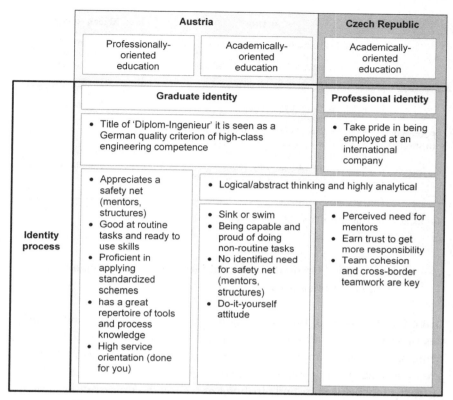

FIGURE 12.5   Identity process of graduates in Austrian and Czech HEI

been remarkably absent from the graduate employability discourse (Clarke, 2018, p. 1932) despite its abundant use and reference in management and psychology literature as a foundation to career success (Fugate & Ashforth, 2003). The findings of this pilot study suggest that there are a number of personal attributes that impact the perception of graduate employability. The ones that were also stated by all interviewed experts were resilience, adaptability, flexibility and responsiveness to the rapidly changing needs of the labour market. Overall, they generally agree that it is vital to possess a set of personal attributes that allows a person to navigate the dynamics of today's world of work. Five of the eight respondents claimed that without those personality traits the level of perceived employability would be substantially reduced even if the perceived degree of possession, position and integration was high. In view of these statements, it was decided that in our case individual attributes do not feed into the identity process but need to be presented on equal terms next to these categories.

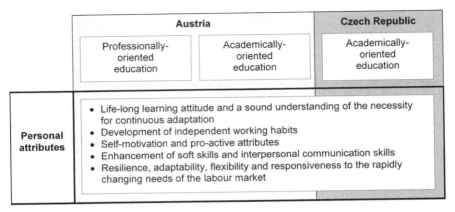

FIGURE 12.6 Personal attributes of graduates in Austrian and Czech HEI

5 An Extended Graduate Employability Model – Conclusions and Practical Implications

Given that the focus of this investigation was placed on assets and capabilities that impact the perception of graduate employability, no attention was being paid on labour market factors. In sum, the framework was adapted in several aspects. First, it was found that elements of human and social capital, individual behaviours and attributes as well as the process of becoming a graduate were classified as equally important and not necessarily feeding into each other. Hence, in view of the identified equal relevance of these assets this frame depicts four stand-alone categories, namely possession, position, integration and engagement. Arguably, being partly interwoven these blocks cannot be analysed wholly on their own given that their boundaries are sometimes blurred and a clear distinction is not possible. Yet, the authors present them in four distinct categories to demonstrate that they are all given equal weight based on the data. Second, it was identified that the processual approach and the individual behaviours in terms of career management strongly interrelate with both graduate and professional identity features, which is why these two categories were merged in one. This category is referred to as 'identity process' given that it not only incorporates the social process of becoming a graduate but also the one of becoming a professional.

Hereby, CMC was found to be a crucial enabler for becoming integrated into newly emerging identities. To dynamically gather, synthesise and analyse educational and occupational information during the transition period was identified as a vital ingredient for employability. For this reason, this third category is specified as 'integration', so to say the capacity to construct, contextualise and redefine different identities in line with the required portfolio, the disciplinary context and specific sector. In addition, 'integration' addresses this constant awareness process with regard to necessary abilities, skills, aptitudes and attitudes to effectively navigate the world of work. In this context, it appeared best to sum up individual behaviours such as career building skills and career self-management under the concept of CMC and put it as 'connecting glue' between graduate and professional identity.

The last adaptation is reflected in the fourth category that the authors capitalise under 'personal attributes'. Here, a proactive stance towards lifelong learning, resilience, adaptability and responsiveness were found to be the most critical assets in terms of personality traits. It came to the fore that engagement goes hand in hand with physical, cognitive and emotional involvement with the specific role performance.

The factors that were found to influence perceived graduate employability in this investigated cross-border region suggest a number of practical implications. First, HEIS not only play a major role in the development of human capital but also in the pursuit of a gradually emerging graduate and/or professional identity. It is for this reason, that programme leaders of the investigated cross-border region may use this knowledge to further enrich their curricular modules of informatics, civil engineering, logistics and mechanical engineering with soft skill elements and career management skills. Incorporating transversal skills such as self-management into the learning experience may bring further benefit to future graduates (Bridgstock, 2009) and force them out of the comfort zone of their respective degree specialisations.

A sharpened awareness of the required personal attributes may also lead to more informed decisions on curricula development, especially in light of the fact that they can be both taught and further developed (Dacre Pool & Sewell, 2007). This may also have the potential to go beyond rigid checklists of specific skillsets and allow for sufficient space for reflective learning and the development of higher-order thinking skills. At the same time, it may be an advantage to strengthen the professional identity already throughout the studies (more internships, stronger ties to the industry, more practice-oriented education, a good mix of academics and practitioners). In this sense, both academic and professional identities may be (re)negotiated and at the same time career adaptability and a dynamic understanding of career development may be encouraged. On a critical note, it needs to be stated, however, that this shift in teaching approaches may hardly work without appropriate training of academic staff. Only if faculty possesses sufficient awareness of the emerging needs of the labour market and can relate to these requirements outside their disciplinary box, they are capable of responding proactively to the complexities of the world of work, be it through interdisciplinary cooperation with T-shaped professionals or cross-disciplinary integration.

Another practical implication can be drawn from the knowledge gained in terms of social capital. Given that a degree in a technical field was perceived as a major asset in this region and even regarded as a key asset of social capital, regardless of status or ranking of the respective HEI, government bodies would be well advised to put increased effort into bringing more persons into science, technology, engineering, mathematical (STEM)fields. Especially in this highly industrialised region that heavily relies on technically qualified staff, the general trend towards massification of HE should be used wisely. This is all the more relevant since it is asserted that the university education system still belongs to 'another world' for many young persons (Bourdieu, Passeron, De Saint-Martin, Baudelot, & Vincent, 1994). Austrian measures that target the social dimension by breaking down social barriers and opening institutions of higher learning to previously underrepresented groups (Gaisch & Aichinger, 2016) may put a special emphasis on those disciplines that are regarded as the biggest social capital, first and foremost the STEM fields. Once in the university system, HEIs may then help those students to build strong networks, long-term interpersonal relationships and a solid basis of shared values, norms, group membership and identification.

Finally, employers may be advised to re-consider their often unrealistic, and at times, excessive expectations in terms of work-ready graduates. It needs to be critically questioned if increasing demands for vocational university approaches to skill development may not carry the danger of a rather inflexible tailor-made job profile with a skill set that is too narrow to be transferred to other contexts (Hansen, 2014). It should also be in the interest of future employers to take on graduates that are well-rounded citizens and critical thinkers capable of contextualising acquired knowledge to a variety of work environments. It is also for this reason that the block 'personal attributes' as presented in this framework is of equal significance and on the same level as the other categories. Consequently, employers should be held accountable for a broader discourse on graduate employability that next to university-specific qualifications related to the professional field also allows for discussions about their own roles in fostering ongoing graduate employability and lifelong learning opportunities.

A genuine discourse on the required features of graduate employability is all the more relevant in view of the growing importance of global markets, international networks and cross-border cooperation where a broader focus on lifelong learning opportunities as well as continuous skill development have become a quality feature for both industry and academia (Yang, 2015; Sin

THE APPLICABILITY OF TWO GRADUATE EMPLOYABILITY FRAMEWORKS 305

& Amaral, 2016). This has led to the fact that institutions and organisations have expressed their readiness to place greater emphasis on educational features along these lines. On a critical note, it needs to be stated that research on policy implementation generally points to difficulties in moving from policy rhetoric to genuine change in practice (Mason O'Connor, Lynch, & Owen, 2011). What may accelerate practical implementation, though, is the recognition that employability is largely dependent on soft skills and graduates' intrinsic personality traits and attitudes towards work. Given that engagement is shaped by family, society and educational institutions, concerted efforts of all stakeholders' involved – academic and administrative staff, management, industries, family environment and students themselves – are needed to fully develop these essentials.

6 Research Limitations and Future Directions

In qualitative research, it is vital to describe a person's view of the world and his or her position taken in a study (Savin-Baden & Major, 2013). In the knowledge that there are no research methods that are entirely "value-free in their applications" (Greenbank, 2003, p. 791), it is all the more important to reveal any biases that could obscure our ability to conduct this pilot study. It is in this spirit, that the authors seek to reveal their positionalities here. We all work at the same HEI, namely University of Applied Sciences Upper Austria, which has – despite its practice-oriented orientation – established its own department for higher education research. Our main research interests lie at the interface of educational sociology, higher education systems and governance and leadership. Our team consists of higher education researchers, academics and research associates that are socialised in a variety of disciplines (sociology, economics, socio-linguistics, knowledge media and educational science). Thus, despite – or precisely because of – the diverse range of ontological and epistemological positions we are keenly aware that our own beliefs, situated knowledge, values and competency impact our sense making in a myriad of ways. The same goes for the methods we choose and the lenses we adopt during the interpretation of our findings. It is for this reason that we continuously seek to challenge our preconceptions and engage in a constant process of critical reflexivity in full awareness that multiple realities are socially constructed and co-constructed between the researchers and the informants (Lincoln & Guba, 1985).

Throughout our research, we adopted both an emic (inside) and etic (outside) position (Morris, Leung, Ames, & Lickel, 1999). While our emic stance translated in our eagerness to understand what was going on at the investigated setting from the vantage point of the insiders, our etic position allowed us to look at what was going on from a researcher's point of view. Here, our aim was to relate the phenomenon of interest to the literature. In this sense, we position our research in what Madill, Jordan, and Shirley (2000, p. 9) have termed a "contextual constructionist approach" which assumes that there are always multiple interpretations that strongly depend on the position of the researchers and the social context of the research.

In view of its qualitative nature and the fact that it is a pilot study, this contribution has a limited sample size. Further, the focus of the investigation was placed on technical disciplines and degree programmes only, which were additionally narrowed down by a regional perspective in the cross-border region of Upper Austria and the Czech Republic. Future research may open up the scope and include non-technical degree programmes. In addition, the geographical lens may be extended and adopt further regions. The applicability of the graduate employability frameworks may be tested in future quantitative studies.

References

Andrews, J., & Higson, H. (2008). Graduate employability, 'soft skills' versus 'hard' business knowledge: A European study. *Higher Education in Europe, 33*(4), 411–422.

Bandura, A. (1986). *Social foundations of thought and action: A social cognitive theory.* Englewood Cliffs, NJ: Prentice-Hall, Inc.

Blasko, Z., Brennan, J., Little, B., & Shah, T. (2002). *Access to what: Analysis of factors determining graduate employability.* London: HEFCE.

Bodea, C. N., Dascalu, M. I., Velikic, G., & Stancu, S. (2016). Lifelong learning and employability in the Danube region countries: Influences and correlations. *Amfiteatru Economic Journal, 18*(43), 521–536.

Boden, R., & Nevada, M. (2010). Employing discourse: Universities and graduate 'employability'. *Journal of Education Policy, 25,* 37–54.

Bogner, A., & Menz, W. (2009). The theory-generating expert interview: Epistemological interest, forms of knowledge, interaction. In A. Bogner, B. Littig, & W. Menz (Ed.), *Interviewing experts* (pp. 43–80). London: Palgrave Macmillan.

Bourdieu, P., Passeron, J. C., De Saint Martin, M., Baudelot, C., & Vincent, G. (1994). *Academic discourse: Linguistic misunderstanding and professorial power.* Oxford: Polity Press.

Boyatzis, R. (1998). *Transforming qualitative information: Thematic analysis and code development.* Thousand Oaks, CA: Sage.

Braun, V., & Clarke, V. (2006). Using thematic analysis in psychology. *Qualitative research in psychology, 3*(2), 77–101.

Bridgstock, R. (2009). The graduate attributes we've overlooked: Enhancing graduate employability through career management skills. *Higher Education Research & Development, 28*(1), 31–44.

Brown, P., Hesketh, A., & Williams, S. (2004). *The mismanagement of talent: Employability and jobs in the knowledge economy.* Oxford: Oxford University Press.

Chase, S. (2011). Narrative inquiry: Still a field in the making. In N. K. Denzin & Y. S. Lincoln (Eds.), *The Sage handbook of qualitative research* (4th ed., pp. 421–434). Washington, DC: Sage Publications.

Chreim, S., Williams, B. B., & Hinings, C. B. (2007). Interlevel influences on the reconstruction of professional role identity. *Academy of Management Journal, 50*(6), 1515–1539.

Chydenius, T., & Gaisch, M. (2016). Work-life interaction skills: An exploration of definitional and functional perspectives within the Austrian and Finnish ICT Industry. *Business Perspectives and Research, 4*(2), 169–181.

Clarke, M. (2018). Rethinking graduate employability: The role of capital, individual attributes and context. *Studies in Higher Education, 43*(11), 1923–1937.

Clarke, M., & Patrickson, M. (2008). The new covenant of employability. *Employee Relations, 30*(2), 121–141.

Clarke, V., & Braun, V. (2013). Teaching thematic analysis: Overcoming challenges and developing strategies for effective learning. *The Psychologist, 26*(2), 120–123.

Cohen, L., Manion, L., & Morrison, K. (2013). *Research methods in education.* New York, NY: Routledge.

Cranmer, S. (2006). Enhancing graduate employability: Best intentions and mixed outcomes. *Studies in Higher Education, 31*(2), 169–184.

Dacre Pool, L., & Sewell, P. (2007). The key to employability: Developing a practical model of graduate employability. *Education+ Training, 49*(4), 277–289.

Delaney, L., & Farren, M. (2016). No 'self' left behind? Part-time distance learning university graduates: Social class, graduate identity and employability. *Open Learning: The Journal of Open, Distance and e-Learning, 31*(3), 194–208.

Eby, L. T., Butts, M., & Lockwood, A. (2003). Predictors of success in the era of the boundaryless career. *Journal of Organizational Behaviour, 24*(6), 689–708.

Fereday, J., & Muir-Cochrane, E. (2006). Demonstrating rigor using thematic analysis: A hybrid approach of inductive and deductive coding and theme development. *International Journal of Qualitative Methods, 5*(1), 80–92.

Finch, D. J., Hamilton, L. K., Baldwin, R., & Zehner, M. (2013). An exploratory study of factors affecting undergraduate employability. *Education+ Training, 55*(7), 681–704.

Forrier, A., & Sels, L. (2003). The concept employability: A complex mosaic. *International Journal of Human Resources Development and Management, 3*(2), 102–124.

Fugate, M., & Ashforth, B. E. (2003). *Employability: The construct, its dimensions, and its applications.* Paper presented at Academy of Management Conference, Seattle, WA.

Fugate, M., Kinicki, A. J., & Ashforth, B. E. (2004). Employability: A psycho-social construct, its dimensions, and applications. *Journal of Vocational Behavior, 65*(1), 14–38.

Gaisch, M. (2014). *Affordances for teaching in an international classroom. A constructivist grounded theory* (PhD thesis). University of Vienna, Vienna.

Gaisch, M., & Aichinger, R. (2016). Pathways for the establishment of an inclusive higher education governance system: An innovative approach for diversity management. In *38th EAIR Forum* (pp. 1–10). Birmingham: European Higher Education Society.

Gaisch, M., & Aichinger, R. (2018). Second-tier higher education institutions and the diversity challenge: Structural components adopted through a Germanic lens. In R. L. Raby & E. J. Valeau (Ed.), *Handbook of comparative studies on community colleges and global counterparts* (pp. 217–233). New York, NY: Springer International Publishing.

Gaisch, M., & Oellinger, P. (2014). Beyond disciplinary boundaries. dynamics of a design as inquiry project. In M. Ueberwimmer, S. Wiesinger, M. Gaisch, T. Sumesberger, & R. Fuereder (Eds.), *Proceedings of Cross-cultural Business Conference 2014* (pp. 285–293). Austria: Steyr.

Gaisch, M., Rammer, V., Hrušková, L., & Krátká, J. (2017). A cross-cultural study between Austria and the Czech Republic on required competencies beyond technical expertise. In M. Ueberwimmer, S. Wiesinger, M. Gaisch, T. Sumesberger, & R. Fuereder (Eds.), *Proceedings of Cross-cultural Business Conference 2017*. Austria: Steyr.

Greenbank, P. (2003). The role of values in educational research: The case for reflexivity. *British Educational Research Journal, 29*, 791–801.

Harré, R. (1984). *Personal being: A theory for individual psychology.* Cambridge, MA: Harvard University Press.

Hansen, A. (2014, February 26). Universities Australia deal to get students 'work ready'. *The Conversation.* Retrieved from http://theconversation.com/universities-australia-deal-to-get-students-work-ready-23719

Harvey, L. (2000). New realities: The relationship between higher education and employment. *Tertiary Education & Management, 6*(1), 3–17.

Hillage, J., & Pollard, E. (1998). *Employability: Developing a framework for policy analysis.* London: DfEE.

Holmes, L. (1995). *Skills: A social perspective. Transferable skills in higher education.* London: Kogan Page.

Holmes, L. (2012). Realist and relational perspectives on graduate identity and employability: A response to Hinchliffe and Jolly. *British Educational Research Journal, 39*(6), 1044–1059.

Holmes, L. (2013). Competing perspectives on graduate employability: Possession, position or process? *Studies in Higher Education, 38*(4), 538–554.

Holmes, L., Green, M., & Egan, S. (1998). *Graduates in smaller businesses: A pilot study* (Final report on a project funded by the Government Office for London, Management Research Centre). London: The Business School, University of North London.

THE APPLICABILITY OF TWO GRADUATE EMPLOYABILITY FRAMEWORKS 309

Jackson, D. (2016). Re-conceptualising graduate employability: The importance of pre-professional identity. *Higher Education Research & Development, 35*(5), 925–939.

Jackson, V. (2013). *Investigating employability: The perspective of the business school graduate* (Doctoral dissertation). University of Liverpool, Liverpool.

Johnson, J. (2015). *Fulfilling our potential: Teaching excellence, social mobility and student choice* (Cm9141). London: BIS.

King, Z. (2004). Career self-management: Its nature, causes and consequences. *Journal of Vocational Behavior, 65*(1), 112–133.

Knight, P. T., & Yorke, M. (2002). Employability through the curriculum. *Tertiary Education & Management, 8*(4), 261–276.

Lincoln, Y. S., & Guba, E. G. (1985). *Naturalist inquiry.* London: Sage.

Madill, A., Jordan, A., & Shirley, C. (2000). Objectivity and reliability in qualitative analysis: Realist, contextualist and radical constructionist epistemologies. *British Journal of Psychology, 91*(1), 1–20.

Mason O'Connor, K., Lynch, K., & Owen, D. (2011). Student-community engagement and the development of graduate attributes. *Education+ Training, 53*(2–3), 100–115.

McGrath, S. (2009). *What is employability?* UNESCO Centre for Comparative Education Research, School of Education, University of Nottingham.

McQuaid, R., & Lindsay, C. (2005). The concept of employability. *Urban Studies, 42*(2), 197–219.

Minarik, D. (2008). Comparison of Czech and Austrian Foreign Policies and their Politics towards South Asia. *Studies, 42*(2), 197–219.

Ministry of Education, Youth and Sports. (2008). *Higher education in the Czech Republic 2008.* Centre for Higher Education Studies.

Morris, M. W., Leung, K., Ames, D., & Lickel, B. (1999). Views from inside and outside: Integrating emic and etic insights about culture and justice judgment. *Academy of Management Review, 24*(4), 781–796.

Oellinger, P., Lembke; J., Gaisch, M., & Gros Salvat, B. (2014). Epistemological perspectives and intercultural encounters: In pursuit of creative ways to narrow ontological gaps. In Ueberwimmer et al. (Eds.), *Proceedings of Cross-cultural Business Conference 2014* (pp. 337–344). Austria: Steyr.

Okay-Somerville, B., & Scholarios, D. (2017). Position, possession or process? Understanding objective and subjective employability during university-to-work transitions. *Studies in Higher Education, 42*(7), 1275–1291.

Oliver, B. (2015). Redefining graduate employability and work-integrated learning: Proposals for effective higher education in disrupted economies. *Journal of Teaching and Learning for Graduate Employability, 6*(1), 56–65.

Patton, M. Q. (2002). *Qualitative research and evaluation methods* (3rd ed.). Thousand Oaks, CA: Sage.

Pegg, A., Waldock, J., Hendy-Isaac, S., & Lawton, R. (2012). *Pedagogy for employability.* New York, NY: Higher Education Academy.

Plăiaş, J., Pop, C. M., Dabija, D., & Băbuţ, R. (2011). Competences acquired by graduates through marketing higher education – Findings from the employers' perspective. Analele Universităţii Oradea – *Ştiinţe Economice, 18*(4), 762–769.

Riessman, C. K. (1993). *Narrative analysis* (Vol. 30). Thousand Oaks, CA: Sage.

Rothwell, A., & Rothwell, F. (2016). Graduate employability: A critical oversight. In M. Tomlinson & L. Holmes (Eds.), *Graduate employability in context* (pp. 41–63). London: Palgrave Macmillan.

Rott, G. (2015). Academic knowledge and students' relationship to the world: Career management competence and student centred teaching and learning. *Journal of the European Higher Education, 2.*

Savin-Baden, M., & Major, C. H. (2013). *Qualitative research: The essential guide to theory and practice*. London: Routledge.

Schultz, T. W. (1971). *Investment in human capital. The role of education and of research.* New York, NY: The Free Press.

Sin, C., & Amaral, A. (2016). Academics' and employers' perceptions about responsibilities for employability and their initiatives towards its development. *Higher Education, 1–15.* https://doi.org/10.1007/s10734-016-0007-y

Suleman, F. (2017). The employability skills of higher education graduates: Insights into conceptual frameworks and methodological options. *Higher Education, 1–16.* https://doi.org/10.1007/s10734-017-0207-0

Thomas, D. A. (2006). A general inductive approach for analyzing qualitative evaluation data. *American Journal of Evaluation, 27*(2), 237–246.

Tomlinson, M. (2012). Graduate employability: A review of conceptual and empirical themes. *Higher Education Policy, 25* (4), 407–431.

Tran, T. T. (2016). Enhancing graduate employability and the need for university-enterprise collaboration. *Journal of Teaching and Learning for Graduate Employability, 7*(1), 58–71.

Van der Heijden, B. (2002). Prerequisites to guarantee life-long employability. *Personnel review, 31*(1), 44–61.

Van der Heijde, C. M., & Van Der Heijden, B. I. (2006). A competence-based and multidimensional operationalization and measurement of employability. *Human Resource Management, 45*(3), 449–476.

Vanhercke, D., De Cuyper, N., Peeters, E., & De Witte, H. (2014). Defining perceived employability: a psychological approach. *Personnel Review, 43*(4), 592–605.

Yang, W. (2015). Tuning university undergraduates for high mobility and employability under the content and language integrated learning approach. *International Journal of Bilingual Education and Bilingualism, 1–18.* https://doi.org/10.108 0/13670050.2015.1061474

Yorke, M. (2006). *Employability in higher education: What it is – what it is not* (Vol. 1). New York, NY: Higher Education Academy.

CHAPTER 13

Universities in the Complex Setting of the West Bank: Entrepreneurial or Engaged?

Huub L. M. Mudde

Abstract

Palestinian universities lack resources, have restrictive (inter)national mobility opportunities, and are faced with numerous security measures. This paper analyses to what extent entrepreneurial transformation at these universities is taking place and how it is related with the political, economic and cultural complex setting in which they operate. It combines a literature review with findings of a mixed methods study at four universities applying the entrepreneurial university framework of the European Commission and OECD. Findings indicate that staff and students are more negative than positive about the entrepreneurial status of their institutions, with students being more critical than staff. At each of the universities, international donor supported entrepreneurial activities are starting up as a way to overcome youth unemployment. The author concludes that Palestinian universities are to be understood as engaged universities that increasingly stimulate their students to act entrepreneurially. Rooted in the context of the Palestinian cause, they contribute socially and culturally to their local communities. Furthermore, the author states that in a developing context the notion of an entrepreneurial university as an important contributor to innovation through research does not apply. He calls for rethinking the innovation-driven Triple Helix concept when applied in low-income countries, with 'donor-pushed' and 'society-driven' as new typologies for stakeholder cooperation.

Keywords

entrepreneurial university – Palestinian Territories – entrepreneurship education – higher education – employment – engaged university

© KONINKLIJKE BRILL NV, LEIDEN, 2020 | DOI: 10.1163/9789004422582_014

1 Introduction

Palestine, formally known as the Occupied Palestinian Territories, is operating in a context of political tension, affecting the social and economic lives of its citizens. More than 50 years of Israeli occupation has led to economic stagnation, disrupting labour and trade flows and constraining private sector development (CIA, 2017; UNCTAD, 2017). The economy is not sustainable, largely dependent on donor funding and not competitive, ranking 107 of 148 countries according to the Competitive Industrial Performance Index (UNIDO, 2017; World Bank, 2017b).

The Palestinian labour force is characterised by high unemployment, large differences between men and women, a large informal economy and many people outside the formal labour force. In this challenging context, attention for entrepreneurship is growing rapidly. Palestinian universities are starting to offer entrepreneurship education to develop the entrepreneurial mindset of graduates, and are encouraging students to become self-employed. Making students more entrepreneurial asks also for an entrepreneurial university (Röpke, 1998), but how are Palestinian universities coping with this role in a context of scarce resources, when freedom of action and movement is restricted, and economic prospects are gloomy?

This paper analyses to what extent entrepreneurial transformation of universities in the West Bank is taking place and how this relates with the political, economic and cultural complex setting in which these universities operate. It is inspired by a mixed methods study at four universities (see Table 13.1).

In this chapter, the HEInnovate assessment framework for European entrepreneurial higher education institutions (European Commission & OECD, 2013) is applied and Gibb's definition of entrepreneurial universities has been used. This definition refers to an academic organisation that is designed for staff and students to "demonstrate enterprise, innovation and creativity" (Gibb, 2013, p. 1), that creates public value, partners with local, regional, national and international stakeholders, and that is able to effectively operate in a dynamic context. The concept of entrepreneurial university is however challenged by ideas of the 'engaged university'. These are universities that are dedicated to achieving social and cultural local impact (ACEEU, 2016). This poses the question whether universities in Palestine can best be characterised as entrepreneurial or engaged.

The remainder of this paper is structured as follows: first, the interrelations are explained between entrepreneurship education, entrepreneurial university and the economic context, and how the concept of entrepreneurial university differs to the concept of engaged university. The paper continues by

UNIVERSITIES IN THE COMPLEX SETTING OF THE WEST BANK

TABLE 13.1   General profile of the five universities assessed

Name	Your of foundation	Total number of students (2017)	Total number of academic staff (2017)	Academic profile	Formal status
An-Najah National University (ANNU)	1977 (1918)	20,452	1,080	Comprehensive	Private
Al-Quds University (AQU)	1984	11,982	470	Comprehensive	Private
Hebron University (HU)	1971	8,700	390	Comprehensive	Public
Palestine Technical University Kadoorie (PTUK)	2007 (1930)	7,091	238	Technical	Governmental

SOURCE: WEBSITES OF THE RESPECTIVE INSTITUTES AND STRATEGY DOCUMENTS, CONSULTED IN 2017

exploring the specific situation of the West Bank and the Palestinian higher education. In addition, the findings are structured around cases of four universities and ends with a discussion and conclusions.

2   Literature Review

Substantiated by the importance of entrepreneurship for the employability of graduates and for economic development (Röpke, 1998; European Commission & OECD, 2014), universities globally pay increasing attention to entrepreneurship education. This education is seen as a way to develop the entrepreneurial mindset of students and to encourage them to become self-employed (Gibb, 2013). 'Entrepreneurship', and thus the associated competences and skills, is used in the dual meaning of being 'enterprising' as well as starting up and running a business (Gibb, 2002; European Commission & OECD, 2014, p. 5).

Entrepreneurship education is just one element of an entrepreneurial university. Another feature of an entrepreneurial university is that it is designed to encourage and support individual entrepreneurial behaviour (Röpke, 1998; Clark, 2004; Coyle, Gibb, & Haskins, 2013; Aranha & Garcia, 2014). Entrepreneurial activities are not in isolation from other university operations, but leadership, governance, education, research and community services are together geared towards achieving the entrepreneurial agenda of the institution (Gibb, 2013; European Commission & OECD, 2014). The entrepreneurial university concept goes beyond the stimulation of entrepreneurship, creation of business and commercialisation of knowledge, and developing individual entrepreneurial competences and skills. It is geared towards achieving the strategic goals of the university (Gibb, Hannon, & Robertson, 2012; Coyle, Gibb, & Haskins, 2013). An entrepreneurial university is an academic organisation that creates public value in partnership with local, regional, national and international stakeholders, and that is able to effectively operate in a dynamic context (Gibb, 2013, p. 1). A university needs to have a certain level of autonomy to become entrepreneurial (Clark, 1998, 2004; European Commission & OECD, 2014). They are considered entrepreneurial when they are able to diversify their funding base by increasing non-public sources through commercialisation, in alignment with their academic operations (Clark, 2004).

In 2013, the European Commission and OECD developed an online self-assessment tool for European entrepreneurial higher education institutions named HEInnovate that operationalises the concept of entrepreneurial university on seven dimensions.[1] First, the university leadership and governance are stimulating and creating a stategic setting for entrepreneurial behaviour of its staff, students and external relations. Leadership is one of the important drivers of entrepreneurial transformation of universities (European Commission, 2012; Coyle, Gibb, & Haskins, 2013; Gibb, 2013). Second, the organisational capacities, in particular finance and human resources, are in place for implementing the entrepreneurial agenda of the university. Third, teaching and learning strenghtens entrepreneurial mindsets of all students. Fourth, the university has a programme in place for preparing and supporting those students, staff and alumni that want to start-up a business. Fifth, the university strategically cooperates and exchanges knowledge with a diversity of stakeholders for the benefit of social, cultural and economic development. Sixth, the university has an active internationalisation policy of staff and student mobility, international research and partnerships. And seventh, the university is a learning organisation that uses the results of its entrepreneurial strategy and activities for continuous improvements. The disinction in the HEInnovate framework between 'entrepeneurial teaching and learning' and 'preparing and supporting entrepreneurs' aligns with the earlier mentioned difference

UNIVERSITIES IN THE COMPLEX SETTING OF THE WEST BANK 315

between entrepreneurship in the meaning of being enterprising and of creating a business venture.

The origin of the concept of entrepreneurial university is understood in the context of knowledge-based economies with the seminal work in the late nineties by Etzkowitz in the United States and Clark in Europe (Clark, 1998; Etzkowitz, Webster, Gebhardt, & Cantisano Terra, 2000). Universities are challenged to deliver relevance in research and teaching in a setting of growing global competition in the knowledge economy (Coyle, Gibb, & Haskins, 2013). They are seen as important drivers for economic growth and innovation (Fayolle and Redford, 2014).

Etzkowitz (2004) poses that the interaction with industry is the real lever towards becoming an entrepreneurial university. A strong 'interdependence' with industry and government is a key phenomenon of entrepreneurial universities (Etzkowitz, 2004; Clark, 2004). Private sector, government and academia together shape the economy. Such a Triple Helix can be university-pushed, government-pulled or corporation-led (Etzkowitz & Zhou, 2007). In the university-pushed model, universities are initiators of regional innovation through commercialisation of knowledge and job generators. In the government-pulled model, government is the most important actor and initiator of economic development. In this model, universities are under the control of government and supportive to regional development by helping existing industries and contributing to policy. The corporation-led model supposes industry to be the driving force of technological innovation with universities contributing to innovation.

Critics of the Triple Helix model argue that more stakeholders play a significant role in innovation and shaping the economy, in particular civil society. Civil society is important from the perspective that the public uses and applies knowledge and as such is part of the innovation system (Carayannis & Campbell, 2012). In developing countries, international donor agencies contribute as well. They support financially, and offer expertise and an international perspective (Beugré, 2017). This leads to quadruple or even quintuple helix models. This broader societal view aligns with a shift from a narrow focus on university's economic functions to its broader social and cultural roles (Cai & Lui, 2016). The concept of entrepreneurial university with its emphasis on the business and economic dimension of higher education is challenged by ideas of the civic or engaged university. Goddard and Kempton (2016, p. 13) characterise a civic university as an institution in which the structure, education and research are intertwined with the socio-economic development of the society in which they operate: whilst research is designed for "socio-economic impact," education is meant to "produc[es] well rounded citizens as graduates." With the main characteristic of civic universities being engaged with the community, the terminology of engaged or civic universities is interchangeable. The Accreditation Council for Entrepreneurial and Engaged Universities (ACEEU, 2016) describes engaged universities being dedicated to "continuous improvement and the generation of greater social and cultural impacts for the city and region" (p. 5). Related to these concepts, and relevant for assessing the Palestinian universities is the concept of 'anchor' institution defined by the Work Foundation (2010, p. 3):

> anchor institutions do not have a democratic mandate and their primary missions do not involve regeneration or local economic development. Nonetheless their scale, local rootedness and community links are such that they are acknowledged to play a key role in local development and economic growth, representing the 'sticky capital' around which economic growth strategies can be built.

Goddard, Coombes, Kempton and Vallance (2014) indicate that in particular in weaker economies, like in Palestine, universities are among the most important anchor institutions. They can "act as a source of stability in local economies, buffering against the worst effects of periodic downturns" (Goddard & Kempton, 2016, p. 7).

The above poses the question how universities in Palestine can best be characterised, operating in a setting of economic stagnation and occupation: are they entrepreneurial or engaged? What can we learn from understanding university transformation processes in other economically vulnerable societies?

3   Employment and Entrepreneurship in the West Bank

Palestine is considered to be a factor-driven economy, characterised by high rates of agricultural self-employment and a large number of small manufacturing and service firms (Porter, 1990; Porter, Sachs, & McArthur, 2002). However, due to the occupation, access to natural resources and upscaling through export is severely hampered. UNCTAD (2017) concludes that 50 years of occupation have resulted in 'de-development' of the Palestinian economy and undermining of the agricultural and industrial sectors. In 2017, around 2.9 million people lived in the West Bank, of which an estimated 18% lived below the poverty line (PCBS, 2017; CIA, 2017).

The Palestinian labour force is characterised by high unemployment, large differences between the sexes, a large informal sector, and many people outside the formal labour force (see Table 13.2). More than 150,000 people in the

UNIVERSITIES IN THE COMPLEX SETTING OF THE WEST BANK 317

TABLE 13.2   Employment indicators of the West Bank, Palestine

Population size	2.9 million	
Labour force	8,44,000	
Unemployment rate	women: 29.8%	men: 15.5%
Unemployment rate of graduates	25.20%	
Average of Unemployment Duration	women: 10.9 months	men: 3.7 months
Informal employment	women: 51.5%	men: 66.8%
Outside labour force	women: 82.3%	men: 27.3%

SOURCE: WEBSITES OF THE RESPECTIVE INSTITUTES AND STRATEGY DOCUMENTS,
CONSULTED IN 2017

West Bank are unemployed (PCBS, 2017), excluding those who have dropped out of the labour market and are no longer seeking employment. This equates to, according to the ILO (2016), 1.44 million Palestinians.

In this challenging context, the attention for entrepreneurship is growing rapidly in Palestine. The Global Entrepreneurship Monitor pictures however a problematic entrepreneurial situation, characterised by high numbers of business closures, relatively low activity rates, and a large proportion of necessity entrepreneurship: there are 67 necessity-driven entrepreneurs for each 100 opportunity driven entrepreneurs (MAS, 2013). The overarching majority of businesses are small-scale enterprises with an average of four employees (UNIDO, 2014). In recent years, initiatives have been taken in support of entrepreneurship. Palestine has risen on the Doing Business Index (from 140th to 114th in the annual ranking of 190 economies) (World Bank, 2017a), indicating a better regulatory environment for starting, running and dissolving a business.

4   Higher Education in Palestine

The higher education sector in Palestine is relatively young with the first universities founded in the 1970s (European Commission, 2012). Whilst these universities were established to provide higher education to young Palestinians at a time where it was becoming increasingly difficult to study abroad, their foundation is understood within the Palestinian state-building strategy. The universities were meant to preserve the Palestinian identity and acted as cradle for political activists (Taraki, 2015). Only after the Oslo Accords of 1993, the Palestinian National Authority was established and became responsible for various sectors, including education. Since then, the number of higher education institutions has increased to 49, enrolling 213,000 students. All of them predominantly focus on education with the research function underdeveloped, dependent on external funding. No support mechanisms exist for researchers who would like to protect their Intellectual Property as a first step towards commercialisation. Universities are self-managed, autonomous institutions, supervised by the Ministry of Education (European Commission, 2012).

University operations are constrained by the occupation in several ways. Financially, because the under-resourced Palestinian National Authority structurally contributes less to higher education than budgeted, leaving the universities largely dependent on income out of tuition fees (European Commission, 2012), project funding and sponsoring. In addition, international students and staff exchange is hampered due to limitations in mobility. Carrying out technical research and equipping laboratories is difficult because the import of an extensive amount of dual-purpose goods is prohibited. These are goods that have a security risk according to Israel, because of a potential use for military purposes (Niksic, Eddin, & Cali, 2014).

Little information is available on the entrepreneurial status of Palestinian universities. A study undertaken in 2015 by Morar at one university in the West Bank concluded that entrepreneurship development was in its early stage. In 2016, Palestinian students assessed the entrepreneurial status of seven universities in the West Bank using the HEInnovate framework (European Commission & OECD, 2013). The results showed that the entrepreneurial status of these universities was weak. They concluded that there is no clear entrepreneurial university model across Palestinian universities. Furthermore, publications from the European Commission (2012) and Khatib, Tsipouri, Bassiakos, and Haj-daoud (2013) indicate that cooperation between the private sector and higher education is limited. Companies are hardly involved in curriculum development and higher education's contribution to innovation by businesses is minimal.

5 Methodology

This chapter is inspired by a mixed methods study at four universities (see Table 13.1) applying the entrepreneurial university framework HEInnovate of the European Commission and OECD with its seven dimensions already mentioned (2013). The framework has been operationalised by identifying per dimension a set of variables and indicators (Table 13.3). The study combined structured questionnaires allowing for a quantitative inter-university comparison, with interviews and content analysis to explore the phenomenon of 'entrepreneurial university' within each university-specific context.

UNIVERSITIES IN THE COMPLEX SETTING OF THE WEST BANK

TABLE 13.3   Variables per dimension of the HEInnovate framework

Dimension of framework	Variables
Leadership and governance	Strategy; High level commitment; Coordination; Support to faculties; Relation to wider regional, social and community environment
Organizational capacity	Funding; Internal cooperation; Recruitment; Staff development; Incentives and rewards
Teaching and learning	Formal learning; Informal learning; Validation of entrepreneurship learning outcomes; Collaborating and engaging with external stakeholders; Research
Supporting entrepreneurs	Attention for entrepreneurship awareness; Business creation support; Business start-up training; Mentoring; Access to finance; Access to business incubation facilities
Knowledge exchange	Collaboration and knowledge exchange with industry, society and the public sector; Active involvement in partnerships; Links with incubators, science parks and other external initiatives; Staff and students opportunities to take part in innovative activities; Knowledge exploitation
Internationalization	Internationalization strategy; International mobility of staff and students; International staff; Internationalization in teaching; International research
Monitoring and evaluation	Impact of entrepreneurial strategy, personnel and resources, teaching and learning, start-up support, knowledge exchange activities, and internationalization

SOURCE: ADAPTED FROM HEINNOVATE (2013)

Per university, data were collected from four groups of respondents: leadership, academic staff, students and external stakeholders (see Table 13.4). In total, 200 students filled out a structured questionnaire with statements on their own institution, and 56 staff members filled out a similar questionnaire. Each dimension of the European Commission/OECD framework was captured in a sub-set of statements. A five-point Likert scale was used for all the statements, with one indicating total disagreement, and five indicating total agreement with the statement presented. The two questionnaires (for students and staff) were tested for validity and reliability using factor analysis. Each sub-set of statements had its own validity score, because it is based on a different

TABLE 13.4   Number of respondents per university

	ANNU	AQU	HU	PTUK
Number of staff respondents	–	23	6	27
Number of student respondents	56	62	55	27
Number of interviews with staff and leadership	13	9	10	11
Number of FGDs with staff	1 (4 staff members)	0	0	1 (5 staff members)
Number of FDGs with students	2 (6+17 students)	2 (8+6 students)	1 (6 students)	1 (20 students)
Number of interviews with external stakeholders	3	1	5	1

dimension of the European Commission/OECD framework. All scores – Cronbach's alpha – were 0.7 or far above, indicating that the factors are reliably measured by the relevant questions in the questionnaire.

In addition, 125 people were interviewed or took part in focus group discussions. Interview and focus group data were analysed in two steps. First, per university, data were summarised by using a data-matrix that related the information received with the dimensions of the European Commission/OECD framework. This resulted in a university-specific narrative that was complimented by data of the various internal documents, allowing for triangulation and interpretation of the survey results. The narratives represented a balanced picture from the perspective of all four groups of respondents. Subsequently, the university-specific narratives were aggregated using the same dimensions of the European Commission/OECD framework.

6   Findings

The empirical findings describe how the four Palestinian universities scored on the seven dimensions of the European Commission/OECD framework, include a narrative of each of the universities, and conclude with a summary.

UNIVERSITIES IN THE COMPLEX SETTING OF THE WEST BANK

6.1 *Perception Scores*

Students and staff have been asked to score statements related to the entrepreneurial status of their university on a scale from one to five. Table 13.5 presents the means per dimension of the framework, i.e., the total scores of the respective sub-set of statements divided by the number of statements.

TABLE 13.5   Mean per dimension of the analytical framework, students and staff, by university (n = 256)

	ANNU		AQU		HU		PTUK
	Students (n=56)	Staff (n=23)	Students (n=62)	Staff (n=6)	Students (n=55)	Staff (n=27)	Students (n=27)
Leadership and governance	2.37	3.18	2.51	2.83	2.61	3.40	3.19
Organizational capacity	2.46	3.12	2.54	3.05	2.72	3.37	3.11
Entrepreneurial teaching and learning	2.48	3.02	2.55	2.89	2.70	3.28	3.22
Preparing and supporting entrepreneurs	2.42	2.85	2.44	2.70	2.56	3.15	2.89
Knowledge exchange and collaboration	2.51	2.87	2.42	2.74	2.59	3.28	3.12
Internationalization	2.71	3.01	2.54	2.61	2.46	2.90	3.05
Measuring impact	2.58	2.59	2.30	2.42	2.50	2.88	3.23
Total mean	2.50	2.95	2.47	2.75	2.59	3.18	3.12

On a Likert scale of five, a mean of three is regarded as average. Only the cumulative responses of Palestine Technical University Kadoorie (PTUK) staff and students were slightly above this average (3.18 and 3.12 respectively), indicating that this is the only university at which the respondents had a slightly more positive than negative perception on the entrepreneurial status of their university. Additional analysis of variance indicated that there are statistically significant differences between students and staff. Students scored significantly lower than staff on all of the seven categories of the framework with the exception of the category 'Measuring of Impact'. That category does not show significant differences. A closer look at the student responses leads to the conclusion that there are no statistically significant differences between students by department, by sex or by number of years studying at the university. The same applies to staff. Hence, there are very small differences between how groups of respondents perceived the entrepreneurial status of their university with two exceptions: PTUK respondents perceived their university as more entrepreneurial than respondents from other universities. Furthermore, students had a more critical view than staff.

6.2   *An-Najah National University: For the Sake of Academic Excellence*

At the time of data collection, the mission of An-Najah National University (ANNU) was different from the mission of other Palestinian universities. It put emphasis on scientific excellence in education and research with an international outlook. University leadership stressed that ANNU was focusing on being an academically strong institution and was proud of the quality of its students, stating that ANNU attracted the best high school students. The university ranked first or second among all Palestinian universities with respect to the quality of its programmes and several of its programmes were internationally accredited.

During the last few years, entrepreneurship started to get greater attention. Teachers increasingly challenged students to develop their own projects instead of relying on finding a job. In addition, the university website gave prominent attention to entrepreneurship. It stated that "An-Najah aims at pushing the wagon of the Palestinian economy onward, therefore; it builds ties with the local community through carrying out pioneering projects and supporting entrepreneurs by offering them the needed resources and facilities" (ANNU, 2017). The university leadership realised that entrepreneurship activities at ANNU needed to be structured more: around ten units were working on entrepreneurship but there was no coordination.

However, both staff and students were critical. Staff indicated that the structure and culture of the university was not conducive for swift, entrepreneurial decision making. They considered ANNU as being bureaucratic and hierarchical with a lack of client orientation. According to students, ANNU was not focusing on entrepreneurship and they were not offered support (see Table 13.5: the student mean was 2.50). They found it important to develop entrepreneurial skills, but indicated that if they wanted to develop in that area, they

UNIVERSITIES IN THE COMPLEX SETTING OF THE WEST BANK

sought support outside the university. ANNU had no entrepreneurship awareness programme for students, hardly offered business development support, and attention for entrepreneurship in formal education was absent in many faculties or limited in others.

Some initiatives, however, focused on improving relations with industry. The Business Innovation & Partnership Center of the University (called NaBIC) was a kind of technology transfer office that maintained relations with industry. Furthermore, the Palestine Bank funded ANNU staff to spend one semester at a company. In this way, staff had the opportunity to enrich its practical experience and to feed this back into teaching. In addition, from the four universities studied, ANNU was the only one with several years of experience in running a business incubator. A local branch of an international IT company had its office within the premises of this incubator. Already in 2005, the Korean Palestinian Information Technology Institute of Excellence, which was hosted at the university, established the externally funded IT Incubator. Operating formally outside the university structure, the incubator was open for students, but not focusing on them. It operated in relative isolation from the regular university operations. In 2017, eight projects were incubated, none of them by students.

6.3   Al-Quds University: Entrepreneurial out of Necessity

The existence of Al-Quds University (AQU) is strongly related with the Palestinian cause. Naming the university Al-Quds, the Arabic name for Jerusalem, is a statement in itself. At the time of the study, the university had a campus in the old centre of Jerusalem and was as such one of the few Palestinian organisations that could voice the interest of Palestinians within Israel. This came with a price: economically non-viable operations like the Jerusalem campus were kept open because of political reasons. Deteriorated by minimal governmental support, AQU structurally lacked financial resources. Out of necessity, the university had an active, entrepreneurial income generation strategy through developmental projects, sponsorships and above all being attractive to students. Around 70% of the annual income was from tuition fees. On campus, many buildings were named after wealthy individuals, mainly from the Middle East, who sponsored the facilities. Income out of spin-offs, business development services or joint ventures was insignificant. Directly related to the need for income, was a positive attitude of the university administration towards staff seeking opportunities. Colleges were actively developing externally funded new initiatives. Staff indicated that the university had 'something entrepreneurial' because it was able to attract an increasing number of students although it was struggling in many ways (mainly financially). What was missing however was coordination and strategic mutual enforcement of the variety of these entrepreneurial initiatives.

The university recently paid more attention to increasing the employability of its graduates by linking education with industry, stimulated by the university strategy that focused on income generation, innovation, start-ups and job creation. The best example included the Dual Studies programme in Electrical Engineering and Information Technology that started in 2015 to maximise the possibility of graduates to get a job. These programmes were initiated by the German Institute for Development Cooperation (GIZ) that funded programmes to strengthen the employability of graduates. During the full Bachelor programme, students spent three months on campus, then three months at the company for which they got paid. In 2017, 80 companies were envisaged to be partners for more than 60 students. AQU considered the programme successful, because of the number of companies involved and employers were positive about graduates meeting their criteria. Stimulated by the success, a similar programme in international business started in 2016 and there were plans to use the same concept for Master level programmes.

In 2017, AQU started another novel initiative to reduce the gap between university and industry. It established a joint venture with a private company based in Dubai for the production and selling of personal care products made from Palestinian organic ingredients. This initiative derived from university research and production began in 2018. It was meant to become a place to train students with possibilities for employment.

However, students complained and were less positive about the entrepreneurial status of AQU (see Table 13.5: the student mean was 2.47). They indicated that teaching was – with exceptions – theoretical with a focus on memorising. Entrepreneurial skills were not given attention. They stated that this was the general approach in Palestine, also at high school. There was no programme (curricular or extra-curricular) offered to students for making them aware of the opportunities and challenges for becoming entrepreneur. There was no programme in place for supporting interested students to set-up a business. Support was given, but this was ad-hoc and dependent on individual faculty members.

AQU was actively engaged with many partners in society. Respondents stated that partnerships were important because they helped increase employability of graduates and could generate income. Another important reason for

AQUS active partnerships was political: AQU operated in Jerusalem as one of the few Palestinian organisations whilst the Palestinian Authority could not. International partnerships were plenty; mainly project-based and externally funded, but international mobility of staff and students was limited due to travel restrictions. In 2017, three foreign students were able to get a visa to study at AQU.

6.4 Hebron University: A Strategic, Top-down Entrepreneurial Change

At the time of data collection, Hebron University (HU) was strongly embedded in the local community, literally in the centre of the city, and intertwined with the local social and cultural network. An example was the annual Hebron Grape Festival organised by the university in collaboration with the Municipality that promoted Palestinian agriculture. The city was in an economically vibrant region with many small, family-owned businesses and several companies, in particular in agribusiness. Founded in 1971 as an Islamic college, HU was rooted in Palestinian Islamic traditions with an academic origin in culture and arts. This was appreciated by many Palestinian parents. They considered HU to be a trustworthy place for their daughters, in some departments there were more than 70% female students. With around 9,000 students, it was a relatively small university.

In 2016, HU formulated a new, five-year strategic plan with the vision of becoming a global university by 2020. In his foreword, the university chairman explicitly referred to entrepreneurship as a way to increase employability of the graduates: "Hebron University aims at offering all students a learning community [...] by integrating the culture of leadership and entrepreneurship in various disciplines of the university curricula in a market where job opportunities are becoming less whilst opportunities for entrepreneurship are increasing" (HU, 2017, p. 2). To coordinate the implementation of this strategy, an entrepreneurship executive committee was established and chaired by the Vice President of Academic Affairs. As a first step, the university started to adapt the university bylaws, regulations and policies with the aim of supporting the faculties to become more entrepreneurial. Next, a strategy for the entrepreneurial development of students was agreed upon. The university discovered that most of the graduates lacked the entrepreneurial skills needed for establishing new businesses or projects. Therefore, the university was planning to start developing the entrepreneurial mindset of students by offering short extra-curricular training to 400 students. This was completely new for HU, because it had neither a programme nor stand-alone activities in place aiming at entrepreneurship awareness of students. This innovation process was stimulated and supported by a British Council funded project aimed at developing Palestinian graduates with entrepreneurial employability skills and attributes. In this project seven Palestinian universities, among which HU, got support from three British universities in developing policies, pedagogical practices and support structures for students.

Only recently, HU started to develop curricula on entrepreneurship in combination with capacity building of teaching staff. In September 2017, HU started to offer an elective course 'Entrepreneurship and Innovation'. At one faculty, the final research project of the Bachelor program had been reoriented into a hands-on project in which students had to find a company and make a business plan. In 2017, 94 students participated. A bottleneck for introducing more entrepreneurial teaching was that the experience and skills were lacking on how to facilitate experiential and practical learning of students. Staff also mentioned that they got no support from the university to strengthen entre-preneurial skills of students. Undertaking practical work needed transport and budget which was scarce.

Staff as well as students expressed the desire to have a business incubator at the university. This was also understood by the university leadership: an analysis of strengths and weaknesses of HU executed in 2016 indicated that the university did not have incubators to host innovative business projects and that there were no regulations for supporting start-up small and medium enterprises. Therefore, the Strategic Plan 2020 included actions to establish an IT Incubator and a Business Incubator. In addition, regulations were meant to be developed to support and implement innovative projects of students and staff. In addition, HU signed an agreement in 2017 with the Hebron House of Commerce to enable HU students to use their business incubator. This part-nership also included a first business competition and business plan develop-ment training for students.

Although HU had many partnerships, institutional collaboration with com-panies seemed limited. Only recently, HU put more attention to cooperation with companies, mainly in the framework of projects funded by among oth-ers the World Bank and the Netherlands. The university-industry relations were mainly one-way partnerships in which the university asked for student support. Business representatives stated that they offered traineeships to stu-dents out of social responsibility. They found it important to decrease the gap between the graduate's skills and the company needs, but stressed that there were very little job opportunities. Collaborative research in support of innova-tive business was the exception to the rule.

UNIVERSITIES IN THE COMPLEX SETTING OF THE WEST BANK 327

6.5 *Palestine Technical University Kadoorie: Entrepreneurial Leadership*

PTUK became a university in 2007, but its origin dates back to 1930 as an agricultural college. In the twentieth century, PTUK lost access to most of its land and transformed into a technical college. At the time of this study, PTUK was in a better financial position than other universities because salaries of all staff were paid by the Palestinian Authority.

In 2013, a new university president came into office, actively pushing an innovation and entrepreneurship agenda. Known as one of the Palestinian leaders in innovative thinking and education development, he considered himself a change agent. Under his leadership, many new education programmes started. The student body increased with more than 60% in five years to about 7,000 students. This growth was because of a rapid increase of the number of Bachelor students on top of a stable number of students in vocational engineering education. Deans expressed that there was a strong sense of cooperation among the management of PTUK because it was a new, upcoming university; they stated that "we need to work as a team, otherwise it does not work." There was a top-down coordinated strategy implementation with all deans involved. These developments seemed to pay off with staff and students perceiving PTUK as more entrepreneurial than how respondents from the other three universities perceived their universities (see Table 13.5: staff scored 3.18 and students scored 3.12).

Under a new Innovation and Education Technology Center, in 2016, PTUK set in place a six month extra-curricular business ideation programme for students. At the end of this programme, students were presenting their ideas in front of potential investors. Typical for this programme – and similar Palestinian programmes – was the terminology: instead of naming it 'business ideas', students were stimulated to develop 'project ideas', being entrepreneurial (start-ups) or scientific (applied research). Staff and students referred to 'projects' instead of 'start-ups'. The core functionality of PTUK's programme was a database and online platform that allowed online support and evaluation of the ideas that students included in the database. By mid-2017, 148 students had included 47 projects in the database, of which 24 were entrepreneurial projects (40 students) and 23 scientific projects (108 students). At the time of this study, one project was about to receive funding from the Palestinian Higher Council for Innovation. In addition to the ideation programme, PTUK was starting up business incubation initiatives. An incubator was in place but with minimal activities. A second incubator focusing on agricultural start-ups, meant to open its doors in 2018, was made possible through external funding.

TABLE 13.6   Summary of entrepreneurial university assessment of the four Palestinian universities

	ANNU	AQU	HU	PTUK
Leadership and governance	Focusing on 'scientific excellence', no strategy towards becoming an entrepreneurial university	Strategy 'Creating a culture of Innovation and production', focusing on income generation, innovation, start-ups and job creation	In early stage of coordinated strategic change to become more entrepreneurial	Entrepreneurial vision and personal involvement of the University President
Organizational capacity	No income out of business development	An active entrepreneurial income generation strategy to overcome difficult financial situation; First attempt to raise income out of business development	Realization by university leadership that regulations and incentives need to be in place for staff to act entrepreneurially	Less focus on income generation because (relatively) better financial position
Teaching and learning	Increasing number of entrepreneurship courses in several colleges, in particular Faculty of Engineering and IT	Purposefully introducing market-oriented experiential learning models; A few entrepreneurship courses	Introduction of new 'Entrepreneurship and Innovation' elective course	A few entrepreneurship courses, in particular at the College of Technology; Staff trained on entrepreneurship

(cont.)

TABLE 13.6   Summary of entrepreneurial university assessment of the four Palestinian universities (*cont.*)

	ANNU	AQU	HU	PTUK
Supporting entrepreneurs	IT Incubator started in 2005; No entrepreneurship awareness and -development program for students	No entrepreneurship awareness and - development program for students; 2 incubators about to start	No entrepreneurship awareness and - development program for students	Business ideation program for students offered (RAE3); Incubator recently in place
Knowledge exchange	Technology Transfer Office in place (NaBIC); Cooperation with companies as location for training and final graduation project	Companies contributing in Dual Studies program; Cooperation with companies as location for training and final graduation project	Cooperation with companies as location for training and final graduation project	Cooperation with companies as location for training and final graduation project
Internationali-zation	No double or joint degree programs with universities abroad; Mobility is scarce	Master study on Entrepreneurship in Fashion with Staffordshire University (UK) being developed; Mobility is scarce	Two double degree programs with universities abroad; Mobility is scarce	No double or joint degree programs with universities abroad; Mobility is scarce
Monitoring and evaluation	No measurement of entrepreneurial performance	No measurement of entrepreneurial performance	Baseline study on students' entrepreneurial skills foreseen & repeat research to measure impact	No measurement of entrepreneurial performance

Recent initiatives had been introduced with the intention of making education more market-oriented. Supported by GIZ, the Fashion Design department trained students to be self-sufficient and worked 'extremely closely' with fashion industry. At the College of Technology, the vocational education programmes were practice-oriented and seven faculty members were trained to deliver the entrepreneurship course in an interactive, entrepreneurial manner. Students were however critical, stating that although individual teachers challenged them to create their own projects, development of entrepreneurial skills was hardly given attention. They had limited understanding on what it would take to be an entrepreneur.

Relevant for all four universities was that they benefited from a recent Dutch funded project aimed to make their agricultural related education and research more demand-driven. A new, joint agribusiness Master programme was developed in close cooperation with Palestinian companies in which more emphasis was given to practical work.

7   Discussion

The cases demonstrate that the autonomy of the institutions allowed each university to make different choices with lack of funding and youth unemployment as imperatives for change. These choices varied from positioning the university as academically strong (ANNU), to being opportunity driven (AQU), a locally rooted teaching university (HU), to a technology driven innovative institution (PTUK). At each of the universities, entrepreneurial activities were starting up mainly in the area of education. Entrepreneurship seemed to be presented as 'the' remedy for employment creation and economic growth, strongly promoted by the donor community. Entrepreneurship courses were set-up at all universities as well as incubators to help students to start-up their businesses. The four cases demonstrate that a diversity of initiatives were taken by the universities to develop entrepreneurial attributes of all students and linking education with industry. This is appropriate in the problematic economic context of Palestine.

From an 'entrepreneurial university' perspective, were the universities also designed to encourage and support individual entrepreneurial behaviour (Clark, 2004; Coyle, Gibb, & Haskins, 2013; Aranha and Garcia, 2014)? Did the universities systematically promote among their staff and students entrepreneurial attributes like opportunity identification and implementation? "Performing entrepreneurial activities does not automatically transform

UNIVERSITIES IN THE COMPLEX SETTING OF THE WEST BANK 331

a university into an entrepreneurial university" (Sam & Sijde, 2014, p. 901): one can only speak of an entrepreneurial university when "the entrepreneurial activities create added value for education and research and vice versa."

The question whether the Palestinian universities were designed to encourage and support individual entrepreneurial behaviour (Gibb, 2013) should be answered negatively. Nor are the Palestinian universities to be understood from the traditional, economically dominated view of entrepreneurial universities as contributors to innovation and business development with innovative research (Etzkowitz, 2004). The private sector in West Bank is small, university research is limited and the economic outlook of Palestine is worrisome at the least. Only in the case of HU has a strategic entrepreneurial transformation process started. At PTUK, developments were going fast and ingredients were in place to become an entrepreneurial university, in particular the personal leadership of the university president (European Commission and OECD, 2012; Coyle, Gibb, & Haskins, 2013; Gibb, 2013), and the academic technology base of the institute with its focus on innovation (Clark, 1998). At the other two universities, entrepreneurial activities were being undertaken but not as a coordinated, strategic intention. The case of AQU demonstrates that entrepreneurial strategic behaviour at most of the Palestinian universities was fuelled by financial necessity. Parallel to the high percentage of necessity entrepreneurs in the country, entrepreneurial, opportunity seeking behaviour of university leadership and staff was also a choice out of necessity.

All new, entrepreneurial activities found at the universities were initiated by or at least fully compliant with international donor agencies supporting Palestine. Donors stimulated universities to cooperate more with industry. They pushed universities to be innovative in education in order to increase the chances for (self-)employment of graduates. Thus, different from engagement with industry being the lever of change (Etzkowitz, 2004), entrepreneurial transformation of Palestinian universities was an external process initiated by donor agencies. The typology of Etzkowitz and Zhou (2007) on stakeholder cooperation of university-pushed, government-pushed and corporation-pulled, needs 'donor-pushed' as additional typology explaining stakeholder cooperation in West Bank.

The donor dominance is reflected in the terminology used within the universities. Students, stimulated by the universities, stated that they intended to run their own 'project' after graduation. Staff and students did not refer to 'business' or 'start-ups'. They grasped the opportunities offered by donor project funding and as such demonstrated calculated, entrepreneurial behaviour feasible within the context of Palestine.

The question arises whether the concept of entrepreneurial university is suited for describing the Palestinian universities. Whilst the concept is intertwined with the role of universities in knowledge economies (Clark, 1998; Etzkowitz et al., 2000), the Palestinian economy is factor-driven with predominantly small-scale enterprises and agricultural production. In this context, entrepreneurship is framed as developing entrepreneurial attributes of the youth. This is reflected in the focus of Palestinian universities on entrepreneurship education, more than on entrepreneurial university transformation.

The concept of 'anchor institution' (Work Foundation, 2010) does apply. The cases of the four universities indicate that they were locally rooted in the West Bank and played an important role in local development. They were responding to societal changes, acted as employers and sources of income for many, creating public value and cooperating with a variety of stakeholders. As such, the Palestinian universities can be considered as engaged with structure, education and research intertwined with the socio-economic development of the West Bank (Goddard & Kempton, 2016). University strategy and leadership priorities – as important conditions for being entrepreneurial – need to be understood against the backcloth of the Palestinian cause. This fits within the strategy to 'resist by existence' captured in the Palestinian concept of 'sumud', which stands for a strong determination to stay in the country and on the land (Rijke & Teeffelen, 2014). The economically not viable campus of AQU in Jerusalem is a case in point. Also the attention for student employability can be explained from the vision and mission of the universities to build the capacities of the young people of Palestine for the benefit of the future of a Palestinian nation. Entrepreneurship education is brought in as a new instrument in this ongoing political, cultural and economic struggle.

8   Conclusions

Palestinian universities operate in a complex setting of a frustrated economy and an explosive political situation. They lack resources, have restrictive national and international mobility opportunities, and are faced with numerous security measures. Their prime focus is on education and they have limited research capacities and tradition. In this context, differences among the universities in West Bank are limited when assessing their entrepreneurial status. Stimulated by donor agencies, all are starting entrepreneurship activities for students with the ambition to help overcome youth unemployment. All try to improve working relations with industry, and all are struggling financially. Differences between the universities of how staff and students perceive the entrepreneurial status of their respective institutions are minimal. In general, one is more negative than positive, with students across the board being more critical than staff.

This leads to the conclusion that entrepreneurial activities are taking place at all universities, but more than being entrepreneurial, the Palestinian universities are to be understood as engaged universities that increasingly stimulate their students to act entrepreneurially. Rooted in the context of the Palestinian cause, they contribute socially and culturally to their local and regional communities (ACEEU, 2016).

The theoretical implication from this paper is twofold. First, it carefully considers labelling a university 'entrepreneurial'. Globally, all universities perform entrepreneurial or entrepreneurship development activities, but that does not yet make them strategically and organisationally entrepreneurial. Second, the notion of entrepreneurial university as an important contributor to innovation through research does not apply in a developing context with predominantly young teaching universities. This leads to the conclusion that the innovation-driven Triple Helix concept needs rethinking when applied in factor-driven economies. In a context in which government institutions are often weak, private sector is small, universities are young, under-resourced and focusing on teaching with weak research capabilities, 'donor-pushed' and 'society-driven' are useful typologies explaining stakeholder cooperation for economic development and innovation.

Note

1 In 2018, an eighth dimension was added: 'Digital Transformation and Capability' (https://heinnovate.eu).

References

ACEEU. (2016). *Standards & guidelines engaged university accreditation.* Amsterdam: Accreditation Council for Entrepreneurial and Engaged Universities (ACEEU).

ANNU. (2017). An-Najah National University website. Retrieved December 20, 2017, from https://www.najah.edu/en/

Aranha, E. A., & Garcia, N. (2014). Dimensions of a metamodel of an entrepreneurial university. *African Journal of Business Management, 8*(10), 336–349.

Beugré, C. D. (2017). *Building entrepreneurial ecosystems in Sub-Saharan Africa. A quintuple helix model.* New York, NY: Palgrave Macmillan.

Cai, Y., & Lui, C. (2016, June 15–17). *The entrepreneurial university as an institutional entrepreneur in regional innovation system development: The case of Tongji creative cluster in Shanghai.* Paper presented at the UNIKE Conference, Copenhagen, Denmark.

Carayannis, E. G., & Campbell, D. (2012). Mode 3 knowledge production in quadruple helix innovation systems. Twenty-first-century democracy, innovation, and entrepreneurship for development. In E. G. Carayannis & D. Campbell (Eds.), *Mode 3 knowledge production in quadruple helix innovation systems* (SpringerBriefs in Business, Vol. 7). New York, NY: Springer. doi:10.1007/978-1-4614-2062-0_1

CIA. (2017). *The world factbook west bank.* Retrieved May 20, 2017, from https://www.cia.gov/library/publications/the-world-factbook/geos/we.html

Clark, B. R. (1998). *Creating entrepreneurial universities. Organizational pathways of transformation.* Oxford: Pergamon, for the International Association of Universities IAU Press.

Clark, B. R. (2004). *Sustaining change in universities. Continuities in case studies and concepts.* Maidenhead: Open University Press.

Coyle, P., Gibb, A., & Haskins, G. (2013). *The entrepreneurial university: From concept to action.* Oxford: National Centre for Entrepreneurship in Education (NCEE).

Etzkowitz, H. (2004). The evolution of the entrepreneurial university. *International Journal Technology and Globalisation, 1*(1), 64–77.

Etzkowitz, H., Webster, A., Gebhardt, C., & Cantisano Terra, B. R. (2000). The future of the university and the university of the future: Evolution of ivory tower to entrepreneurial paradigm. *Research Policy, 29*(2), 313–330.

Etzkowitz, H., & Zhou, C. (2007). *Regional innovation initiator: The entrepreneurial university in various triple helix models.* Paper presented at the Triple Helix VI Conference, Triple Helix Association, Singapore.

European Commission. (2012). *Higher education in the occupied Palestinian territory.* Brussels: European Commission.

European Commission & Organisation for Economic Cooperation and Development (OECD). (2013). *HEInnovate.* Retrieved 2013, 2014, 2015, from www.heinnovate.eu

European Commission & Organisation for Economic Cooperation and Development (OECD). (2014). *The entrepreneurial higher education institution. A review of the concept and its relevance today.* Brussels & Paris: European Commission and OECD.

Fayolle, A., & Redford, D. T. (2014). *Handbook on the entrepreneurial university.* Cheltenham: Edward Elgar.

Gibb, A. A. (2002). In pursuit of a new 'enterprise' and 'entrepreneurship' paradigm for learning: Creative destruction, new values, new ways of doing things and new combinations of knowledge'. *International Journal of Management Reviews, 4*(3), 233–269.

UNIVERSITIES IN THE COMPLEX SETTING OF THE WEST BANK

Gibb, A. A. (2013). *Developing the entrepreneurial university of the future. key challenges, opportunities and responses.* Paris: OECD.

Gibb, A. A., Hannon, P., & Robertson, I. (2012). *Leading the entrepreneurial university. Meeting the entrepreneurial development needs of higher education institutions* (Updated edition). Oxford: Said Business School, University of Oxford.

Goddard, J., Coombes, M., Kempton, L., & Vallance, P. (2014). Universities as anchor institutions in cities in a turbulent funding environment: Vulnerable institutions and vulnerable places in England. *Cambridge Journal of Regions, Economy and Society, 7*(2), 307–325.

Goddard, J., & Kempton, L. (2016). *The civic university. universities in leadership and management of place.* Newcastle: Newcastle University.

Hebron University. (2017). *Strategic plan 2020.* Hebron: Hebron University.

ILO. (2016). *Labour market transitions of young women and men in the occupied Palestinian territory. Results of the 2015 school-to-work transition survey* (Work4Youth Publication Series No. 40). Geneva: International Labour Organization.

Khatib, I., Tsipouri, L., Bassiakos, Y., & Haj-daoud, A. (2013). Innovation in Palestinian industries: A necessity for Surviving the Abnormal. *Journal of the Knowledge Economy, 4*(4), 492–510.

MAS. (2013). *The Global Entrepreneurship Monitor (GEM): Palestine country report 2012.* Ramallah: Palestine Economic Policy Research Institute (MAS).

Morar, V. (2015). *Progression towards an entrepreneurial university model.* Maastricht: Maastricht School of Management.

Niksic, O., Eddin, N. N., & Cali, M. (2014). *Area C and the future of the Palestinian economy.* Washington, DC: World Bank.

Palestinian Central Bureau of Statistics (PCBS). (2017). *Labour force survey: Annual report: 2016.* Ramallah: Palestinian Central Bureau of Statistics (PCBS).

Porter, M. E. (1990). *The competitive advantage of nations.* New York, NY & London: The Free Press and Macmillan Press.

Porter, M. E., Sachs, J., & McArthur, J. (2002). Executive summary: Competitiveness and stages of economic development. In M. E. Porter, J. Sachs, P. K. Cornelius, J. W. McArthur, & K. Schwab (Eds.), *The global competitiveness report 2001–2002* (pp. 16–25). New York, NY: Oxford University Press.

Rijke, A., & Teeffelen, T. V. (2014). To exist is to resist: Sumud, Heroism and the everyday. *The Jerusalem Quarterly, 59,* 86–99.

Röpke, J. (1998). *The entrepreneurial university: Innovation, academic knowledge creation and regional development in a globalized economy.* Marburg: Marburg University.

Sam, C., & Sijde, P. V. (2014). Understanding the concept of the entrepreneurial university from the perspective of higher education models. *Higher Education, 68*(6), 891–908.

Taraki, L. (2015). Higher education, resistance, and state building in Palestine. *International Higher Education*, 18–19.

UNCTAD. (2017). *Report on UNCTAD assistance to the Palestinian people: Developments in the economy of the occupied Palestinian territory*. Geneva: UNCTAD.

UNIDO. (2014). *Technology transfer for recycling of building material waste, Gaza Strip, and support to the marble stone industry in the west bank*. Vienna: United Nations Industrial Development Organization (UNIDO).

UNIDO. (2017). Competitive industrial performance Palestine. *Competitive Industrial Performance (CIP) index*. Retrieved February 20, 2018, from https://stat.unido.org

Work Foundation. (2010). *Anchoring growth: The role of 'anchor institutions' in the regeneration of UK cities*. London: The Work Foundation Alliance Limited.

World Bank. (2017a). *Doing business 2018. Reforming to create jobs. Economy profile West Bank and Gaza*. Washington, DC: World Bank.

World Bank. (2017b). *Palestine's economic outlook*. Washington, DC: World Bank.

Printed in the United States
By Bookmasters